THELYPHTHORA
or
A Treatise on Female Ruin

VOLUME II

TAKEN FROM MY LIBRARY SHELF
AND REPRINTED IN LIKE FORM
Original Fonts Version

Don Milton

All Text, Images, and Text Images
Copyright 2009 Don Milton
All Rights Reserved

Dedicated to the men who lost their lives, their livelihood, and their place in history because they chose the Bible, not custom.

Trust in the LORD with all thine heart;
and *lean not unto thine own understanding*.
In all thy ways *acknowledge Him, and He shall direct thy paths.*
Proverbs 3:5-6

ABOUT THE EDITOR/PUBLISHER

For the last ten years, Don Milton has pastored ChristianMarriage.com, an online ministry dedicated to providing theological answers to questions about marriage. Pastor Don has published numerous books on the topics of Courtship and Christian Marriage as well as Law & Justice. He recently published his own novel, The Prince of Sumba, Husband to Many Wives, and is currently working on a historical novel. He received his Bachelor of Arts in Linguistics from the University of Washington in 1987.

Don has a wonderful wife and three children. He would like to have more.

Other Books Published by Don Milton

Title	Author	Availability
Prince of Sumba Husband to Many Wives	Don Milton	Now
Exhortatory Address to the Brethren in the Faith of Christ	Martin Madan	Now
A Dialog on Polygamy	Bernardino Ochino Don Milton	Now
Letters to Joseph Priestley	Martin Madan	May 2009
Thelyphthora Volume II A Treatise on Female Ruin	Martin Madan	May 2009
Thelyphthora Volume III A Treatise on Female Ruin	Martin Madan	May 2009
Juvenal and Persius Volume I	Martin Madan	May 2009
Juvenal and Persius Volume II	Martin Madan	May 2009
John Milton on Polygamy	John Milton	May 2009
Many More Titles	Don Milton & Others	Fall 2009

To Purchase Books or to Contact Don Milton
Visit - DonMilton.com or write:

Don Milton
PO Box 10162
Scottsdale, AZ 85271-0162

ABOUT MARTIN MADAN

In 1746, thirty-five years before the Reverend Martin Madan wrote this book, he founded the London Lock Hospital. London Lock was the first voluntary hospital that treated venereal disease.[1] Shortly after Madan founded the Lock Hospital, the institution opened a new building and it became known as *The Female Hospital*. He then began to hold worship services in areas of the hospital *that afforded him the ability to preach as well as to lead a congregation in the singing of hymns* but soon it became crowded, so he set out to build a chapel. With donations from wealthy patrons he was able to build a chapel that seated up to eight hundred people.[2] This may not seem large compared with today's mega-churches but it's still a very large fellowship and it was one of the largest of his day. The wonderful thing about Madan's chapel was that it received enough in tithes to become a strong source of support for the hospital.[3] It was there that the singing of hymns first took hold as part of Christian worship.[4] The members of Lock Chapel sang from a hymnal that Madan, himself, had published. He published the hymnal as a benefit to future generations as well as to raise money for the hospital.[5] From the Chapel at the Lock, hymn singing spread quickly throughout the English speaking world with Madan's hymnal the standard. His mastery of musical worship brought thousands to the Chapel at the Lock and his hymns have brought many more thousands to a saving knowledge of our Lord.[6] In less than thirty short years from the first printing of Madan's hymnal, fully two thirds of the hymns sung, even in the parishes of the Church of England, had been lifted; *word for word, note for note, from Madan's own hymnal*. Madan's hymnal had in fact become the core of the Church of England's hymnal.[7] The Baptists' hymnal came out twenty five years after Madan's.[8] The hymnal that he published was called A Collection of Psalm and Hymn Tunes Never Published Before, the proceeds from which were for the benefit of the Lock Hospital.

Madan held the position of Chaplain at the Lock till the day he died. This was partly due to the fact that he eclipsed all of his contemporaries in promoting, as well as defending, the faith. It was Madan who defended Whitefield and the Methodists against the vicious satire of playwright, Samuel Foote, in 1760, (See his Exhortatory Address to the Brethren in the Faith of Christ at the back of this book) so it was not surprising that he continued to defend the faith and biblical morality till the day he went to be with the Lord."[9]

Four years after the publication of this book, Madan excoriated another group of rascals, the judges of England, for their inconsistency in rendering justice. In his seminal work, *Thoughts on Executive Justice*, he outlined the need for sure and swift punishment of criminals. After his death he was falsely accused of having favored hanging for theft, but he stated in the very book that they quoted out of context against him, that he agreed with the maxim that '*a less punishment, which is certain, will do more good than a greater [punishment], which is uncertain.*'[10] After another two years Madan defended the faith against Unitarian, Joseph Priestly in his *Letters to Joseph Priestley*. Another two years and Madan published his translation of Juvenal and Persius from Latin to English with copious explanatory notes. Today it remains unmatched in thoroughness.[11] On occasion Madan still preached at the Lock Chapel and yet he still found time to write dozens of letters excoriating those who would gamble on the horse races.[12]

Despite all these accomplishments, not to mention his many published sermons, Christian historians have failed to chronicle his ministry in their accounts of the great evangelists of the Eighteenth Century, not to mention the great legal minds of the Eighteenth Century. This and other books in this series, will attempt to correct that deficiency, a deficiency which has left an important part of Church history unrecorded; the transition from singing Psalms to singing hymns. And it was that transition that the Lord used to spark the great revivals of the hundred years that followed Madan's ministry. Prior to Martin Madan's successful promotion of hymn singing, there were only random cases of hymn singing. A church here, or a church there would allow hymn singing, and Christians at non-church venues as well as at dissenting churches sang hymns. However, it took the success of the Reverend Martin

Madan's chapel and its music to make it acceptable. The new hymn singing combined biblical concepts with calls to repentance into a moving form of worship. The hymn provides a way for biblical concepts to be presented in poetry set to music. Many lost souls have been deaf to all other forms of preaching, but have been converted by the hearing of a single hymn.

As you read this book, may you be blessed in knowing that its author was the man who polished some of the most famous words in today's hymnals, the man who composed and arranged the music behind many of those hymns, and the man who cared for and counseled the cast aside women of his time; Martin Madan, the Father of the Evangelical Hymnal.

The preceding *About Martin Madan* section as well as the following footnotes are used with permission, having been gleaned from Prince of Sumba, Husband to Many Wives, Chapter 12 - Martin Madan, A Memory of Love by Don Milton - Copyright 2009

1. "The first special hospital was the Lock Hospital near Hyde Park Corner, founded in 1746 by Martin Madan, who became its first chaplain."
A History of English Philanthropy
by Benjamin Kirkman Gray
London - P.S. King & Son, Orchard House, Westminster - 1905

The following is an account of some of the types of patients that could be found at the Lock Hospital.

"There are merit-mongers, among the most abandoned sinners. Two women were, some time since, admitted into the Lock Hospital, in order to be cured of a very criminal disease. Mr. Madan, who visited them during their confinement, laboured to convince them of their sin and spiritual danger, 'Truly,' said one of them, 'I am by no means so bad as some of my profession are : for I never picked any man's pocket, in my life.' The other said, 'I cannot affirm that I never picked a man's pocket; but I have this in my favour, that I never admitted any man in my company, on a Sunday, until after nine at night.'
The Works of Augustus M. Toplady page 168.
You will remember Toplady as the writer of that famous hymn,

Rock of Ages. He was a very close friend and admirer of the Reverend Martin Madan, having also preached at the Lock Chapel.

Good News from Heaven; or, the Gospel a Joyful Sound. At the Lock Chapel, near Hyde Park Corner, June 19, 1774. By the Reverend Augustus Toplady.

Recorded on page 375 of The Monthly Review Volume 52 1775

Madan wrote a tract concerning the sequence of events that led to the conversion of one such prostitute. Despite her conversion and new way of living, she soon died of the illnesses she acquired as a prostitute. This is chronicled in: *A Remarkable and surprising account of the abandoned life, happy conversion, and comfortable death of Fanny Sidney, a young gentlewoman, who died in London in April, 1763, aged 26 years.* By the Reverend Martin Madan

2. "The Lock Chapel was (officially) opened March 28, 1762" but the Reverend Martin Madan conducted services prior to that in other areas of the institution that afforded him the ability to preach as well as to lead the congregation in the singing of hymns.

Dictionary of National Biography - Edited by Sidney Lee - McMillan and Co.1893 - Page 288

Through Martin's exertions a new chapel, capable of seating 800 persons, was erected in the garden of the hospital, he himself contributing 100 pounds.[100 pounds converts to $20,000 in today's U.S. dollars. University of Michigan conversion table.] It was opened on March 28, 1762 and by 1765 was entirely free of debt.

The Madan Family and Maddens in Ireland and England By Falconer Madan 1933 - Page 112

3. "In the case of the Lock Hospital, the musical movement coincided with the Evangelical. Its chapel was used not only by its inmates, but by a strongly contrasting *West End Evangelical congregation who rented sittings.*"

These rented pews helped pay for the expenses of the hospital.

The Princeton Theological Review - Volume XII - 1914

The Princeton University Press - Princeton, N.J. - Page 87

4. "He (William Romaine) held the extreme Calvinistic position as to the exclusive use of inspired words in Praise, and was able to impose his views upon his own congregation. But he could not

stay the rising tide of Hymn singing or make a breach between the Gospel and the Hymns of the Revival. *In Martin Madan the new Hymn singing found an effective sponsor.* The humorous and sturdy John Berridge was as early on the field as Madan, but less effective."
The Princeton Theological Review - Volume XII - 1914
The Princeton University Press - Princeton, N.J. - Page 73,74
5. In the preface to the Hymnal that the Reverend Martin Madan published, "The Collection of Psalm and Hymn Tunes sung at the Chapel of the Lock Hospital" Mr. Madan writes:
"I have at last, with no small care and trouble, completed this Book of Tunes for the use of the Chapel; and as the publication of them may be of service to the Charity, I must desire your acceptance of the Entire Copy, hoping that, by the sale of this Music, some addition may be made to your fund for maintaining and promoting the charitable work which you have undertaken."
6. The Church of England's hymnal began with Martin Madan's Collection of Psalms and Hymns (1760).
The New Schaff-Herzog Encyclopedia of Religious Knowledge by Johann Jakob Herzog, Philip Schaff, and others. Copyright 1909
7. In 1788, the publisher of the fifth edition of the Church of England hymnal, "appropriated fully two thirds of the contents of Madan's Collection."
The Princeton Theological Review - Volume XII - 1914
The Princeton University Press - Princeton, N.J. - Page 76
8. The first Baptist hymn-book was Rippon's (1787).
The New Schaff-Herzog Encyclopedia of Religious Knowledge by Johann Jakob Herzog, Philip Schaff, and others. Copyright 1909
9. It was Martin Madan who defended Whitefield and the Methodists against the vicious satire of playwright, Samuel Foote in his Exhortatory address to the brethren in the faith of Christ published in 1760
10. Thoughts on Executive Justice with respect to our Criminal Laws Published in 1785 - Page 63
11. A New and Literal Translation of Juvenal and Persius; with Copious Explanatory Notes, by which these difficult satirists are rendered easy and familiar to the reader. In Two Volumes.

About the Author - Martin Madan

By the Rev. M. Madan -Printed for the Editor, at Mr. Lewis's, No 157, Swallow-Street, Near Piccadilly MDCCLXXXIX (1789)

12. "It was formerly the abode of the celebrated [famous] Dr. Madan [Martin Madan], of whom we have given an account. During his residence here, [Birmingham, England] he interposed his authority as a magistrate, to prevent the introduction of illegal games into the town during the race week; he gave notice to those persons, who were in the habit of letting [renting] their houses for this purpose, that it was contrary to the laws of their country, and if they persisted in doing it, they must take consequences. Several tradespeople, who disregarded this notice, were sent to prison, which so exasperated the inhabitants, that they burnt his effigy, near the spot where the pump now stands."

Some Particulars Relating to the History of Epsom by Henry Pownall 1825

"I possess twenty-three letters from him to George Hardinge, Esq., M.P., July 9, 1789-March 14, 1790, [Against illegal gaming] written in good spirits and with some wit."

The Madan Family by Falconer Madan 1933

"Mr. Madan, however, the most respectable clergyman in the town, [Birmingham] preaching [1787-1789] and publishing... [against Priestley's Unitarianism] ...I addressed a number of "Familiar Letters to the Inhabitants of Birmingham," in our defence."

An Appeal to the Serious and Candid Professors of Christianity By Joseph Priestley - Page 105

A BRIEF NOTE ABOUT 18TH CENTURY FONTS

It would be silly to think that anyone fluent in English could not easily identify an "s" or an "f" by context or read the letters "c" and "t" when joined by cursive at the top instead of the bottom. Therefore, I will not entertain such thoughts. May you have much pleasure reading this great 18th century work.

THELYPHTHORA;

OR,

A TREATISE ON

FEMALE RUIN,

IN ITS

CAUSES, EFFECTS, CONSEQUENCES,
PREVENTION, AND REMEDY;

CONSIDERED ON THE BASIS OF THE

DIVINE LAW:

Under the following HEADS, viz.

MARRIAGE, ADULTERY,
WHOREDOM, and POLYGAMY,
FORNICATION, DIVORCE;

With many other INCIDENTAL MATTERS;

PARTICULARLY INCLUDING

An Examination of the Principles and Tendency of
Stat. 26 GEO. II. c. 33.

COMMONLY CALLED

THE MARRIAGE ACT.

IN TWO VOLUMES.——VOL. II.

THE SECOND EDITION, ENLARGED.

———What in me is dark
Illumine, what is low raise and support;—
That, to the height of this great argument,
I may assert ETERNAL PROVIDENCE,
And *justify* the ways of GOD to MEN.

MILTON.

LONDON:
Printed for J. DODSLEY, in Pall-Mall.
M.DCC.LXXXI.

CONTENTS OF VOL. II.

CHAP. VI.
Of DIVORCE — — Page 1

CHAP. VII.
Of MARRIAGE, *considered in a civil View, as* the OBJECT *of* HUMAN LAWS.—EXAMINATION *of the* PRINCIPLES *and* TENDENCY *of the* MARRIAGE-ACT — 34

CHAP. VIII.
Of SUPERSTITION, *more especially relating to the Subjects treated in this Book* — 91

CHAP. IX.
Of GOD'S *Jealousy over His Laws* — 212

CHAP. X.
Of POPULATION.—*Comparison of the* JEWISH LAW *with* OURS — — 245
APPENDIX *to Chap.* X. *on* PENANCE *and* COMMUTATION — — 273

CHAP. XI.
CONCLUSION — — 278

APPENDIX, N° I.
The Case of HANNAH, 1 Sam. i. — 349

APPENDIX, N° II.
Extract from BARBEYRAC *on* GROTIUS 362

MEMORANDUM.

"The grand question to be tried is——

"Whether a SYSTEM filled with *obligation* and *responsibility*, of MEN to WOMEN, and of WOMEN to MEN, even unto *death* itself, and this established by INFINITE WISDOM, is not better calculated to prevent the *ruin* of the *female sex*, with all its horrid consequences, both to the public and individuals, than a SYSTEM of *human contrivance*, where neither *obligation* nor *responsibility* are to be found, either of MEN to WOMEN, or of WOMEN to MEN, in instances of the most *important* concern to BOTH, but more especially to the *weaker sex* ?"

See Vol. i. Pref. xxiii, xxiv.

ERRATUM.

The reader is desired to rectify a mistake, p. 144, relative to the King of *Portugal*'s marrying his *niece*. The fact is this: there was a double *incest* in the royal family of *Portugal*, which, with the help of *papal dispensations*, seems to bid fair for arriving at what was antiently practised in the royal house of the *Ptolemies*, where Ptolomy Ceraunus married his *sister Arsinoe*, as did afterwards *Ptolomy Philadelphus*—(such incestuous marriages being allowed in Ægypt.—See Ant. Univ. Hist. vol. ix. p. 376, 379.)

The princess of *Brazil*, eldest daughter of *Don Joseph* the Ist—King of *Portugal*—married her *uncle Don Pedro*, her *father's brother*, anno 1760, she being in the twenty-sixth year of her age, and he about forty-three.— See Lev. xv. ii. 14.

Feb. 21, 1777, the *prince* of *Beira*, their son, married the *infanta Maria Benedicta*, his aunt—i. e. his *mother's* youngest *sister*—she being then in her thirty-first year, and *he* in his sixteenth.—See Lev. xviii. 15.

See Ann. Reg. 1777, Tit. *Chronicle*, 170—and Tit. History of *Europe*, 1777.

THELYPHTHORA.

CHAP. VI.

Of DIVORCE.

STILL on this subject, as on all the rest, we must keep the holy *scriptures* alone in our view; as the will of GOD, touching this, and all things else, is only to be known from the revelation which He hath been pleased to make of it in His WORD.

The first marriage we read of, was between our first parents *Adam* and *Eve*; and on that occasion, we find the will of THE MOST HIGH, with respect to the *indissolubility* of the marriage, declared by the mouth of *Adam*, Gen. ii. 23, 24.—*This is now bone of my bones, and flesh of my flesh; she shall be called* WOMAN, *because she was taken out of* MAN. *Therefore* (or, for this cause) *shall a man leave his father and mother, and shall* CLEAVE *unto his wife, and they shall be one flesh.* These are not to be looked upon merely as the words of *Adam*, but of HIM that made them *male* and *female*, declared by *Adam*. See *Matt.* xix. 4, 5; where CHRIST quotes this primary law of marriage, and abfolute prohibition of *divorce*, thus—*Have ye not red, that he which made them at the beginning made them male and female, and faid, For this caufe fhall a man leave father and mother, and be joined* (προσκολληθησεται) *unto his wife, and they twain fhall be one flefh*. Comp. 1 Cor. vi. 15, 16. The conclufion which CHRIST draws from this inftitution is as follows—*Wherefore they are no more twain, but one flefh: what therefore* * GOD *hath joined* (συνεζευξεν, *yoked* as it were) *together, let not man put afunder*. By this it appears, that when once a man and woman have become *one flefh*, they, by *this act*, though two diftinct and independent perfons before, are fo indiffolubly *one*, in confideration of the *divine law*, that neither the parties themfelves, nor any other perfon, or power upon earth, *can put them afunder*. It is not by the ordinance of man that they are joined together, but by the ordinance of GOD; therefore OUR SAVIOUR faith, *What* GOD *hath joined together* (by pronouncing them

---

* It is to be obferved, that OUR LORD, in his quotation of the paffage, which contains the *primary* inftitution of the *marriage-union*, introduces not the leaft hint, as if fome outward ceremony of man's device, was neceffary, either to the *perfection* or *indiffolubility* of the contract in GOD's fight—nor is there fuch a thing to be found in any other part of the *Bible*.

one

one flesh) let not man put asunder.—But was this rule to be understood in so absolute a sense as to admit of no relaxation or exception whatsoever?—No: We read of *one*, which was allowed to be a dissolution of the marriage-bond, and that was—*the woman's uniting herself to another man than her husband*; this is the true scriptural idea of נאף—*adultery*. The moment this happened, the husband was totally released from all * obligation to her,

---

* Dr. *Ayliffe*, as cited in *Burn's Ecclef. Law*, Tit. *Marriage*, says—that " a divorce *a vinculo matrimonii* cannot be for *adultery*, for that the offence is after a just and lawful marriage;" and cites 1. Inst. 88.

This was the doctrine of Father *Soto* at the council of *Trent*, adopted by that Synod, and decreed, with an *anathema*, against all who should say *that the church had erred in so determining*.

This doctrine of the " contract not being dissolved by the *adultery* of the wife, so as that the husband might marry again," was vehemently opposed by the *Lutherans*, who did maintain, that " *adultery* was a cause of divorce *a vinculo matrimonii*." *Bucer*, in the book which he wrote for the use of *Ed.* VI. Ann. 1550, recommends, that " a *second* marriage might be *lawful*, after a divorce for *adultery*." Burnet, Hist. Ref. vol. ii. p. 156. However, this kingdom has adopted the *doctrine* of the *Papists*—wherefore the *Ecclesiastical Courts* can go no farther than a divorce *a mensa et toro*, in cases of *adultery*; nor can the injured husband get rid of the *adulteress*, so as to marry again, without a special *Act of Parliament*, which now takes place of the *Pope*'s dispensation for that purpose;—a mode of remedy this, instituted of man, not of GOD—profitable to those who are to receive their fees—*expensive* to those who are to pay them;—so expensive, as to be *totally* out of the reach of the generality, who are, by these means, deprived of that relief which they are *ipso facto* entitled to by *nature*, *reason*,

her, or union with her; and, as appears also from the mind of GOD, afterwards declared in the farther promulgation, and more explicit revelation of His law, might not only

reason, and *scripture*.—Compare Matt. v. 31, 32. with Jer. iii. 8. and consider well כרת—to *cut off*; and ἀπολυειν —to *set loose*, or *release*.

These words are of much stronger import than ἀφίημι —to *send away*, or *dismiss* from *cohabitation*—which we are to understand to be the meaning of St. *Paul*, 1 Cor. vii. 11. γυναῖκα μη ἀφιέναι—and ver. 12. μη ἀφιέ]ω αυ]ην; this certainly answers to the idea of a *dismission* from *cohabitation*, or a divorce *a mensa & toro*—but ספר כריתת —.*libellum excidii*, or bill of *cutting off*, must be meant of the *bond itself*, and so is it always to be understood in the Hebrew scripture. This was in the husband's own power, without the interference of any, unless of the *witnesses* before whom perhaps it might be signed, though certainly *lawful* in GOD'S sight, in no case, where the marriage itself had been just and lawful — παρεκ]Ὁ λογȣ πορνειας, as the infallible interpreter of the *divine law* speaks, Matt. v. 32.—*except for the cause of fornication*:—there the idea of divorce is expressed by ἀπολυω—"Ὁς ἂν ἀπολύση τὴν γυναῖκα αὐτȣ, &c. Now ἀπολυω signifies to *loose*—*set loose*—or *release* as from a bond, and so to divorce a wife by *loosing the bond of marriage*, which, that it might be done *on account of fornication* before, or *adultery* afterwards, is surely as clear as the sun; for saying that a thing may not be done, except for *one reason only*, is saying that for *that reason* it may be done, or language must lose its meaning. The fathers at *Trent* were hard put to it to make a decree upon the subject, for they had the scripture, the opinions of *St. Ambrose*, many of the *Greek* fathers, and the practice of the *eastern* church, against them; so they *splitted the hair*—not by condemning those who say that " matrimony may be *dissolved* by *adultery*, and another con-" tracted"—which *Ambrose*, &c. maintained;—but, by condemning those who say "the church may err in teach-" ing otherwise." The truth of the matter was, that
by

only *put her away*, but, if he chose to bring her to a public trial, have *her*, and the *man* who defiled her, *put to death*. This, as appears from the whole tenor of the law as delivered

by declaring *adultery* to be no cause of divorce *a vinculo matrimonii*, they reserved the lucrative business of *dispensation* in the hands of the *Pope*; who, arrogating to himself a power of trampling on all the laws of heaven and earth, readily enough granted *divorces*, with *or without* cause, to such as were able to pay for them, either in money, or by adding to the power, wealth, and territory of the church.

In 1548, the *Marquis of Northampton* was divorced from his wife, whom he convicted of *adultery*; but the divorce being only *a mensa & toro*, the question was, whether he could marry another wife? And in the beginning of king Edward's reign, a commission was granted to *Cranmer*, *Archbishop of Canterbury*, the Bishops of *Durham*, *Rochester*, to Dr. *Ridley*, and six more, to examine and try the question; but before it could be determined, the *Marquis* married solemnly *Elizabeth*, daughter to *Brooke* Lord *Cobham*; for this he was put to answer before the council: He there said, " he thought,
" that, by the word of GOD, he was discharged of his
" tie to his former wife; that the making marriages in-
" dissoluble, was but a part of the Popish law, by which
" it was reckoned a *sacrament*; and yet the Popes,
" knowing that the world would not easily come under
" such a yoke, had, by the help of the *Canonists*, in-
" vented such distinctions, that it was no *uneasy* thing
" to make a marriage void among them: that the con-
" dition of this *church* was very hard, if, upon *adulteries*,
" the *innocent* must either live with the *guilty*, or be ex-
" posed to temptations to the like sins, if a separation
" only was allowed, but the bond of the marriage con-
" tinued undissolved."

However, as things had proceeded so far before the *delegates*, it was ordered that *he* and his *new wife* should be *parted*, till the matter should be determined. In conclusion, the whole question was divided into *eight queries,*

livered by GOD to *Moses*, and by him delivered and explained to the people, was the *only* legal cause of *divorce*, where the marriage was at first just and lawful. This certainly was, as well where the woman's act of incontinency was committed before marriage, and found out afterwards, as where it was committed afterwards.

The word πορνεια, which the Evangelist makes use of Matt. v. 32. and not μοιχεια, which more particularly answers to the Hebrew נאף—*adultery*, has occasioned some to think, that it relates to an act done by the woman *before* marriage, but found out *afterwards*, for which he might *put her away*, and not only that, but might have her *stoned to death*, if he chose to make her a *public example*, as appears Deut. xxii. 21. However this supposition may be true, yet it cannot be the *whole truth*, for the word must equally relate to an act done after *marriage* or *espousals*, as appears from *Joseph*'s

queries, which were put to some learned men (who, does not appear); who returned their answer in support of the *second marriage.*—In fine, the whole was determined in favour of the *Marquis*, and he allowed to cohabit with his second wife.—See this whole matter in *Burnet's Hist. Ref.* second part, p. 56, 57, 58. and *Coll.* to Part 2. B. i. N° 20. See also vol. ii. p. 192, 256.

Burnet, Art. Ch. of Eng. p. 289, 3d edit. observes, that—" the notion of a separation for *adultery*, and yet
" the bond of marriage continuing, was never known
" till the *Canonists* brought it in; but the indissoluble-
" ness of the marriage, even for *adultery*, was never set-
" tled in any council till that of *Trent.*"

intention

intention with regard to his *espoused wife Mary* *.—*He being a just* and holy man, and therefore not willing to marry † a woman whom he thought to be an *adulteress*, yet unwilling to expose her to public shame, or to *make her a public example*, was *minded to put her away privily*. Matt. i. 19. I take πορνεια, which we render *fornication*, to be like the word ακαθαρσια—*uncleanness*, a general term inclusive of all illicit *commerce between the sexes*, of which *adultery* is a species; therefore used by our Lord to include every species of criminality in the wife, which is mentioned in the Old Testament: as—First —her having had commerce with another man before any betrothment, espousals, or marriage with her present husband. See Deut. xxii. 13—21. Secondly—after being *betrothed*, ver. 23, 24. Thirdly—after marriage, ver. 22. Πορνεια has evidently this sense, 1 Cor. v. 1. As Christ most probably spake in *Hebrew*, it is to be supposed, by the *Evangelist*'s delivering to us the word πορνεια, that Christ expressed Himself by

---

* Under the law of *Moses*, a *virgin betrothed* was reckoned the *wife* of him to whom she was *espoused*, and was to be *stoned to death* if she wilfully lay with another man. *Deut.* xxii. 23, 24.

† The text says —πριν η συνελθειν αυτες—*before they came together she was found with child*, &c. Συνελθειν is—to have *matrimonial commerce*—congredi—coire—which consummates marriage, and makes the parties *one flesh*. Matt. i. 18. 1 Cor. vii. 5. See *Parkh*. Gr. & Eng. Lex. and *Leigh*'s Crit. Sacr. sub. voc. Συνερχομαι.

the word זנה, which signifies *whoredom* in general.

When we speak of *divorce*, we must always pre-suppose a lawful marriage, I mean such a one as is lawful according to the law of GOD. Those which were forbidden of GOD in those positive laws, Deut. vii. 3. with respect to connections with the *heathen*, as well as those which we find prohibited *Lev.* xviii. by reason of *consanguinity* and *affinity*, were not only *voidable*, but *void* * in themselves, after they were forbidden by those positive laws. But amongst all those laws, there is not the least trace of forbidding marriage, or enjoining *divorce*, on account of any *pre-engagement* whatsoever on the *man's side*—nor was such a thing ever known, till the *Church* of *Rome* first invented, and then established

---

* The laws against marriages with *heathen* women, must not be understood to affect the validity of marriages with such as were proselyted to the worship of the true GOD, from the worship of *idols*. Such women, being out of the *mischief* which those laws were enacted to provide against—that of corrupting and turning their husbands from GOD to *idols* (see Deut. vii. 4.)—were certainly out of the *intention* of it, and were indeed as much members of the church of GOD, as the *Jewish* women themselves were. Such were *Rahab*—*Ruth*, and others mentioned in scripture as married to men in the *holy line*. See Pf. xlv. 10, 11. Of this number we must also reckon *Solomon's* wife *Naamah*, the *Ammonitess*, (the mother of *Rehoboam*) whom *Solomon* married † before he came to the throne of *Israel*, when his heart was filled with zeal for GOD's law—the neglect of which, in his more advanced years, plunged him into gross idolatry. See 1 Kings xi. 1, 2, 3.

† See 1 Kings xiv. 21. 2 Chr. xii. 13. Comp. with 2 Chr. ix. 30.

it by *Canon Law*. Wherefore all our *divorces* on that account, which we derive from human invention and *church-power*, are without GOD's authority, therefore unlawful in His fight, as *putting afunder* those who ought not to be feparated. Had the law of GOD forbidden a man to have *more than one wife* at a time, all but the *firſt* muſt have been *put away*, and that by the ſentence of the magiſtrate, for the ſame reaſon that the *Jews*, in *Ezra*'s time, were commanded to *put away* the *idolatrous* women whom they had married; becauſe it would have been contrary to GOD's poſitive law * to have kept them

—ſee

---

* The law againſt marrying with *Heathens*, though poſitively enacted, Deut. vii. 3. yet ſubſiſted before, as may appear from what JACOB's *ſons* ſaid, Gen. xxxiv. 14. to *Shechem* and *Hamor* on the ſubject of *Dinah.—We cannot do this thing, to give our ſiſter to one that is uncircumciſed, for that were a reproach* (or diſgrace, חרפה) to us. *Shechem* was an uncircumciſed Heathen, and therefore his *lying with Dinah*, the daughter of *Jacob*, could not make her *Shechem's* lawful wife—it was no other than a *pollution*—ver. 13. The deceit which *the ſons* of *Jacob* made uſe of to wreak their revenge, and the murders which they committed on the *Shechemites*, after having diſabled them from all ſelf-defence, by ſtratagem, and *that* effected by a notorious abuſe and proſtitution of the ſacred rite of *circumciſion*, muſt be allowed to be one of the fouleſt acts recorded in Scripture; and as ſuch, it appears to be mentioned by *Jacob*, ver. 30. and again, ch. xlix. 5, 6. 7. where he fixes a *curſe* upon the principles on which they acted.

On the other hand, as GOD often ſerves the purpoſes of his *Providence* by the wickedneſs of men, as well as by their good actions, we may view the matter as a puniſhment on *Shechem*, for violating the laws of hoſpita-

lity,

— see before vol. i. p. 133. So *John the Baptist* told *Herod*, who had married his brother *Philip*'s wife—" *It is not lawful for thee to have her.*" Matt. xiv. 4. ἐχειν αυτην— to *retain* her. He was doubtless bound to *put her away*, since GOD himself had, as it were, *forbidden the banns* (Lev. xviii. 16.) even supposing the brother had been dead; for he had a daughter by *Herodias* living, named *Salome*, who would have been heiress to *Philip*. Numb. xxvii. 7, 8. See *Josephus*, Ant. Lib. xviii. 6, 4. *Doddridge*, vol. i. 166. *note* a. But as *Philip* was then living, *Herod* also sinned against the *seventh* commandment, in *taking* her at first; and therefore it was *unlawful for him to have her at all.* So in the case of *Abimelech*, who had taken *Sarai* the wife of *Abram*, he is commanded to put her away, and *restore her to her husband*, on pain of death. Gen. xx. 7. In all cases where the *taking* was forbidden, as well in *heathen* and *idolatrous*, as in *incestuous* connections, the *retaining* seems to be unlawful, as a constant repetition, and continuation of the for-

lity, in defiling a *virgin* who appears to have trusted herself under his protection, ver. 1. (Comp. ver. 7. latter part.) and then, with the rest of the *Shechemites*, profaning the holy rite of circumcision, by receiving it only for carnal and worldly ends, ver. 23, without the least view to it, as the holy ordinance of JEHOVAH, or as the seal of his covenant with those who duly received it. This affords an awful and instructive lesson to all, who take on them, either the *profession*, or, more especially, the *ministry* of religion, with wordly views, or to answer some *secular* or *sinister* purpose.

bidden act: but where the taking is no where forbidden, there is no *allowed* cause of *divorce*, or putting away, *except for the cause of fornication*, or the woman's having suffered herself to be *defiled* by another man, either *before* or *after* their coming together.

If we take the words of the primary institution merely by themselves, and judge of them by their *sound* (as the *Papists* do—*Hoc est corpus meum*—in support of the ridiculous lye of transubstantiation) they may be said to intimate that a man shall have but *one wife*, not only at *once*, but, as some have contended, as long as he lives; and thus *second* marriages are forbidden: but if we consider them as explained by GOD himself in the subsequent parts of the scripture, they appear to mean that a man shall *cleave* to *any* and *every* woman that he marries, and not *put her away except for fornication*. I conclude this to be the import of the law, because, if it was meant to forbid *polygamy*, and to enjoin the *divorce* of a *second* woman taken, living a *first*, we should somewhere have met with an explicit determination of the matter; but such a thing, or even an hint or trace of it, is not to be found. So far from it, GOD, in that declarative law, Deut. xxi. 15. absolutely ratifies the *second* marriage as much as the *first*, not only by declaring the issue of the *second* equally inheritable, but even to take place of the other as to the right of the *first-born*, if *born first*. This could not be, if taking the *second* was a forbidden act; such

second

second taking, being prohibited, would have been *null* and *void*, as in other inftances, and the man would have been commanded to have put away the *fecond* wife and her children, as was done in the cafe of other forbidden contracts. See *Ezra* x. 3. The direct contrary appears, for on the footing of that law, the man could no more *divorce* the *fecond* than he could the firft; GOD calls them both נשים—which word, though, when it ftands by itfelf, it denotes the *female fex in general*, like the French *Femmes*, yet in the connection it ftands here, like the word * *Femmes* alfo, denotes *women in a marriage relation*, or *wives* as we tranflate it. GOD likewife determines the iffue of both to be *equally legitimate*, by making them *equally inheritable*. This law was fubfequent to the *Adamic* law, could not contradict it, therefore muft be looked upon as entirely confonant with its whole intention; for GOD cannot contradict himfelf. That GOD made general laws fubject to certain exceptions, on particular occafions, and for particular purpofes, is very plain; we have an inftance of this, Deut. xxv. 5. where a *brother* was to marry his *brother's widow*, though againft the *general law*, Lev. xviii. 16; but this particular cafe was excepted out of that *general law*, for a particular purpofe, which appears in the law itfelf (fee before vol. i. chap. iv.) but where this was not the cafe, there the

---

* Quand un homme aura *deux Femmes*. Fr. Tranfl.

general

general law was to be observed. The permissions of *divorce* which respected the *bond-maids*, Exod. xxi. 11. the *captive-women*, Deut. xxi. 14. seem also exceptions to the *general law*; but these are things peculiar to the *Jews* at that time, and cannot concern us. Therefore, as we live under the *general law* against *divorce*, delivered Gen. ii. 24. which equally binds all mankind, it is most assuredly as unlawful to abandon *one wife* as *another, except for the cause of fornication*. All *divorces* of *human invention*, fall as much under the interdict of GOD's law *now*, as in the days of CHRIST's dispute with the *Pharisees*; wherefore a *divorce*, which declares the nullity of a *polygamous* marriage, is not only without all foundation from GOD's word, but is an arraignment of the wisdom and holiness of GOD, as well in permitting, as in ratifying, blessing, and owning such contracts to be valid in all respects. That He did all this is manifest, as hath at large been proved, nor is there a single instance to the contrary throughout the *whole bible*.

* When *King Henry* VIII. was about to divorce *Queen Catherine*, all manner of people were consulted: among the rest, the *Jewish Rabbins*; who gave it under their hands, in *Hebrew*, that " the laws of *Leviticus* and *Deuteronomy*
" were *thus* to be reconciled—that the law of marrying the
" *brother's wife*, when he died without children, did only
" bind in the land of *Judea*, to preserve families, and
" maintain their successions in the land, as it had been
" divided by lot. But, that in all other places in the
" world, the law of *Leviticus*, of not marrying the bro-
" ther's wife, was obligatory." *Burnet* Hist. Ref. p. 88.
2d edit.

This

This matter is not a mere speculative point, but of the most important concern; for if women, taken by men already married, were not *lawful* wives in GOD's fight, then *commerce* with them was *illicit*, and the issue must be *illegitimate*, and, if so, *uninheritable*. —Whither will this carry us? Farther, I dare say, than the most zealous *anti-polygamists* mean it should, even to the bastardizing the MESSIAH Himself. Unless an after-taken wife be a *lawful* wife to the man who takes her, notwithstanding his *former wife* be living, whether we take our LORD's genealogy on His *supposed father*'s side with *St. Matthew*, or on His mother *Mary*'s side with *St. Luke*, *Solomon* the ancestor of *Joseph*, and *Nathan* the ancestor of *Mary*, through whom our LORD's line * runs back to *David*, being the children of *Bathsheba* (whom when *Da-*

---

* *David* being, by GOD's own appointment, seated on the throne of *Israel*, which was settled on him and *on his seed*—became the *common ancestor* in whom the whole *royal family* might be said to center, and from whom the succeeding kings must make out a *legal* title—this is probably the reason why (Acts ii. 29.) he is styled *the Patriarch David.*

It is true that *ten of the tribes* were *rent out of the hands of Solomon*, 1 Kings xi. 31. but the kingdom of *Judah*, including the little tribe of *Benjamin*, still remained, which was inherited by a regular succession of *David*'s lineal and lawful descendents, till it centered in the person of the *Man* JESUS, as to the *hereditary right*, though the *possession* of it had been long interrupted, and, according to that antient prophecy of *Jacob* (Gen. xlix. 10.) the *sceptre* and *lawgiver* were departed from *Judah*, when *Shiloh* came to set up a *kingdom not of this world*. Comp. Is. ix. 6, 7. Dan. ii. 44. with John xviii. 36.

vid

vid married he had also *other wives* by whom he had children) muſt fail in their *legitimacy*, conſequently all that could be claimed from the common anceſtor *David* muſt be defeated; for if there be a failure *here*, nothing can ſet it right even to the *lateſt poſterity*. We muſt therefore either allow that *polygamous* marriages were valid and lawful in the ſight of God, or deny Christ to be the *ſon of David*; for in the language of ſcripture, a *baſtard*, or one corruptly born, is *not a ſon**. So the *apoſtle*, *Heb.* xii. 8. *Then are*

* i. e. Not in a proper, *legal*, or *inheritable* ſenſe.—In common acceptation the word בן may denote a *boy* or *male child*, of which an *harlot*, or even an *adultereſs*, may be delivered, (ſee Judges xi. 1. and 1 Kings iii. 20, &c. 2 Sam. xi. 27) as the word *ſon* may among us—ſtill this word is ſeldom uſed by us without ſome note of diſtinction, where a *baſtard* is ſpoken of—ſuch as *natural* or *baſe-born ſon*; ſo a *female baſtard* is ſeldom called *daughter*—but *natural* or *baſe-born daughter*. The *Hebrew* word, Deut. xxiii. 2. for one *corruptly* or *ſpuriouſly* born, is ממזר, which is thus explained by *Le Clerc*:—" Hoc eſt—natus
" ex illegitima uxore, qualis erat peregrina mulier,
" quam Hebræus fortè compreſſiſſet, nec tamen duxiſſet,
" aut meretrix, aut cujus matrimonium lege vetitum
" erat. Selden de Jur. Nat. & Grot. lib. v. c. 16."——
" A *baſtard* is one born of an illegitimate wife, as of a
" *ſtrange woman* (or foreigner) whom a *Jew* might have
" accidentally lain with, and yet could not have married;
" or an harlot, or one whoſe matrimony was forbidden
" by the law."——The Greek νοθος, a *baſtard*, is oppoſed to υιος, a *ſon*. The Hebrew בן is uſed alſo for the *male* offspring of a *brute*, (ſee Zech. ix. 9. בן אתנות —to which the υιον υποζυγιε, Matt. xxi. 5. anſwers)—it therefore ſeems to denote, in a general ſenſe, *male offspring* of any kind; but in the true, legal, and proper ſenſe of it, when applied to the *male offspring* of mankind, frequently to denote *lawful iſſue*, in oppoſition to that which is *corrupt* or *ſpurious*.

ye

ye bastards and not sons—νοθοι και ȣ'χ υιοί.—Nor could he be hereditary *king of Israel*. To make out His title to this, all his ancestors up to *David* must be proved to be *David's* lawful and *inheritable* issue, for that is one meaning of *the seed of David according to the flesh. Rom.* i. 3; as we should say, in modern language—*heir of his body lawfully begotten*. This could not be on any other footing than a *polygamous* marriage being as lawful as any other in the sight and judgment of the MOST HIGH; otherwise *Solomon* was νόθος και ȣ'χ υιος —*a bastard and not a son*—through whom must be derived the heirship to *David* on CHRIST's supposed * *father's* side. So likewise was *Nathan* a *bastard and not a son*, through whom CHRIST's heirship to the throne of *Israel* must be derived on the side of His mother the *Virgin Mary*. It is sufficient to prove one link in the chain of CHRIST's genealogy from *David* faulty, to defeat all His title to the appellation of *Son of David—King of Israel*. We might go farther, and say that *Rehoboam,* the immediate descendent from *Solomon*, was also a *polygamist*. He took *Mahalah*, then *Abihail*, then *Maachah* the daughter of *Absalom* (whom, it is said, *he loved above all his*

---

* It is to be remarked, that the *Angel*, which is recorded to have appeared Matt. viii. 20. emphatically styles *Joseph*, ΥΙΟΣ ΔΑΒΙΔ—SON OF DAVID—a clear proof, that the whole line from DAVID had been kept pure from all *illegitimacy* and *bastardy*; but this could not have been, if the *Jewish* law, like ours, bastardized the issue of a *polygamous* contract, of which there were so many instances in the family between DAVID and JOSEPH.

other

other wives) by whom he had *Abijah*, his successor in the throne of *Israel*, and who stands on record as a *lawful* descendent of *David*. Matt. i. 7. See 2 *Chr*. xi. 18, 21, 22.

We might also reckon the good *king Josiah* among the *polygamous* kings of *Judah*; we read of *two* of his *wives*, 2 Kings xxiii. 31, 36. the name of one was *Hamutal*, the daughter of *Jeremiah* of *Libnah*, by whom he had *Jehoahaz*; and the name of the other was *Zebudah*, the daughter of *Pedaiah*, of *Rumah*, by whom he had *Jehoiakim*, the father of *Jeconiah*, who is found, *Matt*. i. 11, 12, in the line of CHRIST's ancestors from *David*. For the character of *Josiah*, see 2 Kings xxiii. 25. *Like unto him there was no king before him, that turned to the Lord with all his heart, and with all his soul, and with all his might, according to all the law of Moses, &c.*

Now, to go no farther, if a *polygamous* marriage was *unlawful*, and of course *null* and *void* before GOD, then was not CHRIST legally descended of *the house and lineage of David*, but from a spurious issue, not only in the instances abovementioned, but also in others which might be mentioned. So that when CHRIST is supposed to condemn *polygamy* as *adultery*, contrary to the institution of marriage, and to the *seventh* commandment, He must at the same time be supposed to defeat * his own title to the character of the MESSIAH, concerning whom GOD *had sworn* to *David*, that *of the fruit of his loins, according to the flesh, He would raise up* CHRIST *to sit on his throne.* See *Acts* ii. 30. with *Pf.* cxxxii. 11. *The fruit of his loins* in this place, and *the seed which shall proceed out of thy bowels,* 2 *Sam.* vii. 12. are expressed, 1 Chr. xxii. 9. by—*Behold a* SON *shall be born unto thee*—which, though *primarily* spoken of *Solomon, ultimately* points to CHRIST, as 2 Sam. vii. 14. with Heb. i. 5. demonstrably shew. Therefore CHRIST is emphatically styled THE SON OF DAVID.

How would all this stand by *our* law? *Decius*, a nobleman of large estate, having this, as well as his honours, limited to him *and the heirs of his body*, marries *Decia*, by whom he has no issue; then, living *Decia*, he marries *Portia*, by whom he has a son. *Decius* dies. This son cannot inherit the estate and honours of *Decius*, as heir of his body, nor can this be done by any of the descendents of that son to the latest posterity. The reason of which is, that we deem a *po-*

---

* Filius qui petit hæreditatem tanquam filius, debet probare filiationem. "A son who seeks an inheritance, or estate by succession, as a *son*, ought to prove *sonship*." This maxim of the *civil law* was also among the *Jews*; they excluded, on the authority of Deut. xxiii. 2. from all the privileges of the *Jewish* commonwealth, both civil and religious, not only all illegitimate issue, but even that whose legitimacy was any ways doubtful. See Univ. Hist. vol. iii. p. 117. note L. Comp. Judg. xi. 1, 2. Also Ezra ii. 62. Neh. vii. 64.

lygamous

lygamous marriage no marriage at all, but *null and void* to all intents and purposes whatsoever; but not so the *law of* God: which is *wisest and best*, must be left to the consideration of the *judicious* reader.

There is a remarkable circumstance in *David*'s history, which I cannot help observing on this occasion, which is, that the adulterous offspring of *David* by *Bathsheba*, the wife of *Uriah*, begotten by *David* during the life-time of *Uriah*, is mentioned *twelve* times in *eight* following verses, 2 Sam. xii. 15, &c. and is not once called בן—*a son*, but הילד—*the man-child*. The prophet *Nathan* indeed says, ver. 14.—הבן הילוד לך—*the son which is born unto thee*—which carries with it a sharp reproof of *David*, who, before he came to a sight and sense of his sin, might have called it so himself; but after he was awakened to a due sense of his iniquity, not all the torments which he endured while the child was *sick*, nor the news of its death, ever induced him to call it בני "*my son*," but הילד—*the man-child*. How differently did he express himself on the news of the death of *Absalom*, 2 Sam. xviii. 33, and 2 Sam. xix. 4. where *eight* times in *two* verses he repeats—*O Absalom, my son! my son!* &c. I'll venture to suppose that, if *David* had been asked the cause of this distinction, we should have reason to think he saw a most important difference, between a *child* begotten in *adultery*, and a *son* begotten and born under *polygamy*.

I think the prophet *Nathan* used the word

son in an *improper* sense, as abovementioned, and for the reason there given; because the *child*, being begotten in *adultery*, was a *bastard, not a son*, in the legal sense of the word. בֵּן—*a son*, is from the root בנה, which signifies to *build*, as an *house, a city*, &c. therefore בֵּן—*a son*, is so called, in the true legal and proper sense of it, because he *builds up or continues* his *father's house or family* *. The *child* therefore of *David's* adulterous intercourse with *Bathsheba*, was not properly *a son*. And the *Holy Spirit*, ver. 15, when He returns to the narrative of GOD's dealings with *David* for his iniquity, saith, *And* JE-HOVAH struck, (not הבן—*the son*, but) הילד —the *man-child*, (see Exod. i. 17, 18.) which *Uriah's wife bare unto David:* and we do not find this unhappy offspring ever mentioned afterwards, either by *David* or his *servants*, by any other name. We use the word *son* much in the same sense with the *Hebrew* בֵּן, to denote *lawful issue*. If a man makes a will, and leaves his estate and effects to *his son or sons*, no bastard could take under this description, the word *son* only denoting *lawful issue*. Hence no *bastard* can have any ancestors to whom he can inherit or be *an heir*—but, as saith the *apostle, Gal.* iv. 7. If *a son then an heir*, which explains what he means (Rom. viii. 17.) by saying—*If children then heirs*, &c.; for it is as true in the scrip-

---

* In this sense the word בֵּן seems emphatically used Gen. xxii. 2, 12, 16.

tures

tures as in our law—" *qui ex damnato coitu* " *nascuntur, inter liberos non computantur*"— " those who are born from illicit *commerce* " are not reckoned amongst children." It follows, therefore, that our LORD's ancestors, *Solomon, Nathan, Abijah*, &c. in the direct line from *David*, must all be deemed of GOD the issue of *lawful* marriage, otherwise He is not the *Son of David*—the *King of Israel*. The lawfulness of *polygamy* must of course be established, or the whole of *Christianity* must fall to the ground, and CHRIST not be *He that was to come, but we must look for another.* Matt. xi. 3.

Our *divorces, causâ præcontractûs*, or because of an antecedent contract on the man's side, are without the *divine authority*, and stand wholly on the inventions of men upon the subject of *polygamy*; these originate from the received notion that though *polygamy* was " allowed under the Old Testament, it " is forbidden under the *law of the New* " *Testament*;"—wherefore all *polygamous* contracts are *null* * *and void* in themselves, and
the

---

* I do not find that the *ecclesiastical courts* have gone any farther in such a case, than merely pronouncing a polygamous contract *null and void*, ab initio — I cannot meet with any instance of their punishing a man as an *adulterer* or *fornicator*.

These courts are called *spiritual*, because they take cognizance of offences of a spiritual and religious kind, and they profess to judge by the *law of* GOD—but where is there to be found, in all the *law of* GOD, either a precept or example to justify this sort of divorces, *causa præcontractûs?* The truth is—they make void the *law of* GOD

the parties entering into them are to be divorced. But as there is *no law* in the New Testament which is not in the Old Testament, the latter must for ever remain as the invariable rule of right; wherefore all *divorces* whatsoever, which have not their grounds and reasons in the *divine law* which was delivered by *Moses*, are encroachments on the *divine prerogative*, and amount to the sin of—*putting asunder those whom* GOD *hath joined together*.

Polygamy on the man's side (for that is the sense in which I would be understood to use the word throughout this whole book) is no cause of *divorce*, either with regard to the former or to the after-taken woman; had it been so, we surely should have found some instance of it in the *History of the Church*, from *Adam* to the time of the *prophet Malachi*, that is to say, in the space of about 3600 years. Nor is it to be imagined, that GOD should suffer His own *chosen* people to have continued in the open and avowed

---

GOD *through their traditions*; and a man who is *divorced* on such an account may very justly, with a little variation, apply to the *judge* who pronounces the *sentence* of *divorce*, what was said by *Paul* to the *high-priest* ANANIAS on another occasion, Acts xxiii. 3. *Sittest thou to judge me after the law, and commandest me to be* DIVORCED *contrary to the law?* The right of the *ecclesiastical powers* to *divorce* the man, and the right of the *civil powers* to *hang* him, are equally without all foundation in the *divine mind* and *will*, as revealed in the scriptures, and are built on that πρωτον ψευδος of the council of *Trent*, concerning the " unlawfulness of *polygamy* to " *Christians*."

practice

practice of living with *more wives than one*, if the very first positive law, which is evidently the foundation of all others upon the subject, was intended to forbid or prevent such a practice; as little is it to be conceived, that He should make laws for the regulation of it, if He had forbidden the very *thing itself* to be done at all.

As to the *divorces* which *Moses* permitted, it was a mere *toleration*, to avoid worse consequences, if those *hard-hearted Jews* had been forced to keep their hated wives. It was no repeal, or even suspension, of God's positive law, but only operated as an exemption from the censure and animadversion of the magistrate*; it was no less a breach of God's law in those who did it, than if such *permission* had never been given; as our Lord evidently shews in His discourse with the *Pharisees*, in his exposition and application of the antient *law of* God, and in the conclusion which He draws from it. So, though our *ecclesiastical* courts take upon them to pronounce a contract *null* and *void*, which is entered into with a *second* wife, living a first, yet this does not affect the matter in the sight of God, they are not the less *husband and wife*; for being joined together according to His institution, and thus being pro-

---

* It would have been very injurious to have punished the *women* who left their husbands under a *bill of divorce*, even though they went to another man, seeing this was by the husband's own act and deed; for—*Volenti non fit injuria*.

nounced by Him *one flesh*—the command is—*let not man put them asunder.*—All such *divorces* are therefore *null* and *void*, and as ineffectual to dissolve a marriage in the *sight* of GOD, as *Moses's* bill of divorcement was. On the footing of GOD's law, *Jacob* could no more have abandoned *Rachel*, his *second* wife, than *Leah* his *first* * ; nor could *Elkanah* have any more divorced *Hannah* than *Peninnah*—nor could King *Jehoash* have put away either of those *wives* which *Jehoiada* the high-priest had taken for him. Why? because GOD's primary law was, that *a man shall cleave to his wife, and they shall be one flesh*; or, as it is expressed in that explanatory passage, Deut. xxii. 29. *She shall be his wife*, BECAUSE HE HATH HUMBLED HER, *he may not put her away all his days*. This positive command of GOD stands *unrepealed*, for the reason on which it is apparently

---

* *Abraham's* putting away *Hagar*, is not the least exception to the rule here laid down, for this was done by the IMM DIATE COMMAND of *Heaven*, not only to deliver *Sarah* from the insolence of *Hagar*, and *Isaac* from the *persecution* of her son *Ishmael*, (comp. Gen. xxi. 9. with Gal. iv. 29.) but to hold forth, in a *prophetical* type and figure, what was to come *to pass in the latter days*, when the seed of *Abraham*, according *to the flesh*, should be rejected for their *unbelief*, and *persecution* of the true *Isaac*, and the *spiritual* children of *Abraham* (see *Gal.* iii. 7.) be called to *inherit the promises*. See this whole matter opened and explained—Gal. iv 22, &c.

Besides, it may be observed, that here is nothing said of a *bill of divorce*, the word made use of is גרש—which signifies to *expel*, *drive*, or *thrust out*, or, as we should phrase it—*turning her out of doors*—and is applied to *Ishmael* as well as to *Hagar*, ver. 10.

founded

founded muſt be the ſame for ever, and bears a direct and abſolute teſtimony againſt all *divorces* of human invention, whether by thoſe of old who made the law of GOD *void through their traditions,* and *taught for doctrines the commandments of men,* or by their *ſucceſſors* of more *modern* date, and actually confines them to thoſe caſes *only* which are mentioned in the *word* of GOD. It cannot be ſhewn from that *word,* that a man's having a *wife,* and afterwards (living the firſt) marrying another, is a cauſe of *divorce* from *either,* or that *ſuch* marriage was deemed *null* and *void,* or forbidden, or even *found fault* with, much leſs *condemned,* in any one ſingle inſtance; but it is very eaſy to ſhew the direct contrary, that is to ſay, that whereever *any man* received the perſon of a virgin into *his poſſeſſion,* he (if ſhe was not betrothed or eſpouſed to another) by that *ſingle act* made her *his wife,* and was abſolutely forbidden to *put her away all his days:* this, let the man's *ſituation* be what it might. GOD made *no* difference, and thoſe who *do,* not only have no authority but their own, but uſe that authority (like the *Phariſees* of old) in direct oppoſition *to,* and defiance *of,* GOD's expreſs command. They may be ſaid to *make the hearts of thoſe ſad, whom* GOD *hath not made ſad,* Ezek. xiii. 22. by making that *ſinful* which GOD hath not made *ſinful,* (for *where there is no law, there is no tranſgreſſion)* and this *by their lyes*—and *to ſtrengthen the hands of the wicked,* by releaſing them from

the

the indissoluble obligations which GOD's law lays them under, and thus facilitating the designs of *seduction, lewdness*, and *debauchery*, which GOD's law was evidently made to prevent.

One safe rule whereby we may judge of the laws delivered by *Moses*, as binding or not on *Christian* men, I take to be this—namely—the considerations on which such *laws* were given; and the reasons on which they are grounded. For instance—the reason for establishing the *ceremonial* law, was to set out and shadow forth *good things to come*—Heb. x. 1.—therefore when those *good things did come*, that law had done its office, answered its end, therefore *waxed old and vanished away*. Heb. viii. 13. So there were many political institutions, adapted particularly, some to the situation of the *Jews* during their *journeyings* through the *wilderness*—others to their subsequent abode in the *land of Canaan*—calculated for their government with respect to the peculiarity of their situation, not only with regard to themselves, but to that of the *nations* about them. These being *local*, and peculiar to their dispensation, as well under the *theocracy* administered by *Moses*, *Joshua*, and the following *judges*, as under the government of their *kings*, are not binding on *Christian* men, whose situation, from the very nature of the thing, can never be the object of those *local*, or *temporary statutes*.

But when we find a *law* given, which is
of

of perpetual and *univerfal* concern, fuch as relates to the prefervation of *millions* from deftruction—to the defence of the *weak* againft the *ftrong*, and the fupport of GOD's moral government in the world, in one of the greateft of all concerns to fociety, the *commerce of the fexes*, there, as the *reafons* of thofe laws can never ceafe, thofe *laws* themfelves muft be of univerfal and perpetual obligation. Otherwife it would be making *laws* which are not commenfurate with the *reafons* on which they are founded, or, in other words, GOD's governing His people for a limited time, and then leaving them without any government but *their own*.

We admit that GOD's law ftill condemns *whoredom*, *fornication*, and *adultery*, and hold thofe marriages to be illegal, which the law of *Mofes* hath made fo, on account of *affinity* and *confanguinity*; but we renounce the pofitive law which binds for ever the *virgin* to the man who has *humbled* her, though this very law was evidently enacted to prevent thofe mifchiefs which arife from *feduction*, and is, in the very terms of it, clearly in affirmance of that *primary* and *univerfal* law, *They fhall be one flefh*: but as there is the fame reafon for the *continuance* of this law, as there was for *giving* it at firft, namely to prevent *whoredom* and *fornication*, and all the mifchiefs which are the confequences of *taking* women and then *abandoning* them, it is doubtlefs among thofe *indelible* ftatutes, which are as unalterable as the reafons on which the *all-wise* LAW-GIVER founded them. As nothing can make a *marriage* in GOD's fight but His *own* inftitution, fo nothing can make a *divorce* lawful before Him but His *own* authority. To affert the contrary, is to fet man's law above GOD's law; which is in effect to take part * with the *man of fin, the fon of perdition, who oppofeth and exalteth himfelf above all that is called* GOD, *or that is worfhipped; fo that he, as* GOD, *fitteth in the temple of* GOD, *fhewing himfelf that he is* GOD. 2 *Theff*. ii. 4. One character of this *man of fin* was, that he fhould *think to change times and laws*. Dan. vii. 25.—Our LORD's oppofite character to this is very apparent in all He faid and did, but no where more fo, than in what He faid on the fubject of *divorce*, in His difpute with the *Pharifees, Matt.* xix. 4, &c. He there fhews from the *divine law*, what *makes a marriage*, and, taken in connection with chap. v. 32. what *diffolves it*, and authorizes *divorce*—while we, like the *Pharifees*, make and unmake marriages juft as we pleafe, and, if we do but fteer clear of a *prieft* and an *human ceremony*, may *take* and *put away* as many women as we can feduce. —Methinks a *Jew* might exclaim againft us in the words of *Shylock*——

"O father *Abraham*, what thefe Chriftians are!"

---

* The Council of *Trent* actually pronounced an *anathema* againft any who fhould fay, that the " church " might not difpenfe with fome of the *impediments* men- " tioned in *Leviticus*, or add others." *Brent*. Tranfl. of *Polano*, 784.

Efpecially

Especially if he took *his Bible*, and contrasted the *law of Heaven* to our laws, as they *now* stand, relative to the subject of marriage.

Even the antient * *Goths* may serve to shame us—for they obliged him who debauched a *virgin*, to marry her, if she was equal to him in rank; if not, he was constrained to give her a fortune equal to his own condition; if he could not give her such a fortune, he was *condemned to death*, because a woman thus dishonoured had no chance of obtaining an husband without a *fortune*, and because it was by marriage only that a state could be properly peopled. See *Alex.* Hist. Wom. vol. i. p. 148.

So in the business of *adultery:*—the antient *Germans* allowed the husband to assemble the relations of the adulteress, in their presence to cut off her hair, strip her naked, turn her out of his house, and whip her from one end of the village to the other. A woman thus publicly exposed, could never wipe away the stain of so foul an infamy, nor could any motive ever prevail on another to marry her, though youth, beauty, fortune, and every advantage combined to allure him.

---

* As may, in many respects, the *Hottentots*; for, as *Kolben*, in his History of the *Cape of Good Hope*, informs us — they suffer no *promiscuous* intercourse with their women — they punish *adultery* with *death* — they allow the validity of *polygamous* marriages—in all which particulars, they follow, though they know it not, the law of *Moses*—whereas *we Christians*, to whom are committed the oracles of God, directly counteract it in these very important particulars.

Ib.

Ib. p. 151. We CHRISTIANS, *reward* the *adulteress* with a *divorce*, which enables her to become the legal property of the *adulterer*; that is to say, if the injured husband can afford the enormous expence of it, if not, he must be plagued with the woman during life. But to return——

The mischiefs arising from *unlawful divorce*, (for such I call *all putting away* which is not authorized by the *divine law*) are dreadful to think of, none can enumerate them, unless they could distinctly count the miseries of *prostitution*. This can exist on no other foundation than men *taking* women, and *putting them away* just *as* and *when* they please; a practice as contrary to the *primary* law of nature established at the beginning, as to every thing CHRIST laid down on the footing of that law in His discourse with the *Pharisees*. I will allow, that, here and there, instances may be found of *females*, who owe their ruin to their own vicious inclinations, and who have nobody to blame but themselves; but for *one* instance of this sort, *hundreds* owe their destruction to the baseness and treachery of their *seducers*. The *divine law* was levelled at both these cases—if a virgin *played the whore* by prostituting *herself*, it was a *capital offence*—if a man enticed a *virgin*, &c. he was to *endow her to be his wife*, and not *put her away all his days*. While these *laws* were in force and vigour amongst the *Jews*, as to the observance of them, there could be no *whore among the daughters of Israel*,

rael, Deut. xxiii. 17. When *Moses* found it necessary in *some cases*, mentioned *Deut.* xxiv. 1. *to suffer them to put away their wives*, the same *hardness of heart* which occasioned this measure of *policy*, (for so it certainly was) led them to abuse it to purposes of great licentiousness, of which *adultery* grew to be the consequence, as may appear from *Deut.* xxiv. 4. a scripture little considered and understood, but the basis of what CHRIST said to the *Pharisees*, Matt. xix. 9.—Still we read of no *brothels*, no public *prostitutes* of the *daughters of Israel*. If the wife, who was unjustly *divorced*, *married another man*, she committed *adultery*, the man who married her committed *adultery*, and the first husband, by being the *cause*, was liable to the guilt of such *adultery*; and though the severity of the law, as to the *temporal* consequences, was suspended by the *bill of divorcement*, yet in GOD's account the primary *law of marriage* was violated, the law of the *seventh* commandment broken, and the delinquents were answerable at the bar of the divine justice, as transgressors of the *divine law*. So said the law itself, as explained by CHRIST, Matt. v. 32. xix. 9. Mark x. 11. Luke xvi. 18.

Now to apply this.—The *obligation* created by the law of marriage is one and the same for ever, so must all those laws be, which GOD gave by *Moses* to explain and enforce it; as Exod. xxii. 16. Deut. xxii. 28, 29 [*].

Our

[*] Dr. *Alexander*, Hist. of Wom. vol. ii. p. 236. speaking of the privilege of *divorce* among the *Jews*, adds, in allusion

Our laws and cuſtoms may be compared to the *bill of divorcement*, which *put aſunder thoſe whom* GOD *hath joined together*; ſo that *if a man take a virgin*, (not betrothed) *and lie with her*, he is under no obligation to her whatſoever, he may put *her away for every cauſe*—ſhe may go and *be another man's wife*; and this, ſo far from being reckoned *adultery*,

alluſion to the law of Deut. xxii. 28, 29.—" But he
" who deflowered a virgin forfeited it, and the law ob-
" liged him, in compenſation for that injury, not only
" to pay her father fifty ſhekels of ſilver, but to marry
" and retain her for life." " Was it *poſſible*," ſays he,
" to deviſe a law that more ſtrongly protected female
" chaſtity?"—It certainly was not poſſible—and the abolition of this law is equally ruinous to the female ſex, and an inſult to that GOD who ſo graciouſly conſulted their ſecurity and protection. This is beſt accounted for, by conſidering that our preſent *ſyſtem* of law, with reſpect to the *commerce of the ſexes*, has, in a great meaſure, been handed down to us from the *church of Rome*—that the churchmen thereof, in former ages, had the framing and faſhioning matters as they pleaſed — that as all marriage was forbidden them, they took ſpecial care to make themſelves amends, by keeping thoſe laws out of ſight, which, had they been retained, muſt have ſadly interrupted their monſtrous debaucheries, as well with regard to *virgins* as *married women*, " which were often carried to ſuch lengths as we ſhould
" ſcarcely credit (ſays our author) were we not aſſured
" of them by the moſt authentic records." Had the law of *Lev.* xx. 10. been retained, the churchmen could not very *ſafely* have defiled *other men's wives*—and as they could not take any woman for their *own*, the laws of *Exod.* xxii. 16. and *Deut.* xxii. 28, 29. could not poſſibly be obeyed—therefore it was expedient to leave them out of their ſyſtem. They now, from long diſuſe, have ſunk into oblivion, and perhaps there are thouſands of thoſe, who call themſelves *Chriſtians*, who do not recollect that there are ſuch laws as theſe in the *Bible*.

as by God's law it certainly is, is accounted a *virtuous* action; it makes her *an honest* woman, as the *phrase* is; such a marriage (though doubtless *adultery*, in the sight of God, in the man who by *putting her away caused her to commit it*—in the man *who marries her who is so put away*—and in the woman who *marries another man*, living the first who possessed her) is accounted a *cleanser*, as it were, of all former *defilement*, takes out the *spots* from the woman's character, and has been by some ludicrously styled " the " *fuller's earth* of reputation." All this monstrous wickedness is, as to the guilt of it, as much kept out of our sight, by our laws and customs, as the guilt of the divorcing *Jews* was kept out of theirs by the *bill of divorcement*. Well might our Blessed Lord say, *Luke* xvi. 15. *That which is highly esteemed among men is abomination in the sight of* God! The place which those words stand in, shews them to relate in a particular manner to what He says at the 18th verse, touching the point of *unjust divorce*, they stand in the same context; which plainly reaches from the words—*And He said unto them*, ver. 15. to the end of ver. 18.

As to the consequences of such *taking* and *unjust divorcement*, with respect to far the greater number of *seduced females*, who (abandoned to all that *infamy, want, disease*, and even *death itself* can bring upon them) are—

<blockquote>
At once the *prey* and *scorn* of all they meet,
Swarm in each brothel, and infest each street—
</blockquote>

Vol. II.   D   as

as I shall consider their situation, with its effects and consequences, both to themselves and the public, in the conclusion of this work, I will say no more of it here, but proceed to consider the *commerce of the sexes*, as it concerns society in general, and is therefore the object of human laws, more particularly with regard to *marriage* as a *civil contract*.

CHAP. VII.

Of MARRIAGE *considered in a* CIVIL VIEW, *as the* OBJECT *of* HUMAN LAWS.—— EXAMINATION *of the* PRINCIPLES *and* TENDENCY *of the* MARRIAGE-ACT.

HAVING before considered *marriage* as a *divine institution*, as ordained of GOD, and by Him defined in what it shall consist (see before vol. i. p. 18—20) I cannot help once more observing, that, in this view of it, no human power has the least authority *

to

---

* Some have properly distinguished marriage as *two-fold*, consisting in a *two-fold bond*, called *vinculum internum*—an internal bond, and *vinculum externum*—an outward, or external bond. The first of these arises from the *union* of the *male and female* in *one body*, and is rendered *indissoluble* by the command—*they shall be one flesh*. Compare Gen. ii. 24. with 1 Cor. vi. 16. This cannot
be

to interfere, so as to make that *null* and *void* which GOD hath made *valid* and *binding*; or to say that those are not *one flesh* whom His *word hath made so*; or to *put asunder* those whom GOD, by his own ordinance and command, hath *joined together*. Nor hath any human legislature the least authority to determine who *shall*, or who *shall not*, marry together, unless its law be declarative *of* or coincident *with* the *law of* GOD.

But forasmuch as *marriage* must, in the very nature of the thing, concern the outward order of *society*, it becomes, in that point of view *only*, an object of human laws in the light of a *civil* contract; the recognition of which, as to *civil* purposes, is of much consequence to the *state*; therefore certainly every state has a power, not only to require such recognition, but under such *terms*, and under such *conditions*, and by such *means*, as may appear to the legislature most

be dissolved during the lives of the parties, but by an act of *adultery* in the woman, which totally vacates it, and releases the man from all obligation whatsoever. The *vinculum externum*, or *outward* bond, arises from the recognition of the other by some outward rite or ceremony in the sight of men. This, as to the mode of administration, is different according to the various customs of mankind, and is the *object of human laws*; but the other is one and the same, as to its essence and obligation, in all ages and places, and no more controulable, in these respects, by *human laws*, than any other works of *creation* or *providence*. To assert the contrary, is that species of *atheism* which strikes at the wisdom, holiness, perfection, purity, and stability of the DIVINE LAW, as well as at the uncontroulable *sovereignty* and *immutability* of the DIVINE LAW-GIVER.

D 2   expedient

expedient for the security of inheritances, family descents, pedigrees, and other wise purposes, which are to be answered thereby, still not interfering with the *thing itself* as between GOD and the *parties*, but leaving this as it stands in the *Bible*.

This distinction has not been attended to as it ought, therefore the laws of this country, like the laws of most others, have intrenched on the *divine law*, making crimes, and ordaining punishments, which are not only unwarranted by it, but are directly opposite to it: as a proof of this, we need only turn to the *Statute Book*, and read 31 Hen. VIII. c. 14. which made it " *felony* for a
" man in *holy orders* to marry, both in him,
" and in the woman." So 1 Jac. I. c. 11. which enacts, that " if a man, being mar-
" ried, shall marry another woman, his first
" wife being alive, he shall be deemed a
" felon, and suffer death as such."—The first of these two laws was repealed long ago, but the latter is still in force, and, but for the *benefit of clergy*, a man who had *two wives*, would be sent to the *gallows* with *murderers* and *highwaymen*, though there is no more warrant for this in the word of GOD, than there was for making a *priest* a *felon* for marrying at all, or for *burning* a man under the writ *de hæretico comburendo*, for being such an *heretic* as to deny that a piece of *wafer*, after a *priest* has muttered some words over it, is a *human body*. Vulgar errors, while remaining merely in the minds of
men,

men, however they may affect the individuals who believe them, may be very *harmless* things with respect to those who are wise enough to search and think for themselves, and therefore differ in judgment; but when they are obtruded upon the consciences of men, armed with the terror of sanguinary laws, even unto death itself, they are formidable to the last degree; and those are to be remembered as some of the best friends to mankind, who have had the *wisdom* first to form their own opinions by the scripture of truth, and then the *courage* to attack, and the *success* (under Providence) to defeat, some of these *monsters*, though doubly guarded and defended by *laws* of *church* and *state*. No opinions, however sacred in the estimation of mankind, can in the least affect the truth of GOD with respect to the *moral* world, any more than different systems of *philosophy* can affect or change the smallest atom in the visible creation—GOD's government over *both* is utterly unassailable by mortals, unchangeable by human power or wisdom. The *phænomena* of day and night, depend not on the systems of the *Ptolemaic*, *Cartesian*, or *Newtonian* philosophy, but on the wisdom and power of him who *created all things*, and *upholdeth them by the word of His power*. So with respect to *marriage*, which is as much an ordinance of GOD, as the ordinances of the material heavens are, (Jer. xxxi. 35, 36.) it is, with respect to itself, as uncontroulable by human power, as the rising or setting of the *sun* and *moon*. Errors in philosophy cannot change these—errors in divinity cannot affect the other: therefore that which constituted a *marriage* at the *beginning*, will constitute it to the *end*, though every legislature upon earth were to combine in a law to make it *null* and *void*.

I am now led to speak of a *law*, which I cannot mention, or even think of, but with indignation, I mean 26 Geo. II. c. 33. intitled *An Act to prevent Clandestine Marriages*. —This law seems to me, and I am by no means singular * in my opinion of it, to go farther than any other upon the subject ever went, by striking in the very terms of it at the *Divine institution*, so as to render it *null and void to all intents and purposes whatsoever*, if certain circumstances invented by the human legislature † are not complied with.

As

---

* I have been credibly informed, that the late *Duke of Bedford* attempted an abolition of the *Marriage-act*, and that he lost a motion made in the *House of Lords* for that purpose but by one voice.—My informant was present at the time.

† Among the *Romans*, the *Papian* law declared those marriages illegal which had been prohibited, and yet only subjected them to a penalty; but a *senatus consultum*, made at the instance of the Emperor *M. Antoninus*, declared them *void*; there then no longer subsisted any such thing as a *marriage, wife, dowry*, or *husband*. See *Montesquieu, Spirit of Laws*, Book xxvi. c. 13. By this it appears, that the *heathenism* of our *Marriage-act* is by no means unprecedented. To this another precedent may be added from the *Popish council of Trent*, where, after many long arguments pro and con, *clandestine*

As far as this law was meant to *prevent clandestine marriages*, from which, as the preamble sets forth, "great mischiefs and inconveniences have arisen"—it was within the jurisdiction of the legislature to enact it; that is to say, so far as the matter related to *marriage* in the light of a *civil contract*; but when it makes the marriage *null* and *void* to all *intents* and *purposes whatsoever*, so as to release the parties from the *bond of marriage*, with respect to each other in the sight of GOD (for nothing less can be understood by those words) it *puts asunder* those *whom* GOD *hath joined together*, and amounts to a *repeal* of the law and ordinance of THE MOST HIGH; for, by this act, parties who are actually married in the sight of GOD, and in

---

tine marriages were at last decreed to be *null* and *void*. However, this was by no means done unanimously, many dissented, and thought that the *church* had no authority in the matter, it being a *divine*, not an *human* ordinance, and, according to a saying of *Pope Innocent* III. " not to *be dissolved by any power of man.*" When the day came for giving their voices for the decree (Nov. 11, 1563) Cardinal *Varmiense* would not be present, thinking the church had no authority in the matter, and saying that if he were present, he should be forced to declare, for the satisfaction of his own conscience, that " the synod had no power to make that " decree." Cardinal *Morone* said, that it pleased him, if it pleased the *Pope*. *Simoneta* said, it did not please him, but referred himself to the *Pope*. Of the others, fifty-six did absolutely deny, and all the rest did approve it. See *Brent. Hist. of Coun. of Trent*, fol. 671, 783. However, they declared clandestine marriages to have been true and lawful, so long as the *church* did not disallow them, and *anathematized* him who did not hold them for such. Ib. 784.—What trifling with GOD's law and men's consciences!

their *own consciences*, are set *free* from each other—the man may abandon his *wife*, the *wife* leave her *husband*, and marry *another man*. *Let not the husband put away his wife*, 1 Cor. vii. 11.—and *Let not the wife depart from her husband, but and if she depart, let her remain unmarried*, ver. 10, 11.—have now no place, where the institution of GOD is *only* concerned; for it is not the ordinance of GOD, but complying with the *terms* of an *act of parliament*, which makes a *marriage*, and which said terms are not one * of them found in the *Bible* as constituting *marriage* in the *sight of* GOD. If after the words "such marriage shall be null and void," there had been added, "as touching and concern-
"ing such or such civil rights, privileges,
"or

---

* It must be allowed that Sect. 10, which concerns the marriage of *infants under age*, without *consent of parents and guardians*, has some authority from the scriptures, but it goes too far;—the scriptures give a power to the *father* of a *woman, being in her father's house in her youth*, to vacate *any vow* she made without her father's *knowledge or consent* (Numb. xxx. 4, 5.) and of course any *betrothment* or *espousal* which she had entered into, *per verba de futuro*, or *de præsenti*, but could not vacate an *actual marriage*, the *act* which constituted this, was *irrevocably* gone and past, and had transferred all *dominion* over the woman, into the hands of the *husband*. See before vol. i. p. 26. It is to be observed, that the power *over vows* was confined to *fathers only*, and this only in the case of *daughters*—or to *husbands* in the case of *wives*, which last superseded all authority which could be derived elsewhere. See Numb. xxx. 6, 7, 16. Gen. iii. 16. latter part, Gen. ii. 24. Pope *Paul* IV. made a constitution, ann. 1557, that marriages made by sons before the age of thirty, and of *daughters* before the
age

"or immunities, given to married persons by any law, statute, or custom of this realm," this might have fallen within the line of *human* jurisdiction; but to affect the *divine institution itself*, so as to make that *null* and *void* which GOD hath ratified by saying—*they shall be one flesh*, is a sacrilegious attempt to repeal the law of Heaven, just as much so as interfering with any *other* ordinance of GOD, as to its *validity*, unless administered according to *act of parliament*.

The *Popes* of *Rome* have made very free with the laws of GOD, even to the striking the *second* commandment out of the *Decalogue*, because it bore a little too hard on the *idolatry* of the *church* of *Rome*; but instead of *one*, we have struck out *many* of GOD's commandments—*viz.* Gen. ii. 24. Exod. xxii. 16. Deut. xxii. 28, 29. because *clandestine marriages* bore hard upon the pride and ambition of the *nobility and gentry*.——— But to return to the main point—

age of twenty-five, without consent of father, or of him in whose power they were, should be void. *Brent. Hist. Counc. Trent*, 407. The same *Pope* sent a *monitorie* to Dame *Joan* of *Arragon*, wife of *Ascanius Columna*, that she should not marry any of her daughters *without his leave*, or if she did, the matrimony, though *consummated*, should be *void*. Ib. 749. Our law seems to quadrate exactly with this *papal monitorie*, in assuming a power to *vacate* marriages, which are not made by *leave of the parliament*, even though consummated. Pope *Paul's monitorie* was a bold encroachment on the divine prerogative, but that of the *British parliament* was much more so;—the first respected the individuals of a single family—the latter those of a whole nation.

To

To illustrate what has been said on the subject of intermeddling with GOD's ordinances, let us suppose a case—*Baptism is a divine ordinance*, ordained, both as to the *sign* and *thing signified*, by CHRIST according to the *prophecies* of the Old Testament. The words by which this ordinance was set forth, are to be found Matt. xxviii. 29. *Go ye therefore, and teach all nations, baptizing them in the name of the Father, and of the Son, and of the Holy Ghost.* This is the *whole* ordinance of *baptism*, and our *church* rightly declares—Can. xxx.—that " when the *minister*, dip-
" ping the infant in water, or laying water
" upon the face of it, hath pronounced these
" words — *I baptize thee in the name, &c.*
" the infant is fully and perfectly baptized,
" so as the *sign of the cross* being afterwards
" used, doth nothing add to the perfection
" and virtue of *baptism*; nor, being omitted,
" doth detract * any thing from the effect
" and substance of it."—Now let us suppose that *ministers* should scruple to use the *sign of the cross* in *baptism*, that this should grow so general, as almost to amount to an abolition of the ceremony; this being complained of to the *higher powers*, they enact a law for the restoration of it, in which is the following clause—" And be it further enacted by the

* Why is this ?—Because the *ordinance of baptism* is simply *that* which GOD hath *made it*. For the same reason, marriage is simply *that* which GOD *hath made it*. Therefore no additions of man's invention, or the want of them, can affect the *marriage union* (any more than the *baptism)* in GOD's sight.

" authority

" authority aforesaid, that no persons who
" shall be baptized, not having the *sign of*
" *the cross* made upon their foreheads, shall
" be deemed or reckoned members of the
" *Christian* church, but such *baptism* shall
" be *null* and *void to all intents and purposes*
" *whatsoever.*" Can any person, who has a true regard for the word and ordinances of GOD, maintain that such a law could in the least affect the state and condition of a person so baptized, before GOD, or that he would be, in the divine account, less a *member* of the *Christian church* because of such a law? Would it not be a sacrilegious attempt to alter GOD's own ordinance, and to make it subject to the law and will of man, and as such to be despised and abhorred by all the faithful?—Where then is the difference?—GOD is as express and determinate as to the *one* marriage ordinance, as to the *one* ordinance of *baptism:* therefore by no rule of sound reason can it be proved, that *both* are not equally out of the reach of *human* authority, so as that *man* can neither *add* to nor *diminish* from either, in the sight of GOD.

That human authority may order an outward *marriage ceremony,* or a public *baptism,* to be used or administered at such a given time or place, I do not dispute; nor do I doubt but those may be punished who transgress such order—but that such things can affect the validity of a *divine institution,* with respect to *itself,* must surely be denied by all who will allow GOD to have a sole exclusive

jurisdiction

jurifdiction and authority over His own appointed ordinances. When therefore GOD fays that if a man lies with a *virgin not betrothed, fhe fhall be his wife,* BECAUSE HE HATH HUMBLED HER, *he may not put her away all his days,* which is but an explanatory way of faying—*they fhall be one flefh*—an human law which adds—" provided fuch and
" fuch conditions be obferved, as *banns* or
" *licence,* otherwife fuch marriage fhall be
" *null* and *void to all intents and purpofes*
" *whatfoever* (which is but an explanatory
" way of faying they fhall *not* be *one flefh*")
is as palpable a denial of GOD's *inftitution,* as to its *validity,* as can well be conceived; as alfo an abfolute contempt of the words of CHRIST, in the conclufion which he draws from the *divine* declaration—*What* GOD *hath joined together let not man put afunder.* It would be a moft abfurd attempt, and what all the world befides would laugh at, if the *parliament* of *Great Britain* were to pafs an act to alter the laws of *France* and *Spain*; but it is more abfurd, and what we ought to grieve at, becaufe it is wicked, when men enact laws which in their aim and tendency would alter or repeal the fixed, eftablifhed, and immutable *laws of heaven.*

The folemnity of that fort of engagement which the fcriptures call *betrothing,* infomuch that it was *death* to defile a *betrothed virgin,* was held in great veneration in the *church* of *Ifrael;* fo was it amongft us antecedently to what is called the *Marriage-act,*
26 Geo,

26 Geo. II.—our *ecclesiastical* courts * would have compelled the solemnization of a marriage so contracted by *verba de futuro* or *verba de præsenti* (but more especially where it became a marriage *de facto* by *carnal knowledge*) in *facie ecclesiæ*: but all this is now set aside, and the most *solemn* contract that can be entered into between the parties, signifies just nothing at all; they may forsake each other just as they please, for it is enacted, that,
" in *no case whatsoever*, shall any suit or pro-
" ceeding be had in any *ecclesiastical* court in
" order to compel a celebration of *any* mar-
" riage in *facie ecclesiæ*, by reason of any
" contract of matrimony whatsoever, whe-
" ther *per verba de præsenti*, or *verba de fu-*
" *turo*, any law or usage to the contrary
" notwithstanding." Here, we may say, is
a *coup de grace* given to the small remains of

---

* When I mention *ecclesiastical courts*, I would not be understood to mean that even their *being* and *establishment* is of any *divine right*, much less their *jurisdiction* and *proceedings*; they certainly were the inventions of the *Popes* of *Rome*, as instruments and executioners of their oppression and tyranny over the persons, properties, consciences, and lives of mankind; their jurisdiction in matrimonial affairs was finally settled by the *council of Trent*, which decreed, that " If any say, that matri-
" monial causes do not belong to ecclesiastical judges,
" let him be accursed."—See *Brent. Hist. of Counc. of Trent.* 784. This horrible and antichristian decree (for no trace of such a thing is to be found in the scripture) bears date ann. 1563, about three hundred years after *Pope Innocent* III. had thrown the ordinance of *marriage* as a *sacrament* entirely into the hands of the *priests*.

female

female security which had been preserved * in our laws; for now, let the contract be *what it may*, the injury arising from the breach of it ever so great, the consequences to the *enticed virgin* ever so horrible, it is out of her power even to aim at that justice which the law of GOD so positively commands to be done. This *act* of *parliament*, taken all together, amounts to a repeal and utter abolition of the law of GOD, almost in every point where marriage is concerned. First—as to *betrothment*, which I take to answer, in some measure at least, to what we call a contract *per verba de futuro*, as where the man says—" I *will* take you to be my wife," and the woman says—" I *will* take you to be my " husband." This was held so sacred by the ordinance of GOD, and persons *thus contracted*, were in GOD's account so bound to each other, that a *defilement* of the *betrothed woman* was reckoned the *defilement* of a *man's wife*. Deut. xxii. 23, 24. Nor could such a woman contract marriage with any other man—Exod. xxii. 16. Deut. xxii. 28.—of course the man who had *betrothed* the wo-

---

* Promises of marriage to a woman, have, in all well-regulated states, been considered as *sacred*, and the breach of them punished by a variety of methods. The *Prussian* laws do not endeavour so much to punish the breach of promise, as to enforce the performance of it—which they do by religious admonitions, by imprisonment, by a fine of half the man's fortune, or a certain part of his daily labour, or, if he runs away to avoid the marriage, by marrying the woman to him by proxy, and allowing her a maintenance out of his effects.—See *Alexander's* Hist. Wom. vol. ii. p. 268.

man was bound, and therefore compellable by the law, to carry *such a contract* into execution. On this principle our *ecclesiastical* courts proceeded, till the *parliament* tied up their hands, and took the business of *marriage* into their *own, any law* (either of GOD or man) *or usage to the contrary notwithstanding*.

Espousal—I take to answer, in some degree, to our contract *per verba de præsenti*, as when the man says to the *woman*—" I *do* take thee to be my wife," and the woman says—" I *do* take thee to be my husband."—If the *betrothment* by words in the *future tense* amounted in GOD's sight to so solemn and binding a contract, a contract arising from words in the *present tense*, must, if possible, be *more so*; for this is the other contract so far *executed*—therefore, *a fortiori*, the *ecclesiastical* courts would compel the parties to a public recognition of this contract in the *face of the church*; but this is also set aside, and made *null and void to all intents and purposes whatsoever*.

But farther—*marriage* itself, which, according to the *Bible*, is the consummation of the whole by *carnal knowledge*, which makes the parties in the sight of GOD, and by His positive command, *one flesh*, even this signifies no more than the others—our *ecclesiastical* courts heretofore called this by its right name, a *marriage de facto*—or *in fact*—and so they well might; for it is the only ordinance of *marriage* which GOD ever revealed:

—where

—where this happened, *divorce* or *putting away* was forbidden—*A man shall forsake father and mother, and cleave to his wife, and they shall be one flesh*—*What therefore* GOD *hath joined together, let not man put asunder.* But we may say of all these *bonds*, as was said of the *seven green withs* wherewith *Samson* was bound—*Judges* xvi. 8, 9.—that as a *thread of tow is broken when it toucheth the fire*, so were * *they* broken.

If these matters above mentioned were overlooked, or not sufficiently considered, at

* A flagrant instance of this appeared in the year 1772; when " a cause of great consequence was deter-
" mined in *Doctors Commons*, and a *marriage* that had
" been *solemnized* in the church, by licence, and *con-*
" *summated*, was declared *null and void*, in conformity
" to a *clause* in the *marriage-act*. It appeared that the
" husband had obtained the *licence*, by swearing that
" the person, for whom the licence was required, was
" of *age*, when she was not." See Gent. Mag. for 1772, p. 149. The writer of which observes—that
" to bastardize the issue of such marriages, seems to
" have something in it repugnant to the sacred insti-
" tution." This is a *mild* way of censuring so *monstrous*, so *wicked*, so *diabolical* a sentence, which can hardly be outdone by the *church* of *Rome* itself. The *judge* who pronounced it could not do otherwise, being bound in his decision by the *clause* in the *marriage-act*—but what a law must that be, which tends to divorce, *a vinculo matrimonii*, those, who by the *law of heaven* are indissolubly *joined together as one flesh!*

Let any man produce, if he can, a more palpable *treading under foot*, a more daring *annihilation* of the *positive commands* of GOD—a more evident defiance hurled at the DIVINE LAWGIVER HIMSELF! Yet this *law*, this *very law*, under which an infinity of such sentences of divorce may be pronounced, still is suffered to subsist, and hold its *empire* over the DIVINE AUTHORITY!

the

the time of the passing of *the act*, it is highly proper that they should now be considered; and the act repealed, at least be * materially altered from its present state of direct opposition to the *word and will* of GOD.

How the law stood before the passing this *act of parliament*, may be gathered from the following short case, 2 Salk. 438, and cited by *Dr. Burn*, Eccl. Law, Tit. *Marriage*, p. 30. *Wigmore's case. Holt*, Ch. J. said—
" By the *canon* law, a contract *per verba de
" præsenti* is a *marriage*—so is a contract
" *per verba de futuro*, if the contract be exe-
" cuted, and he *take* her; this is *a marriage*,
" and they *cannot punish for fornication*, but
" only for not solemnizing the marriage
" according to the forms prescribed by law,
" but NOT SO AS TO DECLARE THE MAR-
" RIAGE VOID."

We have several statutes against *clandestine* marriages; as 6 and 7 Will. III. c. 6; 7 and 8 Will. III. c. 35; 10 Ann, c. 19; also *ecclesiastical* laws, as Can. 62, 63; but no law

---

* *Dr. Alexander*, after observing the pains which were taken to promote marriage among the *Romans*, says—
" It has generally been thought sufficient to stain, with
" some degree of infamy and dishonour, all kinds of
" illicit connection between the sexes, to make the way
" to the enjoyment of lawful love as easy and accessible
" as possible, and to trust the rest to nature. In this
" last respect the *English* legislature seems of late to have
" acted contrary to the common maxim, and thrown a
" variety of obstacles in the way of matrimony; but
" should decrease of people be the consequence, that
" body, it is presumable, are too wise to persist in a
" voluntary error." Vol. ii. p. 245—246.

till 26 Geo. II. ever presumed to *vacate* the contract between the parties, or to declare the marriage *null and void to all intents and purposes whatsoever*, even though the *ceremony* itself was not red, as in *Wigmore*'s case; where, though the husband had a *licence* from the *bishop* to marry, yet *Wigmore*, being an *Anabaptist*, married the woman according to the *forms* of his *own religion*.

I cannot think of the *marriage-act*, as it is called—though it may more properly be styled the *anti-marriage-act*—without recollecting *Horace*'s

> Nil mortalibus arduum est
> Cælum ipsum petimus stultitiâ.
>
> *No work too high for man's audacious pride,*
> *Our folly would attempt the skies.*

To the case above mentioned, I will add a transcript from *Dr. Burn*, Eccl. Law, tit. *Marriage*, p. 17. that the *reader* may be still farther convinced of our departure from that reverence towards the *divine law*, which our *ecclesiastical* courts once had it in their power to shew—" Heretofore, if any having con-
" tracted matrimony *de præsenti*, and being
" convented before the *ecclesiastical* judge,
" did refuse to execute the sentence given by
" him to celebrate the matrimony accord-
" ingly; after lawful admonition given in
" that behalf, he or she so refusing might
" for their contumacy therein be excom-
" municated, and be imprisoned on a writ *de*
" *excommunicato capiendo*, until he or she did
"submit

" submit to obey the monition of the ordi-
" nary in that behalf.

" But as for persons who had contracted
" spousals *de futuro*, if either of them did
" refuse to perform their promise, the judge
" was not to proceed to the *significavit* into
" chancery for an *excommunicato capiendo*, but
" rather to absolve that *cursed* party which
" contemned the censures of the church, al-
" beit there be no cause of favour, but for
" fear of further mischief, by * compelling
" them to go together which did hate one
" another: yet was not this froward party
" to be thus dismissed, but was to suffer pe-
" nance for the breach of his promise: nor
" was he or she to be dismissed or absolved,
" if those spousals *de futuro*, by reason of
" *carnal knowledge*, or some *other act* equi-
" valent, DID BECOME MATRIMONY; for
" in that case, as in the former, where spou-
" sals were contracted *de præsenti*, the dis-
" obedient party was to be *excommunicated*,
" *apprehended*, *and imprisoned*, and not to be
" *absolved* or *released* before satisfaction, or
" death, or other *just* cause of divorce.

" But now, by 26 Geo. II. c. 33. no suit
" or proceeding shall be had in any *eccle-
" siastical court*, in order to compel a cele-
" bration of *any marriage in facie ecclesiæ*,
" whether *per verba de præsenti*, or *per verba
" de futuro*, which shall be entered into after
" March 25, 1754."

* This was something like *Moses*'s sufferance of *divorce* among the *Jews*, for the *hardness of their hearts*.

Such *was* the law—fuch *is* the law—*now* as contrary to the law of GOD, as it was once conformable to it; for as far as the *ecclefiaftical* courts went, they acted conformably to the *divine law:* but they did not proceed, unlefs there appeared fome contract *per verba de futuro,* or *per verba de præfenti*; whereas GOD's law, more extenfively calculated to preferve the *female fex* from feduction and ruin, determined the *carnal knowledge* of a *virgin,* in*all cafes, *to* "*amount to matrimony,*" where fhe was *not betrothed* to another, and compelled the public recognition of it, by the only means whereby, in thofe days, fuch recognition feems to have been made, that is to fay, by the payment of the מהר or *dowry* into the hands of the father, (fee Exod. xxii. 17. Deut. xxii. 29.) moft probably in the prefence of *witneffes*; which feems to have been the cafe in all public tranfactions among the *Jews.* See *Ruth* iv. 9, 10, 11. If. viii. 2. Jer. xxxii. 10, 12, 25, 44.

So that though *betrothing* or *efpoufals* might, and in moft cafes, as among us, did, go before *marriage,* and create a folemn contract between the parties; yet where this was not the cafe, the man's taking poffeffion of the *woman's perfon,* though he had never feen her before that inftant, created the indiffoluble bond of *marriage* between them in the fight of GOD; as appears, Deut. xxii.

---

* *i. e.* In all cafes not excepted *by law*, as thofe Lev. xviii. 6—18. Deut. vii. 3. Comp. Gen. xxxiv. 14.

28, 29. The reason there given is, because HE HAD HUMBLED HER. Whereas we mistake the *betrothment or espousals* for the *marriage* itself, and suppose, that where *these* are not, there *marriage* is not: but the contrary appears in the passage of *Deuteronomy* above cited. In the very nature of things it must be so, otherwise a *lesser* contract by *words* is of higher validity than a *greater* by *deed*, and the *promise* of the woman's person more binding than the *actual possession* of it; which, tho' a *solecism* chargeable on human systems relating to marriage, cannot be chargeable on those which are the contrivances of *infinite wisdom*. The more we examine the former, the more shall we discover of the leaven of the *Pharisees, who made the word of* GOD *of none effect through their traditions.*—The more we examine the law of GOD, the more shall we be apprized of its harmony and consistency with itself, as well as with the peace, good order, and welfare of human society; more especially with regard to its care and watchfulness over those who stand most in need of its protection, the *weaker sex*, which, as matters are now ordered, seem of less value than the *beasts of the field.*—If a man goes into his neighbour's field, and wilfully *maims* or *wounds* his cattle, it is *felony* without benefit of clergy; but to *seduce*, and *debauch* his daughter, and then to look upon himself as free from all *legal* obligation to marry her, is the grand privilege which he finds annexed to our repeal of the laws of Heaven.

Heaven. As for the sufferer, if she be poor, so that her maintenance depends upon her character, this being gone, she must starve for want of employment, or plunge herself into the * depths of prostitution to get food and raiment.

With regard to the business of *clandestine marriages*, how far they are or are not " mis-" chievous or inconvenient to the *kingdom*," may admit of much doubt; much may be said on both sides of the question: but I cannot help thinking with the learned Judge *Blackstone*, who thus expresses himself on the subject, vol. i. 438. *Quar. Edit.*—" Re-" straints upon marriages, especially among
" the lower class, are evidently detrimental
" to the public, by hindering the increase
" of people; and to *religion* and *morality*, by
" encouraging *licentiousness* and *debauchery*
" among the single † of both sexes, and
" thereby

---

* What is said by If. xlii. 22. may be well applied to describe the wretchedness of ruined and deserted *females* in this country—viz.—" *a people robbed and spoiled*, " *they are all of them snared in holes* (חורים Speluncis. Pagn. " —*dens*— which are *dark and secret places*) *and they are* " *hid in prison-houses: they are for a prey, and none deli-* " *vereth; for a spoil, and none saith—Restore.*" See *Taylor* sub voc. חור, No. III.

† I am afraid, that what this learned and excellent writer here observes, is not to be confined to *licentiousness* and *debauchery* among *single persons* only; for the *marriage-act*, by throwing the inclinations of children and wards, as well as their persons, under the absolute power of parents and guardians till the age of *twenty-one*, has, in many instances, proved fatal to their future peace. I cannot express my meaning better, than in the words of the ingenious *Marquis of Beccaria*, in his *Essay*

on

" thereby destroying one end of society and
" government, which is—*concubitu prohibere*
" *vago.*"—It is beside my purpose to enter deeply into the consideration of this law in a temporal view; but it hardly can be supposed to increase *marriage*, unless in the *parish-registers*, by many persons marrying in the parish churches and chapels, because they cannot marry elsewhere. Doubtless numbers there are who would have married elsewhere, but now never marry at all, because their peculiar circumstances or situations may be such, as to prevent their compliance with the *terms* of the *act*; many of whom are most probably hurried by their passions into something worse than a *clandestine marriage*.

That ingenious foreigner *Mr. de Lolme*, in his *Examen Philosophique des loix relatives aux marriage*, ch. 4. and 5, proves, that " every
" obstacle to marriage is a *vice* in govern-
" ment, and an injury to the rights of citi-

---

on Crimes and Punishments, c. 31. " CONJUGAL FIDE-
" LITY," saith he, " is always greater, in proportion
" as marriages are more *numerous* and *less difficult*. But
" when the interest or pride of families, or paternal
" authority, not the inclination of the parties, unite
" the sexes, *gallantry* soon breaks the slender ties, in
" spite of common *moralists*, who exclaim against the
" effect, while they pardon the cause."

I much doubt, whether every sessions of parliament, for some years past, has not afforded melancholy proofs of the truth with which the noble *Milanese* made the above observation. I should except the *last*.—But this was so extraordinary, as to be mentioned in some of the *public prints*, as almost a WONDER—*inter mirabilia anni* MDCCLXXX.

" zens."

" zens." Under this head he shews, that the "English act of parliament of 1753, is "contrary to the law of nature," and explains the reasons of that truly *Patrician* act.

The passing such a law as this, in a maritime and commercial *island*, whose *external* strength, by which it can annoy its numerous enemies, and whose *internal* strength, by which it is to defend itself against their invasions, must depend on the numbers of its people, is surely a capital *solecism* in our political system. The wiser *Heathens* took every measure they could, to discourage celibacy, to promote marriage, and, of course, to increase the numbers of their people. *Plato* lays it down, that in a well-ordered republic, the first consideration should be to make laws for the promotion of marriage, that every one should marry, not merely to please himself, but as a benefit to the public; therefore he would have every unmarried man punished annually by a fine of so many *drachmæ*, and some mark of infamy, who lived to thirty years of age without marrying. De LL. lib. vi. *Lycurgus*, the *Spartan* lawgiver, would not admit unmarried men to the public games, spectacles, and feasts. Plut. in *Lycurg.* and an action was given against those who did not marry at all, or too late to have children. Among the *Romans*, they were liable to a mark of ignominy or disgrace set on them by the *Censors*. Val. Max. lib. ii. c. 9. *Augustus* rejected the testament of a man who died under a state of celibacy.
Ib.

Ib. lib. vii. c. 7. On the other hand, married men (especially those who had children) had many privileges—they were exempted from being sent on embassies, and had the first voice in all public decrees or sentences. In any canvassing or making interest for magistracy, or any other office, the number of children which a man had, was considered as a very prevalent recommendation. Appian, lib. ii. de Bell. Civ. In all the public theatres, they were seated in an honourable place. *Suet. Augustus* was for their receiving presents every year. They were exempt among the *Spartans* from keeping watch, if they had *three children*; if *five*, from all public offices whatsoever. *Herod.* l. iii. The like privileges were among the *Romans* with respect to the *tutelæ* and *curatelæ*—wardships and guardianships—from the burden of which a man was exempted at *Rome*, if he had *three* children—in any other part of *Italy*, if he had *four*—and in all the provinces, if he had *five*. Instit. lib. i. tit. 25. *Athenæus* speaks of a festival, at which the women laid hold of all the *old batchelors* they could find, and dragged them round an altar, beating them with their fists.

Many more instances might be mentioned, to shew what all wise states have thought on the subject of marriage; that it was the means of enriching them with people, and therefore all encouragement was given to it: whereas we have, by *act of parliament*, narrowed, in many instances, its bounds within the circle of family pride, and personal avarice;

rice; and in order to this, have laid difficulties in its way which are *insuperable* to thousands, who might otherwise have contributed their portion of increase to the public riches.

I have elsewhere mentioned the late *Duke of Bedford*'s motion for a repeal of the marriage-act—*His Grace* spake near *three* hours upon the subject, and in the course of his speech expatiated much on the preference which is given to private inclination, humour, pride, and caprice, beyond public utility—" The *riches* of this, as of every coun-
" try," said he, " are the *people*.—The grand
" object, which we are to consider, is this—
" the law in question, by being restrictive of
" marriage, must in course be restrictive of
" population.—What is the consideration of
" this or that individual, where the welfare
" of the public, which is chiefly promoted
" by the increase of the people, is at stake?
" I have a daughter" (meaning the present amiable *Dutchess of Marlborough)* " who is
" deservedly my delight; any misfortune
" which could happen to her by an impru-
" dent or unsuitable marriage, would be a
" most sensible affliction to me; but," said the noble *patriot*, " what is this to the
" public? What is it to the public whom
" she may marry—or whom any body's
" daughter or son may marry? Population is
" the grand point to be considered with re-
" spect to the public; therefore an Act,
" which makes public utility subservient to
" the

" the mere confideration of preventing here
" and there a private inconvenience, is an
" impolitic, an injurious, a mifchievous law;
" it ought never to have been made, it ought
" now to be repealed."

This is pretty near the fubftance of what was reported to me to have been the conclufion of *his Grace's* fpeech on the occafion. However, his motion was loft by *one* fingle voice. He faid, that " he fhould make it " again the next year"—but, before that time, he went out of adminiftration, and he dropped his intention, as perhaps having little hope of fucceeding as a private *Lord* in oppofition, after having failed while in public office.

Whatever may be the fuppofed ill confequences of *clandeftine marriages*, however " mifchievous or inconvenient to the king- " dom" they may, in fome inftances, have been found, yet no mifchief or inconvenience could poffibly arife from them, which might not have been obviated without intrenching on GOD's prerogative, without attacking the validity of His holy ordinances. The fixty-fecond *canon* prohibits " minifters from fo- " lemnizing matrimony without *licence* or " *banns*, or at any other times than between " eight and twelve in the forenoon"—the breach of this *canon* is attended with the " fufpenfion of the offending minifter for " three years *ipfo facto*," but it does not offer to affect the *validity* of the contract between the parties. The 6th and 7th of W. III.

W. III. c. 6. ordains a penalty on the minister for marrying without licence or banns, of one hundred pounds, and for the second offence to be suspended, *ab officio et beneficio*, for *three years*. By the 7th and 8th of W. III. c. 35. the penalty of one hundred pounds is extended to every offence of the minister, likewise ten pounds is laid on every man who is married without *banns* or *licence*. The 10th of Anne, c. 19. has a clause to prevent *clandestine marriages*, and lays one hundred pounds on the minister—and if such marriage be *solemnized in any gaol*, by any minister who is a prisoner there, one hundred pounds upon him, and one hundred pounds upon the gaoler suffering the marriage to be solemnized in the prison without *banns or licence*.—These were revenue acts, and only attacked *clandestine marriages* with a view to the duties payable on licences; but still they keep clear of calling in question the *validity* of the *marriage*, wheresoever or howsoever solemnized. This was reserved for the 26th of Geo. II. c. 33. which, as has been observed, is levelled at the validity of the *ordinance itself*, if not administered as therein required. To prevent *clandestine marriages* by punishing the *minister*, either by pecuniary or even corporal punishment, or to lay a fine on the parties so married, would not have exceeded the authority of the legislature, any more than by interfering in any other matter of outward order and decency; but when they declare—*such marriage null and void to all*

all intents and purposes whatsoever, so as utterly to dissolve the contract between the *parties*, they interfere with GOD's own immediate ordinance, which mortals have no right to do. Human legislators may have power over *ecclesiastical* persons, to provide that they discharge their office, but have no power themselves to interfere in holy things. When King *Hezekiah* began the reformation of the *Jewish* church, and brought in the *priests* and *Levites*, and gathered them together, and gave them order to execute their office, he did lawfully and rightly. But when King *Uzziah* himself attempted to burn incense before the LORD, thus interfering with the appointed ordinance of GOD, which made it only *lawful for the priests the sons of Aaron* to burn incense, he did wrong, he exceeded his own authority, and usurped the authority of GOD, and GOD struck him with leprosy to the day of his death. Comp. 2 *Chr.* xxix. 4, 5. with 2 *Chr.* xxvi. 16, &c.

If the parliament were to lay a duty upon the register of every *baptism*, and, in order to secure it, were to lay a *penalty* on every *minister* registering a baptism on *unstamped* parchment, they would have authority so to do; but if they went on, and said, that " *all bap-*
" *tism so registered* should be *null and void* to
" all intents and purposes whatsoever, so that
" children so registered should be no mem-
" bers of the *Christian* church," such a law would be as absurd and shocking as the *marriage-*

riage-act is, but not at all a greater insult upon the *divine ordinance* of *baptism*, than this is upon the divine ordinance of *marriage*.

So with regard to the LORD's *supper*, if an act was made that for greater *decency* and *order* in the administration thereof, the minister should give notice on the *Sunday* before, upon a penalty of £. 5 for every omission; no doubt the parliament might make such a law; but if the act went on and said, that " where any persons shall receive the *sacra-* " *ment* from the hands of any minister who " hath neglected to give such notice afore- " said, such receiving shall be *null* and *void* " *to all intents and purposes whatsoever*; and " no benefit accrue to the *receivers* thereby" —how would such a law as this be distinguishable, in point of folly and impiety, from the *act* which we have been considering? No distinction in these respects can be fairly made, till it can be proved, that the sacrament of the LORD's *supper* is an appointed ordinance of GOD, but that the *ordinance* of *marriage* is not. In the mean time, I must profess my *faith* to be, that the *parliament* of *Great Britain* had no more a right to pass the *marriage-act*, in its *present form*, than it had to pass an act to * repeal the *ten commandments*.

I don't

---

* We can hardly read over the impious decree of *Darius*, the king of *Persia*, which is recorded Dan. vi. 7. without shuddering.—To make a *statute*, that—" who- " soever shall ask a petition of any God or man, for
" thirty

I don't mean, by any thing I have said, to put *ministers*, in the business of *solemnizing marriages*, on the same footing with *priests* under the law of *Moses*, with regard to the ceremonial ordinances; these last were ordained and appointed of GOD to those services, which shadowed forth *good things to come*; but it does not appear, that either the *priests* under the Old Testament, or the *apostles* or other *ministers* under the New Testament, were ever employed in *marrying* people (as it is called) or had any thing to do in the matter. *Marriage* was appointed, and its essentials settled, before there was a *priest*, or *church*, or *ceremony* so much as mentioned, wherefore nothing of this kind can be wanting to its completeness and perfection in the sight of GOD. The interference of *priests*, and the appointment of a set form of words to be read over the parties by that *priest*, are

" thirty days, save of the king, he shall be cast into the " den of lions"—was an attack on the crown and dignity of the *Divine Majesty*, horrible to conceive.—But by what *logic* can it be proved, that the *Medo-Persian* monarch had not as much right to do this, as a *British legislature* to invent *impediments to marriage*, which are unknown to the scriptures; to make that *null* and *void*, which GOD's law ratifies and confirms; and thus to *put those asunder*, whom the express command of the MOST HIGH indissolubly *joins together?* However ignorance may be pleaded in excuse of the poor idolatrous *Heathen* —this but aggravates our guilt; for we have the *oracles of* GOD *committed to us*, and to be ignorant of their contents, is of itself a GREAT crime—disregarding them, still a GREATER—acting in opposition to them, GREATEST of all!

purely

purely of human, and comparatively (as I shall shew in the sequel) of modern invention, therefore can have no more effect upon the *divine ordinance* itself, as between GOD and the parties, than the other human inventions of services for the *burial of the dead*, and the *administration* of the *sacraments*, can have upon the *state of the dead*, or on the *validity* of the *sacraments*, to those who receive them: if it were otherwise, the efficacy of GOD's ordinances no longer depend on *His appointment*, but on the *will of man*. A *Papist* may be brought to believe that the *validity* of the *sacrament* depends on the *intention* of the *priest*; but to believe this, is not a greater error, than to believe that *any* ordinance of GOD whatsoever depends on any thing else, as to its *validity* and *efficacy*, but the mind and will of GOD as revealed in His word:— If He has said *they shall be one flesh*—it is not for man to say *they shall not*—if He has thus *joined them together*, it is not for *man to put them asunder*.

Now, to apply what has been said to the subject of this chapter, it will be necessary for us to keep the ideas of marriage, as it is a *divine ordinance* with respect to GOD, and as it is a *civil contract* with respect to the public, distinct in our minds. It is the *first* only which constitutes the indissoluble union in GOD's sight, but it is the *second* which recognizes and ratifies that union in the sight of the world; and this is a sort of security which (as so much depends upon it with respect

spect to *society*) the world has a right to require, consequently to exact, and those who wilfully refuse to give it, deserve to lose every privilege and benefit which are annexed to it. Were the consciences of men what they ought to be, the fear and love of GOD would reign within them, and a strict observance of His commandments be the measure and rule of all their dealings towards GOD and each other. But in this corrupt state of things this is not the case, therefore human laws are necessary to enforce the *divine law*, in no instance, perhaps, *more* necessary than in the case before us. If no contract of a public nature was insisted upon, but all left to the private agreements and determinations between the parties, men might take women, and women men, and keep or put one another away as humour or fancy suited;—the woman who was the wife of A. to-day, might become the wife of B. to-morrow; in short, it is impossible to *conceive*, much more so to *express*, the confusion which must ensue * on such a plan. Therefore, when human laws are made to exact a public

---

* We should be living like the *Zaporavian Cossacks*, who have no marriages among them, nor any domestic œconomy, but merely take their women as they want them, for the purposes of propagation, without any distinctions of propriety whatsoever. So far from cohabitation, they do not even suffer the women to live among them; and they are so far from knowing their own children, that it is no uncommon thing for a *brother* to have children by a *sister*, or a *father* by a *daughter*. See *Voltaire* on the *Russian empire*.

contract between the parties in the face of the world, which contract cannot be broken nor dissolved but for the *one cause* which GOD's word allows, such laws are in affirmance of the law of GOD, and therefore are righteous laws; and, as such, ought to be obeyed; nor have any persons a right to that respect, and to those privileges, which are due to *married* persons, who despise such *an ordinance* * *of man* as creates a *civil contract* in the sight of the world, by way of recognition of that

---

* The words of St. *Peter* are πάση ἀνθρωπίνη κτίσει—the word κτίσις is here applied to *magistrates* (as appears from the context) whose offices are *created* by men.—So the *Romans* say—creare consulem—to *create* a consul;—*creare* regem—to *create a king:* but though the offices of particular magistrates are of human *creation*, and are different in various countries, *yet there is no power but of* GOD, *the powers that are, are ordained of* GOD. Rom. xiii. 1. Therefore St. *Peter* commands obedience to magistrates for *the* LORD's *sake*. Also the particular mode or form of government may be ἀνθρωπίνης κτίσεως— of *human creation*, yet government itself is of *divine authority*.—See Gen. iv. 7. See on the word κτίσις, *Leigh, Crit. Sacra*, and Mr. *Parkhurst's* excellent and ingenious Gr. and Eng. Lex. to the New Test.

Yet, forasmuch as for the necessities of government, the *magistrates* must make or *create* laws and civil institutions, I cannot see why every *human law* may not be styled ἀνθρωπίνη κτίσις, and this place of St. *Peter* be understood as including *magistracy* itself, and the *ordinances created* by that magistracy. *Bishop Sherlock*, in his *Discourses*, vol. iv. *Disc.* xiii. p. 368, &c. first edit. gives a very different signification of the ἀνθρωπίνη κτίσει, and finds fault with the rendering it—*ordinance of man*. However, on the most mature consideration, we cannot but pronounce, that the *novelty* of the *Bishop*'s interpretation, far exceeds its *solidity*; and *that* for more reasons than it is to our present purpose to enter upon.

private contract which they have entered into between themselves in the fight of GOD. Those who wilfully live together, as *man* and *wife*, without this, are deservedly reckoned infamous, and as deservedly cut off from the benefits of marriage, so far as *civil society* is concerned: therefore to discourage, and even to *punish* such a conduct, is certainly within the authority of all *civil government*, nor would any government be justified in not doing it, for without this, men and women would be living like the beasts of the field. No fault is therefore to be found with our laws for enforcing the public recognition of GOD's *ordinance*, but for not enforcing it in *all cases*, and for making it *null and void* in *any*, where GOD's law hath not made it so. Instead of shutting up the *ecclesiastical* courts against the complaints of deserted females, or preventing their enforcement of *that redress* which GOD's law commands, every *court* in *Westminster Hall*, and every *magistrate*'s house in the kingdom should be open to them, and on pain of death, or at least of perpetual imprisonment till compliance, every man who had *seduced* a woman, whether with or without a promise of *marriage*, should be obliged to wed her publicly. Under what *rite or ceremony* this is done, is of very little consequence, so that it be effectual for the notoriety of the contract, and the prevention of causeless divorce. That which makes the *marriage* before GOD is the same every where, that which recognizes it in the fight of men,

F 2   is,

is, and may be different, but all tending to one point, that of affording to the state, as well as to the parties themselves, such a security for their cohabitation, as is necessary for the peace, good order, and welfare of the whole. Something like what *Q. Curtius* reports *Alexander* to have said when he cut the famous *Gordian* knot, I would say on the *tying* the *nuptial knot*, as far as public ceremony is concerned—*so it be done, no matter how.* The interference of *priests*, and the *service* which is red over the *married couple*, are purely of human invention, no such thing appears in the scripture, and therefore, though both subject to human controul, yet neither being of *divine appointment*, can have any effect on that which *is*, so as to *add* to it, or *diminish* from it in the sight of GOD. As I shall have something very particular to observe on this subject under the head of *superstition*, I shall say no more upon it in this place, than that all attempts to alter, change, or *make void* a *divine institution*, as to its force, power, and efficacy, with respect to *itself*, before GOD, are so far from being binding on the consciences of men, that they ought to be abhorred. The only matter in which the 26 Geo. II. c. 33. seems to be deficient, is, that it does not more plainly express its meaning and tendency, and after the words—
" such marriage shall be *null and void* to all
" intents and purposes whatsoever," it does not add—" any thing in the scripture to the
" contrary notwithstanding"—it *all but* says
this

this in the clause about *precontracts*, and it must *quite mean* this, for the act to have its full force and effect.

Still the *divine law* is one and the same, still therefore ought it to *commend itself to every man's conscience in the sight of* God. 2 Cor. iv. 2. and this upon its *own* authority.—If, therefore, human laws have put *marriage*, as to itself, on a different footing than it stands upon in God's word; if impediments to *marriage* have been raised up by human contrivance, which are not * to be found in that word; in these, and the like instances, human legislature exceeds its authority.

When a man, having *one wife*, takes *another* to her, the *ecclesiastical* courts pronounce such second *marriage null and void*—our courts of *criminal judicature* pronounce him a *felon*—but if God's word be the *criterion* of right and wrong, our laws have no more authority to say that a man shall not have *two wives*, than the *Popish* laws have to say that a *priest* shall not have *one*, neither have our *ecclesiastical* courts any more authority to *divorce* such *second* woman from the man who has *married* her, than the *Pharisees* had to *put away a wife*

---

* The council of *Trent* made a *decree*, that, " if any " shall say, that the *church* hath not power to add *im-* " *pediments* which are *not* in the book of *Leviticus*, and to " dispense with those that *are*—*let him be* ACCURSED."— I believe it may readily be granted, that both *church* and *state* have *equal* authority in the matter. See Brent, Counc. Trent, p. 784.

for every caufe; for no fuch caufe of *divorce* is to be found in GOD's word. Such a thing would never have been thought of, had the *Bible* maintained its due weight in the church—then had not men dared to have made matters of *divine inftitution* fubject to their caprice—changeable with their fancies, as if the fixed and unalterable will of GOD was as variable as their own. To fet this matter in its true light, let us reflect a little on the changes which have been made, touching * GOD's inftitutions

---

* Here we might mention the marriage of *Henry* VIII. with *Catherine of Arragon*, his brother *Arthur's* widow, which was had and folemnized " by the counfel and advice of the moft wife and graveft men of thefe realms, and by the deliberate and mature confideration and confent of the beft and moft notable men in learning, in thofe days, in *Chriftendom*." (See preamble to ftat. 1. *Mary*, c. i. fec. 2.) This very marriage, after twenty years cohabitation, and iffue had, was diffolved by *divorce*, and declared by *act* of *parliament* (25 *H.* VIII. c. 22.) " to be *againft the laws of Almighty* GOD, and therefore utterly void and of no effect." This was in 1533. Twenty years afterwards, in 1553, the faid marriage was " definitively, clearly, and abfolutely declared, deemed, and adjudged to be, and *ftand with* GOD's *law*, and *His moft holy word*, and to be accepted, reputed, and taken of good effect and validity, to all intents and purpofes." When Henry VIII. wanted a divorce from *Catherine* of *Arragon*, on the footing of her having been his brother *Arthur's* wife, it was held, that, " *Confent* without *confummation* made a marriage, compleat." When he wanted to get rid of *Ann* of *Cleves*, ten years afterwards, then the direct contrary doctrine was held—and " no marriage was compleat without confummation." See *Burnet Hift. Ref.* p. 281, 2d edit. In the year 1536, in the cafe of *Ann Boleyn*, it was *judicially* determined that a *precontract*,

though

ftitutions in this country—31 Hen. VIII. c. 14. makes *a priest* that marries, as also *his wife, felons*; and so even to affirm that a *priest* might marry *by the law of* GOD, with death and forfeiture of estate.—5 and 6 of Ed. VI. c. 12. repeals all this, and declares it "as " lawful for *priests* as for all other *Christian*

though no actual marriage or consummation followed, was a ground of divorce from a subsequent marriage though consummated—the direct contrary was determined by act of parliament in 1540, four years afterwards." See *Burnet*, p. 203, 283. These contrarieties and contradictions were the product of that *worldly wisdom*, which is always found to accommodate itself to the *times*; and, wherever *power* or *interest* seem to direct its operations, is the most flexible of all principles.—It is a perfect *Gnatho*, and may say—

> Quicquid dicunt laudo—id rursum si negant, laudo id quoque.
> Negat quis? Nego. Ait? Aio. Postremo, imperavi egomet mihi,
> Omnia assentari. is quæstus nunc est multo uberrimus.   *Ter. Eun.* Act. ii. Sc. 2.

> " Whate'er they say I praise it; if again,
> " They contradict, I praise *that* too : does any
> " Deny? I too deny :—Affirm? I too
> " Affirm :—and, in a word, I've brought myself
> " To say, unsay, swear, and forswear, at pleasure :
> " And that is now the best of all professions "
>   COLMAN.

How much better than all this do we represent the *divine law*, when we suppose it to attend on the times, and to change with the opinions of men? Thus Cardinal *Cusanus* said judicially in the council of *Trent*, that " the understanding of the scripture must be *fitted to the* " *time*, and expounded according to the *current rites*; " and that it is not to be marvelled at, if the *church* in " one time expoundeth in one fashion, at another in " another." *Brent.* Council. Trid. 159.

" men, to marry." See *Art. Ch. of Eng.* 32. These two contrary propositions were determined with *equal* solemnity by the two above-mentioned *kings,* by and with the advice of their several parliaments, and this all within the space of thirteen years. Then came *Queen Mary,* in 1553, and *priests* could not marry—In 1558 the embargo was once more taken off, on *Queen Elizabeth's* accession, and then *priests* might *lawfully* marry. See *Ratification* of the 39 Articles of Religion.

So with regard to the sacrament of the LORD's *supper*—to deny the doctrine of *transubstantiation,* was *heresy;* for which the offender was to " *be burnt* to death, and " forfeit as in cases of high treason." This was *law* and *sound divinity* in 1539, 31 Hen. VIII. c. 14.; but in the year 1547, 1 Ed. VI. all was repealed and set aside. In 1553 *Queen Mary* came to the crown, and all revived again; hundreds were *burnt alive*— but in 1562, 5 *Eliz.* this monstrous doctrine (with the laws which taught and supported it) was abolished, and declared to be " un- " proveable by holy writ—repugnant to the " plain words of scripture—to overthrow " the nature of a *sacrament*—and to have " given occasion to many superstitions." See *Art.* 28. *of the Ch. of Eng.* Amidst these strange, confused contradictory systems of religious opinion, what part may we suppose to have been taken by the great and unchangeable JEHOVAH? shall we imagine Him

such

such an one as ourselves? that he was of one mind in the reign of Hen. VIII.—of another in the reign of Ed. VI.—that he changed again at the accession of *Queen Mary*, and veered about again in the reign of *Queen Elizabeth*. Absurd as such questions may appear, they are not more so than to imagine His mind and will can change on one subject more than on another. To affirm, therefore, that His will can change touching the institution of *marriage*, either with respect to the *thing itself*—the *impediments* against it—or cause of *divorcement* from it; that these were one thing in the days of *Moses*—another in the days of JESUS CHRIST, and as many others as the fancies of men chose to make them, in the several periods of the *Christian church*, just as *Papists* or *Protestants* happened to be uppermost, and to get the *legislative* power into their hands; and especially since the invention of *marriage-ceremonies* to be performed by *priests*,—must involve the *affirmant* in difficulties from which he can never extricate himself, but by totally renouncing so unscriptural, so senseless an *hypothesis*, and allowing that *marriage*, as in GOD's sight, in all the respects above mentioned, stands on the same foundation as ever—*the word of* GOD. Dryden says somewhere—" GOD never meant " His works for man to mend." This is doubtless as true of *His law* as it is of his other *works*; concerning *this* we may also say—*He spake, and it was done, He commanded,*

and

and it stood fast. The rejection and contempt of *this law,* are the causes of numberless evils, which it was revealed and established to prevent in that most important business the *commerce of the sexes.*—*Adultery,* or the defilement of a betrothed or married woman, is, by God's law, a capital offence, to be punished with the *death of both the parties;* but being no crime at all in the eye of our *penal statutes,* it stalks abroad as it were at noonday, fearless and careless, and seems now to be a fashionable method of a *wife*'s getting rid of her *husband,* that she may marry her *gallant.*

Men being under no obligation by *our* law, as by God's law, to marry *virgins* they *seduce*—and if *married* men, being under a legal disability so to do—turn these deluded and helpless females out upon the wide world, either to starve, or to support a wretched existence by *prostitution.* God's law positively says, that *every man,* be his situation what it may, shall protect the virgin he seduces—that he never *shall put her away all his days.* So that (as in the case of *adultery)* we do *not punish,* as a public offence, what God *condemns*—and we do *punish,* in other cases, what God *commands*; for if the *married* man who seduced a *virgin,* &c. was to *marry her,* he would (but for the benefit of the *clergy)* be hanged for his pains. We may laugh at the absurdities of *Popery,* and condemn those tenets of the *church of Rome* which gave birth to the 31 Hen. VIII. c. 14.

wherein

wherein a *priest's* living with a *wife* is made *worse* than keeping a *concubine*, the first being made felony in the *first* instance, the other not till a *second*; we may reproach such monstrous opinions with every term which can express abhorrence and detestation; but are our laws less absurd, less contradictory to every principle of the *divine law?*—We make laws to hang a man for having *two wives* of his *own*—let him only debauch an *hundred wives* of *other people*, and he's safe from all *criminal* * prosecution!

---

* The remedy by *civil action* is certainly open, but attended with great *expence, trouble,* and *loss of time*; and however such *damages* may be given as may in some measure satisfy the *plaintiff*, on these accounts, and be some punishment to the adulterer; yet what can restore the *husband's* lost peace of mind, both with respect to his seduced, debauched, and ruined wife, and to any children she may have brought him, which now he is to maintain and provide for as his own, under the dreadful apprehension that they are the bastards of *other* people? Still even this poor remedy is out of the reach of numbers, who cannot afford to go to law. As to *divorce*, this is so far from any *punishment* on the *woman*, as matters are now managed, that it is the very thing she desires; for by this she can marry a man whom she *likes better* than her husband. It is indeed so far beneficial to the injured husband, that it releases him from the *adulteress*, and so far may be looked upon as some remedy for his misfortune; but when the great expence of coming at it is considered, the steps which must be taken before it comes into parliament, and the cost afterwards, it is out of the reach of the common sort of men. The *physician* who was to prescribe a *pearl* of a hundred pounds value, to be dissolved in some liquor which cost also a hundred pounds, and taken for the cure of a disease which a poor man is afflicted with, would adapt his medicine about as well to the circumstances of his patient,

secution! We also determine that if a man hath *two wives*, he is a capital offender; but let

patient, as our *divorces* are to the relief and release of injured husbands. However, it is not the *king's* "*soit fait comme il est desiré*," which makes the *divorce* valid in the *sight of* GOD, though it certainly is the dissolution of the *civil contract*;—by the law of GOD the *divorce* was *ipso facto* in the power of the husband the moment the *act* of *adultery* came to his knowledge, and if he *put away his wife*, and *married another* (even upon the principles of *monogamy*) he *did not sin*; to say otherwise, would be to contradict the scripture, and to deprive a man of a positive right, which GOD and nature have invested him with. I would wish to apply this to the case of every *poor* man among us, who though not *so poor* as to be able to swear he is not worth *five pounds*, yet poor enough to have a *divorce*, in the usual way, out of his reach.— Why is such a one to be forced to live with an *adulteress*? to maintain, by the sweat of his brow, the children of other people? to suffer all the miseries and inconveniences which a profligate wife may bring upon him? The reason once might be, because the church of *Rome* denied *adultery* to be a cause of divorce *a vinculo matrimonii*, without the POPE's *dispensation*, and a poor man could not pay for it.

The reason now is, because we are treading in much the same steps, and deny *adultery* to be a cause of divorce *a vinculo matrimonii*, without *an act of parliament*, the expence of which only the rich can afford.

This is not among the *oppressions* which *Solomon saw under the sun*, for it never existed, till *Christian* churchmen took upon themselves to trample under foot those rights of mankind, which the laws of *Heaven* had invested them with, and to direct and govern the opinions and consciences of men as might best serve the sordid views and interests of that *kingdom of this world*, which they first set up, and then called it THE CHURCH.

'Tis true, the whole fabric was shaken to its very foundations, by the zeal and activity of the Protestant *reformers*, so as to be demolished within this kingdom; but the *rubbish* is not all yet cleared away; and, among other things, that of declaring *adultery* no cause of divorce

let him *debauch* and *ruin* an hundred *virgins*, or keep a *dozen concubines*—he shall be free!

vorce *a vinculo matrimonii*, contrary to Jer. iii. 8. with Matt. v. 32.

I do not mean that any man should be able to divorce his wife, without some *public* act of notoriety ; for this would subject women to divorces on stories invented, or suspicions entertained, which may be groundless, and only to serve some *sinister* purpose—but that, where *adultery* is absolutely proved, there, as the contract is *ipso facto* dissolved, such dissolution should be allowed in such a manner as to lie within the reach of every man. One thing may be observed—that if *adultery* be not a cause of divorce *a vinculo matrimonii*, on the authority of the scripture, no POPE's *dispensation*, or ACT OF PARLIAMENT, can make it so ; but if it be a cause of such divorce, all men are equally entitled to the benefit of it.

The reason which the *canonists* give for *adultery*'s not being a cause of divorce *a vinculo*, &c. is very curious, viz. " *because the offence is after a just and lawful mar-* " *riage.*" See before p. 3. n. This is what makes the offence ;—if no marriage, there can be no adultery : so that to make that which comes into the very *essence* of the crime, an exemption from the punishment of it, was no better than a bad excuse for retaining the power and lucre of dispensation in the hands of the *Pope*.

The passage Jer. iii. 8. above referred to, sets the matter in a very different light. GOD says, that for the *adultery* of backsliding *Israel*, (meaning the ten tribes*)* He not only שלחתיה had *put her away*, but He had *given her* a bill of כריתת *divorce, excision*, or *cutting off*. Comp. Is. l. 1. All this most evidently is to be understood in a figurative sense, but shews that *adultery* is a cause of *excision* or *cutting off a vinculo*, &c.

On the whole of scripture, taken together, on the subject, it seems that the law inflicted death on *adultery*, and if the injured husband prosecuted, that sentence must be inflicted by the judges ; or if he did not chuse to make his wife *a public example*, he might in a more *private* manner *put her away*, and *give her a bill of excision*. Comp. Matt. i. 19.

I will

I will not say—" *Risum teneatis?*"—but rather—" *Quis talia fando temperet a lachry-mis?*"——

These things, and others which might be observed on these subjects, may serve to shew how far *superstition* hath supplanted the religion of the *Bible*, and the *traditions* of men the *commandments* of GOD. What makes matters even still worse, is, that the authority of CHRIST is pleaded for much of this. He who came to *fulfil the law*, is represented as an *innovator* and *destroyer* of it. His *apostles* are called in as His *coadjutors*:—though, when we hear them speak for themselves, they utterly disavow the charge—" *I came not to destroy the law*," saith CHRIST—and saith *St. Paul*, in his *own* name, and in those of his *fellow-labourers—Do we destroy the law through faith? God forbid!—Yea—we establish the law.—*Was *such* the language of all our *municipal* laws, it would be happy for the world, as the torrent of *lust, profligacy,* and *cruelty*, could no longer ravage far and wide, and spread its desolation over thousands and tens of thousands of deluded and forsaken *females,* and, by *their* means, over the young and thoughtless of the other sex. Then might we hope that the pure truth of God might find its way back to the now dark regions of *Asia*, which, till then, is humanly speaking, impossible; and the followers of *Mahomet* would no longer have it in their power (like *Cerinthus*) to charge the GOD of the *Christians* " with opposing the
" GOD

"God of the *Jews*."—Even * *China* itself might listen to the truth, when unadulterated with human inventions, unsophisticated with *pious lyes*. Whereas they may now say to us, as Christ said to the *Pharisees*—*Ye have made the commandment of* God *void by your traditions*. Matt. xv. 6. *Ye teach for doctrines the commandments of men.* Mark vii. 7.

I do not mean by this, that any *missionary* would be justified in allowing the laws of the *seraglio*, or of the *haram*, as agreeable to

---

* *Montesquieu* is for giving physical reasons for permitting *polygamy*, or prohibiting it, in different countries, according to the heat or cold of the climate. Thus, says he, " the law which permits only *one wife*, is phy-
" sically conformable to the climate of *Europe*, and
" not to that of *Asia*. This is the reason why *Ma-*
" *hometanism* was so easily established in *Asia*, and with
" such difficulty extended in *Europe*; why *Christianity*
" is maintained in *Europe*, and has been destroyed in
" *Asia*; and, in fine, why the *Mahometans* have made
" such progress in *China*, and the *Christians* so little."
He well adds—" Human reasons, however, are subordi-
" nate to that *Supreme Cause*, who does whatever He
" pleases, and renders every thing subservient to His
" will." Sp. of Laws, vol. i. 372. Octavo, Eng.
book xvi. c. 2. Again he says—book xix. c. 18. " It
" is almost impossible for *Christianity* ever to be esta-
" blished in *China*," for which he mentions several reasons, and, among the rest—" the marriage only of one
" wife."—" As for the *Indians*, travellers inform us,
" that the chief reason why several of their *princes* have
" refused to embrace the *Christian* religion, hath been,
" because, among other conditions, it was required
" of them to admit no more than one woman to their
" bed." *Puffend.* b. vi. c. 1. § 16.

the

the law of God. Buying women as *slaves*, and shutting them up as *prisoners*, forcing them against their inclinations, and detaining them against their consent, under bolts and bars—the mutilating men, and making them *eunuchs*, that they may be guards and centinels over these unhappy women, is all monstrously inhuman, wicked, and abominable, and so ought to be represented. It is so far from having a single ingredient in it of the true idea of the holy ordinance of *marriage*, that it is no other than a most horrid scheme of *rape* and *debauchery*, and these multiplied according to the number of those wretched *females* who become the hapless victims of the pride, lust, and tyranny of their oppressors.

Where each fair neck the yoke of slavery galls,
Clos'd in a proud SERAGLIO's *gloomy walls;*
And taught, that levell'd with the brutal kind,
Nor sense, nor souls, to women are assign'd.
DUNCOMBE—*Feminiad,* p. 8.

Was the truth of God received, did real affection unite the parties, the prison-doors would be thrown open, the unhappy guards dismissed, and numbers bless the day, when choice established the union, when faithful-

* Lady M. W. M. letter 41, says to the Countess of B——— "But you'll object, that men buy women *with an eye to evil.*" "In my opinion, they are *bought* and *sold,* as publicly and as infamously, in all our *Christian* great cities."

nefs was fecured by affection, and all feduction and dereliction prevented by the guardianfhip of the *divine law*. On the other hand, were a *miffionary* to go into thofe countries where *polygamy* is allowed, and open his commiffion with declaring, that—" though " *polygamy* was *allowed* under *the law*, yet " Christ forbad it under *the gofpel*."—he would go with *a lye in his right hand*. If. xliv. 20. He would have nothing to do but to take the plan of the *marriage-act* in his *left*, and tell the people, that " unlefs *banns* " were publifhed in the *mofque*, or *ten* * *zinger* " *lees* were given to the *Mufti*, or fome leffer " fum to the *chief Imams* for a *licence*, and " unlefs the ceremony be performed in fuch " a particular place, the marriage is *void* to " *all intents and purpofes* whatfoever, the po- " fitive inftitution of God to the contrary " notwithftanding." This would make the *lye* complete, and probably procure the † *miffionary*,

---

* About *ten guineas* Englifh.

† Since I finifhed the manufcript of thefe papers, I have met with a book, which made a great noife in *Europe* at the latter end of the laft century; its title is— *Polygamia Triumphatrix*, in which is the following remarkable paffage: " Taceo quod multi Gentiles, & " Turcæ, apud quos *polygamia* viget, ad Chriftianam " fidem fint acceffuri, fi *polygamia* apud nos non effet " prohibita. Sicuti conftat uti vir diffufiffimæ erudi- " tionis *Gifbertus Voetius* teftatur, quod totum regnum " *Tonchinum* una cum rege ad Chriftianam fidem fuiffet " converfum, nifi Jefuitæ in fuis concionibus jamdum " converfos a polygamia dehortati fuiffent, & regi ipfi " perfuadere voluiffent quod ipfi omnes uxores excepta " unica, fi Chriftianus fieri vellet, fint deferendæ. Quæ

sionary, what he would richly deserve, an hearty *bastinado* for his pains. That any rational

"res adeo movit ipsum regem, ut omnes illos apostolos, uti audire volunt, cum *apostolica*, seu potius *chimærica* doctrina ejecerit. De quo damno ecclesiæ illi hostes, non tantum polygamias, sed etiam matrimonii, respondebunt aliquando in extremo judicio."

"I mention not that many Gentiles and *Turks*, among whom *polygamy* is much used, might come over to the *Christian* faith, if *polygamy* were not prohibited among us. *Gisbert Voetius*, a man of most extensive erudition, testifies, that the whole kingdom of *Tonquin*, together with its *king*, might have been converted to the *Christian* faith, unless the *Jesuits* had in their discourses dissuaded those who had been already converted, from *polygamy*; and even chosen to persuade the *king himself*, that he must put away all his wives except one, if he would become a *Christian*: which so provoked the *king*, that he cast out all those *apostles* (as they would be called) together with their *apostolical*, or rather *chimærical*, doctrine. For which loss to the church, those enemies, not only of *polygamy*, but even of matrimony, will answer at the great day."

Lord *Kaims*, Hist. of Man, vol. i. p. 197, observes, that among the most zealous Christians in the kingdom of *Congo*, polygamy is in use as formerly, when they were *Pagans*; and that sooner than give it up, they would renounce *Christianity*.

Bellarmine, De Matrim. c. 12. very *piously* saith—"Ob *solam polygamiam* infideles a baptismo & toto Christianismo arcendi."—"That infidels who use *polygamy*, are for that *sole cause* to be driven from *baptism*, and from the whole of *Christianity*."—Query—If this be not to *strain out a gnat, and swallow a camel?*

In c. 10. of the same book, the same *Bellarmine* saith—"*Polygamia* non repugnat *juri naturæ*, quod est divinum, quod unus vir ex pluribus fœminis liberos possit suscipere & alere."—"*Polygamy* is not repugnant to the *law of nature*, which is *divine*, that *one man* might beget and bring up children by *more women than one*."

tional beings can be brought to believe such absurdities in any part of the globe, is one sad proof of the ascendency which superstition has over the minds of men, and of the small pains which in general are taken by them to * inform themselves in matters of the highest consequence; of which I shall next proceed to treat, in the following chapter.

I will only observe here, however strange it may seem, that our notions relative to the *commerce of the sexes*, are by far more friendly to † *polygyny*, than the *Turkish* system of *polygamy* is. A *Turk* may take one or more *wives*; but then they are kept in his *haram* as his inviolable property — no eye of a

---

Contradiction must ever be found, where people err from the *one consistent truth of* God.—Hence it is no wonder, that, notwithstanding all the bitterness of that gloomy misogamist *Jerome*, against even marriage itself, in his writings against honest *Jovinian*, that he should say, when writing to *Pammachius — Non damno polygamos.* —" I do not condemn *polygamists*."

* " They tread in the steps of their fathers, never exa-
" mining whether they be right or wrong. Custom and
" education have almost banished reason from the earth.
" The *Hircanians* and *Bactrians* cast their aged pa-
" rents, yet living, to the dogs: which inhumanity,
" when *Stasanor*, the deputy of *Alexander the Great*, en-
" deavoured to suppress, they had like to have deposed
" him from the *government*: so prevalent is the *force* of
" a received *custom* on the minds of the unthinking
" herd." *Turkish Spy*, vol iv. p. 39.

† By *polygyny* (from πολυς, *many*, and γυνη, *woman*) is meant — the having more *women* than one, without *marriage* or other obligation towards them.

By *polygamy* (from πολυς, *many*, and γαμος, *marriage*) is meant — the having more *wives* than one.

stranger

stranger can * ever behold them, and they are maintained and provided for, as liberally as the man's circumstances will permit. Whereas, among us, a man may *take* as many women as he can seduce, and abandon them whenever he pleases; they can claim no property *in him*, nor he *in them*; he turns them upon the *common*, either to starve with hunger, or rot by *prostitution*.—That this is against the law of GOD, is very clear; but there is nothing in our law which can either prevent or remedy it. Had we, at the *Reformation*, adopted the law from *Mount Sinai*, instead of that from the *council of Trent*, relative to *marriage*, such things could not exist.

With regard to the depredations which are made on *married women*, how may the *Mahomedans* † shame us! So sacred are wo-

---

* The distrust of the *Turks* is so great, that they will not permit their wives to see any man whatsoever, no, not their nearest relations; and a woman that should shew her *face*, nay, even her *hands*, would be looked on as dishonoured. *Le Bruyn*, vol. i. p. 453. What would a *Turk* think of *Christian* wives, *as they appear in public places*, where it is even *unfashionable* to have the husbands of their party?

† N. B. " I am much pleased with the *Turkish* man-
" ners; a people, though ignorant, yet, in my judgment,
" extremely polite. A gallant convicted of having de-
" bauched a *married* woman, is regarded as a pernicious
" being, and held in the same abhorrence as a *prostitute*
" with us. He is certain of never making his fortune,
" and they would deem it scandalous, to confer any
" considerable employment, on a man suspected of hav-
" ing committed such enormous injustice." Lady M. W. M, vol. iii. 189. edit. 1767.

men

men in *India*, that, even in the midst of slaughter and devastation, the common soldier leaves them unmolested; the *haram* is a sanctuary against all the licentiousness of victory; and ruffians, covered with the blood of an husband, shrink back, with veneration, from the secret apartment of his wives. But this is not confined to *India*. At *Constantinople*, when the *Sultan* sends an order to strangle a state criminal, and to seize on his effects, the ruffians who execute it enter not into the * *haram*, nor touch any thing belonging to the women. See *Alexander*, Hist. of Wom. p. 191.

In short, we may boast of our *monogamy*, and condemn *polygamy*—but there is not a nation under heaven, where *polygyny* is more openly practised, than in this *Christian* country; for though a man can *marry* but *one* at a time, he may have as great a variety of women as he pleases, without ever *marrying* at all. This is so inveterated by custom, that those laws of *Heaven* which were made to prevent it, seem to be totally forgotten.

* It was a bitter *sarcasm* on the *Christians*, which was uttered by *Mehemet Effendi*, the last *Turkish* ambassador in *France*—" We *Turks*" (says he) " are great
" simpletons, in comparison of the *Christians*. We are
" at the expence and trouble of keeping a *seraglio*, each
" in his own house; but you ease yourselves of this
" burden, and have your *seraglio* in your friends'
" houses."—See Hume's *Essays*, 3d edit. vol. i. p. 252. How far we have been imitating the manners and customs of the *French*, so as to make ourselves objects of the above reflection, I leave to others to determine.

However this *Christian* land may suffer by such comparisons as have been made above, yet I cannot refrain from carrying them still further. The just detestation and abhorrence with which we look on a *Turkish* SERAGLIO, and all the appendages relative to the management of it, ought still to increase, when carried to a survey of our *Seraglios* in *England*; I mean our *public brothels*; where are to be found numbers of young, beautiful, and once modest and innocent *females*, who have been seduced and deserted, and are now driven into the horrid necessity of *common prostitution* to keep them from starving. The doors of these *houses* of *infamy* are open to every *comer*, the women the temporary property of every *visitor*—filthiness and obscenity defile their conversation, and the most abandoned profligacy attends their actions:——these *houses* are accommodated to men of all ranks and degrees, from the highest to the lowest; and, lest the plan of lewdness should suffer by being narrowed within the boundaries of walls, every public street, after a certain time of night, exhibits a kind of *itinerant Seraglio*, where men are saved the trouble of going out of their way; they are met by numbers of women, whose language and behaviour are too shockingly indecent to mention, and who seem so far to have obliterated every trace of *female* delicacy, as to retain nothing which can bespeak them to be women, but their mere shape.

Let

Let us, from these scenes of horror, turn our eyes to the *wards* of a *public hospital*, to which the *harpies* are consigned by the force of a *disease*, which, after having communicated to numbers of men, threatens their own destruction. Here may be seen, *female ruin* in its last stage of ignominy and misery. The bloom of youth, the gracefulness of form, the beauty of features, are fled and gone; and the whole frame dissolving into corruption, rottenness, and dust. The mind, equally contaminated with the body, exhibits a hideous mixture of remorse, ignorance, guilt, stupidity, hardness, and despair.

What can the *Grand Seignior's* SERAGLIO, or the HARAM of a *Turkish Bassa* exhibit, equally horrible, equally disgraceful (not only to all good policy and government, but even to human nature itself) with these *scenes*, which are the objects of common observation in this *Christian* country?

When it is considered, that, all this arises from a *system* of total *irresponsibility* of the *seducer* to the woman he *seduces*, it is reduced to a very *simple* principle, and the *simplicity* of the *remedy* speaks itself.

I will conclude this chapter with a summary of its contents, which are all reducible to one general rule.—GOD's *ordinances*, being of His *own* appointment, are solely under *His* own *authority*; so that *men* cannot change or alter them, either with respect to *themselves* as to the *matter* of them, or as to their *operation, force*, and *effect*. *Marriage* is an ordinance

ordinance of God, of His own appointment, both with respect to the thing *itself*, and its *operation, force,* and *effect,* with respect to *us.*—therefore, as to these, is solely under God's authority, and cannot be changed or altered by human laws. As the substance of the *bread* and *wine* in the Lord's *supper,* remained the *same* after consecration as before it, notwithstanding the bloody edict of Henry VIII. above mentioned; so *marriage* remains, as to the *matter, force, effect,* and *obligation* of it upon the parties, just the *same* in the sight of God *now,* as *before* 26 Geo. II. c. 33.

As no human law can change any *ordinance of* God, so neither can it change any *truth* of God.—I firmly believe, that the 39 articles of the *church of England* contain, in point of doctrine, the truth of God; but I do not believe this one jot the more because they are enacted by authority of *parliament:* nor should I believe it one jot the less, if the efforts of their *Arian* and *Socinian* adversaries were to succeed, and the *parliament* was to declare their obligation upon men's consciences, as well as the articles themselves, and all things contained therein—" *null and void* " *to all* intents and purposes whatsoever; " any law or usage to the contrary notwith- " standing."

There is a *statute* which has been before mentioned, viz. 31 Hen. VIII. c. 14. which makes it *felony, without benefit of clergy,* to assert that the *communion in both kinds is ne-*
cessary

cessary to the laity, or ought to be *administered or received*—but this law could have no effect upon the nature of the ordinance as in God's fight.—So 1 Jac. c. 11. makes a man a *felon, and to suffer death*, for having *two wives* together—but can this be proved to affect such a *marriage*, or to make it null and void or sinful in God's fight? The only way to prove that either of these laws are binding on men's consciences, is, to prove that they harmonize with God's truth as revealed in the scripture, otherwise one is just as much unauthorized as the other.

As to mere *circumstantials*, which respect outward order and deceney, as they are no part of the ordinances themselves, they may be under the appointment and controul of man. So when our *Rubric* says—that there shall be " a table with a fair white linen " cloth upon it," at the administration of the *sacrament of the* Lord's *supper*—and again, with respect to *baptism*—that " without great " cause and necessity, the people shall be " warned that they procure not their chil- " dren to be baptized at home in their " houses"—I see no sort of harm in all this; but if the *act of parliament*, which confirmed the *Rubric*, had gone on—" And be it en- " acted, that if the sacrament of the Lord's " *supper* be administered without such *fair* " *white linen* cloth *upon the table*, or *baptism* " be administered in *private houses*, unless " for such *great cause and necessity* aforesaid, " such sacraments of the Lord's *supper*, and
" *baptism*,

"*baptism*, so administered, shall be utterly
"*null and void* to the receivers of the same,
"*to all intents and purposes whatsoever*"—this
had been an attack upon the *ordinances and
truths* of scripture—not a lawful and authorized *statute*. Let this reasoning be applied
to the question of *marriage*, as it is a * *civil
contract*, and as such the *object of human laws*
—and as it is a *divine institution*, and as
such *not the object of human laws*—then it
may easily be determined how far these
ought to be binding on the consciences of
men, where marriage is concerned.

* The *outward* contract between the parties, is certainly of a *civil* nature, and ought to belong to the *civil
magistrate*. In this respect, the *clergy* have no more to
do with it than they have with *fines* and *recoveries*, or
any other temporal causes. The payment of the מוהר
or *dowry* (see before, vol. i. p.   .) among the *Jews*,
which was in nature of a *civil* contract, was transacted
between the man and the damsel's father; but had nothing to do with the *priests* and *Levites*, nor was it any
part of the *Temple* service.

CHAP.

CHAP. VIII.

Of SUPERSTITION, *more especially relating to the Subjects treated in this Book.*

WHEN man fell from GOD by disobedience, in striving to make himself *wiser* than GOD had made him, and that by means which GOD had forbidden, he lost that image of *knowledge* and *wisdom* in which he was originally created. (Comp. Gen. i. 26. Col. iii. 10.) The only means of any restoration to this, must be by *revelation*; for as man by transgression had brought *darkness* into his soul, as well as *guilt*, this could never have been removed by any powers of the human will or understanding; HE *alone* who created the *material light,* could dispel the clouds in which the human mind was involved, and cause once more the *light of the knowledge of the glory of* GOD to shine into the desolate and benighted heart of man. Nothing could have * discovered any traces of

---

* " God hath given out to us the whole of His *mind*
" and *counsel* concerning us in *writing*, as a merciful
" and stedfast relief against all that confusion, darkness,
" and uncertainty, which the vanity, folly, and loose-
" ness of the minds of men, drawn out and heightened
" by the unspeakable altercations which fall out amongst
" them, would otherwise certainly have run into."
Dr. *Owen* on the Scriptures, p. 28.—to which we may add—which they *have* run into by leaving the *written word.*

the *divine* mind and will, but thofe gracious declarations of them, for which fallen man ftands folely indebted to the free and gratuitous interpofition of divine mercy and goodnefs. *For what man knoweth the things of a man, fave the fpirit of man which is in him? Even fo the things of* GOD *none* (ȣδεις) *knoweth —but the Spirit of* GOD. 1 Cor. ii. 11.—*Who hath known the mind of the* LORD, *and who hath been His counfellor?* Rom. xi. 34.—*My thoughts are not your thoughts, neither are my ways your ways, faith the* LORD; *for as the heavens are higher than the earth, fo are my ways higher than your ways, and my thoughts than your thoughts.* If. lv. 8, 9.—*Canft thou by fearching find out* GOD, *canft thou find out the* ALMIGHTY *to perfection? It is as high as heaven, what canft thou do?—deeper than hell, what canft thou know?* Job. xi. 7, 8.

This is giving us fair warning of our deplorable *ignorance* with refpect to GOD and His *will* and *ways*.—Still—*vain man would be wife, though man be born like a wild* * *afs's colt*.

---

* " How keenly is this comparifon pointed!—*Like
" the afs's*—an animal remarkable for its ftupidity, even
" to a proverb;—*like the afs's colt*—which muft be ftill
" more egregioufly ftupid than the dam; *like the wild
" afs's colt*—which is not only blockifh, but ftubborn
" and intractable; neither poffeffes valuable qualities
" by nature, nor will eafily receive them by difcipline.
" —The image in the original is ftill more ftrongly
" touched. The comparative particle *like* is not in the
" *Hebrew*; it is—*born a wild afs's colt*—or, as we fhould
" fay in *Englifh*—*a mere wild afs's colt.*" HERVEY,
Ther. and *Afpaf.* vol. ii. p. 237. 5th edit. 1777, octavo.

Job

Job xi. 12. His imagination will set to work; and though he be assured that *all scripture is given by inspiration of* God, *and is profitable for doctrine*— therefore is to *teach* us;—for *reproof* (προς ελεγχον)—for reproof *or conviction* of *sin and error*—and therefore to set them before us in their true light;—for *correction*—επανορθωσιν—for setting right and amending that which is wrong;—for *instruction*—(παιδειαν—institution—discipline) *in righteousness*; and all this that the *man of* God *may be perfect, thoroughly furnished unto all good works,* and thus *be made wise unto salvation* (see 2 Tim. iii. 16, 17.)—yet, such is the pride, such the folly of man, he will not be satisfied with what God hath revealed, but would fain make some discoveries of his *own* concerning God and *religion*, which, rather than part with, he will even make the criteria and standards of truth; will endeavour to reconcile his own *inventions* with God's *revelations*; and if this be too hard, the next experiment is to accommodate the *divine revelations* to his *own inventions*. There are no *popular* systems of *religion* and *worship*, where this is not to be found. This was the plan of the *Babel-builders* of old time, and ever since it has been, as *they* were, *scattered over the face of the whole earth.* Gen. xi. 8. The *Heathen*, who had the *volume of nature* open to them for their instruction (Rom. i. 19, 20.) *became vain in their imaginations, and their foolish heart was darkened—professing themselves to be wise, they became fools, and changed the*

the truth of GOD *into a lye,* &c. ver. 22, 25. The *Jews*, with the *written volume* of *divine revelation* before them, set their imaginations to work, trying to find out some *holier* and *better* way to walk and to please GOD than they found there—till they were as much lost to the teachings of GOD's *word*, as the *Heathen* were to the teachings of the *outward creation*—till, as Isaiah, lx. 2. expresseth it—*darkness covered the earth, and gross darkness the people.*—The *Christian* churches began very early to tread in * the same steps, and

to

---

* When we contemplate *Christianity*, as revealed in the Old Testament, and as opened to us in the New Testament, we may truly call it a most noble, most gracious, and most glorious display of heavenly wisdom, an emanation from all the perfections and attributes of the DEITY; suited, *divinely* suited, to relieve the wants, and to heal the misery, of fallen man—to stamp once more the *divine image* on the human soul, and make it *meet to partake of the inheritance of the saints in light.* Col. i. 12.

But if it be considered *only* as it appears when *cauponized* with the vain reasonings of men of corrupt minds —*adulterated* by human sophistry—*perverted* to serve the cause of earthly power and worldly dominion, or to quadrate with human systems—*darkened* by folly and superstition—*disgraced* by the uncommanded austerities of visionaries and enthusiasts—*scandalized* by the monstrous vices of its professors—*wrested* by disputants into palpable contradictions, and made subversive of the *divine law*—but above all, as pressed into the service of fraud, rapine, injustice, and cruelty—it then appears, not only unworthy of the DEITY, but the most mischievous and horrid *superstition* that ever infested the earth. Little better than all this, are the views of it presented to us by the most faithful historians, in their accounts of the *church*, but more especially after the *empire* became
Christian,

to invent schemes of *holiness* and *purity* with respect to *manners*—of *mortification* and *austerity* with regard to *discipline*, and *not sparing of the body* (Col. ii. 23.)—of *rites* and *ceremonies* with regard to *worship*—of human *wisdom* and *science* with respect to *doctrine*—till they even (before two centuries were elapsed) vied with *Babel* itself; and whoever can read Dr. *Mosheim*'s account of the early ages of *Christianity*, without thinking it as great a miracle as any recorded in the *gospels*, that they should ever reach us at all, but more especially in the pure state in which they are among us, will appear to have a talent at accounting for things by *second* causes, beyond the capacity of any writer I yet have met with. Why *Heathens*, *Jews*, and *Christians*, should act so uniformly towards those *revelations which* GOD *at sundry times and in divers manners* (Heb. i. 1.) hath vouchsafed them, is all accounted for on one simple principle—Prov.

Christian, when we read of little else, in general, than the intrigues of *churchmen* against one another, and the rest of mankind, in order to gratify their ambition and avarice—and to satiate their pride, revenge, and cruelty. That the scriptures should be preserved to us entire, when coming through *such hands*, is as evident a miracle, as it would have been to have kept a spark of fire alive in the *heart of the sea*. But here let me mention, with veneration and honour, the comparatively faithful *few*, who, in the face of difficulty, danger, and even *death itself*, maintained their integrity, and *shone as lights in the world*—such are well called—*the salt of the earth* (Matt. v. 13.) for it has been by the *favour* of their *lives and doctrines*, that the whole *mass* has been preserved from total corruption.

xxvii.

xxvii. 19. *As in water face answereth to face —so doth the heart of man to man.* Hence it is, that through all ages of the *church,* those who have invented *systems* for *others,* have constantly been mixing the peculiarities of some or other which they have had invented for *them:*—there is therefore no security to be found from error, until a man is really and truly

Nullius addictus jurare in verba magistri.
Hor.

Friend * *to all sects—but blindly sworn to none.*
Francis.

The *Apostle,* 1 Thess. v. 21. says, *Try—prove—examine*—δοκιμαζετε—*assay,* as refiners do metals, *all things; hold fast that which is good.—Beloved,* saith 1 *John* iv. 1. *Believe not every spirit, but try the spirits whether they are of* God, *because many false prophets are gone out into the world.* But how is this *trial* to be made ?—Not by the poor ineffectual *fire* of *human wisdom*—but by putting what we hear or read into the *furnace* of *divine truth,* by *searching the scriptures,* comparing *spiritual things with spiritual,* and whatsoever will abide this, we may believe to be true; for God's truth, like His *children* that we read of Dan. iii. 27. the more it is *tried,* the more evidently will it appear to be his peculiar care, and the more glorious will it come forth.

* The author means, as far as *Christian love* and *charity* call upon him to be so.

His having raised up men from time to time in all ages of the *church*, who dared † thus to examine into the truth for themselves, and then to attack the *superstition* of the day in which they lived, is to be reckoned among the foremost of those *second causes*, by which the *truth* hath been preserved to us. Yet much remains to be done, and surely none, who call themselves the real friends of mankind, can help wishing for the day, when those shackles which have been fixed upon the consciences of men by *priestcraft*, *bigotry*, and *vulgar error*, shall all drop off, and when men shall be bound, in all their actions towards *Heaven* and *each other*, by the ties of *justice*, *mercy*, and the *love of* GOD—

---

† There are few more beautiful images in any poet whatsoever, than that, by which Mr. *Prior* represents the doubts and fears of the human mind, when determining simply for itself, and the confidence and boldness with which it acts, when it has *vulgar opinion* on its side.

Poor ALMA, like a lonely deer,
O'er hills and dales does doubtful err:
With panting haste, and quick surprize,
From ev'ry leaf that stirs, she flies;
Till, mingled with the neighbouring herd,
She slights what erst she singly fear'd;
And now, exempt from doubt and dread,
She dares pursue, if they dare lead:
As their example still prevails,
She tempts the stream, or leaps the pales.

He then, quoth DICK, who, by your rule,
Thinks for himself, becomes a fool. &c.

ALMA, Canto III.

Matt. xxiii. 3. Luke xi. 42.—when whole *hecatombs* of feduced, ruined, and deferted *females* fhall ceafe to *pafs through the fire* of men's luft to *Moloch*, and to be offered at the fhrine of *proftitution*.

Fable tells us, that *feven* noble *Athenians* were annually given to be devoured by the monfter *Minotaur*; that this inhuman cuftom prevailed until *Thefeus* flew the devourer:—we may fay of our prefent *fyftem* of laws, relative to the *commerce of the fexes*,

————mutato nomine de te
Fabula narratur———

Change but the name, the fable's told of thee.

only with this difference, that *feven* victims fatisfied the *Cretan monfter*, but not feventy— nor feven hundred—nor feven thoufand *feduced virgins* are fufficient to complete the quota which is annually furnifhed, by the *female fex*, of facrifices to the monfter *Proftitution*. So it has long been, and fo it ftill muft be, until a reftoration of GOD's moft *holy* and *beneficent law* fhall take place among us.

Superftition is the offspring of human pride* and *ignorance:* as thefe are to be found

in

---

* Thefe have always been faft friends to each other, and moft determined *foes* to all that can oppofe their influence over the minds of men. The difficulties which they have laid in the way of all difcoveries or revivals of *truth*, in matters of *human fcience* as well as of religion, are manifeft to all who are acquainted with the hiftory

of

in the nature of every child of fallen *Adam*; fo, as thefe are *more* or *lefs* fubdued by the power of the world. When, after the darknefs of many ages, the firft dawn of learning and tafte began to appear in *Europe*, learned men in different countries began to cultivate *aftronomy*: *Galileo*, a *Florentine*, about 1610, introduced the ufe of *telefcopes*, which difcovered new arguments in fupport of the motion of the earth, and confirmed the old ones, which had before been made ufe of by *Copernicus*; but fuch were the pride and ignorance of mankind, and fuch the fury and bigotry of the *priefts*, that *Galileo* was forced to renounce the *Copernican* fyftem as a *damnable herefy*. This very *philofophy* is now, as improved by Sir Ifaac Newton, adopted as the true fyftem of the univerfe. We might here alfo mention that barbarous murder, which was committed on *Vigilius*, a *Chriftian Bifhop*, who was burnt by the decree of the *Roman* church, for afferting the *Antipodes*; a truth which all nations are now fenfible of, fince the improvement of navigation and traffic. See *Turkifh Spy*, vol. ii. p. 92. edit. 1691. By this, and many other inftances which might be given, we may judge how fmall the bias of *popular opinion* ought to be, where *truth* is concerned. This obfervation may be illuftrated ftill farther, if we confider the oppofition given to the introduction of the *Quinquina* or *Jefuits* bark, about the middle of the laft century, now almoft univerfally acknowledged to be one of the greateft and beft remedies in the whole province of medicine;—and, in our time, how were the whole *college* alarmed at the *fever powder* introduced by Dr. *James*, now proved to be almoft a *fpecific* in *inflammatory fevers?*—What abufe and oppofition did Mr. *Sutton* incur, becaufe he introduced a method of preventing patients in the *fmall-pox* from being ftewed to death by the ignorance of *phyficians?*—now this very method is become the moft *approved* practice.

> *Cætera de genere hoc (adeò funt multa) loquacem*
> *Delaffare valent* Fabium.   Hor.

power of divine truth, *superstition* will *less* or *more* bear its sway in religious matters.

By *superstition*, I would be understood to mean—a *devotion which has no foundation in the revealed will of* GOD, and either rests in the *imagination* of the party, or owes its sanction to some *mis-interpretation* or *ill-understanding* of the *revelation itself*. Under the former head, we may rank the various *superstitions* of those nations on whom the light of GOD's revelation, as contained in the *Bible*, hath not yet arisen. Under the *latter* we may include many strange and indefensible *opinions*, which are maintained as so many inviolable *truths*, even among those who are blessed with the *oracles of* GOD, and who profess to believe them. The church of *Rome* abounds in this sort of *superstition*, insomuch that she will plead the *wisdom of* GOD, as revealed in *His word*, for the maintenance of *absurdities* too

> The numbers of like instances we meet
> Would tire the most *loquacious* to repeat.

The author therefore by no means thinks he shall escape the obloquy of the *world*, for daring to publish a *treatise* which militates so diametrically against the inveterate opinions, prejudices, and customs which *folly* and *superstition* have established among us. However, if he be but the instrument of holding forth the *mind* of the *great moral Governor of the universe*, so as to excite the attention of the candid and inquisitive to still deeper researches after it, some abler and more respectable pen may be the means of finishing what is here begun, and men be prevailed upon, to consider the dreadful consequences of a departure from that *divine system*, which was established by *infinite wisdom* for the *preservation* and *continuation* of the human species.

palpable

palpable and grofs to conceal themfelves from the difcovery of our *outward fenfes*; yet believed, or profeffed to be believed, by *whole nations* of profeffing *Chriftians*, who are taught to look no farther than the *authority* of the *church*, and to fubmit their *underftandings* and *confciences* to the dominion of *men* * *like themfelves*. A melancholy proof this of the *fuperftition* and *folly* to which we are expofed, when once we can yield our affent to popular opinion, without giving ourfelves the trouble to *fearch the fcriptures*, as the *Bereans* did (Acts xvii. 11.) and to enquire for ourfelves *whether thefe things are fo*.

Free enquiry, when exercifed with an honeft defire to *know* and *to do the will of* GOD, is not only the *privilege*, but alfo the *duty* of every *reafonable creature*. To believe a *propofition* becaufe it has the fanction of *popular opinion, worldly cuftoms*, and *human laws*, may as well land us in *Popery* as in *Proteftantifm*, or in *Heathenifm* as in *Chriftianity*, or in any thing elfe which it is the fafhion to believe in the country where our lot is caft. *Brethren*, faith *Paul*, (1 Cor. xiv. 20.) *be not children in underftanding, but in underftanding be men*. Saith 1 *Pet.* iii. 15. *Be ready always*

---

* There is fomething very fevere, but very true, in that farcafm on the *ignorance* of *Romifh* priefts, and the *credulity* of the people, which *M. De Voltaire*, in his tragedy of *Oedipus*, puts into the mouth of *Jocafta*——

Nos Prêtres *ne font point ce qu'un vain peuple penfe*;
Notre credulité *fait toute leur* fcience.

to give an answer to every man that asketh you a reason of the hope that is in you—that is, a *scriptural, wise,* and *solid* reason. But how can this be done, unless we acquaint ourselves with some better foundation of *our hope,* than the bare IPSE DIXIT, the mere " SAY SO," of *any* man, or *all* men put together?

One of the worst properties of *superstition* is, that, when it becomes inveterate, when grown old by long custom and usage, having descended from father to son, from generation to generation, it is as difficult to eradicate it out of the *body politic,* as to expel a long-fixed chronical disease out of the *natural body.* In some instances, perhaps in *most,* nothing but *dissolution* itself can effect it. The *Pope's* supremacy and infallibility—the doctrines of masses for the quick and dead—indulgences—*five* of the *seven* sacraments—the celibacy of priests—transubstantiation—the adoration of the host—the worship of images and relics—praying to the Virgin Mary—the invention of purgatory—and other most sacred *superstitions,* are so ingrafted into the very constitution of the *Romish* church, that they can never be destroyed, without destroying that *political fabric,* which they call THE CHURCH, itself. This actually happened at the *Reformation*—these things being abolished, there was an end so far of the *church of Rome.*

When we reflect on the *superstition* with regard to *marriage,* which has so long reigned in the *Christian church*, and is as much interwoven with *our laws*, as the other *superstitions* before mentioned once *were*, we may perhaps fear that this can never be destroyed, without destroying the whole *fabric* of those laws which support it.

Still *superstition* is *superstition*, however venerated or dignified; and every man who endeavours to detect it, and to destroy its mischievous supremacy over the minds of men, is equally a friend to religion and to mankind. The zealots on the side of the *superstition* will make an heavy cry against the *detector*, as the *Papists* did against the *Reformers*, or as the *Ephesians* did against *Paul* when he attacked their *great* DIANA, *whom all* ASIA *and the world worshipped*, (Acts xix. 26, 27.) by teaching, that *they are no* GODS *which be made by hands*. But our glorious *Reformers*, knowing that they had the truth of GOD on their side, boldly pushed on, as *Paul* on the same principle had done before them; nothing could prevail on them to be silent in the important cause which they had undertaken, until, happily for themselves, and for succeeding generations, they found the force of that saying—*Magna est veritas & prævalebit*.—GREAT IS THE TRUTH, AND WILL PREVAIL.

I would not be understood as giving the name of *superstition* to every circumstance of *worship* and *religion* which is not to be found in the *Bible*. *Let all things be done decently and in order*, is the direction of an inspired

Apostle,

Apoſtle, 1 Cor. xiv. 40. Many things may be obſerved and uſed for theſe purpoſes, not only innocently, but with much expediency; and while they are looked upon only in *this* light, they ought to have due reverence, and to be *ſubmitted to for the* LORD's *ſake*. 1 Pet. ii. 13. But when once certain appendages of human invention, are put in the place of, or made to ſuperſede the obligation of *divine inſtitutions*, there they erect themſelves into *ſuperſtitions*, and, ſo far from claiming *reverence*, deſerve * *contempt* and *abhorrence*, more eſpecially when they are attended with *ruin, deſtruction*, and *deſolation* to thouſands, whom the law of GOD was formed to protect and to preſerve.

I have before compared the *divine* inſtitution of *marriage* to thoſe other *divine inſtitutions* of *baptiſm* and the LORD's *ſupper*, as equally ordained of GOD, therefore equally exempt from the controul of man, with reſpect to its *eſſence* and *obligation* in GOD's ſight. Laws which men may make to alter or change theſe, are to be conſidered as *ipſo facto* null and void with regard to the conſcience, otherwiſe the ordinances of Heaven might in time become no ordinances at all. Though

---

* A ſtronger caſe than any above hinted at, meets us in the *holy ſcriptures*. The *brazen ſerpent*, ordained by GOD Himſelf, as a glorious *type* of our *once* CRUCIFIED, but *now* EXALTED SAVIOUR, when, in after times, it was abuſed to the purpoſes of *ſuperſtition* and *idolatry*, was broken to pieces by *king Hezekiah*. Comp. Numb. xxi. 8. John iii. 14, 15. 2 Kings xviii. 4.

the

the *Pope* has banished the *cup* from the administration of the LORD's *supper*, and thus abolished one half of the divine institution with respect to the *laity*, yet this cannot make the least alteration as to the essence and obligation of the thing itself in GOD's sight; the entire *sacrament* remains just where CHRIST left it, though *man has put asunder what* GOD *hath joined together*. So is it with the ordinance of *marriage*—those who are *joined together* by that ordinance by which they are pronounced *one flesh*, are so, and must remain so by virtue of the *divine* command, though all the legislative bodies on earth were to meet together, and make a law to *put them asunder*.

Superstition says otherwise.—It has long taught us to tread the *ordinance* of GOD under foot, to vacate its obligation, to destroy its efficacy, to deny its validity; and *marriage* is now supposed to consist in a *human ceremony*, administered by a *fellow-creature*, and that on such *terms* and *conditions*, as the fancy and imagination of mankind have first *invented* and then *imposed*.

Marriage was instituted, and its *one* ordinance appointed, *thousands* of years before there were buildings called *churches* or *chapels*—*steeples*—*bells*—*Popish priests*—or *mass-books*. It is, as instituted by the GOD of nature, simply *one* and the *same* throughout all ages and generations, therefore *one* and the *same* as to its *import*, *validity*, and *obligation*, in the sight of GOD.

The

The particular laws which it pleased the ALMIGHTY to ordain for the honour of his own *moral government*, and for the *peace, welfare*, and good order of *society* in general, as well as for the protection and defence of the *individuals* which compose it, were clearly revealed by GOD at *Mount Sinai*, and committed to writing by *Moses*. These laws can never alter, much less give way to the *superstitious* inventions of men, but stand on record and bear their testimony against all *ungodliness* and *unrighteousness of men*, notwithstanding a *Popish indulgence*, or the sanction of an *act of parliament* to the contrary. These *laws* declare, that *if any man* be found lying with a woman *betrothed* or *married* to an husband, it is *adultery* in *both*, and BOTH *must* DIE—but if with a *virgin not betrothed, she shall be his wife—he may not put her away all his days*—BECAUSE HE HAS HUMBLED HER. The reason here given is very plain and conclusive, but with *us* it is no reason at all, we (practically at least) read the law thus—*she shall not be his wife—he may put her away when he pleases,* though he has HUMBLED HER—unless a certain human being called a *priest*—reads out of a service-book a certain *form of words*, called a *form of solemnization of matrimony*—in a certain place, called a *parish church* or *chapel*, and all this in compliance with a certain *human law* made for that purpose.— The whole is dependent on the humour of the parties, for if either be base or wicked enough to depart from their *engagement* before

fore God, and to refuse a compliance with the *outward ceremony*, no *legal* restraint is laid on their total departure from each other; they may utterly divorce each other for ever—and *this*, though God's LAW positively forbids it, in words clear and plain as if written with a *sun-beam*.

Notwithstanding what is above observed, that which *was*, still *is*, and ever *will* be, the *Divine mind* and *will* upon the subject of *marriage*, and of that ordinance by which it is effected in the sight of God. No *outward ceremony* could add to its obligation, and accordingly we find no trace of any such thing in the scripture; the ceremonial appointment of the paying the *fifty shekels* to the *damsel's father*, seems to be the only *outward recognition* of the *contract* which appears under the law of *Moses*; but not a vestige do we find of the interference of *priests*, or *rites* and *ceremonies* of *matrimony* being any part of the *temple service*. The *Jews* indeed in after times invented many *rites* and *ceremonies* * upon the occasion;

---

* A particular account of these may be seen in *Broughton*, Hist. Lib. vol. ii. p. 179. None of them are to be found in the law of *Moses*, but consist of various inventions of their own; though one in particular, mentioned Matt. xxv. 1—7, seems to have been borrowed from the *heathen* customs—that of the *bridegroom* conducting the *bride* to his house by the light of torches at night. See HARMER's *outlines*, p. 330. n.

Νύμφας δ' ἐκ θαλάμων, δαΐδων ὑπολαμπομενάων,
Ἠγίνεον ἀνὰ ἄςυ, πολὺς δ' ὑμέναιος ὀρώρει.
Hom. Il. Σ. l. 492—3.

Alon

occasion; but as none of these are to be found in *holy writ*, they cannot be supposed in the least essential to the *ordinance* of marriage. It appears from some passages of scripture, as John ii. 1. Matt. xxii. 2, &c. that it was usual for the parties to call their friends and neighbours together, and to make

> Along the street the new-made brides are led,
> With *torches* flaming, to the nuptial bed.   POPE.

So VIRGIL, Ecl. viii. ver. 29.
Mopse novas incide faces; tibi ducitur uxor.

——————— prepare the *lights*,
O *Mopsus*, and perform the bridal rites.
DRYDEN.

So Æn. iv. l. 18. we find the word *tæda*, a *torch*, put for marriage itself.

Si non pertæsum thalami *tædæque* fuisset.

On which the *Delphin edition* thus comments—
Tædæque.] Facis è *tæda* arbore é picearum genere: pro nuptiis sumitur; quia præferebatur novæ uxori, in mariti domum deducendæ.

And of the *torch*] made from a tree of the *pitch* or *rosin kind* (see *Ainsworth*, sub *Picea*.)—It is *used* to signify *marriage*, because it was carried before the *new-married wife*, when she was to be brought home to the house of her husband.

> Claustra pandite januæ
> Virgo adest, viden' ut *faces*
> Splendidas quatiunt comas?

The virgin comes—ye gates unfold your leaves;
See how the shining *torches* shake their flames.
CATULL. Epithal.

The glorious use which our BLESSED SAVIOUR makes of this custom, in that beautiful and instructive parable of the *ten virgins*, is well known.

a *feast* * or *entertainment* on the occasion; but this was no more a part of the *marriage*, than the *king*'s coronation-dinner is a part of his *title* to the crown; nor can any human ceremony add any more to the validity of a *marriage* in the sight of GOD, than the *coronation* itself does to the *king*'s right to the throne of these realms: this indeed is a solemn recognition, a public notification of something which existed before, but does not in the least add to its validity in the sight of GOD. If a *king* of *England* was to die before his *coronation*, he would die as really *king* of *England* as if he had survived that ceremony, and the crown would equally descend to the heir apparent.—So a man and a woman *joined* together according to GOD's ordinance, though they died before any outward human ceremony, would die just as much *husband* and *wife* in GOD's account, as if all the services which men ever invented had been red over them. This in every case—no prior engagement on the *man's side* was pleadable in bar of the *divine law*; its obligation affected all men alike, nothing could vacate or set it aside more with respect to *one* man than *another*. The words of the law, as hath been before shewn at large, do not authorize any exception, and where any is made, it is not GOD but *man* that makes

* The word γαμος signifies a *marriage-feast* in John ii. 1. So γαμος, Matt. xxii. 2, 3, 4. See *Tobit*. viii. 19, xi. 19.

it,

it, but with no more authority than the *cup* is denied to the *Popish laity* in the LORD's *supper*—this wants scripture for its warrant, and so doth the other.—In short, human authority militates against the word of GOD—*The prophets prophesy falsly,* (saith Jer. v. 31.) *and the priests bear rule by their means—and the people love to have it so.*—No doubt, while they can gratify their passions without the least obligation to protect or provide for as their wives, the *virgins* they debauch, they will love the *superstition* which indulges them, and hate the *law* which restrains them —they will contend for the *rule* of *priests* in the affair of *marriage,* and believe that without their interference, there can be no *marriage allowed,* or *divorce forbidden.*

How this *superstition* should first arise in the Christian church, is very accountable from the propensity of the human mind towards inventions of its *own* in religious matters. The children of *Adam* are very apt to tread in the steps of their *first parents,* and to be *wise above what is commanded.* It flatters the pride of the heart, when some scheme of *seeming piety* is invented, which bids fair to set the *projector,* in his own opinion at least, above the level of more *scriptural professors.* We should never have heard of works of * *supererogation,*

---

* We may observe, that the laws of GOD have been profaned and insulted two ways: 1. By *inventing works* which they have not commanded: 2. By *making sin* where they have made none. As for the trade of *sin-making,* *pererogation,* if there were not a much higher gratification of human pride, and self-conceit, in thinking we do *over and above* what GOD hath commanded, than in walking by the plain written rule of GOD's *word.* We have but to read the histories of the *Popish saints,* and we shall find some uncommanded heights of mortification, bear a price beyond all the *scriptural* self-denial which is to be met with—an hair shirt—a girdle with iron spikes in it—macerating the body by austere fasting—or lacerating the flesh with whips and scourges—together with other uncommanded instances of the αφειδεια σωματος, which the *Apostle* mentions—Col. ii. 23.— will set a *Popish ascetic* into a state of spiritual pride little short of madness:—the cell —the cloyster—*the abstaining from meats, which* GOD *hath created to be received with thanksgiving, of them which believe and know the truth* (1 Tim. iii. 4.); but above all— *forbidding to marry* (ver. 3.) though rendering millions * of men and women useless in their generation,

---

making, it has been a very lucrative branch of commerce to the *church of Rome,* by increasing the demand for *licences, indulgences, dispensations,* &c. I am sorry to be obliged to confess, that our *Protestant church* is not quite clear of this traffic.—If a matter is *evil in itself,* what licence or dispensation can justify it? if it be *not evil,* what need of licence or dispensation? unless it be, that *some* are to gain by the *credulity* of others.

* *Monkery* was pretty well established in the time of *Constantine,* early in the *fourth century.* It began in the *eastern* countries, in *Egypt, Palestine,* and *Persia,* before it was introduced into the *western* parts of the *Roman* empire.

generation, and, as far as in them lies, destroyers of the human species, contrary to the *primary* decree of Heaven, Gen. i. 28.—all these are looked upon as the * heights of *purity* and religious *perfection*.

These things were foreseen and foretold by that *Spirit* which knoweth what is in man —see *Tim.* iv. 1, &c.—The *apostles* were scarcely cold in their graves, when these *seducing spirits, transforming themselves into angels of light,* began to work. One grand design of *Satan,* in all that he does, is the destruction of the *human race;* hence we may account for those plans of *celibacy* which make such a figure in the history of the *Christian* church. Dr. *William Cave,* a celebrated historian of *primitive Christianity,* in *ch.*v. tells us, that " the *Christians* of † those times
" were

In the fourth *century,* the numbers of *monks* and *nuns,* in *Egypt alone,* amounted to *ninety-six thousand.* See *Jortin*'s Remarks, vol. ii. 165, 173.

* How far they proved so, may be seen in *Burnet,* Hist. Reform. vol. i. p. 191, 241—2. and in *Hist.* of *Popery,* vol. ii. p. 431, 432.—When visitors were appointed by Hen. VIII. to enquire into the *sanctity* of the *monasteries*—the above-mentioned authors have recorded the *black return* which was made. See also *Fuller, Church Hist.* lib. vi.

† " The *fathers* began from early times to talk
" weakly and injudiciously upon the subject of *marriage,*
" and to cry up a single life above measure. Till,
" about the time of *Constantine,* notions were enter-
" tained, which afterwards helped to fill the world with
" drones, mendicants, fanatics, and imaginary dæmo-
" niacs, not to mention other bad consequences.

" *Ambrose,* in the fourth century, was a violent
" stickler

" were so far from breaking in upon unchaste
" embraces, that they frequently abstained
" even from *lawful* pleasures, and kept
" themselves even from the *honourable* and
" *undefiled* bed, never marrying all their life.
" We are, says *Octavius*, chaste in our speech,
" and chaste in our bodies, and very many of
" us, though we do not boast of it, do in-
" violably preserve a *perpetual virginity*; and
" are so far from any extravagant desires
" after incestuous mixtures, that many stand
" at a distance from the most chaste and mo-
" dest embraces. Thus *Justin Martyr* tells
" the emperors, that, among the *Christians*,
" there were a great many of either sex, who
" for sixty or seventy years had kept them-
" selves single and uncorrupt, and he wished
" that the like could be shewn in all * other

" stickler for celibacy, and affirms, that *Alexandria*,
" *Afric*, and the *East*, where there was the greatest num-
" ber of *religious virgins*, were *therefore* more *populous*
" than other countries." *Jortin*, vol. ii. 297, 298. A
sentiment worthy *St. Patrick* himself! *Athanasius* also
praised *virginity* very highly, and preferred it to *marriage*, though he thought 'twas *not forbidden*. Du Pin,
Eccl. Hist. vol. ii. p. 47. Eng. transl.

" In the fifth century, *Salvian*, and other celebrated
" writers, gave it as their opinion, that none were
" truly and perfectly holy, but those who *abstained from*
" *matrimony*." Mosh. vol. i. p. 255. In the sixth century began the reign of intellectual darkness, which
lasted for a *thousand* years, under the superstition and
buffoonery of the church of *Rome*, till it began to be
dispelled by the Protestant reformation in the sixteenth
century.

* How gloriously would this have increased the *devil's*
triumph over that primary command—*Be fruitful and
multiply, and replenish the earth!*

VOL. II.   I   " sorts

"forts of men." Here was a foundation laid for people in after times to combine themselves into distinct societies, to consider *marriage* as a less pure state than *celibacy*, and therefore to bind themselves under vows of *perpetual chastity*, as they called it. Indeed so early as the *second* century, there were a set of people who called *marriage* "a *carnal thing*, "and unlawful for *Christians* under the *gos-* "*pel*."

Those zealots among the primitive *fathers* and *Christians*, who thought "marriage for "*once allowable,* yet held it in a *second* * in-

---

* The *Romans* held it dishonourable for a woman to marry twice; they judged it to be a criminal incontinence, and a tacit breach of the promises made in her first marriage. Hence *Virgil*, in those beautiful lines, makes *Dido*, the widow of *Sichæus*, say—

> *Sed mihi vel tellus optem prius ima dehiscat,*
> *Vel Pater omnipotens adigat me fulmine ad umbras,*
> *Pallentes umbras Erebi, noctemque profundam,*
> *Ante pudor quam te violo, & tua jura resolvo.*
> *Ille meos, primus qui me sibi junxit, amores*
> *Abstulit; ille habeat secum, servetque sepulchro.*

> But first let yawning earth a passage rend,
> And let me through the dark abyss descend;
> First let avenging JOVE, with flames from high,
> Drive down this body to the nether sky,
> Condemn'd with ghosts in endless night to lie;
> Before I break the plighted faith I gave:
> No; he who had my vows shall ever have,
> For, whom I lov'd on earth, I worship in the grave.
> DRYDEN.

When we compare this with 1 Cor. vii. 39. Heb. xiii. 4. and other passages in scripture, we shall find, that the notion about *second* marriages, resembled *Heathenism* more than *Christianity.*

"stance *inexcusable.*" Dr. *Cave,* in a very commendable zeal for the *virtues* of these people, throws the best veil he can over their *follies,* and makes the best excuse he can invent for them.—" Indeed it cannot be denied," says he, " but that many of the ancient fathers—*Tertullian, Cyprian, Hierom,* and others, did inveigh against *second* marriages with too much *bitterness* and *severity,* violently pressing many passages in scripture to serve the cause, *straining* the string many times till it *cracked* again, and not sticking to censure and condemn *second* marriages as little better than *adultery.* Hear what one of their *apologists* says to it:—Amongst us, every man remains as he was born, or engages himself in *one* only marriage; for as for *second* marriages, they are but a more plausible or decorous kind of *adultery,* our LORD assuring us, that *whosoever putteth away his wife, and taketh another, committeth adultery:*—which text, as also another of like importance, how perversely he interprets, and impertinently applies to his purpose, I am not willing to remember."

However absurd such an interpretation of the above scripture may appear to us, because we are not involved in all the *superstition* of those days, yet it is not more so than interpreting the words as some of our more modern commentators do, to condemn *polygamy.*—*Putting away a wife by a bill of divorcement, and marrying another,* is at least as good a

phrase

phrase for putting a *dead* woman under ground, and marrying a *second*, as for *taking two wives together*, or for *keeping* a *living* one, and taking another to her.

St. *Jerome* (as he is called) who lived in the 4th, and in the beginning of the 5th *century*, actually wrote against *marriage*, and numbers it among those things which are *per se mala ac vitiosa*—" evil and vicious in " themselves."—See *Beza* on 1 Cor. vii. 1. No wonder that this sour *monk* of *Palestine* should inveigh so bitterly as he did against *second* marriages of all sorts.

It has been remarked, that of all the praisers of *virginity*, JEROME seems to have performed his part the best; who calls *Eustochium* the *nun* his *lady*, because she was the *spouse* of his *Lord*, and reminds the mother of this lady, that she had the honour to be GOD's *mother-in-law*—Socrus Dei. *Jortin*, Rem. on Eccl. Hist. vol. ii. p. 170.

Some of *Jerome's* interpretations of scripture are too curious to be omitted—He says, that the *clean animals* in *Noah's* ark, signified *virgins*; and the *unclean*, those who *married*. He calls *virgins—the vessels made unto honour*— and the *married—the vessels made unto dishonour* (see Rom. ix. 21.); he expounds the *fruit* which encreased an *hundred-fold* (see Mark iv. 20.) of *virgins—the fixty-fold*, of *widows—the thirty-fold*, of the *married—*excluding every where those who have *married more than once*; of whom he says—*Certe in bona terra non oriuntur, sed in vepribus & spinis voluptatum*

voluptatum—" they certainly do not spring up " in *good ground*, but among the *briars and* " *thorns* of *pleasures*." GLASSIUS."

Ambrose, Prefect and afterwards bishop of *Milan*, who also lived in the 4th *century*, was a violent declaimer in favour of *virginity*, and, in a treatise on that subject, he exhorts " girls to enter into *nunneries*, though *against* " *the will of their parents.*" *Jortin*, ib. 176.

The progress of *superstition* in this 4th century, and the erroneous notions which prevailed, excited the zeal of many to stem the torrent. The most eminent of these worthy opposers was *Jovinian*, an Italian monk; who, towards the conclusion of this century, taught first at *Rome*, and then at *Milan*, that " those who passed their days in " unsociable celibacy, were not more ac- " ceptable in the eyes of GOD, than those " who lived virtuously in the bonds of mar- " riage." These and other judicious opinions, which many began to adopt, were first condemned by the church of *Rome*, and afterwards by *Ambrose*, in a council held at Milan, anno 390. The emperor *Honorius* seconded these authoritative proceedings by the violence of the secular arm—answered the judicious reasonings of *Jovinian* by the terror of coercive and penal laws—and banished this pretended *heretic* to the island *Boa*. *Jovinian* published his opinions in a book, against which *Jerome*, in the following century, wrote a most bitter and abusive treatise,

treatise, which is still extant. See *Mosheim*, Edit. *Maclaine*, vol. i. 203, 204.

In the beginning of the 5th century arose *Vigilantius*, a man remarkable for his learning and eloquence, who was born in *Gaul*, and went from thence into *Spain*, where he performed the functions of a *presbyter*. This man, honouring GOD's word above the *traditions* and *superstitions* of those times, boldly stept forth, and bore his testimony against the opinions and manners of the reigning demagogues, and especially on the subjects of *celibacy* and *marriage*, together with the ridiculous austerities of a *monastic life*. There were, among the *Gallic* and *Spanish* bishops, several that sided with *Vigilantius*; but *Jerome*, the great *monk* of the age, assailed this bold *reformer* with such bitterness and fury, that nothing but his silence could preserve his *life*, from the intemperate rage of *bigotry* and *superstition*. And the name of good *Vigilantius* remains still in the *list of heretics*; which is acknowledged to be authentic by those, who without any regard to their own judgment, or the declarations of scripture, followed blindly the *decisions of antiquity*. See *Mosheim*, vol. i. 255, 256.

Jerome's Epistle against *Vigilantius* is a curiosity in its kind, and may be found in the *collection* printed at *Tournay*, duodecimo, p. 601. He sets out with observing how many " *monsters* have appeared in the world, " such as *Centaurs*, *Syrens*, *Cerberus*, the
" *Chimera*,

"*Chimera, Geryon,* &c." At laſt *Vigilantius* is introduced as one of the greateſt *monſters* of all, " who," he tells us, " with an " unclean ſpirit fights againſt the Spirit of " CHRIST; for that he calls continency, " hereſy—and *chaſtity,* the ſeminary of luſt." —In ſhort, the poor man had written on the behalf of marriage, and plainly ſaw what muſt be the end of the pretended ſchemes of *chaſtity,* which the *monks* had eſpouſed. But *Jerome* proceeds—" Proh neſas! *Epiſcopos*
" ſui ſceleris dicitur habere conſortes, ſi ta-
" men *Epiſcopi* nominandi ſunt, qui non
" ordinant *Diaconos,* niſi prius uxores dux-
" erint, nulli cælibi credentes pudicitiam,
" & niſi prægnantes viderint uxores clerico-
" rum, infanteſque de ulnis matrum vagi-
" entes, CHRISTI ſacramenta non tribuunt.
" Quid facient orientis eccleſiæ? Quid
" Ægypti & ſedis apoſtolicæ, quæ, aut vir-
" gines clericos accipiunt, aut continentes,
" aut, ſi uxores habuerint mariti eſſe deſiſt-
" unt? Hoc docuit *Dormitantius* libidini
" fræna permittens, & naturalem carnis ar-
" dorem, qui in adoleſcentia plerumque fer-
" veſcit, ſuis hortatibus duplicans, immo
" extinguens coitu fœminarum: ut nihil ſit
" quo diſtemus a porcis, quo differamus a
" brutis animantibus, quo ab equis de qui-
" bus ſcriptum eſt—*Equi inſanientes in femi-*
" *nas facti ſunt mihi: unuſquiſque in uxorem*
" *proximi ſui hinniebat.* Jer. v. 8. Hoc eſt
" quod loquitur per David Spiritus Sanctus
" —*Nolite fieri ſicut equus & mulus quibus non*
" *eſt*

" *est intellectus* & rurfum de *Dormitantio* &
" fociis ejus—In chamo & freno maxillas
" eorum conftringe, qui non approximant
" ad te."—" O abominable fhame! he *(Vi-*
" *gilantius)* is faid to have *bifhops* partners of
" his wickednefs, if fuch are to be called
" *bifhops,* who do not ordain *deacons* unlefs
" they firft be *married*—believing there is no
" chaftity in a *fingle man*; and unlefs they
" fee the wives of the clergy pregnant, and
" infants crying in the arms of their mo-
" thers, they do not commit to them the
" power of adminiftering the *facraments* of
" CHRIST.

" What muft the *Eaftern* churches do?
" What thofe of *Ægypt* and of the *apoftolical*
" *fee*—(i. e. *Rome)*—who receive *clergy* that
" are *virgins,* or continent, or who, if they
" have *wives,* ceafe from being hufbands?

" Thus taught *Dormitantius*" (N. B.—a *filly pun* on the name of *Vigilantius)* " giving
" the reins to licentioufnefs; and doubling,
" by his exhortations, the natural ardor of
" the flefh, which ufually grows warm in
" youth, yea, even extinguifhing it by in-
" tercourfe with women. So that there
" may be nothing in which we fhould be
" diftinguifhed from *fwine,* or in which we
" fhould differ from *brute beafts,* and even the
" *horfes*—concerning which it is written—
" *Raging for women, they are become to me as*
" *horfes; every one neighed after his neigh-*
" *bour's wife.* Jer. v. 8. This is what the
" HOLY SPIRIT fpeaks by DAVID—*Be ye*
" *not*

"*not like to horse or mule, which have no understanding*—and again, concerning *Dormitantius* and his *fellows*—*Constrain their jaw-bones with a bit and a bridle, lest they approach unto thee.*" Pſ. xxxii. 9.

The *reader* has here a ſample of the ſpirit of thoſe times with regard to *marriage*, particularly of the *clergy*; likewiſe of the candour, fairneſs, and good manners, with which thoſe were treated, who dared, like *Vigilantius*, to ſtep forth in the cauſe of *ſcripture, common ſenſe,* and *truth,* againſt *ſuperſtition, folly,* and *error*; alſo of the ridiculous *abuſe* and *perverſion* of ſcripture, in order to maintain the reigning *ſuperſtition*. Laſtly, we may obſerve, in what *Jerome* ſays, about "the *biſhops* refuſing to ordain *deacons* unleſs *their wives were with child,*" &c. that a little *lying* and *ſcandal* was eſteemed of ſingular uſe. See *before*, vol. i. p. 285. n.

It ſhould ſeem that the ſeverity with regard to *ſecond* marriages was afterwards relaxed, as to the *laity* at leaſt; but a *third* was prohibited by ſeveral councils; and the emperor *Leo,* in the 9th century, publiſhed an edict, ſubjecting thoſe who married *thrice,* to the penalties which had been decreed againſt them by the *antient councils*. However, this *emperor* was fairly caught in his *own ſnare*; for when he wanted to revoke that edict in his own caſe, the *clergy* would not ſuffer it.

The *emperor Leo,* who reigned at *Conſtantinople,* married *four* times, for which the then Patriarch excommunicated him. He
begged

begged to be restored, but in vain; upon which he deposed *Nicolaus Mysticus*, who had excommunicated him, from the *patriarchate*, confined him to a monastry, and placed one *Enthymius Syncellus* in his room. This occasioned a schism in the church, some of the *clergy* siding with *Nicolaus*, some with *Enthymius*. Though *Enthymius* restored *Leo* to the communion of the faithful, yet he resolutely opposed him, when, by the advice of the senate, he was about to publish an edict, declaring it *lawful* to marry a *fourth* time. Nor would the *clergy* suffer the *emperor* to revoke his *former edict* against those who married *thrice*. See *Ant. Univ. Hist.* vol. xvii. p. 79. See a full account of this matter in *Du Pin*, Eccl. Hist. Eng. Transf. vol. iii. p. 1, 2.

By all this we may learn, how early the *mystery of iniquity* began to work, in a combination of *church and state*, against the prerogative of *Heaven*, with respect to *marriage*, by men taking upon themselves to decide upon the *lawfulness* or *unlawfulness* of marriages, either independently on the scriptures, or in total opposition to them; likewise to misinterpret and misapply them to justify their proceedings.

But to return to the primitive *Christians*. Had these people attended properly to the scriptures, instead of the workings of their own imaginations, they would not have been led into a disparagement of *marriage*, either when entered into in *one* or *more* instances. As to *marriage* itself, it was instituted when

man

man stood in the *likeness and image of* GOD, in a state of much higher *purity* and *holiness* than any can now know on *this side heaven*; therefore it must have been in all respects consistent with *such* a state. *One* of the *two* persons recorded in scripture to have been *translated into heaven, that he should not see death* (Heb. xi. 5.) was a *married* man; nor did he keep himself " from the *honourable* " and *undefiled* bed;" for it is said, Gen. v. 22. *And* ENOCH *walked with* GOD, *after he begat Methusaleh, 300 years, and begat sons and daughters.*

As to *second* marriages, the calling them " *adultery and whoredom*," was a monstrous *superstition*, amounting to a denial of the scriptures, which absolutely allowed them as *lawful* and *good*, even on the *woman's side*. Thus *Paul*, in allusion to the law of *Moses*, Rom. vii. 3. *So then if while her husband liveth she be married to another man, she shall be called an adulteress; but if her husband be dead, she is free from that law, so that she is no adulteress, though she be married to another man.* And again—*The wife is bound by the law as long as her husband liveth; but if her husband be dead, she is at liberty to be married to whom she will,* &c. 2 Cor. vi. 14. Comp. 1 Tim. v. 14.

So that we see what little dependence is to be placed on *primitive fathers* and *Christians*, or indeed on any thing else but the written word of GOD itself—compared with itself—explained by itself. The truth we come at by thefe means is fure and ftedfaft, and may fafely be relied upon, though all the world fhould agree to think otherwife.

Dr. *Cave*, who, as was obferved, has endeavoured to foften the * abfurdities of thefe *good* folks as much as poffible, fays, p. 90. "Though the fathers and antient councils "were thus fevere in this cafe (of *fecond* "marriages) yet the rigour of their cenfure

---

* Dr. Jortin, Remarks on Ecclefiaftical Hiftory, vol. iv. p. 376, fays, that—"our *Cave* may be called, the *white-* "*wafher of the ancients.*"—See before p. 122. If Dr. *Cave* had concealed their follies and weakneffes, he would have faved himfelf and his readers a good deal of trouble, which might have been more profitably employed, than in framing excufes for abfurdities, which had better be forgotten, as meriting *oblivion* rather than *apology*.

The farther we fearch, the more will the number of their abfurdities increafe upon us : witnefs fome of the *fathers* and *moralifts*, mentioned by *Athanafius Vincentius*, in his Notes on *Theoph. Aletheus*; who held, that, "Scortatio cum propriâ uxore committi poteft, cum non "liberorum quærendorum caufâ, fed ad explendam li- "bidinem, vel cum pregnante aut lactante res habetur." "That a man may be faid to commit *whoredom* with his "*own wife*, when he hath intercourfe with her, not for "the fake of having children, but to fatisfy his *defires*, "or when fhe is with *child*, or gives *fuck*." If this be the cafe, how is *marriage* any remedy againft *fornication* ? and what becomes of the *apoftle's*—*If they cannot contain, let them marry; for it is better to marry than to burn?* 1 Cor. vii. 9. How can a man *burn* the lefs for having a wife, if he is to have no accefs to her for many months together, or indeed, on fuch principles, *not at all*, after fhe has done breeding ? Yet fuch was the wifdom of *Ambrofe, Jerome, Origen*, and others, who, in fuch inftances, by becoming *wifer* and *holier* than the fcriptures, were the inftruments of *Satan*, to enfnare the confciences of thofe who had folly enough to believe what they faid. Comp. 1 Cor. vii. 5.

"will

" will be much abated, if what some tell us
" be true, that *many* of their passages are not
" levelled against *successive* marriages, but
" against having *two wives at the same time*;
" for, as a learned man has observed, there
" were *three* sorts of *digamy:* 1. A man's
" having two wives at once: 2. When, the
" former wife being dead, he married a *se-*
" *cond* time: 3. When a man on slight cause
" put away his wife by a bill of divorce,
" and married another."—With regard to
this *last*, it certainly could not be inveighed
against too severely; for it is contrary to the
very institution of marriage, that a man *should
put away his wife* for *any* cause, except for fornication*; as Christ proves to the *multitudes*,
Matt. v. 32. and to the *Pharisees*, Matt. xix.
4, 5, 6.

As to the two first, namely, " a man's
" having two wives at once, and a man's
" marrying a *second* after the death of his
" *first*," however Dr. *Cave*, or any other of
their *apologists* may endeavour to " abate the
" asperity of their censures," they *both* were
esteemed by the antient *Christians* and primitive *fathers equally* * unlawful; which is
not

---

* *Athenagoras*, in the second century, in an apology
for the *Christians*, which he presented to the Emperor
M. Antoninus, asserts—"that the devils were ruined by the
" love that they bare unto women— commends virginity,
" and condemneth *second marriages*, calling them—an
" *honest adultery.*" See *Du Pin*, vol. i. p. 56. English
Transf.

In the *Neocæsarienfian* council, anno 314, it was decreed

not to be wondered at, when *marriage* itself was so much spoken against, as a state of *less* * purity and perfection than *celibacy*, consequently the *more* and the *oftener* a man engaged in *marriage*, the more *impure* he must be. But the truth is, that there is *no* impurity whatsoever in *marriage*, though *often* or but *once* entered into. *Abraham*, who had *more wives than one at a time*, is not recorded as *less* pure than *Isaac*, who appears to have had but *one*; nor is *Isaac* said to be *more* pure than his son *Jacob*, who had *four*; we read of them all in an equal state of *glory in the kingdom of heaven*, Matt. viii. 11. but of no reproof on God's part, or sorrow or repentance on their part, on account of their different *situations* while *on earth*.

The *superstition* of its being sinful to have *two wives* in *succession*, remained a great while

---

creed—" *Presbyterum* convivio *secundarum nuptiarum* " interesse non debere." " That a *presbyter* ought not " to be present at a feast of *second nuptials*." The *canonists* said, that " an *iteration* of marriage was contrary " to all honesty; or, if it could be admitted into the " number of *honest things*, it must be called *honest whore-* " *dom*. Some said, that though it might be lawful, " according to *St. Paul*, yet it was *fere fornicatio*— " *almost fornication*."

* This notion, and all its pretensions to *purity*, was no better than *Heathenism*; for among the *Romans*, " when the bride was brought home to her husband's " house, she was not to touch the *threshold*, but was " lifted over it by main strength, because the *threshold*, " being sacred to *Vesta*, a most *chaste* goddess, ought " not to be defiled by one in *such* circumstances." Broughton, Hist. Lib. vol. ii. 179.

in the church; however the Proteſtant reformation helped us to the *ſtat.* of Edw. VI. (ſee before vol. i. p. 199) which diſſipated men's fears upon that ſubject; but with reſpect to having *two wives at a time*, we are ſtill taught to look upon it in as horrible a light, as the primitive *Chriſtians* did on having a *ſecond* after the death of the *firſt*. This *ſuperſtition* has been ſo uniformly and ſucceſsfully kept alive, that the reprobation of *polygamy* in the *Chriſtian* church (our weſtern part of it at leaſt) is as *univerſal*, as the belief of *tranſubſtantiation* or *purgatory* was before the Proteſtant *reformation*. In ſhort, the *ſuperſtition* is inveterate, we may almoſt be ſaid to ſuck it in with our mother's milk; it faſtens upon us in our very infancy, it grows up with us—we know not how to get rid of it, nor ever ſhall, till, as at the above glorious period, men will dare to ſearch, think, and judge for themſelves, and thus emancipate their underſtandings from the ſlavery of *vulgar* * prejudice and *popular* opinion.

The

---

* In Mr. *Coxe's* Sketches of *Switzerland*—an entertaining, inſtructive, and ſenſible performance, lately publiſhed—he ſpeaks of the Abbey of *Einſidlin*, in the canton of *Schweitz*, and adds—" The ridiculous tales
" they tell of the origin and aggrandizement of this
" abbey, are ſo many melancholy inſtances of the cre-
" dulity of the darker ages. That they are ſtill be-
" lieved in the preſent *enlightened* century, muſt be at-
" tributed to the force of habitual prejudice; and at
" the ſame time proves, how difficult it is for the hu-
" man mind to ſhake off thoſe ſuperſtitious errors,
" which

The Statute de Bigamis, 4 Edw. I. c. 5. ousted a man of his clergy, if he had been

"which it has early imbibed under the sanctified name
"of religion." P. 75, 76.

Another instance mentioned of the force of custom and prejudice over the human mind is to be found p. 488.

"At *Basil* the clocks go an *hour* faster than those of
"the rest of *Europe*. Several reasons are assigned for
"this; one is, that the *sun-dial* on the outside of the
"*cathedral*, by which the *town-clock* is regulated, de-
"clines somewhat, as the building does, from the east,
"which occasions a variation from the true time.

"A motion has often been made, in the sovereign
"council, to have the town-clock regulated properly,
"but constantly rejected. The people would think
"their liberties invaded, if such regulation was made.

"A few years ago, it was secretly agreed by some
"leading men in the town, to have the dial turned
"half a minute each day, till the shadow should im-
"perceptibly point to the true hour. This expedient
"was accordingly put in practice, and the town-clock
"had already lost *three quarters of an hour*; when an
"accident discovered the plot, and the magistrates were
"compelled to place the dial in the place in which it
"stood before, and to have the town-clock regulated
"by it as usual. Indeed long-established customs,
"however indifferent or ridiculous, are apt to lay so
"strong an hold on vulgar minds, as to become some-
"times dangerous, always difficult to be altered;—I
"need not remind you how long it was before we could
"be persuaded in *England* to reckon our years accord-
"ing to the general mode of computation received by
"the rest of *Europe*."

Thus far Mr. *Coxe*—to whose last observation, I cannot forbear adding an anecdote of a certain pious old woman, who could not be persuaded, but that "all our
"national troubles and misfortunes, which have be-
"fallen us since the year 1751, have been so many
"judgments upon us for striking *eleven days* out of the
"*kalendar*, and, by this means, having *fewer Sundays*
"than we had before."

twice

twice married—the 1 Jac. c. 11. would *hang* a man that has *two wives*, but for the benefit of clergy; and no doubt these laws have, in their several days, served to strengthen the cause of *superstition*, by annexing public *infamy*, as well as *punishment*, to the supposed crimes of *bigamy* and *polygamy*. With regard to *adultery*, or with respect to the seduction and debauchery of *virgins*, and then abandoning them, the *adulterer* or *seducer* may be found in what is called the *best companies*; be treated with civility, and even respect; while the *polygamist* is arrested for *felony*—sent to prison—tried before a court of criminal judicature—rendered infamous for life, and, thanks to the benefit of the clergy, that he is not dragged to a *gibbet*, and put to death!

The foundation of all this is, the *wisdom* of man exalting itself against the *wisdom* of GOD; hence it is that men devise laws which are contrary to the law of GOD; and the opposition which *superstition* has taught us to make to *nature, reason,* and *scripture,* obtains the * sanction of vulgar opinion on the side

---

* " All men are full of themselves and their own
" principles: and the *Nazarenes* of the *West* are so brimming with them, that there is no room left for instruction of amendment. Like the *Chinese*, they
" boast of their own science and wisdom, reputing all
" the rest of the world *ignorant* and *blind*.

" They are so *narrow* in their *tenets*, so *dogmatical* in
" their *decisions*, and so *conceited* of all, that it is difficult for a man, who has conversed in a freer air, to
" frame himself to their rules." *Turkish Spy,* vol. iv. p. 125.

of falshood and error. That *superstition* should lead men to reject the law of GOD, *to make void the commandments of* GOD, *through their traditions*, under a notion of greater *sanctity*, is not at all surprizing, when the *pride* and *ignorance* of the human heart are duly considered. The instances which are recorded of it, concerning the *Pharisees* of old time, are written for our instruction and admonition: the severity with which CHRIST treated them on this account, ought to stand as a warning to us, lest we also *come into the same condemnation*.

Among the various instances which we find of this in the New Testament, there is not a more striking one, nor one more illustrative of what I have been saying, than that which appears Mark vii. 9—14. where our LORD convicts the *Pharisees* of a rejection of the *fifth* commandment, in favour of a *superstition* of their own, which, though it had a better foundation than most of their *traditions*, with respect to the *act* itself (see 2 Kings xii. 9.) yet, as they abused it, it became a direct contrariety to the express and positive law of GOD. CHRIST tells them in plain terms as much, ver. 9. *Full well do ye reject the commandment of* GOD, *that you may keep your own traditions.* When *Jehoiada* the *high-priest* ordered a chest to receive the money, through *an hole in the lid,* which the *people* gave towards the repairs of the temple, he did *well*—and those who gave of their substance for this purpose did also *well;*—but when in after time these *gifts* were preferred before the relief of a *sick, necessitous,* and *aged parent,* whom the *fifth* commandment enjoined them to *honour*—with their substance doubtless, as well as in all other respects—then they did *ill,* by preferring the observance of an *human tradition,* before the express injunction of the *divine law.*

To appoint an *outward* means of recognizing a *marriage,* and not leave people to take *one another's words* (as the saying is) is very proper, and, in this mixed state of things, *necessary* for the *good of the whole*; but to put the ceremony in the place of God's *institution*—to declare a marriage *null and void* without it, to *all intents and purposes whatsoever*—to set the parties free from the obligation which they are under towards God and *each other* by the divine command—is as direct a breach of the command of God in this respect, as the *Pharisees* were guilty of in the *other,* and our Lord's reproof of the *Pharisees* equally belongs to *us*—we certainly *make void the law of* God *through our traditions, and teach for doctrines the commandments of men.*

There is no avoiding *superstition,* neither is there any deliverance from being led by it into thinking we do the *will of* God, when we are only doing the *will of man,* and that in contrariety to the *divine will,* while, like those of old, our *fear towards* God *is taught us by the precepts of men.* If. xxix. 13. and while, like *dead fish* with the stream, we are

K 2   carried

carried down with the tide of vulgar error and popular opinion.—*Ye do err, not knowing the scripture.—Search the scriptures*—was the advice of Him *who spake as never man spake*. When we are wise enough to follow this counsel, worldly systems and human inventions may, and will suffer in our opinion, and we may be led to grieve at the folly and *superstition* which are to be found in them; but we shall be overpaid for any uneasiness of this sort, by the pleasure we must receive, in beholding the beauty, harmony, and order that are to be found in the word of God. We shall then see, that the misery and destruction of so many of our defenceless fellow-creatures, in the points before complained of, are owing to the rejection of that *divine* system of *justice*, *mercy*, and *truth*, which, if observed in all its parts, has so wisely and amply provided for their *protection* and *preservation*.

As *superstition* blinds the *conscience*, and misleads the *judgment*, so it *hardens the heart*, and renders it unimpressible by the calls of pity and compassion—*cruelty* will triumph over *mercy*, and the most horrid *barbarities* pass for the fruits of *heavenly zeal—The time cometh, when whosoever killeth you will think that he doeth* God *service.* John xvi. 2.

<blockquote>
Tantum *religio* potuit suadere malorum!
Virg.

Such dreadful ills from SUPERSTITION *spring!*
</blockquote>

The history of *Popery* furnishes us with numberless examples of this: let the reader take the following from Dr. *Gedde*'s Tracts, vol. i. p. 412, 413; where, speaking of the execution of *heretics* at an *auto de fe* in *Portugal*, he describes the *delight* with which the crowd of spectators behold the torments which are administered on the occasion to the poor sufferers, and then adds—" That the "reader may not think, that this inhuman "joy may be the effect of a natural cruelty, "that is in those people's disposition, and "not of the spirit of their religion, he may "rest assured that all public malefactors, be- "sides *heretics*, have their violent deaths no "where more tenderly lamented than among "the same people, and even when there is "nothing in their deaths that appears in- "human or cruel."

By the way, what a state of infatuation must we be in, to open the door again for the admission of *Popery* into this country, by repealing any part of those salutary laws which were made for its exclusion! One should think that this country had suffered enough from the *spirit* and *temper* above described, to make us dread every step which can lead to their re-admission. To suppose, what many profess to believe, that *Popery* is not *now* just what it was in *Queen Mary*'s days, is to suppose that *Popery* is not *Popery*; which is an absurdity as great as to *imagine* that a *thing* is not *itself*.—But I should ask the reader's pardon for digressing from the main

main point before us; which I trust I shall easily obtain, when he considers how naturally a writer on *superstition* is led to the mention of *Popery*, which is no other than a *confluence* of every species of it.

As for the *Popish laity*, the scriptures are taken out of their hands, and they are left at the mercy of their *priests* (who are generally as ignorant * as themselves) for the interpretation of their *creed*; this chiefly consists in *human tradition*, and detached parts of the scripture, explained or translated as the *church* pleases, and made to prove *any thing*, or *every thing*, or *nothing*, as may best serve the purposes of *superstition* and *priestcraft*, and maintain their absolute dominion over the *understandings* and *consciences* of mankind. The *Protestant* church of *England* has distinguished herself for her moderation, arrogating to herself no absolute dominion in *matters of faith* over the *consciences* of her children. She withholds no part of the scripture either from their *eyes* or *ears*—puts the *Bible* into their hands, that they may search for themselves, and orders her *ministers* daily to read portions of it to the people, that those who cannot *read*, may *hear* the things of GOD, and *judge* for themselves. She tells us plainly in her *Articles*, that, " Holy scripture con-
" taineth all things necessary to salvation,
" so that whatsoever is not red therein, nor
" may be proved thereby, is not to be re-

---

* See before p. 99 n.

" quired

" quired of any man that it should be be-
" lieved as an article of faith, or be thought
" requisite or necessary to salvation." *Art.* 6.
—And again, *Art.* 20. " The church hath
" authority to decree rites and ceremonies,
" and authority in matters of faith; and yet
" it is not lawful for the church to ordain
" any thing that is contrary to GOD's word
" written, neither may it so expound one
" place of scripture that it be repugnant to
" another. Wherefore, though the church
" be a witness and keeper of holy writ, yet,
" as it ought not to decree any thing against
" the same, so, besides the same, ought it
" not to inforce any thing to be believed for
" necessity of salvation."

A more unreserved *caveat* against *superstition* cannot easily be penned, nor is it in the power of language to form a more ample licence for *free-enquiry*; if therefore what has been said in the foregoing pages, should be a means of obviating the *first*, and this by promoting the *other*, I shall think myself well paid for the pains I have taken.

As to the *superstition* of imagining that a *church-service* makes the *marriage*, and that without it no *marriage* is valid or binding, or *lawful* before GOD, it is as unscriptural and absurd, as it is mischievous and ruinous to the *weaker sex*. There is not the least trace of such a thing either in the *Old* or *New Testaments*; marriage, with respect to itself, and as between the parties, stood entirely upon the simple institution of GOD, before *priests* or *service-books* existed; therefore nothing can be of the *essence* of it, but what GOD * appointed

* The institution of marriage may be found in those words, Gen. i. 28. *Be fruitful and multiply, and replenish the earth.* But that which constitutes it, as to the *matter* of it, in GOD's sight, is his own ordinance delivered by *Adam*, Gen. ii. 24. ודבק באשתו והיו לבשר אחד—*Et adhærebit* IN *uxore sua, & erunt in carnem unam.* Mont.

Our translation—*A man, &c. shall cleave to his wife*—does not convey the idea of the *Hebrew* דבק באשתו—this is literally—*shall be joined or cemented* (προσκολληθήσεται, LXX.) IN *his woman—and they shall become* (i. e. by this union) *one flesh.* This is the one, simple, divine ordinance, and the obligation resulting from it is *indissoluble*; wherefore, saith CHRIST—*what* GOD *hath joined together, let not man put asunder.* The same thing is expressed in other words, Deut. xxii. 29.—*She shall be his woman,* or *wife,* as we call it, (sa femme, Fr.) BECAUSE *he has* HUMBLED HER—*he may not put her away all his days.* Human laws or ceremonies can have no more effect on this, than upon the rising of the sun, or the flowing of the tide: these are not more fixed and unalterable than the other.

The more I have *searched* the scripture, and examined this point, the more fully am I convinced, even to demonstration itself, that as GOD never appointed any other thing as the *matter* of baptism but *water*, poured or sprinkled on the body, in the name of the HOLY TRINITY (for I do not mean to enter into the disputes about the meaning of βαπτίζω) so he never appointed any thing as the *matter* of that *union* by which the man and woman become *one flesh*, but the דבק באשתו—or, as our *canon* law phrases it, *carnal knowledge*; the very essence of which is expressed in the *Hebrew*, though perhaps our translators thought it more *decent* to render it as they have done, without giving the ב its literal and usual import. The προσκολληθήσεται πρὸς τὴν γυναῖκα of the LXX, and the προσκολληθήσεται τῇ γυναικὶ of Matt. xix. 5. taken in connection with the κολλώμενος of *Paul*, 1 Cor. vi. 16. (as has been before observed) amount to the same meaning, carry the same idea, if compared and interpreted

appointed *at the beginning*. When, therefore, it is said—*Isaac brought her into his mother's tent, and took Rebekah, and she became his wife* (Gen. xxiv. 67.) and when *Laban* took *Leah* his daughter, and brought her to *Jacob*, and he *went in unto her*—and when *Laban* gave him *Rachel* his daughter to wife also, and he *went in* also unto *Rachel* —these women severally became the absolute unalienable property of their husbands, they became *one flesh* with them, and what GOD had thus *joined together, no man could put asunder*. Thus the matter stood on the simple ordinance of GOD, and thus, as in GOD's sight, it must stand for ever. The *Jews*, and all other *nations*, have ever looked upon

---

ᶦinterpreted by the *Hebrew* original. To this, we may also add that passage of Eph. v. 31, 32. where the *apostle* introduces no circumstance of *human ceremony* (ver. 31.) in order to perfect the *marriage-union*, or to render it a complete emblem of the *great mystery* which he speaks of (ver. 32.)

As for betrothment, espousals, the payment of the מהר or dower, these were circumstantials, and right and proper, as far as outward order and decency were concerned, but these were not the *matter* of the marriage; for, not only as in the case of our *first parents*, but in many other instances in the scripture, *marriage was* where *these were not*.

Therefore to declare " a marriage (though consum-
" mated by *carnal knowledge*) *ipso facto* null and void to
" all intents and purposes whatsoever," where some outward rite or ceremony of mere human invention is wanting, however it may operate in a *civil* view, can be of no effect in GOD's sight; otherwise the *matter* of the ordinance doth not consist in GOD's *appointment*, but men's *inventions*.

marriage

marriage as an occasion of festivity and rejoicing, and various rites and ceremonies have been invented upon the occasion; so there have been with respect to *baptism* and the LORD's *supper:* but these, like all other ordinances of GOD, stand just where they did, and owe their whole *importance* and *validity* to GOD's appointment, and are neither *added* to nor *diminished* in these respects by any rites or ceremonies which men have invented—to say otherwise is rank *superstition*.

Whether the primitive *Christians* had their marriages with each other solemnized by a *minister* of the church, is a disputed point among learned men. Mr. *Selden*, in his *Ux. Heb.* l. ii. c. 29. says—" it was *sometimes*
" so done, at the desire of the contracting
" parties, but they were under [*] no obliga-
" tion by law so to do, nor did any general
" custom prevail, so as to make it a general

---

[*] In an epistle, supposed to be written by *St. Ignatius* to his disciple *St. Polycarp*—the writer informs the *Christians*, that, " their marriage, when performed according to the *will of* GOD, ought to be solemnized in the presence of the bishop."

But it is much to be doubted, whether this epistle be genuine; and if it be genuine, where is any such " *will of* GOD" in the matter, to be found in scripture ? The above-mentioned epistle of *Ignatius* to *Polycarp* stands on much the same footing, as to the evidence of its genuineness, with that of *Ignatius* to the *Ephesians*, wherein he affirms, that " the *devil* was ignorant of the virginity of *Mary*— " of her child-birth—and of the death of our LORD."— Such horrid stuff as this, is enough to shake the credit of the whole. See *Du Pin*, vol. i. p. 43.

" practice."

" practice."—However, whether this was so or not, signifies not a rush, as there is nothing in the word of GOD to warrant it.

Archdeacon *Reynolds*, in his *Historical Essay on the Government of the Church of England*, helps us to find out how this custom came into the *western churches*, p. 70. " Contracts
" of *marriage*, with all its incidents, were
" long considered as rights of *secular* concern,
" and in the tenth century the laws of the
" empire allowed the *validity* of *marriages*
" which were made without *sacerdotal bene-*
" *diction*, or the intervention of the *offices of*
" *the church*. But in the twelfth century
" *Peter Lombard* discovered the institution
" of *seven sacraments* in the mystical expres-
" sion of the *seven spirits of* GOD, which he
" understood as an assurance of the *seven-fold*
" *operation* of the Spirit in *baptism*—the *sup-*
" *per of the* LORD—*confirmation—penance—*
" *orders—matrimony—*and *extreme unction*;
" and the church of *Rome* soon countenan-
" ced his doctrine. This brought *marriage*,
" which was originally of *civil* jurisdiction,
" under *spiritual* cognizance." A little higher, the learned author observes—" The key to
" the contradictory provisions about mar-
" riage, was, that the court of *Rome* was de-
" sirous to have the scales of domestic peace
" in the *Pope*'s hand, that the *legitimacy* of
" children, and the succession of families,
" should depend upon his favour, that *his*
" *holiness* might separate whom no man
" ought to put asunder, or perpetuate con-
" junctions

" junctions which reason and religion for-
" bid."

This was opposed by the *Albigenses* *, those early *reformers*, who taught, that " the
" consent of a willing couple, without the
" formality of *sacerdotal* benediction, made a
" *lawful* marriage."—This was the doctrine which they taught in the territory of the *Count* of *Thoulouse*, and propagated here about 1175.

The *Lollards* † afterwards declaimed against
celibacy,

---

* The *Albigenses* were a sect or party of *reformers*, about *Thoulouse* and *Albigeois* in *Languedoc*, in the twelfth century, who distinguished themselves by their opposition to the discipline and ceremonies of the church of *Rome*. This drew down all manner of persecution and reproach;—the *Papists* charged them with heresy, and loaded them with all the calumnies that the most vindictive malice could invent—at last the storm fell so heavily upon them, that it ended in their destruction. See *Brough*. Hist. Lib. tit. *Albigenses*.

† The *Lollards* (of which appellation many definitions are given, See *Mosheim*, vol. i. p. 744. note u, edit. Macl.) who arose in the fourteenth century, were charged with " preaching openly many heresies, blasphemies,
" and scandalous defamings, quite contrary to the sacred
" *canons* and *decrees* of the *holy fathers*," and were persecuted accordingly.—Pope *Boniface* IX. in his *Bull* against them (see *Fox*, vol. i. 574.) did not deign to call them *men*, but—" *withered—carnal—damnable* shadows
" and ghosts of men." Their crime was, that they were zealous for the *word of* GOD, and opposed the lyes and superstitions of the day—among other things, the incroachments of the *Pope* with regard to marriage.

That this was one ground of enmity and persecution against these poor people, may appear from the following record—" May 2, 1511. *Six* men and *four* women
" appeared before *Archbishop Warham*, in his manor of
" *Knoll*,

celibacy, the use of the *seven sacraments*, and laid it down as *sound doctrine*, that " if a man and woman came together with an intention to live in *wedlock*, this intention is sufficient, without passing through the forms of the church."—This certainly was *sound doctrine*, because agreeable to the word of GOD; where no other ceremony appears to have intervened, in order to constitute a lawful marriage before GOD.

Mr. *Jacob*, in his *Law Dictionary*, tit. *Marriage*, observes, that " before the time of Pope *Innocent* III. there was no *solemnization* of marriage in the church; but the man came to the house where the woman inhabited, and led her home to his own house; which was all the ceremony then used." See *Lilly*-Abr. tit. Bar. and Femme, p. 225. *Moor* 170.

The learned and accurate Judge *Blackstone*—Comm. vol. i. p. 439. quarto edit.—observes, that—" It is held to be essential to a *marriage*, that it be performed by a *person in orders*; though the intervention of a *priest* to solemnize this contract is merely *juris positivi*, and not *juris naturalis aut divini*: it being said that *Pope Innocent* the *third* was the first who ordained the celebration of *marriage* in the *church*, before

" *Knoll*, and abjured many *errors*: one of which was, that the solemnization of matrimony is not profitable, nor necessary for the well of man's soul." See *Burnet*, Hist. Ref. p. 27. 2d edit. folio.

" which it was totally a *civil* contract." I do not cite these authorities to establish any *article of faith* upon the subject, but merely as historical facts, and to shew how far *superstition* must prevail among us, when it is seriously believed, that no obligation of *marriage* is lawful, binding, or valid, in the sight of GOD, that does not owe its *perfection* to a *ceremony* which never existed till the days of a *Pope* of *Rome*, whose pride and ambition led him to ordain it. When once *Peter Lombard* had found out that marriage was a * *sacrament*, the administration of it by the hands of a † *priest* followed of course; the belief of its absolute *nullity*, without this, was gradually received by the *people*, grew into an *article of faith*, and *superstition* has continued it amongst us to this very hour. The *clergy*,

---

* It is to be remarked, that when the church of *Rome* had turned marriage into a *sacrament*, the words by which one of the *real sacraments* was instituted, as to its administration, were to be borrowed in the solemnization of matrimony, and the *council of Trent* decreed, that " the *parish priest*, having interrogated the man and the " woman, and heard their consent, shall say—" I join " you in matrimony, *in the name of the Father, and of* " *the Son, and of the Holy Ghost*." Comp. Matt. xxviii. 19. The *church of England* follows this *Popish* precedent very nearly; for the *minister*, *or priest*, is to say—" I pronounce that they be man and wife together, " *in the name of the Father, and of the Son, and of the Holy* " *Ghost*."

† This had been gradually making its way for a great while:—from the *priest's* attending to give a *benediction*, to *ceremonies* and *forms* of *words*, it crept on, till at last Pope *Innocent* III. by the help of *Peter Lombard's* invention, fully established it.

by

by this means, became possessed of a fresh source of power and wealth; for, what with the fees, or *offerings* as they were more gently termed, for *marriage* itself, that is, for performing the *ceremony*, the publication of *banns*, *dispensations*, and *licences*, it has proved a sort of *philosopher's* * *stone*.

Still

---

* *Soter*, the fifteenth bishop of *Rome*, at the end of the second century, before the name and authority of *Popes* were assumed, finding that appropriating marriage to the *priests*, promised no small revenue to the *clergy*, ordained, that no woman should be deemed a lawful wife, unless formally married by the *priest*. But this seems only to have been temporary, and was confined chiefly to *Rome*; other parts of the *Christian* world followed their ancient customs. We have seen how this was extended and improved in after ages; and we may observe, that in all the instances of cunning and policy wherewith *churchmen* have wrought for the conversion, or rather *perversion*, of Christianity into a worldly system, which could gratify their pride, satiate their ambition, and fill their coffers, few are to be found which have answered the purpose better, than turning marriage into a *sacrament*, throwing it entirely into the hands of *priests*, and laying it under the power and cognizance of ecclesiastical judges.

By these means, the church of *Rome* fastened an additional bond on the understanding and consciences of mankind, which gave rise to lucrative rites and ceremonies, dispensations, licences, and other modes of increasing the power and wealth of the church.

These were greatly enhanced by the introduction of *impediments*, which are not to be found in God's word, as well as of a power of *dispensing* with those that are positively enacted there; insomuch that Pope *Martin* V. gave a man leave to marry with his *own sister*, as is observed by *Angelus de Clavasio*, in a book called *Summa Angelica*, tit. *Pope*. Pope *Pius* IV. was for dispensing with the *prince of Spain's* marrying with his *own aunt*. PHILIP IV.

of

of *Spain*, married ANNE *Archdutchefs of Auftria*, though she was his own niece. *Guthrie*, Gen. Hift. vol. xii. p. 266. And we have lately feen, if I miftake not, the *Pope's* difpenfing with the marriage of the *king of Portugal* with his own *niece*. Yet they hold it unlawful for *godfathers* and *godmothers* to intermarry, either with the parents or the baptized, by reafon of a certain *spiritual cognation* which is invented between them. So the kindred which doth arife by the *facrament of confirmation*, (fee Brent, Counc. Trent, 785.) But of no fuch thing, of no fuch relation, and, of courfe, of no fuch impediment, do we read in the fcripture.

Had the fimplicity of marriage been adhered to as found in the fcripture, matrimony had never been worth a fingle *fixpence* to the *church*; but as matters have been contrived by the church of *Rome*, and adopted in a great meafure by *Proteftants*, it may be faid of the fums it has produced, as is faid of SOLOMON's *brazen veffels*, 1 Kings vii. 47, *Neither was the weight of the brafs found out*. Pope LEO X. might well exclaim,

> *O quantum profuit nobis hæc fabula Chrifti !*

One thing may be obferved, which is, that in all the departures from GOD's word, either as to *ritual* or *doctrinal* matters, which have been made by the church of *Rome*, there is not one which does not *found in damages*, as our lawyers fpeak, and which does not tend to enrich the *clergy*.

They have ufually acted on the principles of thofe *philofophers*, who hold—that " the emptying of one " veffel may poffibly prove the filling of another;" and they have found this fo uniformly to anfwer the experiments which have been tried on the reciprocal connection between one man's pocket and another's purfe, that what *Horace* has reprefented as the language of his day in *Heathen Rome*, is equally applicable to *Rome Chriftian*.

> *O cives cives quærenda pecunia primum eft,*
> *Virtus poft nummos.*

Ye fons of *Rome*, let money firft be fought,
Virtue is only worth a fecond thought.

As our *Protestant church* has thought fit to adopt some of these lucrative contrivances, so, among the rest, the business of marriage has, in its measure, not altogether been thought *unworthy* of its notice. Our account stands pretty much as follows, viz.

To publishing *banns* in the *church*, in most places, is *one shilling*.

To the accustomed duty to the *priest* and *clerk*, which is ordered to be *laid upon the service-book* during the ceremony. This, in most places, is *five shillings* to the *priest*—and to the clerk *two shillings and sixpence*—making together, inclusive of the *banns*, *eight shillings and sixpence*.

This mode of marriage by *banns*—which was the invention of *Pope Innocent* III. and ultimately fixed, with a *salvo* for the Bishop's dispensation, by the *council of Trent*—usually falls to the share of the common or poorer sort of people.

Those who move in an higher sphere usually marry by *licences*, which, by carrying *stamps* upon them, make a considerable branch of the public revenue (as the same sort of things, under the name of *dispensations*, formerly did of the *Pope's*); one of these, if to marry in a church or chapel, costs about *one pound nine shillings*, besides the above accustomed duty to the *priest* and *clerk*, which on such occasions is *doubled*, or turned into the better and more lucrative article of—*what you please*.

If we go higher still, to the nobility, &c. who chuse to marry in *private houses*, they purchase an *absolution* for so doing, at the *moderate* price of *ten guineas*. *Priest* and *clerk* as before. In short—*Nil nisi cum pretio*.

> For money b'ing the common scale
> Of things by measure, weight, and tale,
> In all th' affairs of church and state,
> 'Tis both the balance and the weight.
> HUDIBRAS.

However, if all this related to a merely civil matter, and people are content to submit to it—very well; but there is *mischief* lurking under all this fair shew of decency and religious ceremony, which is horrible to conceive—for, without these things, marriages are declared to be *ipso facto* null and void to all intents and purposes *whatsoever,*

Still the *ordinance* of GOD was seen to be independent on all this, and to set it aside entirely, * was then too hard even for *Rome* itself (though we have lived to see it done in this enlightened age by a *British parliament*); therefore the laws of the *empire* held, as our *ecclesiastical* laws do to this day, that such a coming together on a previous contract, antecedently to the *ceremony*, was a marriage *de facto* †, or *in fact*, but not *de jure*—was not a *lawful* marriage, as to *civil* purposes—till the *priest* had executed that office which the *Pope* had assigned him, on the strength of *Peter Lombard's* monstrous interpretation of —" the *seven Spirits of* GOD."

In order to preserve and increase such an acquisition of power and wealth to the *church*,

---

whatsoever, *any law* (even of GOD Himself!) *to the contrary notwithstanding*.

The bond and obligation which arise *ex assensu & concubitu* (but especially from the *latter*)—which are the only scripture-ingredients of marriage, as ordained by JEHOVAH HIMSELF, as making the οἱ δυο εις σαρκα μιαν —*the twain one flesh*—are entirely set aside; their living together is *criminal*, though GOD has *sanctified* it; parting, and taking others, is *lawful*, though GOD has forbidden it. What is the legalizing such *divorces*, but *facere non peccatum de peccato*—making that *not sinful* which *is so*? What the stamping illegality and sin on such an union, but *facere peccatum de non peccato*—making that *sinful* which is *not so*?—This, from the pen of a *Bellarmine*, as the prerogative of the *Popes of Rome*, is a justly-abhorred blasphemy—this, enacted by a *British parliament*, is the law of a *Protestant* country!

* This was afterwards (anno 1563) completed by the council of *Trent*.

† See before vol. i. p. 30. 31.

a stop was to be put to *private* * *contracts*, which could bring in nothing to the *men of the craft*; therefore the absolute necessity of publication of † *banns* was instituted in the

* *Tertullian*, who lived in the *second century*, and who fell into the errors of *Montanus*, writes thus: *Penes nos, occultæ quoque conjunctiones, i. e. non prius apud ecclesiam profeſſæ, juxta machiam judicari periclitantur.* TERT. de Pudic. c. 4. "Among us, clandestine joinings together, "that is to say, such as are not first openly professed "before the church, are in danger of being judged lit- "tle better than *whoredom*."—The learned *father* saith well—*penes nos*—*among us*—for no trace of such a thing is to be found in the scripture. Thus early did that *mystery of iniquity* begin to *work*, which in after times made so considerable a part of *ecclesiastical* tyranny over the consciences of men, by rendering the interposition of *priests* essentially necessary to *marriage*, as to its *validity* and *obligation* in the sight of GOD. Thus was a foundation laid for the *desertion* and *ruin* of *seduced* females. See before vol. i. p. 9, 10.

† Upon collecting the whole evidence together, the origin of publication of *banns* appears to be as follows: The *Pope* finding the *sweets* arising from his power of *dispensations* to be very great, and large sums to accrue from them, took care to extend their necessity as far as possible—to this end, degrees of *affinity* and *consanguinity* were extended to the *seventh* degree, and even as far as *any relationship could be traced*, within which, none could marry. Still referring to the *Pope* a power of *dispensation*; which was exercised in a shameful manner; being granted to some whom GOD's word had forbidden to intermarry, and others were *divorced*, for marrying within the *degrees* prohibited by the *Canons*. In order, however, to secure and increase the revenue arising from *dispensations*, *clandestine marriages* were forbidden, and none were to marry without *publication* of *banns*, that they might be deterred from *marriage* without a *dispensation*, if within any degrees of *relationship*; for if this was done without the *Pope's dispensation*, they fell under the *claws* of the *ecclesiastical courts*, and the marriage declared *null*.

beginning of the 13th *century*, and also various inventions in order to legitimate the issue of *concubinary parents*, as they called all those who came together *only* according to the *ordinance* of GOD; one of which may serve as a sample of the rest. " The *ceremony* was, that the *parents*, with the spurious issue between them, had a cloak or coverlid cast over them, while the *priest* was performing the *mass* or *office of matrimony*, and as soon as that was ended, the fruitful mother was delivered of a *lusty* infant under coverture and in *matrimony*." Reynolds, 71. Those who could believe that this ridiculous *farce* could make any difference, either in the state of the *parents*, or in that of the *child*, before GOD, may also believe that a man and woman who come together according to the *ordinance of* GOD, are the more *man and wife* in GOD's sight, *after* a *priest* has said *mass*, or red over a *ceremony*, than they were *before*—both these opinions are equally abhorrent from the truth of the scripture, *one* being no more to be proved thereby than the *other*. The Popish council of *Trent* put the finishing stroke to the whole plan, by *solemnly* and *piously* cursing " all who should condemn the *benedictions* and other *ceremonies*, or that should deny matrimonial causes to belong to *ecclesiastical* judges."

We have now seen the *birth*, *parentage*, and *education* of *marriage-ceremony*, as depending on *ecclesiastical* establishment, and of

2   men's

men's taking upon themselves to interfere with the authority and validity of the *divine* ordinance of *marriage*, which simply consists in the *union* of the *male* and *female*, and GOD's pronouncing them *one flesh*; thus is GOD said to *join them together*, and therefore it is, that no want of a human ceremony can ever *put them asunder*. This is truly and properly the *marriage-contract*, or rather the very *marriage* itself—*betrothment* may precede it, *espousals* may go before it; but whether they do or not, this *is*, as it ever *was*, and ever *will be*, *marriage* in the sight of GOD. All beyond this is matter of ceremony, decency, and prudence; I do not pretend to dispute the * expediency of such things; they are, and may, and must be

---

* " A clergyman, in performing a *marriage-ceremony*, does not confer any right or privilege on the parties which they had not before from nature; but only, in a public manner, witnesses and authenticates the public declaration they make, of having entered into a matrimonial agreement according to the laws and customs of the country. Thus, whether the ceremony be performed by a *clergyman*, or, as it formerly was, and still is, in many parts of the globe, by the *civil magistrate*, neither the act of the *clergyman* or *magistrate* convey any *right*, but enter on public record the recognizance of such parties entering, with mutual consent, on the exercise of a *right* which they have by nature;—as when an heir at law succeeds to an estate, the ceremonies customary in the country where he resides, at entering him *heir*, convey to him no new right to that estate, but only publicly declare, and manifest to his country, that he has entered on the use of that estate, by virtue of his inherent right as heir to it by nature." See *Alexander*, Hist. Wom. vol. ii. 259.

binding, as to the *dowries of wives*—the *legitimation* of children in a *civil* view—their *inheriting* eſtates and honours, and in ſuchlike caſes: but with reſpect to God's inſtitution, it remains *as* and *where* it did, and ſo muſt remain, without any poſſibility of receiving the leaſt alteration, or being at all ſubject to the diſpoſal or inventions of *prieſtcraft* and *ſuperſtition*. Therefore it continues a truth indelibly written in the *oracles of* God, that where parties *come together* under promiſe and intention of *marriage,* ſuch promiſe and intention can never be retracted by the parties themſelves, nor diſſolved by any power on earth, without doing violence to the expreſs and poſitive law of God. Nay I will go farther, and ſay, that though there be no promiſe or intention of marriage, yet if a man *entice a virgin,* or, without previous enticement, *meet with her,* and HUMBLE HER, ſhe ſhall for *that* reaſon *be his wife*; *he may not put her away all his days.* Comp. Exod. xxii. 16. *Deut.* xxii. 28, 29. Were theſe truths as indelibly received, written, and believed within the *conſcience* as they ought to be—

> " So many of the *ſex* would not, in vain,
> " Of faithleſs men, and broken vows, complain."

A man would no more dare to *ſeduce* a *virgin,* and then abandon her, than he would dare to *murder* her? as he would be convinced that the *law* of God as really forbids the *former* as it does the *latter.* If theſe *holy* commandments

commandments were, as they ought to be, the law of the land, the *magistrate*, as in *Israel*, would have such power of *coërcion* in every case, as would render the designs of *villainy*, and the machinations of *treachery*, abortive.

'Till this happy time arrives, we may lament, but cannot remedy, the dreadful evils which attend *seduction* and *dereliction*, and, in the pathetic words of the *Preacher*, say—*So I returned, and considered all the oppressions that are done under the sun; and behold the tears of such as were oppressed, and they had no comforter; and on the side of the oppressor there was power; but they* (the oppressed) *had no comforter.* Eccl. iv. 1.

As to the *superstition* which condemns *polygamy*, and persuades men to believe that *our* Saviour called it *adultery*—as it is the *parent* of an error fatal to the *female sex*, insomuch that if a man already married entices a *virgin*, &c. he is to think himself *bound* to *abandon* her, contrary to the *positive command of* God —I must, in this place, say something more on that subject.

This species of *superstition* is like that which among the primitive *Christians* and *fathers* of the *church*, was held in high esteem and veneration, and which reprobated " *second* marriages as little better " than *adultery*," without all foundation whatsoever from the scripture, when rightly understood. The Old Testament often

* mentions *polygamy*, but never, as has been fully proved, with the least mark of disapprobation or disallowance—though often practised, and this openly and avow-

---

* The first instance recorded of *polygamy* is that of *Lamech*, (see before, vol. i. p. 143,) a cotemporary with *Adam*, and only *six* persons from him in a direct line (see Gen. iv. 17—19.) about 129 years after the creation of the world; a period too inconsiderable in point of time, considering the longevity of mankind in those days, to leave us the least room to imagine, that what had been pronounced by *Adam* on the subject of marriage, as recorded Gen. ii. 24. and by him doubtless delivered to his children, was either misunderstood or forgotten.

Le Clerc, on Gen. iv. 19. is far from condemning *Lamech*, as some have done—his words are, "Hinc porro
" an primus πολυγαμ⊙ fuerit *Lamechus* non satis con-
" stat; nec πολυγαμια eo initio magis vituperari
" potuit, quam fratrum & sororum damnantur matri-
" monia. Sive enim humani generis hoc postulaverit
" propagatio; seu earum, quas duxit *Lamechus* alteri
" alius vir non fuerit, cui collocaretur, mulieribus viros
" numero superantibus; seu quæcunque alia fuerit
" causa in tanta hominum raritate, *Moses* quod multis
" post sæculis gentis suæ factitarunt sanctissimi patri-
" archæ, *Lamecho* vitio vertere non potuit."

" From hence it does not sufficiently appear, whe-
" ther *Lamech* was the first *polygamist*; nor could *poly-*
" *gamy*, in that early time of the world, be any more
" found fault with, than the marriage of brothers and
" sisters be condemned. Whether the propagation of
" the human kind might require this—or one of the
" women whom *Lamech* married, had no other man to
" whom she might be given in marriage, the women
" then exceeding men in numbers—or whatever else
" might be the case in such a scarcity of men—*Moses*
" could not turn that into a *crime* in *Lamech*, which the
" *most holy patriarchs* of his nation practised afterwards
" for many ages."

edly,

edly, by those whom the New Testament sets forth as examples of *faith and holiness* (Heb. vi. 12. Heb. xi. *throughout*, with Heb. xii. 1.) yet never in any one single instance condemned. Laws are made for its regulation, to establish the inheritableness of the issue, to prevent partiality in the disposal of the *polygamist*'s effects among the children which he might have by *two wives*, and to forbid his *forsaking* or even *slighting* a *first* wife, if he took a *second* to her. The New Testament never mentions it at all, either as *good* or *bad*, with respect to itself: therefore our laws against it, or opinions about it, can no more make it *sinful*, than the *silly* notions of the primitive *Christians* and *fathers*, could make it " little bet-" ter than *adultery*" for a man to marry a *second* wife after the death of his *first*, or than the laws of *Rome* can make it *sinful* to deny *five* of *Peter Lombard*'s seven sacraments, or in a priest to marry at all. It is not in the power of men to invent sins, and then charge them upon the consciences of their fellow-mortals to their condemnation before GOD:—the assuming this, is a part of that *spiritual wickedness in heavenly things*, (Eph. vi. 12.) which has long distinguished the *mother of harlots and abominations of the earth*. Rev. xvii. 5. It may be looked upon as one striking evidence of the *Pope*'s being the *man of sin*, described 2 Thess. ii. 3, 4. for it is *opposing and exalting himself above all that is called* GOD, *or that is worshipped; it is, as*

GOD,

GOD, *fitting in the temple of* GOD, *shewing himself that he is* GOD.—— *How shall I curse whom* GOD *hath not cursed? Or how shall I defy whom the* LORD *hath not defied?*—was the saying of a man that *had his eyes open.* Numb. xxii. 31. xxiii. 8. xxiv. 4; but those whose eyes are *blinded* by *superstition,* or fast *closed* by *prejudice,* will take upon themselves to do what *Balaam,* daring and wicked as he was, would not presume to do. The answer which he gave to *Balak*'s messengers, when they importuned him to come and curse *Israel,* was a good precedent for us to follow, whensoever we deliver our opinion on the *lawfulness* or *unlawfulness* of any actions of men, where conscience towards GOD is immediately concerned; and indeed it ought to be the language of all our laws, both of church and state—" If *Balak* would " give me his house full of silver and gold, " *I cannot go beyond the commandment of the* " LORD, *to do either good or bad of my own* " *mind;* but *what the* LORD saith, *that will* " *I speak.*" Compare *Numb.* xxii. 5, 6. with xxiv. 13. However, we are assured that the *curse causeless, shall not come.* Prov. xxvi. 22. Therefore though a man should be burnt at a stake for denying *five* of the *Popish* sacraments, and by us * be reckoned

a *martyr*

* I must confess that I hardly ever read over those words of the *Te Deum* without an heart-felt satisfaction —" *We believe that thou shalt come to be our judge.*" How strangely contradictory are the judgments of men on one another! how much under the power of error, caprice, prejudice,

a *martyr* and a *saint*; or another be *hanged* for having *two wives at a time,* and be accounted

judice, and resentment! The same man shall be *canonized* as a saint by some, and *cursed* as an heretic and apostate by others.

The canon of *St. Victor* calls *Luther* a false teacher and an apostate, and him and his fellow-reformers—*hæretical antichrists.*

The writings of the *Protestants* extol them as reformers of the *Christian* church, and revivers of the great truths of the gospel.

The *Romanists* say, that *Luther* died suddenly in a drunken fit, and went *to hell*—some of them, that he was flown away with by the *devil*—a *cacodæmone* sublatum fuisse asserunt.

Quirinus Cnoglerus has observed, in his *Lutheran Creed,* that he had seen a little *German* book written in praise of SAINT *Martin Luther,* which contained at large the legend of this new *Saint,* canonized by the *Protestant* ministers in *Germany,* wherein were these words—

IN VITA ÆTERNA,
CHRISTUS *habet primas, habeas tibi* PAULE *secundas, At loca post illos tertia,* LUTHER *habet.*

IN LIFE ETERNAL,
CHRIST has the first, and PAUL the second place,
The third is justly by our LUTHER claim'd.
See Gen. Dict. Hist. and Crit. vol. vii. p. 247, 259.

The *Turkish Spy,* vol. i. p. 31. represents a *Jesuit,* as declaring, " that the *wickedest* wretches, and most *detestable* that ever were, were *Judas, Mahomet,* and *Luther*; that these two last, as the most impious, are " the more tormented in hell.

About *ten* years before *Luther's* death, he was taken very ill, insomuch that his life was despaired of The *Papists* not only gave out that he was *dead,* but actually published the following curious account of his *death*; which,

counted a very *great sinner*; yet the curse of the *Papists* could not injure the *first*, nor the bad which, for the entertainment of the *reader*, and as a sample of *Romish* veracity, I will here transcribe.

"A horrible and unheard-of miracle, which GOD,
"evermore to be praised, hath, in the filthy death
"of *Martin Luther*, damned *body* and *soul*, been
"pleased to shew for the glory of JESUS CHRIST,
"and towards the amendment and comfort of the
"godly.

"When *Martin Luther* was taken sick, he desired the
"body of our LORD to be communicated unto him;
"which having received, he soon after *died*. When
"he found the end of his life drawing on, he de-
"sired that they would lay his corpse upon an altar, and
"that paying thereto divine honours, they should wor-
"ship it. But GOD at last, to put a period to his hor-
"rible errors, admonished the people by a mighty mi-
"racle to abstain from that impiety, which the said
"*Luther* had brought in: for his body being laid into
"the grave, there arose such a sudden tumult, horror,
"and earthquake, as if the foundations of the world
"had been shook, so that all that were at the funeral
"were struck with amazement. But lifting up their
"eyes, they saw the *holy host* hanging in the air" [*this you must suppose to be the host he received lately, which would not vouchsafe to remain in such a vile heretic's body.*]
"Therefore, with great devotion of mind, they took
"the most *holy host*, and laid it up in a sacred place;
"which being done, the hellish clatter ceased to be
"heard; but the night following, there was a more
"frightful noise about *Luther's* tomb than before,
"which raised the whole city, astonished and half dead
"with fear: therefore in the morning they opened the
"grave, in which the detestable body of *Luther* was
"laid, but found therein neither body nor bones, nor
"any of the cloaths, but a hellish stench of brimstone
"coming out of the grave, that almost choaked all that
"came near it. With which miracle very many being
"affrighted,

bad opinion of *Papists* and *Protestants* united, in the least affect the *second*. Both would fall by the hand of *superstition*—both testify the horrors of its ascendency over the minds of men—*both stand or fall to his own master.* Rom. xiv. 4.

On the contrary, let us remember, that there is a *curse* which is *not causeless*, and therefore *will come*—no *canons* either of the ancient or modern *Christians*—no human laws,

" affrighted, have amended their lives, to the honour
" of the Christian faith, and glory of *Jesus Christ.*"

This curious writing, with *Luther's* answer to it, is to be found in *Lonicerus's Theatrum Historicum*, fol. 246. and in *Hist of Popery*, vol. ii. p. 316.

After considering these, and many other instances which might be given, who, that values the peace of his own mind, would trouble himself, where *truth* is concerned, a single instant about the suffrages of ignorant mortals, either one way or the other?—Well said *Paul*— *With me it is a very small thing* (ἐλάχιϛον — the smallest—least—either in itself, or *in my concern about it*) *to be judged of you or of man's judgment—but he that judgeth me is the* LORD. 1 Cor. iv. 3, 4. That same LORD will judge *us*—therefore, *to know his will, and to do it,* should supersede all other concerns whatsoever. Then I believe it will trouble us, as little as it now troubles honest *Luther* and his fellow-labourers, whether our fellow mortals *curse* or *canonize* us.——As to the suffrages of men—

> *All your Philosophers agree,*
> *And prove it plain, that one may be*
> *A heretic, or true believer,*
> *On this or t'other side a river.*
> PRIOR's Alma, Canto II.

Making human opinion the standard of *truth*, is like making the *cameleon* a standard of colour.

inventions, customs, or opinions will keep it off, or soften its rigour; for it is written in the New Testament as well as in the Old Testament—*Cursed is every one that continueth not in* ALL *things which are written in* THE BOOK OF THE LAW *to do them.* The man who takes a *virgin* into his *possession*, and then forsakes and abandons her, let his own situation be what it may (the *law* makes no difference) will find, that nothing can vacate the obligation of the *divine commands*, Exod. xxii. 16. (comp. Deut. xxii. 28, 29.) which declare that *he shall* SURELY *endow her to be his wife.* The words מהר ימהרנה are an emphatical reduplication—*dotando dotabit*—*endowing he shall endow her*—which expresses the positive certainty that it *shall* and *must* be so: like Gen. ii. 17. מות תמות—*moriendo morieris*—*dying thou shalt die*; which we, according to our idiom, well translate—*thou shalt surely die.* We may give much the same reason for the reduplication of the words in these passages, as *Joseph* gave for the doubling *Pharaoh*'s dream, Gen. xli. 32. —*For that the dream was doubled unto Pharaoh twice, it is* BECAUSE THE THING IS ESTABLISHED BY GOD, *and* GOD *will shortly bring it to pass.* Equally plain and certain, and even more explicit, is that of Deut. xxii. 29. *First*, we have the *command itself*— *She shall be his wife: Secondly*, the *reason*— *Because he hath humbled her: Thirdly*, the *indissolubility* of the positive *obligation* arising therefrom—*He may not put her away all his days.*

days. To reconcile these *things, which are written in the law,* with our opinions and systems of matrimony, is impossible; these laws are evidently explanatory of the *primary law* of marriage, ours contradictory thereto; for no contradiction can be more apparent, than that which arises between a law, commanding marriage on the simple terms of the original institution—*because he has humbled her*—and thus become *one flesh*—and a law prohibiting marriage but on complicated terms of human invention, and even making void, *to all intents and purposes whatsoever,* the obligation which results *merely* from the *divine command.* When we farther consider this to be the case, in a country where the people profess a belief of the *Bible,* and who read these laws over in the public congregations of the *established church* once in every year, we surely ought to lament the reign of *superstition* in the consciences of men, who pray to GOD *to write His laws in their hearts,* and yet contentedly live under and embrace a system as opposite to those laws, as light to darkness. How can we cast a stone at the *Papists,* for striking the *second* commandment out of the *Decalogue,* while we ourselves strike these commandments out of the *book of the law?* May not they say to us—*Ye hypocrites, first cast the beams out of your own eyes, and then shall ye see clearly to pull out the motes which are in our eyes?*

By *these laws* no man can *take a virgin,* and then abandon her; by our laws a man may

may take an *hundred*, and abandon them all:—By the *first*, therefore, *prostitution* is impossible—by the *second* it is a natural consequence; for by the *one* it never *can* happen, by the other it *does*, and *must* happen every day.

Hence it follows, that the seduction of *virgins* by *single men*, who afterwards *put them away* because they *will not* marry them publicly—and by *married* men, who *cannot* if they *would*—may be looked upon as the two flood-gates of *female* ruin and misery: nothing can ever put a stop to their destructive *deluge*, but the abrogation of *superstitious* laws and customs, and the restoration of the *divine plan* of security and protection, which is so clearly revealed, so positively commanded, by the GOD *of heaven*.

Perhaps some will be ready to say, that, " if virgins will deliver up their persons to " men without the *ceremony* first past, but " more especially to *married men*, where they " know the *ceremony cannot* pass, do they " not deserve to suffer?" Reader, if thou hast found this *severe* question presenting itself to thine imagination, as, if thou art one of those who *are wise in their own eyes, and prudent in their own sight*, (If. v. 21.) trusting in *thyself that thou art righteous*, &c. (Luke xviii. 9.) it may have done more than once, in the perusal of these pages—let me advise thee to lay down *my* book, and take up a *better*; turn to *John* viii. 3. and read attentively to ver. 12.—consider deeply that
short

short history which is recorded there, weigh well the circumstances, mark the characters, apply what is said ver. 7. to thyself, and if thou findest thyself inclinable to *retire* with those *Scribes* and *Pharisees*, leaving the objects of thy contempt and bitter scorn to the mercies, the tender mercies of the GOD who made them, knowing that thou thyself art also in the same *condemnation*—well: if otherwise, let me ask thee—*Is thine eye evil because* GOD *is good?* (Matt. xx. 15.) If He *who knoweth whereof we are made* hath graciously provided against the sad and ruinous consequences of human frailty, even as to this world, by enacting positive laws in order to prevent them, where they must fall the heaviest, and of course most need prevention, is it for thee to find fault with so gracious a dispensation, not considering that thou thyself art a monument of the like mercy? For if GOD had said concerning thee, what I suppose thee to have been saying concerning others; had He made no provision in His providence that thou mightest escape the consequences of thine own frailty, where hadst thou now been?—not censuring and condemning others, but thyself condemned to irretrievable misery, involved in inextricable ruin!—Make not then thyself *wiser* and *holier* than GOD; but lament the ravages of lust, seduction, and prostitution; *let thine eyes* (like the *Psalmist's) gush out with water, because men keep not* GOD*'s law.* Pf. cxix. 136. Prayer-Book translation.

I say

I say not this as allowing it possible for human laws, customs, and opinions, to make any thing sinful, which GOD's law hath not made so; *sin is the transgression of the law — where there is no law there is no transgression — nor is sin imputed where there is no law.* Thus speak the scriptures, as we have before observed; but if *superstition binds heavy burdens, and grievous to be borne, and lays them upon men's shoulders,* the *conscience* must groan under the pressure, till the *weary* and *heavy laden* are released, by the friendly and beneficent hand of *divine truth*. To say that a *virgin*, who delivers herself into the possession of the man of her choice, with an intent to become *his wife*, sins in so doing, unless an *outward ceremony* of man's device be first performed, is to say what the *Bible* has no where said: all that GOD says in such a case is, that they shall be *one flesh*, and that *she shall be the man's wife — he may not put her away all his days.* So that all contrivances which hinder the operation of this law, are not only so many snares laid for the *conscience*, which may enthrall and bring it into subjection to the pride and arrogance of man, but are big with every mischief which the DIVINE LAW was enacted to prevent.

The infamy, which, by this means, is stamped on such an *act*, has occasioned the murder of as many infants by the hands of their mothers, in this *Christian* country, as were probably sacrificed to *Moloch* in the same

same space of territory, by the hands of the heathen priests.

If, in consonance with the DIVINE LAW, such an *act* was deemed to create an *indissoluble union* between the parties, and the *public recognition* of it was to be inforced in every instance, as under the law of *Moses*, this mark of *infamy* would be removed, and, together with it, one of the most horrid of all temptations to one of the most unnatural and dreadful of all crimes.

When *Tamar* is arguing with the incestuous *Amnon* against his unhallowed attempt upon her chastity (2 Sam. xiii.) she might well say—" *And I, whither shall I cause my shame to go?*" for such an act was directly against the positive law of GOD, Lev. xviii. 9.—but where is the authority from scripture to stamp the *infamy* of *whoredom* on the exercise of that right, with which every woman is invested by the GOD of nature, for the propagation and continuance of the human species; I mean, that of bestowing her * person

on

* To say—" This is *sinful* before the *ceremony*, but " *lawful* after the *ceremony*," is to attribute a sort of power of *moral transubstantiation*, either to the *priest*, or to the *ceremony*, or to both: not very unlike that power in the *church of Rome*, of changing one substance into another. To imagine, that, that which is *evil* can become *good* by any invention or power in man, is not less absurd, than to suppose, that a little flour and water becoming a *wafer* by the art of the *baker*, can become the body, flesh, and bones of a man by the art of a priest. See before, vol. i. 46—48. vol. ii. 149. n. *Consider the work of* GOD, saith the *Preacher, for who*

on the man of her choice? Having once done this, if she goes to another (living the first) she is נאפה—an *adulteress*; if she falls into the practice of promiscuous intercourse, going from one man to another, as lust, or gain, or hire, may prompt, she is an *harlot*, or *whore*, in the true sense of the word זונה or πορνη, and under the law would have been put to death—but in the other case, we have no more SCRIPTURE AUTHORITY to call her an *whore*, or to stamp the least *infamy* upon her, than the pious people at *Bourdeaux* had for *stoning* a certain young lady of quality to death, for being suspected to have *fasted* on a *Sunday*. See *Comm. on Essay on Crimes and Punishments*, chap. iii. All these things originated from the ambition and avarice of the *clergy* in the middle ages; who, to lay the rest of the world under contribution in the business of marriage, as well as in many other particulars, made it into a SACRAMENT, obscured the real nature and essence of it, and wrested it out of the hands of the *civil power*, as to the *outward* and *public* recognition of it, to secure it to themselves; after which a man and woman could not marry but for the emolument of the church. A new-married couple were not suffered to cohabit for a given time, unless

---

can make that STRAIGHT *which He hath made* CROOKED? —*i. e.* that GOOD *which* He *hath made* EVIL, *or that* EVIL *which* He *hath made* GOOD? *Eccl.* vii. 13. with *Eccl.* i. 15.

they

they paid the church for a difpenfation, nay, a man was not allowed *chriftian* burial, unlefs he bequeathed fomething to the church.—In fhort, a man " could neither come into " the world, continue in it, nor go out of " it," as a late writer has well obferved, " without being laid under contribution " by the clergy." See *Alex*. Hift. of Women, vol. ii. 259.

Were our laws what they ought to be, were they founded on the bafis of the DIVINE LAW, they would come in aid of *female diftrefs*; they would refcue the poor deferted object of the man's ingratitude and barbarity, from that unauthorized *reproach*, which is found fo fatally intolerable by the weaknefs of the *female mind*; and lay the whole infamy and inconvenience, whatever thefe might be, on the guilty betrayer of an undeferved affection.

I have before faid fomething on Deut. xxii. 21; but on farther confideration of that paffage, am convinced that the woman who is faid to *play the whore in her father's houfe*, cannot mean that her crime confifted in giving her perfon to a man, without a marriage-ceremony red over her by a *prieft*—for no fuch thing exifted in *Ifrael* as the interference of *priefts* in marriage—nor was there any *religious* ceremony whatfoever upon the occafion—the only thing which looks like an *outward* ceremony, is the payment of the מהר or *dower*, into the hands of the father of the *virgin*—but even the *want* of this ceremony did

did not annul the marriage, or render the woman *criminal*, as appears from the cafe of the *feduced virgin*, Exod. xxii. 16. who is not commanded to be *put to death*, as the woman is in the other cafe, and as every *whore* of the daughters of *Ifrael* was. Therefore, in order to render the fcripture confiftent with itfelf, we muft fuppofe that the woman was a *betrothed virgin*, who, between her betrothment and her marriage with the man *who found her not a maid*, had given her perfon to *another*; this in deceit of both—concealing her *betrothment* from the one, and her *defilement* from the other—thus *playing the whore*, and fubjecting herfelf to the law concerning *betrothed* damfels, who, if they fuffered themfelves to be violated, were to be *floned to death*, (comp. ver. 23, 24.) where the man that *lay with her* was alfo to fuffer the fame punifhment—but as the man is not mentioned in this light, ver. 21. we muft fuppofe that he was *deceived*, and had done it ignorantly, therefore innocently; for with regard to capital punifhment, *nemo eft reus nifi mens fit rea*. It is to be remarked, in fupport of the above interpretation, that the *virgins*, Exod. xxii. 16. and Deut. xxii. 28. have the addition of *not betrothed*.

Since I wrote the above, I have looked into Bifhop *Patrick*, and am not a little fatisfied with the interpretation above given of Deut. xxii. 21. as I find it fo exactly harmonizes with the fentiments of that learned prelate. His comment is as follows———

" *And*

" *And the men of her city shall stone her with stones till she die.*] This was the punishment of such *adulteresses*, except only of a *priest*'s daughter, who, if she was guilty of this crime, was *burnt alive*, Lev. xxi. 9.—and it plainly shews he speaks here of a woman corrupted between the time of her espousals, and her husband's compleating the marriage; otherwise he could not have had this capital action against her, &c. And this *Maimonides* saith in *Seder Zeraim*, that from *Moses* to his time, it was never doubted the woman he here speaks of was one that proved false to her husband, *after she was contracted to him.*"

The Bishop, in one part of his note, seems to call it "*simple fornication,*" if the virgin was entirely single and disengaged; which proves how prejudice will affect the minds even of learned and judicious persons; for *fornication,* or *whoredom*—זנה—whether *simple* or *compound*, was *death* to the woman who was guilty of it; which is a conclusive proof, that the *virgins* mentioned Exod. xxii. 16. and Deut. xxii. 28, 29. were not guilty of either, and, of course, that none under the same predicament ought to be infamously styled *whores*, and driven to the desperation of destroying themselves or their children, or both, or be driven out of all civil society, to be vagabonds on the face of the earth; but they should be invested, by the laws of the land, with the undoubted right with which the laws of GOD invest them, and

M 4   thus

thus preserved to their *friends*, the *public*, and *themselves*.

As for *conscience*, or that faculty of *judging* and *determining* on our own actions, and thus *excusing* or *accusing* ourselves, *Rom.* ii. 15.—it is a sort of *judge*, on whose determinations the happiness or misery of the human mind must greatly depend, not only with respect to this world, but with respect also to that which is to come—*For if our heart condemn us,* GOD *is greater than our heart, and knoweth all things—if our heart condemn us not, then have we confidence towards* GOD. 1 John iii. 20, 21.—Of what serious importance must it then be, that the decisions and determinations of this awful tribunal should be founded on the clearest and most incontrovertible evidence? In this respect it may be said to have an advantage over all other courts of judicature which we are acquainted with, and that is, in having access to testimony which cannot lye nor deceive, to RECORDS OF ETERNAL TRUTH, delivered to us, as it were, under the *seal* of HEAVEN ITSELF. Now let us suppose a *judge* seated on the bench—a criminal at the bar—the jury sworn—the witnesses on both sides summoned, and prepared to give their testimony—his *Lordship* stops all proceedings with—
" Gentlemen, I will proceed no farther, I
" will have none of these witnesses exa-
" mined; the case of the *prisoner* at the bar
" is sufficiently related in an article of such a
" *news-paper,* clearly stated in such a *pam-*
" *phlet,*

"*phlet*, and you muft acquit or condemn
"him according to thefe."—I believe the *judge* who could act thus, would be deemed very unfit to be entrufted with the lives and properties of his fellow-fubjects.—In this *judge* we fee a lively emblem of a miftaken, mis-led, blinded *confcience*, which fuffers itfelf to decide on the *lawfulnefs or unlawfulnefs* of any thing before GOD, and in His fight, from the maxims, prejudices, laws, cuftoms, and vulgar errors of fallible men, and not from the infallible *written* teftimony of GOD's moft HOLY WORD.—*It is the* SPIRIT *that beareth witnefs, becaufe the* SPIRIT *is truth.* 1 John v. 6. The not being poffeffed of this authentic teftimony of the mind and will of GOD, or not adverting to it, fo as to make it the *one* rule of our judgment in matters pertaining to the *confcience*, puts the blind *Heathen* and the ignorant *Chriftian* upon a level. We are told in hiftory, that when the *Carthaginians* were defeated by *Agathocles*, tyrant of *Sicily*, they imputed their misfortune to the anger of *Saturn*, who was one of their tutelar deities, and this anger they imagined to have arifen from a neglect which they had been guilty of towards him, with regard to the facrifices which were offered him. In antient times it was ufual to facrifice children of the moft noble families to him, but for fome years paft, in thefe facrifices, they had fubftituted children of mean extraction, fecretly bought and bred up for

that

that purpose, in the room of those nobly born. This they now considered as a departure from the religion of their forefathers, and consequently were conscious of having given their Deity just cause of offence. To expiate the guilt of so *horrid* an *impiety*, a sacrifice of 200 children of the first rank was made to the bloody God; and above 300 other persons, in a sense of their dreadful neglect, voluntarily offered themselves as victims, to pacify, by the effusion of their blood, the wrath of this Deity. See Univ. Hist. vol. xvii. p. 447, 448. Such were the determinations of *conscience*, when without revelation.

When we consider the behaviour of the *Portugueze*, which we have seen mentioned before (p.   .) or reflect on the rivers of *Protestant* blood which were poured forth at * *Paris* in 1572, * or in *Ireland* in 1641, by the

---

** On the 24th of *August*, 1572, at *Paris*, were *massacred*, in the dead of the night, not less than 25,000 *Huguenots*. For this execrable action Pope Gregory XIII. ordered a public thanksgiving, and sent a legate to Charles IX. to intreat him to continue it. On *October* 23, 1641, about 100,000 *Protestants* were either burnt or buried alive, drowned, or ripped open, &c. by the Papists in *Ireland*. See Sir *John Parsons*'s History of the *Massacre*, taken from examinations upon oath.

Before this, in the *Low Countries*, from the first edict of *Charles* V. anno 1530, to the year 1558 inclusive, there were hanged, beheaded, buried alive, or burned, 50,000 persons, besides the multitudes put to death in *France*. See *Brent* Counc. Trent. 413.

Six hundred of the *Albigenses* were put to death in one day

the hands of the *Papists*—and all for *conscience* sake—we have but to compare the *Chris-*

day by *Philippus Augustus*—and the *Waldenses* smothered in the caves whither they fled to hide themselves. Ib. 414.

These are but a small part of the cruelties of that bloody *superstition* of that *mother of harlots and abominations of the earth*—Rev. xvii. 5.—of whom we may truly say, in the language of the Poet,

Tristius haud ILLA *monstrum, nec sævior ulla*
Pestis & ira Deûm Stygiis sese extulit undis.
    VIRG. Æn. iii. l. 214, 215.

A heavier scourge was ne'er design'd,
By HELL ITSELF, to plague mankind.

In short, had *Satan* gone to *Rome*, and summoned a *conclave* of *seven spirits more wicked than himself* to his assistance, they could not have devised a plan more subversive of the gospel, more opposite to the scripture, more destructive of the liberties, lives, and properties of mankind, than that *superstition*, which has *blasphemously* dignified itself with the appellation of the HOLY APOSTOLICAL CATHOLIC FAITH.

The scourge and curse it has been to this country, made our *ancestors*, at the glorious *revolution*, frame laws for it's total exclusion; we, their children, are beginning to repeal those laws, under a notion of favouring *religious liberty*, and that *Popery* is not now what it was formerly; but let such *Patriots* go to the *Tower*, and order one of the *lions* to be let out of his den upon him, and he will find how little change of nature has been wrought in the animal by his confinement. I suppose there is hardly an instance upon record of the craftiness of *Popery*, which transcends that of persuading people to believe things to be true, which the evidence of all experience, and of even their own senses, declares to be false. If *Popery* appears to be different from what it was, this proceeds not from any alteration in the thing itself, but from want of power to exert it's intolerant spirit. However, as CONGREVE's *Maskwell* says—" *Qui vult decipi decipiatur*"—" If we will not hear " the serpent hiss, we must be stung into repentance."

tian

tian who does not advert to his *Bible*, with the *Carthaginian* who had no *Bible*, and we shall find a like cause producing like effects, though certainly the one is more inexcusable than the other. Yet in both cases it must be said—*A deceived heart hath turned him aside, that he cannot deliver his soul, nor say, Is there not a lye in my right hand?* If. xliv. 20.

For my own part, I am perfectly convinced, that there is nothing so absurd, so wicked, or so foolish, which the human mind is not capable of being persuaded of, in religious matters especially, when once it delivers itself up to the dictates of *superstition;* for saying this I appeal to those *histories* of the globe which have accurately set forth the various religions, manners, customs, opinions, and laws of its inhabitants. There is one use to be made of these things, which is, to be thankful to the *Bestower of every good gift*, who is the *Fountain of all Wisdom*, that He hath been graciously pleased to cast our lot under the illumination of the *holy scriptures;* that He hath given us His *word, which is truth,* to guide us *into all truth.* This should awaken in us a jealousy over ourselves—knowing the liableness of the human mind to be deceived—which should lead us to try and examine whatever is objected to our belief, or recommended to our practice, by the unerring rule of God's revelation.

Could this have been done at *Carthage*, no children had been sacrificed to *Saturn*—had this been done by the *Papists* in *France* and *Ireland*, no massacres of *Protestants* had disgraced the *Christian* name—and were it now done among us as it ought to be, no *brothels* would teem with harlots—no streets swarm with *prostitutes*—no *wretched infants be butchered* by the hands of their *more wretched mothers*;—the honour of the *married wife* would be secured, the ruin of the seduced *virgin* be prevented. *Adultery* and *whoredom* would no longer dare to face the light, but be consigned to those realms of darkness from whence they came. On the other hand, while we are taught to believe that *sinful* which God has commanded—that *lawful* which God has forbidden, we are as fatally under the power of *superstition*, not only as the *Papists*, but as the very *Heathen* themselves; nothing can really and truly distinguish us from *either*, but an unreserved adherence to those *commandments*, which in so many instances we have *made of none effect by our traditions*.

When we lay *no obligation* on the man who seduces a *virgin*, to marry her, we *make void the law* of God, which positively declares He *shall*—when we *permit the man to put her away*, and deprive her of that recourse to justice which the law of God affords her, we vacate the *divine law*—when, in the case of a man already *married*, we divorce a *virgin*, which he has seduced, entirely from him, forbidding him (and this under pain of death, 1 Jac. chap. 11.) to do her *that* justice which

the

the *divine law* as positively commands, as in the case of a *single man*—we *command* what God *forbids*, and *forbid* what God *commands*.

In short, our *superstition* and the *superstition* of *Rome* go hand in hand; and, however we may be shocked at that monstrous position, which is mentioned by the Reverend *Mr. Porteous*, in his masterly and excellent *sermon on Toleration* (lately preached and published in *Scotland*, on account of the *Popish* bill) that " If the Pope was to command a thing " to be done, and *Jesus Christ* was to forbid " it, yet the *Pope* must be obeyed"—this is not more really horrid, in *sense*, though perhaps it may in *sound*, than saying—where *human laws* command things which are inconsistent with or opposite to the law of God, yet they are to be obeyed. Few would be so daring as to *say* this, but it is practically declared throughout our whole system, as relative to the *commerce of the sexes*.

As to *polygamy*—which is certainly one *link* in the *chain* of God's dispensations, as so absolutely necessary to prevent, in many cases, the *desertion and prostitution* of women, as well as to preserve *men* from vice and profligacy, under various circumstances of unavoidable difficulties and temptations, which *necessary* separation may render them liable to (see before, vol. i. p. 175—177.) the causes of which may fall short of being grounds for utter divorce—it is, considered in itself, one

of

of the last things which a man should think of, who wishes and aims at the happiness of a domestic life. The weight and burden of a double * family, the distractions which most probably *must* be the effect of jealousy between the women, each envying the other her share in the husband's affections, must be productive of disputes, quarrels, and perpetual disquiet. We see this to have been the case even amongst the best people, who were *polygamists*.—What were *Abraham*'s trials, which arose from his connection with *Hagar?*—What those of *Jacob*, from the jealousy and discontent of *Leah* and *Rachel?* So *Elkanah* suffered not a little at the treatment which his favourite *Hannah* received from her rival *Peninnah*—and indeed it is so much in the nature of things, that matters should fall out alike in all times, where there

* This indeed is an objection which arises from the state of *luxury* into which we are fallen; for their plurality of wives was far from being either a charge, or an incumbrance, to the *Jews* of old time, considering their *simple* way of living. The domestic affairs were the province of the women, whilst that of the husband was the business of the *fields* and *vineyards*. Dressing of victuals, the care of the children, spinning, carding, weaving, and the like, are often mentioned in the sacred books as the occupation of women; whilst their husbands chose the more laborious works. See Univ. Hist. vol. iii. p. 146. A great number of children was esteemed, not a *burden*, but a peculiar *blessing*. See Ps. cxxvii. 3, 4, 5; and, where industry prevails throughout, children may be as truly looked upon as the riches of a *family*, as the numbers of industrious people are as the riches of a state. The more working bees there are, the richer the hive.

are

are the same *causes* to produce the same *effects*, that one should imagine most men, who consulted the peace, quiet, and comfort of * themselves and families, would subscribe to *Horace's*

Felices

* I would not press this argument too far, lest it prove too much; for, to say truth, how few *happy* marriages (comparatively) do we see in the world? but how many very *unhappy* ones have arisen from *second marriages?* Where the wife has died, leaving a family of children, and the husband has married again, either to a *widow* having children of her own, or to a *single woman* who brings a *second brood*, what miseries have arisen to the husband and his children by a former wife, through the jealousy and envy of the mother-in-law with respect to her own offspring? Yet all this has nothing to do with the *lawfulness* or *unlawfulness* of the matter itself. Nor is it fair to conclude against what is *essential*, from that which is *accidental*—it is certainly *possible* that *one wife* may make a man's life completely miserable, if she be such an one as *Solomon* mentions, *Prov.* xxi. 19. and xxv. 24.—it is also *possible* that a man might be very happy with *more than one*, if each be like what the same divine *penman* describes, *Prov.* xxxi. 10. &c. Yet, in either case, marriage, as *to itself*, stands just as it did, and is, *in itself*, just what the word of God makes it. We can only say, that, in the present corrupted and distracted state of things, all conditions of life have their inconveniences and distresses: those usually feel the most of them, whose connections in the world are most extensive.

The late excellent *Dr. Hartley* of *Bath*, in his *Observations* on *Man*, p. 230. on the question whether " the " confining *one* man to *one* woman during life (except " in the case of the woman's *adultery*) be calculated to " produce the greatest possible good, public and pri- " vate?" " Here" (saith he) " we must own our- " selves utterly unable to form any exact judgment. " It is impossible to determine by any computation, " which, in all the ways in which marriage has been or " may be regulated, is most conducive to happiness
" upon

Felices ter & amplius
  Quos irrupta tenet copula; nec malis
Divulsus querimoniis,
  Suprema citius solvet amor die.

Thrice happy they, in pure delights,
Whom love with mutual bonds unites;
Unbroken by complaints or strife,
Ev'n to the latest hours of life.
FRANCIS.

It is most readily to be allowed, that such people can have nothing to do with *polygamy*, except it be to abhor and execrate the very thought of it.

The expediency or inexpediency of a thing, and its lawfulness or unlawfulness, are, however, very different considerations; *all things are lawful for me,* faith the *Apostle* (1 Cor. vi. 12. x. 23.) *but all things are not expedient.*—The *inexpediency* of *polygamy* in *most* cases is self-evident, but in *no* case can its *unlawfulness* be made to appear from the *law of God;*—as to the *law* of *man*, it can no more make it *sinful*, than it can make *marriage* itself *sinful*. A *clerk* who married in the reign of Hen. VIII. when this was made *felony without benefit of clergy*, was no more a *sinner* in the sight of GOD, than the *clerk* who married in the reign of Edw. VI. when the marriages of *priests* were declared to be as lawful as those of other men. So a man who has *two wives* is no

---

" upon the whole. This would be too wide a field,
" and where also we could have no fixed points to guide
" us:—here therefore we seem particularly to want a
" *revelation* to direct us, and therefore are under a *par-*
" *ticular* obligation to *abide by its award.*"

more a *sinner* now, than he would have been in the days of the *Patriarchs*, or of the *Jewish theocracy*—GOD's law was the rule of conscience *then*, and no other ought to be so *now*; men can no more *make sins*, than they can *forgive sins*—THE LORD *is our judge*—THE LORD *is our lawgiver*—THE LORD *is our king*. If. xxxiii. 22. Every attempt, therefore, to make things *sinful* which HIS LAW hath *not* made so, however it may appear under the specious guise of *piety* and *purity*, and be recommended to our belief and practice by the teaching and example of *men like ourselves*, it is no other than *Satan transformed into an angel of light*, and availing himself of the weakness and *superstition* of the human mind, to make us *believe a lye*.

In some cases *polygamy* is not only lawful, but *expedient*.—For instance—a man marries a woman, with whom he cohabits, and after a few years, or even months, she falls into raving *madness*—proper help is sought to, but in vain—it appears to be constitutional, from a family disorder—she is confined in a madhouse—pronounced incurable. In such a case as this, no one end of marriage can possibly be * answered to the husband. Other cases

---

* Such a case as this, was put to *Timothy*, Bishop of *Alexandria*, viz. " Supposing a *wife* to be perfectly " *foolish* and *mad*, so as to be confined, Whether an " husband, who says he cannot *contain* himself, may " lawfully marry another wife ?" He answers, that, " this action would be *adultery* in him, and that no-
" thing

cases * might be put of equal difficulty with respect to him—in all which, the expediency of

" thing else is to be said upon the question." This his *Popish* relator ranks among many *judicious* answers.

Another question asked this *judicious Timothy*, was, " Whether a person that fasted in order to communion, " having by chance swallowed down a drop of water, " either in bathing himself, or in washing his mouth, " ought to *communicate* or no?" He answers—" He " ought to do it so much the rather, because 'tis the " *devil* that uses this artifice to hinder his receiving the " communion." See Du Pin, vol. ii. p. 195. Engl. Transl.

* When the case above mentioned—those others which are to be found, vol. i. p. 175—177.—and many suchlike *situations*, are considered—the question, whether " *polygamy* is or is not forbidden by the LAW OF HEA- " VEN," may, perhaps, assume an *importance* in the opinion of the *reader*, which it had not before; and fully justify the *author* in the pains he has taken to settle that matter on the BASIS OF THE DIVINE LAW.

If it be *totally* forbidden, it can be in *no case* allowed— and if so, men must submit, without murmuring or disputing, to the holy and sovereign WILL OF HEAVEN; and, let the inconveniences of their situation be what they may, it is their duty to suffer them *all* with the most unreserved and unlimited resignation.

On the other hand, if it appears that the *thing itself* is no where forbidden, but allowed—it then must *be lawful*.—The contrary position can have no other ground, than the folly and superstition of the human mind, no other obligation than the tyranny of *custom*, sanctified by *human law*—this, to the distress and destruction of thousands.

I remember, once conversing in *France* with a *Capuchin* friar—and observed he wore *sandals*, which left his feet exposed to the rigour of the *cold season*—on asking him whether this was not attended with great distress and inconvenience? he answered—" Yes—that " many of his order had lost their toes, and some their " lives, by *mortifications* which were caused by the severity of a frost."—" Why then, in such seasons at " least, of taking *another wife* is self-evident, and from nothing more than its being GOD's own appointed remedy against the sad consequences of *lust*—*If they cannot contain, let them marry, it is better to marry than to burn.* 1 Cor. vii. 9. To say that a married *Jew,* under such circumstances, might have applied this remedy *under the law,* but a *Christian* cannot *under the gospel,* is to place us

" least, will ye not wear *shoes* and *stockings* like other
" people?" " No—*our rule* forbids it."—" Can you
" really suppose," replied I, " that GOD can require
" this at your hands? or that there is any *merit* in thus
" exposing yourselves to misery, and even death itself,
" merely because men like yourself have commanded it?
" —it is more like *self-murder* than *religion.*"—Here the *father* grew a little angry—however I pacified his wrath, by wrapping an half-crown up in a piece of paper (for they must not *touch* money) and putting it into his hand—he departed, shaking his head at my profaneness, and assuring me, that I " should have the prayers of all his
" convent."

How much wiser are we than this poor *friar?* he would sooner die of a mortification in his feet, than quit his *sandals* and wear *shoes,* because his *rule* forbids it!—We had sooner see men in situations which expose them to distress and destruction, and women irretrievably ruined by thousands, because *our rule* must be observed, instead of permitting them to apply the remedy which GOD hath graciously afforded, the *expedience* of which is, in numberless cases, as self-evident, as the *friar's* making the *change* which I recommended to him.

However, determining to trace the whole matter to the fountain-head, I have endeavoured to leave nothing unsaid upon the subject, which might tend to elucidate it:—its importance is *inconceivably* great—and if we chuse to wear *sandals,* because *Saint Somebody or other* found out that we must not wear *shoes*—we must abide by the consequences.

under a worſe bondage than the *Jews* were, when under *the yoke which neither they nor their fathers could bear.* Acts xv. 10. Common ſenſe, reaſon, nature, here coincide with ſcripture in the reprobation of ſuch an idea. The man may be forced into *whoredom*, and he ſhall be *free;* but if he *marry* he ſhall be *deemed a felon,* and *ſuffer death as ſuch,* ſays the *pious* ſtatute of 1 *Jac.* c. 11.

The caſe of a *married woman* under ſuch circumſtances is very different, becauſe the law poſitively forbids any *ſecond* union with *another man, living her husband.* See Rom. vii. 3. But then let it be remembered, that if the privileges of *women* are circumſcribed by a ſtricter rule than thoſe of the *men,* ſo are their *paſſions;* theſe are uſually as much weaker than the *paſſions* of men, as their bodily ſtrength is weaker than the ſtrength of men. I now ſpeak of *women* as to their natural ſtate, not as corrupted and debauched in their minds by the adventitious circumſtances of bad education, and led aſtray by bad example. If *girls,* as ſoon as they can read, are to have amorous *romances* and *novels* put into their hands, perhaps obſcene and filthy books, where *leſs diſguiſe* is uſed than in the former—if they are taught to reliſh the lewdneſs of the ſtage, and to mix in the diverſions of public aſſemblies, where men (like *Milton's* toad at the ear of *Eve*) make it their buſineſs to defile the purity of *female minds* by very impure converſation—it is no wonder that the rule which I have laid

laid down, should be found liable to many exceptions; but I have no doubt of its being subscribed to by every man, whose happy lot it is to have married a *sober*, truly-*modest woman*. Were it otherwise—did the *passions* of the weaker sex equal the *passions* of men—had not Providence most graciously ordained a considerable disparity, as one means of maintaining the subordination which women are under—the whole world must be thrown into confusion. We may easily judge of what consequences must ensue, by taking a survey of the distraction of those families, where the *natural balance* has been destroyed.

With regard to *superstition*, it takes so many shapes, and appears in so many forms, that one may say—

Quo teneam vultus mutantem Protea nodo?   HOR.

———while it changes thus, what chains can bind
These various forms; this *Proteus* of the mind?
                                        FRANCIS.

Still it is uniform * in leading men from

* When we consider the various mazes of *error* into which mankind are led by the single principle of *superstition*, it may remind us of that beautiful thought in *Horace*, Sat. iii. lib. ii. l. 48. &c.

———*Velut sylvis, ubi passim
Palantes error certo de tramite pellit.
Ille sinistrorsum hic dextrorsum abit; unus utrimque
Error, sed variis illudit partibus.*

As in a wood two travellers may stray,
Both lose the path, each take a different way;
By one *same error* both may be misled,
Though their lost steps in *various mazes* tread.

truth

truth to falshood—in usurping an empire over the human mind, which is inimical to GOD's glory, to the reverence we owe His commandments, as well as to the solid peace, comfort, and happiness of mankind. Whether therefore *superstition* appears in the shape of a brazen image of an old man at *Carthage*, receiving infants into his arms, and letting them drop through into a pit of fire—or of an old man, made of flesh and blood, at *Rome*, commanding people to renounce the evidence of their outward senses—or of a *primitive* father of the *Christian church*, declaring against *marriage* as " unlawful under " the gospel," and that " all *second* mar-" riages are only a more specious and de-" corous kind of *adultery*"—or of a grave and learned English statesman, enacting a law to *put those asunder whom* GOD *hath joined together*—or of a reverend divine, whether *Popish* or *Protestant*, maintaining that certain moral actions which GOD *allowed*, and in some cases *commanded under the law*, are *sinful under the gospel*—*superstition* is still the minister of *Satan*, who is the *God of this world*, (2 Cor. iv. 4.) carrying on his grand design to destroy the *human species*; nor is there so probable a way of effecting this, as in interfering with those wise regulations which the *Most High* hath made for the preservation of the *female sex*, as may appear from much that has been said, but from more which will be said in the conclusion of this treatise.

It is greatly to be lamented, that *superstition*

tion has found its advocates, not only among the *defigning* and *weak*, but even among the learned, and wife, and pious part of mankind; many melancholy inftances of this ftand upon record, not only in the annals of *Popifh*, but of *Proteftant* literature. Here I find myfelf conftrained to animadvert on fome paffages of the *two fermons* * before mentioned,—with a few ftrictures on which, I fhall conclude this chapter.

The learned and pious *author* feems, in a note at the bottom of one of the pages, to infinuate that no marriage is valid in the fight of GOD, where the " ceremony doth not " pafs through the hands of a *prieft*; who," he tells us, " *acts in* GOD's *ftead.*"—Where is fcripture-proof for this? No where— There is not a fingle inftance of fuch a thing either in the *Old* or *New Teftament*; neither the *priefts* nor *Levites* under the *law*, nor the *apoftles* and other *minifters* under the *gofpel*, appear to have interfered in any *one* inftance, nor is fuch a thing given in commiffion to any of them. Their feveral offices are moft minutely fet forth in all the duties of them, but not a word about their *marrying people*; I am therefore apt to think, that the maxim —*de non apparentibus & non exiftentibus eadem eft ratio*—is very applicable on this occafion. If fuch a thing had been, we muft have met with it, when the adminiftration of the public ordinances by the hands of the *priefts* and

* See vol. i. 262.

Levites was fixed under the Old Testament, to whom it was *death* to *add to*, or *diminish from*, the settled institutions of GOD. As for the passages in Gen. i. and ii. on which our author rests so much of his doctrine, particularly, GOD's *bringing the woman to the man and blessing them*, and therefore *priests* are to do the same—he might with equal strength of argument say, that because we are told, Gen. iii. 21. *Unto Adam and his wife did the Lord GOD make coats of skins, and cloathed them*, therefore we are only to *wear skins, and those* are to be *put on* by a *priest*.

However, if this author's doctrine be true, I defy him to shew the record of one single *lawful* marriage (that of *Adam* and *Eve* not excepted) throughout the whole *Bible*; for there is not one mentioned in which a * *priest* appears to have been concerned: quite the contrary; the simplicity of the primary institution is uniformly preserved throughout the

---

* It should seem, that, among other things which the church of *Rome* borrowed from the *Heathens*, this of marriage by a priest was one. *Soter*, Bishop of *Rome*, in the end of the second century, seems to have taken the hint from that species of marriage among the *Romans*, which was called *confarreation*, (See before, vol. i. p. 33.) from the *bride-cake* of *salted bread*, which was eaten on the occasion, and was a ceremony observed at the marriages of the *pontiffs* and other *priests*, as also at the marriages of those persons whose children were intended for the *priesthood*. These marriages were always celebrated by *a priest*. " And here we discover," says a late author, " the first instance of *priests* having cele-
" brated the rites of that institution." See Alex. Hist. Wom. vol. ii. 251. *Chambers*'s Dict. tit. *Confarreation*.

whole.

whole, and probably would have been so still, if *Pope Innocent* the IIId had not thrown marriage into the hands of the *priests*, on *Peter Lombard's* finding it out to be a *sacrament*. This was the origin of so universally bringing an *human ceremony* into the place of a *divine institution*, and of course involving millions of the *weaker sex* in ruin and destruction, by supposing God's ordinance not binding, as in His sight, without the interference of *human invention*.

Drawing any acts of God into precedents, without His authority so to do, may appear to be very *pious*, but is in fact very *profane*, seeing that this cannot easily be done, without *adding* to, or *diminishing* from, what He hath expressly commanded. This is a rock on which our author's scheme must split; for he maintains that—" 'Tis not the form
" of words, which this or that church may
" make use of in a matrimonial ceremony,
" that constitutes the marriage" *(i. e.* in the sight of God; for as to the *civil contract*, they certainly constitute this)—which is very true; but not so what follows—" but
" it is the act of joining together, and pro-
" nouncing them *one* in the name of God,
" by one that is commissioned to act in His
" name."—In the first place, no such commission, with respect to marriage, ever did exist, nor, without a *new revelation*, ever can, as the smallest trace of such a thing is not to be found in that revelation which we are already possessed of. *Secondly*, The *Bible*, gives

gives a very different account of the matter; for the exprefs and pofitive command, Deut. xxii. 29. faith—*She fhall be his wife*; not "becaufe a *prieft* joins them together, or pro-"nounces them one in the name of GOD," "but תחת אשר ענה — BECAUSE *he hath humbled her.* Quòd eam compreffit. Mont. Here then is the *act* of marriage itfelf, by which they become *one flefh*; therefore *he may not put her away all his days.* Such is the pofitive precept of GOD—and yet it is to be fuppofed of *no* validity whatfoever, unlefs * ratified by fome ordinance of *human contrivance*

---

* When OUR SAVIOUR is converfing with the woman of *Samaria*, (John iv.) he fays to her—"Thou haft "had *five hufbands*, and he whom thou now haft, is "*not thine hufband*"—from whence fome have inferred, that fomething befides *cohabitation* is neceffary to conftitute a marriage in the fight of GOD. But let us fuppofe, that *four* of this woman's hufbands were dead, or had divorced her for *adultery*, that, under either of thefe circumftances, fhe had married a *fifth hufband*, whom fhe had deferted, and lived in *adultery* with another man. She certainly had had *five hufbands*, and the man with whom fhe now lived in *adulterous commerce*, perhaps clandeftinely, could not be properly ftyled *her hufband*, nor fhe *his wife*. See *Rom.* vii. 3. She therefore faid *truly*, that fhe had *no hufband*—having left him who was her *lawful* hufband, and living with an *adulterer*, who *was not*.

As this fcripture does not explain itfelf, we can only guefs at its meaning; but then our conjectures fhould be regulated by the whole *analogy* of fcripture, and not be the furmifes of our own fancy. *We* fhould fay (judging from the circumftances of things among *us*) that a woman who lived with a man without fome religious ceremony performed, had *no husband*; but this cannot be the meaning of this place, becaufe the divine *law* conftituted no religious ceremony whatfoever on

the

contrivance—such I muſt call the intervention of a *prieſt*, till I can find it in the ſcripture.—Without this, ſaith our author—" they both live in an * habitual ſtate of *fornication* and *whoredom*."—If ſo, what are we to think of the *patriarchs* and others whom we read of in the Old Teſtament, and whoſe marriages are particularly related? *Iſaac* and *Rebekah*, for inſtance? All we read of their *marriage* is—that, *Iſaac brought her into his mother's tent, and took Rebekah, and ſhe became his wife.* Gen. xxiv. 67. So *Jacob* and *Leah*—*And it came to paſs in the evening, that he (Laban) took Leah his daughter, and brought her to him (Jacob) and he went in unto her.*—*Going in unto* a woman is † equivalent to ענה—*humbling her*, or *lying with*

the occaſion. The whole legality of a marriage among the *Jews* depended on the ſtate of the *woman*, either as excepted againſt or not by the *law*, or as *betrothed* or not to *another man*—not on any religious ceremony—otherwiſe we muſt invalidate every marriage which is recorded in the word of GOD.

* He might as truly have ſaid, that they both live in an habitual ſtate of *burglary* and *houſebreaking*; there is juſt as much ſcripture-authority for this as for the other.

In ſhort, this is the very *lye* which the church of *Rome* wiſhed to have believed, in order to frighten people into the hands of the *prieſts*, in the lucrative buſineſs of marriage-ceremonies, diſpenſations, &c. thus diſhonouring and annulling the *poſitive* inſtitution of the MOST HIGH.

Hoc ITHACUS *velit & magno mercentur* ATRIDÆ.

† This appears from many paſſages of ſcripture, where the words בא אל are to be underſtood in this ſenſe. Comp. Gen. vi. 4. xxix. 21, 23, 30. xxx. 3, 4, 16. xxxviii.

with her. Comp. Gen. xvi. 2. xxx. 3. 2 Sam. xvi. 21. with 2 Sam. xii. 11. 2 Sam. xx. 3. 1 Chron. ii. 21. So in the case of *Jacob* and *Rachel*—*And he (Laban) gave him Rachel his daughter to wife also, and he (Jacob) went in also unto Rachel.* See Gen. xxix. 23, 28, 30. So *Boaz* and *Ruth*, ch. iv. 13. Many more instances might be cited; but I humbly conceive these are very sufficient, to prove, that a *marriage* may be *valid* in the sight of GOD, where there is no *church*—*chapel*—*priest*—or *outward ceremony* administered by a *priest*; if not, then I will agree that these good folks lived in " an habitual state " of *whoredom* and *fornication*." But, by the leave of this learned author, and with all due deference to " *Dr. Hickes's* excellent treatise " on the *Christian* * *priesthood*," there is another

---

xxxviii. 2, 18. Prov. vi. 29. & al. So Calasio, sub voc. —בוא—אשה אל בא—ingressus est ad mulierem—*id est* —Coivit. That this is what makes the *actual marriage* in GOD's account, and is the only ordinance essential thereto, is clearly to be gathered from Deut. xxi. 13. where it is said, that after the *expiration of the month*, which was allowed the *captive-damsel* to bewail her friends, &c. *after that,*

לאשה לך והיתה ובעלתה אליה תבוא
uxorem in   tibi   erit &   ejus eris maritus &   eam ad   ingredieris.

thou shalt GO IN *unto her*, *and be* or *become her husband*, *and she shall be* or *become thy wife*—or *a wife to thee*. GOING IN *unto her*, and *being* or *becoming* her *Lord*—בעל —or *husband*—and her being or becoming *his woman*, or *wife*—are here, as elsewhere, equivalent terms. See before vol. i. p. 43—45.

* Bishop *Bonner*, in *Q. Mary's* reign, made a long speech to the Convocation, in which he compared *priests*
to

other infuperable difficulty in this fame *priestly* fcheme of marriage; which is, that however the *Jews* might have found fuch a perfon under the *Mofaical* difpenfation, I am afraid, after that was at an end, if people had ftaid to the *Virgin Mary*, in three points, and afterwards added—" The dignity of *priests*, by fome means, paffeth
" the dignity of *angels*; becaufe there is no power given
" to the *angels* to make the body of CHRIST, which the
" leaft *prieft* may do on earth, and the higheft *angel* in
" heaven can not do. Wherefore *priefts* are to be ho-
" noured before all *kings* of the earth, *princes*, and
" *nobles*; for a *prieft* is higher than a *king*, happier than
" an *angel*, and *maker* of his *Creator*." Crit. Hift. of Eng. p. 151.

All this is as *wife*, *true*, and *fcriptural*, as to contend that no marriage is valid in the fight of GOD without the intervention of a *prieft*. Let it once be proved from the *Bible*, that *priefts made marriages*, or interfered in them in any one inftance, and I will not only fubfcribe to all *Dr. Hickes* fays in his " excellent treatife," but alfo to all Bifhop *Bonner* faid in his *excellent fpeech*.

If the reader will look into Lord *Sommers's* Tracts, vol. iii. p. 237, 238. he will find " *two* excellent trea-
" tifes" of Dr. *Hickes* mentioned, in which, as appears by the tranfcripts from them, this learned and zealous *Proteftant* divine perfectly harmonizes with *Bifhop Bonner*—as to *priestly* dignity—and as for a *bifhop*, " he is
" to be honoured as GOD; and he who makes himfelf
" a judge of a bifhop, makes himfelf a judge of GOD—
" and he who refifts a *prieft*, is guilty of greater treafon
" than he who refifts the king, the *prieft* being the king's
" fuperior." Of prayers for the *dead*, he fays, " There
" is the fame ground for thofe prayers, as for our com-
" mon *Chriftianity*. We believe thofe prayers are ac-
" cepted, which defire GOD to hear the faints for us,
" to fend the deceafed in CHRIST a good trial." Ib. 236. I cannot help confidering fuch fort of divines as *mules*, neither *Papifts* nor *Proteftants*, but between both; though rather partaking moft of the *former*, efpecially where *toleration* is concerned.

till they could have found a *priest* to marry them, they never could have married at all, but muſt have contented themſelves with living *ſingle*, or " in an habitual ſtate of " *whoredom* and *fornication"*—becauſe, under the *Chriſtian* diſpenſation, we read of no *ſuch* officer in the *church*. We read of ἀποϛολοι —men *ſent* immediately by CHRIST to *teach all nations, baptizing them in the name of the Father, and of the Son, and of the Holy Ghoſt* —therefore eminently ſtyled—*apoſtles*. We likewiſe find *one* added to their original number, whoſe commiſſion, received immediately from CHRIST himſelf, runs in theſe remarkable words, (Acts xxvi. 17, 18.) *To the Gentiles I ſend thee, to open their eyes, to turn them from darkneſs to light, and from the power of Satan unto* GOD, *that they may receive forgiveneſs of ſins, and inheritance among them which are ſanctified by faith that is in Me.* In all this there is not a word about *prieſthood* or *marriage*. We likewiſe read of Επισκοποι, over-*ſeers*, which we call *biſhops*—of Πρεσβυτεροι, *elders*—Διακονοι, *deacons*;—but in all that is ſaid about them (and their ſeveral *offices* are very particularly mentioned, as well as their *characters* and *qualifications)* not the leaſt hint appears of their interference in the affair of *matrimony*. See Eph. iv. 11, 12. For any man, or ſet of men, to tell us that they are commiſſioned from GOD, to do a thing, which is not ſo much as mentioned in *any commiſſion* which they can produce from the ſcripture, as ever having been given to any

man

man upon earth, may charitably be supposed an imposition on their own understandings; but when forced on the belief of others, it is an insult on the understandings of the rest of the world. It is even worse still, for it is acting with the consciences of men, as the *old prophet* in *Bethel* acted towards the *man of* GOD *who came out of Judah to Jeroboam*; it is *lying* to them in *the name of the* LORD. See 1 Kings xiii. 18.

As for a *priest*, there *is* not, nor *can* there be, such a minister or officer of the *Christian* church. *For every priest* (whether highpriest or *other*, compare Heb. v. 1. with Heb. x. 11.) *taken from among men, is ordained for men in things pertaining to* GOD, *that he may offer both gifts and sacrifices for sins; and by reason hereof he ought, as for the people, so also for himself, to offer for sins. And* EVERY PRIEST *standeth daily ministring and offering the same sacrifices, which can never take away sins—But this man* (CHRIST JESUS) *after He had offered one sacrifice for sins, for ever sat down on the right hand of* GOD—*for by* ONE OFFERING *He hath perfected for ever them that are sanctified.* Of course, *there remaineth no more sacrifice for sins*, (Heb. x. 26. latter part) no more order of *priesthood* among men. The truth is, that the whole *priesthood* under the *law* centered in CHRIST under the *gospel*; He is in *reality* what the former was in *type and figure.*—The *Levitical* priesthood, with every circumstance relative thereto, was *a figure for the time then present*, (Heb. ix. 9.)

The

The Holy Ghost thus signifying, that the way into the holiest of all was not yet made manifest, while as the first tabernacle was yet standing, ver. 8. But CHRIST *being come, an high-priest of good things to come,* &c. *now once in the end of the world hath appeared to put away sin by the* SACRIFICE OF HIMSELF. See Heb. ix. 11, &c. To imagine, therefore, that He appointed an *order of men* to offer *gifts and sacrifices for sins* (which is the scripture-definition of the *priest*'s office) besides having no warrant from the scripture, is to imagine CHRIST'S ONE SACRIFICE of HIMSELF *imperfect,* and to stand in need of something else to make it effectual—this runs us directly into what the *church of England* [Art. 31.] very properly styles—" the blasphemous *fables and dangerous* " *deceits*" of the sacrifice of the *Popish mass,* wherein a man professes to *offer* CHRIST over again, and very consistently styles * himself a *Priest!*

* Or rather is so styled by the church of *Rome*; for in the council of *Trent* is a decree in the following terms, *viz.* " The sacrifice and the *priesthood* are united in each " law; therefore there being a visible sacrifice in the *New* " *Testament*, that is, the *Eucharist,* it must be confessed, " necessarily, that there is a visible and external *priest-* " *hood*, in which power is given, by divine institution, " to consecrate, offer, and minister the *Eucharist,* and " to remit and retain sins." Though this decree contains almost as many *lyes* as *words*—yet it was followed by an horrible *anathema* on all who should deny it. *Brent*, Hist. Council of *Trent*, 738, 739. Another *anathema* of the same council, is against—" those who " should say that CHRIST, by these words—DO THIS IN " REMEMBRANCE OF ME—hath not instituted *priests,* " and commanded them to *offer.*" Ib. 574.

In one sense, *every Christian* believer is a *priest*; that is to say, in the spiritual sense described, 1 Pet. ii. 5. *Ye also, as lively stones, are built up a spiritual house,* an HOLY PRIESTHOOD, *to offer up* SPIRITUAL SACRIFICES *acceptable to* GOD *by* JESUS CHRIST. So St. John, (Rev. i. 5, 6.) *Unto Him that loved us, and washed us from our sins in His own blood, and hath made us* KINGS *and* PRIESTS *unto* GOD *and His Father, to Him be glory and dominion,* &c. The appellation of KINGS, as well as that of PRIESTS, equally belongs to all *Christian* believers alike, but to no outward order, or particular set of men among them, in any exclusive sense whatsoever.

The pride and insolence of *churchmen* began very * early to work, and to aim at that dominion

---

* Those vile *forgeries*, which bear the name of the *Apostolical Constitutions,* (the authors of which, it is pretended, were the *twelve apostles*, and *St. Paul,* gathered together, with *Clemens* their *amanuensis*) repeat it over and over, lest *Christians* should forget it, that "a bishop "is a god, a god upon earth, and a king, and infinitely "superior to a king, and ruling over rulers and kings." They command *Christians* to give him tribute as to a king, and to reverence him as a god, &c. Jortin, vol. i. p. 154.

Many passages there are in *Cyprian*'s writings, who lived in the *third century*, containing high notions of *episcopal* authority and *ecclesiastical jurisdiction.* While he strenuously opposed the dominion of *one Pope,* he seemed to make as many *popes* as *bishops,* and mere *arithmetical noughts* of the rest of the *Christians*. Ib. vol. ii. p. 75.

But there is a Popish writer named *Alanus* de *Rupe,* who, in an "excellent treatise on the *dignity and excellency of* the *Christian priesthood,*" leaves the blasphemy of *Bonner,*

minion over the consciences of men, which has been brought to so thorough a perfection by the *Popes* of *Rome*, though so formally *renounced* by an holy *apostle*—2 Cor. i. 24. The first step to making men *do* WHAT the *clergy* pleased, was to make them *believe* AS

Bonner, *Hickes*, &c. far behind; for he makes, in a passage I have now before me, a *priest greater than* GOD *himself*. "Quilibet *sacerdos* habet potestatem patris, & " (salva semper Dei reverentia) habet majorem poten-
" tiam quam Pater omnipotens in mundi efficientia.
" Nempe Pater septem dies laboravit, tam in opere
" creationis quam distinctionis, sed sacerdos celebrans
" quilibet, quantumque parvus, majus his omnibus
" facit.
" Pater enim ibi facit creata, sed sacerdos increatum.
" Ibi Deus producit effectus, sed sacerdos causa causa-
" rum generat.
" Quanta est igitur distantia Dei a mundo creato,
" tanta est excellentia operis sacerdotalis super opus
" creationis. Unde definitivé dico, quod majus est
" opus sacerdotis, quam habere potentiam creandi creata
" tot mundorum quot sunt substantiæ in mundo, &c."

" Every priest hath the power of a father, and (with
" reverence to GOD be it spoken) hath *greater power*
" than the *Father Almighty* had in making the world.
" For the Father (GOD) *laboured* seven days, as well
" in the work of creation as distinction; but a *priest*
" celebrating (the mass) though ever so inconsiderable
" in himself, doth greater things than all these; for
" there the Father makes created things, but the *priest*
" what is uncreated. There GOD produces effects,
" but the *priest* generates the cause of causes.

" As much distance, therefore, as there is of GOD
" from the created world, so far is the excellence of the
" sacerdotal work above the work of creation. Whence,
" I definitively say, that the work of a *priest* is greater,
" than to have a power of creating the creatures of as
" many worlds, as there are substances in the world,
" &c."

they pleafed.—So early as the *fecond* century, "the *Chriftian* doctors had the good fortune to perfuade the people, that the minifters of the *Chriftian* church fucceeded to the character, rights, and privileges of the *Jewifh priefthood*, and this perfuafion was a new fource of *honours* and *profit* to the facred order. This notion was propagated with induftry fome time after the reign of *Adrian*. Accordingly the *bifhops* confidered themfelves as invefted with a rank and character fimilar to thofe of the HIGH-PRIEST among the *Jews*, while the *prefbyters* reprefented the PRIESTS, and the *deacons* the LEVITES." Mofheim, vol. i. p. 88, 101. Thus did they "extend the limits of their authority, turn their *influence* into *dominion*, their counfels into laws, and openly afferted, at length, that CHRIST had impowered them to prefcribe to His people *authoritative rules of faith and manners.*" Ib. 88. The hiftory of the church ftill fhews us, how *fuperftition* enlifted on the fide of *church power*, refifted the authority of fcripture-evidence, "made the obfervance of human rites and ceremonies neceffary to *the attainment of falvation.*" Ib. 296.—till, in the 12th century, *Pope Innocent* the third turned marriage into a facrament, and threw it into the hands of *priefts*, on whofe adminiftration of certain human rites and ceremonies, its validity before GOD was fuppofed to depend; fo that parties *joined together* otherwife than by this means, were deemed

to

to live in " an habitual ftate of whoredom
" and fornication."

When I think on thefe things, I can hardly, with any degree of gravity, tranfcribe what our author lays down as an axiom, " That neither the woman can give herfelf " to the man, nor can her father or friend " give her to him *immediately*, but the hands " of the *prieft only*." The *Rubric* fays, that " the *minifter*, receiving the woman at her " father's or friend's hands, fhall caufe the " man with his right hand to take the wo- " man by her right hand, and fay after him," &c. This is a very decent and harmlefs part of the ceremony — but when we are told, that " the woman *can* neither *give herfelf*, " nor the man *take her*, but at the hands of " the * *prieft only*," we are, I fuppofe, to underftand this to be fo *effential* to *marriage*, that, without it, it is not *valid* in the fight of GOD. Here is fomething very *ferious* indeed; for what muft become of people who do not ufe this ceremony? are they to be deemed to " live in an habitual ftate of *whore-* " *dom* and *fornication?*" The *Quakers*, for † inftance?

---

* So the *Papifts* contended againft the *Reformers*, that GOD's pardon could not be obtained, without *prieftly* abfolution. See *Burnet, Hift. Ref.* 364, 2d edit.

† On this plan, what muft be faid of thofe who married during the times of the *grand rebellion*, when marriages were performed by the *juftices of the peace*, and this for about eighteen years together? Thefe *marriages* were declared valid by the act of 12 Car. II. c. 33. which confirms all that were thus had and folemnized from

stance?—they muſt all, who marry among them, be loſt eternally—for *fornicators and whoremongers have no inheritance in the kingdom* of GOD. 1 Cor. vi. 9. So that this gentleman's notions, like the *Pope's* bulls, carry an *anathema* wherever they are departed from. To invent a ſcheme, for which there is not a tittle of evidence from the *Bible*, and then poſitively aſſert it to be the only one by which *marriage* can be *lawfully* contracted, was worthy the *haughtineſs* of a *Pope*, but not quite ſo becoming the *decent humility* of a *Proteſtant divine*; more eſpecially when the *Bible* is by no means ſilent on the ſubject of *marriage*, but furniſhes us with a ſtream of evidence concerning it, which evidently runs in another channel.

When we are commanded to be *followers of thoſe who through faith and patience inherit the promiſes* (Heb. vi. 12.) we can hardly ſuppoſe that GOD would ſet before us, for our *imitation*, a people who "lived in an "habitual ſtate of *whoredom* and *fornication*," and yet we do not find one ſingle inſtance of their marrying according to our author's plan; they certainly *could* and *did* "receive "their wives from the hands of the fathers "or friends, and not from the hands of a "*prieſt*" at all. *Jacob* received *Leah* immediately from her father *Laban*; thus he after-

---

May 1, 1642, to the year 1660. But this could not ſalve the matter, nor prevent the bitter conſequences of *marrying* without a *prieſt*; which, if what this *author* ſays be true, muſt be bitter indeed!

wards

wards received *Rachel*. *Isaac* is no where said to receive *Rebekah*, nor *Abram* to receive *Sarai* " by the hands of a *priest*." Nor does this appear to have been the case, either before or after the giving of the law, in the Old Testament; neither is there the smallest trace of it throughout the New Testament. So that all this learned *author*'s discourse about *priests* and *marriages*, stands on no better foundation than the *Pharisees* traditions, which were *invented* by one set of men, *handed* down from them to another, and *believed* by the superstitious and ignorant of succeeding generations, till they gained an authority in some cases equal to, in others above, the *written word* of GOD.

Our author very truly says in a note—" It
" was therefore death under the law of *Mo-*
" *ses*, for any *stranger*, that is, one who was
" not of the *priestly* order, to invade the
" *priestly* office (Numb. xviii. 7.) which
" was actually and dreadfully executed upon
" self-sufficient *Corah* and his *deistical* com-
" pany (Numb. xvi. 3. and 32.) nay, so
" very sacred was the office of the *priesthood*,
" that even *kings* themselves were immedi-
" ately and signally punished by GOD him-
" self, for usurping it under the law of *Mo-*
" *ses*, as we may read (2 Chr. xxvi. 18, 19,
" 20.) in the case of *king Uzziah*."

Here I would observe, that, if it was so penal to usurp the *priesthood* under the law of *Moses*, which *priesthood* was only typical of the

the *priesthood* of CHRIST, may it not be worth the while of this *author* to consider what it must be to usurp the *priesthood* of CHRIST itself? The *apostle* shews, Heb. vii. that the typical *priesthood* passed in succession from one man to another, therefore there was always an order of men *called of* GOD, and appointed to that office; for no man could take *that honour to himself, but he that is called of* GOD, *as was Aaron.* Heb. v. 4. The same *apostle* points out a very remarkable difference with respect to the *priesthood* of CHRIST—which is, that it all resides in Him, and cannot *pass to any one else. They truly were many priests, because they were not suffered to continue by reason of death; but this man, because He continueth ever, hath*—ἀπαράϐατον Ἱεροσύνην—a *priesthood which cannot pass from* HIM *to any other.* This is a truth of the last importance, for our salvation depends upon it, as may be gathered from the words of the next verse (see Heb. vii. 23, 24, 25.) When therefore persons assume an office, which is no where said in the New Testament to belong to any but the GREAT HIGH-PRIEST, who is the glorious *antitype* of the whole *Jewish priesthood*, and when they mean any thing by the " *Christian* " *priesthood*" but the *priesthood* of CHRIST himself, which is ἀπαράϐατος, *impassable* from Him to any, may we not reasonably doubt, whether " *Corah* and his deistical company " were the only self-sufficient invaders of " the *priestly* office?" This doubt will be
soon

soon cleared up, if what is said Heb. vii. viii. ix. x. touching the difference between the *priesthood* under the *law of Moses*, and the priesthood of JESUS CHRIST under the *oath* of JEHOVAH, be duly considered and attended to.

But our author proceeds—" Is it not in
" conformity to GOD's bringing the first wo-
" man to the first man, that the minister,
" *who acts in* GOD's *stead* in *our ceremony*,
" gives the woman to the man, and after-
" wards joins them in GOD's * name, not
" his *own*, when he says—" Those whom
" GOD hath joined together (not I) let not
" man put asunder."—You see that neither
" the woman can give herself to the man,
" nor can her father or friend give her to
" him immediately, but by the hands of the
" *priest only*, who receiving her, as our *Ru-*
" *bric* says, from them, gives her to the
" man; which shews, that the compilers

* The unauthorized use of the *names* of the *divine persons* in the holy and *blessed Trinity*, when the *priest* joins the parties in matrimony, is copied, as we have seen (before, p 140. n.) from a decree of the *Popish* council of *Trent*, who gave the following *wicked* reason for their introduction—they said, that—" the use of
" these words was decreed to *no other end*, but that in a
" short time it might be made an *article of faith*, that
" *those words* pronounced by the *parish priest* were the
" *form of the sacrament*." So that what the *Papists* invented in order to make the people *believe a lye*, is here treated as an *essential* part of the *ceremony*, or rather of the very *marriage itself!* See Brent. Hist. Coun. Trent. p. 791.

" of

" of our *matrimonial* form were better * ap-
" prized of the divine inſtitution of mar-
" riage,

* The old proverb faith—" Give the Devil his due :"
—therefore it is not quite handſome, to attribute this ingenious inſight into the *divine inſtitution of marriage* to " the compilers of our matrimonial form," for they plainly borrowed the chiefeſt part of our *proceedings* from the church of *Rome*. When the *council* of *Trent*, building on *Pope Innocent* the IIId's foundation, (ſee before p. 137—139) were determined to give a finiſhing ſtroke to religious liberty, by throwing the conſciences of men into the hands of *churchmen*, and to make the *marriage-union* no longer dependent on GOD's *word*, but on *man's law*, they eſtabliſhed a decree as follows :

" And becauſe prohibitions do no good, the *ſynod* doth
" COMMAND, that the matrimony ſhall be denounced
" in the church *three feſtival*-days (we ſay *Sundays*)
" before it be contracted, and, no impediment being
" found, ſhall be celebrated in the *face of the church*;
" where the *pariſh-prieſt*, having interrogated the man
" and the woman, and heard their conſent, ſhall ſay,
" —*I join you in matrimony* (we ſay, " I pronounce
" you to be man and wife together") *in the name*
" *of the Father, Son, and Holy Ghoſt*, and ſhall uſe
" *other words* accuſtomed in the province. Not-
" withſtanding, the *ſynod* doth refer it to the *will of*
" *the biſhop* (here's a ſalvo for *licences*) to *omit the*
" *banns*; but doth declare thoſe to be *incapable* of
" marriage, who attempt to contract it without the
" preſence of the *pariſh-prieſt*, or another *prieſt* of
" equal authority, and of two or three witneſſes;
" *making void* and *nullifying* ſuch contracts, and pu-
" niſhing the tranſgreſſors." Afterwards it faith,
" The *ſynod* will have this decree to be in force with-
" in thirty days after it ſhall be publiſhed in every
" pariſh.—*Brent*. 785.

To hear a grave and learned *Proteſtant divine* comment on all this *Popiſh* rubbiſh, juſt as ſolemnly as if it was a decree of Heaven, affords no ſmall proof of the force
of

" riage, as well as of the sacred importance
" of the *priest's office,* than some among us
" at present seem to be."

If our compilers of the marriage ceremony, meant to represent what was done in *Paradise,* at the first institution of marriage, they have acquitted themselves very aukwardly, for there is not a single circumstance alike.

As to the "*minister's* acting in GOD's stead" —I do not find that GOD did any thing but *bring her to the man,* whereas with us the man brings the woman to church, and sets her before the *minister*—nor did GOD *speak* on the occasion—whereas the *minister* reads a long ceremony, attended with many * circumstances

of prejudice and superstition: and indeed, were not the subject too serious for such an expression, might be called *ridiculous.* The above is nearly the model of our *marriage plan,* as it stands at present, and thoroughly vacates the *divine obligation* arising from the *divine command.*

* *Burnet,* in his preface to *Hist. Ref.* observes, that the " primitive *Christians* brought in many rites of
" *Heathenism* into their worship."—The use of the *ring* in marriage, seems to have been derived from this source, for that it was an *heathen* custom appears in *Hooker,* Eccl. Pol. fol. edit. 1723, p. 267. The *Jews,* not improbably, borrowed it also from the *Heathen*; for that the *bridegroom* put a *ring* on the *bride's* finger is certain. *Broughton* Hist. Lib. vol. ii. 179. We take it from the church of *Rome.*

Mr. *Chambers—*Dict. under the word *Ring—*gives us ths following account :—

" A second kind of *rings* were the *annuli sponsalitii,*
" *wedding-rings.* Some carry the origin of this custom
" as far back as the *Hebrews,* on the authority of a text
" in *Exod.* xxxv. 22.—*Leo* of *Modena,* however, main-
" tains

cumstances which are entirely the invention of the *compilers*—therefore the " minister's " acting in GOD's stead" without being commanded so to do, either by precept or example from GOD's *book*, is, if very closely attended to, and examined upon the footing of scripture, not quite so like what passed in *Paradise*, as what was transacted on a certain occasion which our *author* has mentioned, concerning certain " self-sufficient intruders" into an office which did not belong to them, not being especially appointed thereunto by GOD *himself*. If the *state* chuses that the *civil contract*, which is to give the security which it requires for the marriage of the parties, should pass through the hands of a

" tains that the antient *Hebrews* did not use any nup-
" tial *ring*. *Selden*, in his *Ux. Heb.* lib. ii. c. 14.
" owns, that they gave a *ring* in the marriage, but that
" it was only in lieu of a piece of money of the same
" value, which had used to have been given before.
 " The *Greeks* and *Romans* did the same; and, *from*
" *them*, the *Christians* took it up very early, as appears
" from *Tertullian*, and in some antient *liturgies*, where
" we find the form of *blessing* the nuptial *ring*." Godwyn, (Rom Antiq. p. 68.) from *Aul. Gell.* tells us, that, " at the *Roman* marriages the man gave, in token
" of good-will, a *ring* unto the *woman*, which she was
" to wear upon the *next finger* unto the *little finger* of
" the *left hand*, because unto *that finger* alone proceeded
" a certain artery from the *heart*."—How far the reason of wearing the *ring* on that particular finger, with regard to the artery, has any foundation in fact, I know not; but we *Christians* place the ring on the same *finger* of the woman. The use of the *ring* in marriage is, therefore, not one of those *circumstances* which are to be reckoned among the *inventions* of our *compilers* of the *marriage-ceremony*.

minister

minister in a church, in the presence of the congregation, a decent proper ceremony compiled for that purpose is certainly expedient—but when we are told of a *divine institution*—the *importance of the priest's office*—his *acting in* GOD's *stead,* and in GOD's *name*—we must require plain *scripture*-proof for all this; but more especially when we are informed, that all this must be complied with on pain and peril of *eternal damnation*; for that must be the consequence of living in " an habi-" tual state of *whoredom* and *fornication*," which our *author* hath peremptorily declared to be the case of all, who are not pronounced *man and wife* by the " *mouth* of a *priest.*"

I should not have said so much on this *author*'s doctrines upon the subject of *marriage,* were they not embraced so generally among us; they have, since *Pope Innocent* the IIId. laid the foundation of them, by throwing *marriage* into the hands of *ecclesiastics,* been growing in credit, till at length it became, among the generality, almost established as an *article* of *faith,* and now confirmed by act of parliament, 26 Geo. II. c. 33. that, " where there is no ceremony " performed by a *priest* (and *this* under cer-" tain *conditions* of *human invention)* there is " no *marriage* *," consequently the *divine institution,*

---

* A recent and most melancholy instance of this mischievous and antiscriptural *lye,* as to its tendency with regard to the principles and practices of mankind, has appeared in the sad and deplorable catastrophe of the unfortunate

inſtitution, with all its weight of obligation, is entirely vacated and ſet aſide, nor can the ſcripture be brought, with its due authority, to reſcue thoſe from deſtruction and perdition, who have a right to its protection. How ſubſervient this human *marriage*-ſcheme has been made, by the *father of lyes*, to the intereſts of his kingdom, in the promotion and increaſe of *whoredom* and *proſtitution*, I need not be at much pains to prove; the *eyes* and *ears* of every man who walks the ſtreets of our *metropolis* after ſun-ſet, will be very ſufficient judges of the matter from their own obſervation.

I will now ſhut up my remarks on our learned *author*, with citing *entirely* a very awful paſſage, which he has tranſcribed *partially* at the concluſion of his *two diſcourſes*. *I teſtify unto every man that heareth the words of the prophecy of this book, if any man ſhall* ADD *unto theſe things,* GOD *ſhall* ADD *unto him the plagues that are written in this book.*

---

unfortunate Miſs *Ray*, and of her ſtill more unfortunate admirer Mr. *H.*—Had the *divine law*, and not *Popiſh* tradition, been made the *baſis* of *our laws* with reſpect to *marriage*, he would have been taught to have conſidered her ſituation as that of the *wife* of the *noble Lord*, by whom ſhe had ſeveral children, and with whom, it was ſaid, ſhe had cohabited from the age of ſixteen, to the *fatal* moment which firſt brought Mr. H. to her acquaintance—he could never have thought of ſoliciting her hand in *marriage*, and conſequently of indulging ſuch a reſentment, on her perſiſting in a refuſal, as at laſt ended in his becoming her *murderer*, and, *intentionally*, his own —but he was awfully reſerved for the hands of the *public executioner!*

And

And if any man shall TAKE AWAY *from the words of the book of this prophecy,* GOD *shall* TAKE AWAY *his part out of the book of life, and out of the holy city, and from the things which are written in this book.* Comp. *Rev.* xxii. 18, 19. with Deut. iv. 2.

" The church of *England*, though she does not consider marriage as a *sacrament*, yet looks upon it as an institution so sacred, that it ought always to be celebrated by an *ecclesiastical* person. And by several canons of our church it is declared, to be no less than prostituting one's daughter, to give her in marriage without the blessing of a *priest*. But marriages without this sanction are not therefore *null and void*. For, though the positive *law of man* ordains marriage to be made by a *priest, that law* only makes marriages otherwise solemnized *irregular*, but does not dissolve them." *Broughton* Hist. Lib. tit. *Marriage.* This passage in Mr. *Broughton* is confirmed by authorities cited in the *margin* of his book; and serves to prove the sentiments of the *church of England*, with regard to *marriage*, antecedently to the *marriage-act*—the passing of which has overturned every part of the *divine institution*, as being of any obligation merely in *itself*, so that *marriage* is now more like a *creature of the state* than an *ordinance of Heaven*.

However, it does appear, that though the *church of England* made some *canons* in very early days which favoured of *superstition*, yet
she

she has uniformly maintained so far the honour of the *divine institution*, that an *irregularity* (even the want of a *priest*) in the administration of the ceremony which was to attend the solemnization of it, did not *vacate* the obligation of the thing itself. See before p. 49, 50.

To conclude—If *superstition* consists in believing certain religious tenets which have no foundation or warrant from the scripture, as well as in setting up human tradition as a rule of faith and practice in religious matters—if *heresy* consists in *adhering* to certain positions and doctrines as so many *religious truths*, which are *inconsistent* with, and in many respects *opposite* to the mind and will of GOD, as revealed in the scripture—I will leave it to the discretion of the reader to determine, under which of the *two* he will rank the following positions, which are deducible from the systems of *law* and *divinity* in this kingdom.

That a man can seduce a *virgin*, and *lie with her*, and yet she not be his *wife* in the sight of GOD, and the man not be compellable to make her so in the face of the world.

That *no union* is binding on the parties, unless authorized by *human laws*.

That a man and woman may *divorce* each other, so as that the woman may marry again to another—if not joined by *act of parliament*.

That *polygamy*, though allowed of GOD under

under the Old Testament, was forbidden by JESUS CHRIST under the New Testament, and is therefore *sinful*, and if so, *damnable*.

That where a man has *two wives of his own*, he shall be deemed a *felon, and suffer death as such*—but if he debauch ever so many *wives* of *other men* he shall be *free*.

That it is a greater crime to be a *polygamist* in *one* instance, than to be a *whoremonger* in an *hundred* *.

That

---

* This and the following paragraph may remind us of an *apothegm* of Cardinal *Campegius*, about the time of the *reformation*, who said—" Multo gravius esse peccatum " quod sacerdotes fiant mariti, quam si plurimas domi " meretrices alant."—" It was a *much more grievous sin* " that priests should *marry*, than that they should *keep* " *many harlots*."

However shocking the *Cardinal's* sentiments may seem to us, yet they are not at all more opposite to scripture, than ours upon the subjects here mentioned: and may serve to shew, how far superstition and prejudice may lead those who leave *the word of* GOD, turn their *ears from the truth, and are turned unto fables*, 2 Tim. iv. 4.

Some time before the *reformation*, the magistrates of the *Swiss* cantons made an edict that—" Every *priest* should " be bound to have his proper *concubine*, that he might " not ensnare the chastity of modest women."

Hugo, Bishop of *Constance*, in his letter to *Zuric* against *Zuinglius*, says—" though this seemed a ridiculous de- " cree, yet it was necessary to be made, nor could be " changed, unless that as much as was constituted in " favour of *keeping concubines*, were at that present con- " verted unto *lawful matrimony*." See *Brent*. Hist. Counc. Trent. p. 17.

As for *Luther*, because he wrote against the celibacy of the *priests* and *monks*, the nuncio of *Pope Adrian* to the diet of *Noremberg*, anno 1523, represented him as " treading in the way that *Mahomet* did long ago, per- " mitting carnal inclinations to be satiated." He also observed,

That it is more criminal to marry *two wives*, than to defile and then abandon ever so many *virgins*.

That human laws, maxims, customs, inventions, and prejudices, are to supersede the obligation of the *divine law*.

That JESUS CHRIST has taught a more *pure* and *perfect* system of morals than is contained in the *law* of the Old Testament.

That *therefore* men are to govern them-

---

observed, that "religious men forsook the cloisters, and returned to the world—that *priests* married, to the *great disgrace and contempt of religion*—wherefore it was necessary that some orders were taken, that these *sacrilegious marriages* might be dissolved, the *authors* severely punished, and the *apostates* reduced under the power of their superiors." Brent. 25, 26. After this, anno 1530, the Emperor *Charles* V. made an edict, that the married *priests* should either forsake their wives, or be banished. Ib. 57.— One accusation against good *Bishop Cranmer* was, that he had been *twice married*: that he had kept a wife *secretly* in the time of Hen. VIII. and *openly* in the reign of Edw. VI. Rapin vol. ii. p. 44. In 1554, *seven Bishops* were deprived by special commission, for having defiled their functions by contracting marriage, in *contempt* of GOD, and manifest *sin of their own souls*, as well as to the *grievous* offence of all orders of people, both *clergy* and *laity*. See *Burnet* Hist. Reform. 274, 275. Part II.

When *Gregory* VII. or *Hildebrand*, made his decree against the marriage of *ecclesiastics*, he branded it with the odious title of *the heresy of* the NICOLAITANS. Hist. of Popery, vol. i. p. 331.

I mention these things, to shew further, what absurdity, folly, and wickedness men may fall into themselves, and lead others into, when *human imagination* usurps the place of *divine wisdom*, and we cease to cleave to the *divine testimony* as the only *rule of right and wrong*, though under notions of stricter *purity* and more exemplary *holiness*.

felves by some *precepts* of Christ, not by the *moral law* of the Old Testament. See vol. i. p. 303, 327.

I could almost here adopt the words of the *Marquis* of *Beccaria*, in his ingenious *Essay* on *Crimes* and *Punishments*, and say of such positions as these, as he does of certain modes of prosecution—" What a labyrinth of ab-
" surdities! absurdities, which" (it is to be hoped) " will appear incredible to happier
" posterity. The *philosopher* only will be
" able to read in the nature of man, the pos-
" sibility of there ever having been such a
" system!"

When the *reader* has revolved the above positions, and perhaps others which may incidentally arise from them, within his mind, he will most likely begin to see, farther than he did before, into that *mystery of iniquity*, which, mixing its baleful influence in the corrupt minds of men, transfuses itself as well into their *religious*, as into their *worldly* systems; and renders *both*, as far as they are connected with each other, either *independent* on, *inconsistent* with, or *opposite* to, the plan of the *divine government*; and these in more respects than we are apt to imagine, till we examine into, and seriously consider the subject, on the footing of the *divine law itself*; and weigh the importance of the *law*, as well as of our obedience to it, by that *holy jealousy* over it, which the Great Law-giver Himself hath manifested in His *word*.

This *jealousy* of God over *His laws*, as a necessary appendage to the preceding pages, shall be the subject of the next *chapter*.

CHAP. IX.

Of God's *Jealousy over His Laws.*

THIS title may be said to form a considerable part of the subject of *holy writ*, and indeed to pervade, and, like the *warp* through the *woof*, to run throughout the whole. The more we contemplate those authentic records of the mind and will of God, the more awfully shall we find this truth illustrated both by precept and example. —I *the* Lord *thy* God *am a jealous* God, *visiting the sins of the fathers upon the children, unto the third and fourth generation* of them that hate me. *Exod.* xx. 5.—and again, Nah. i. 2. God *is jealous, and the* Lord *revengeth; the* Lord *revengeth and is furious, the* Lord *will take vengeance on His adversaries, and He reserveth wrath for His enemies.*

An exemplification of this character of the *holy* God, began with the *first* act of man's *disobedience—By one man sin entered into the*

the world, and death by sin. Rom. v. 12.—*The wages of sin is death.* Rom. vi. 23.—*In the day thou eatest thereof thou shalt surely die.* Gen. ii. 17. Nor was this *death* a mere *personal* punishment, inflicted merely on the person of the *first* offender—but on his *whole posterity:* —*In Adam all die.* 1 Cor. xv. 22.

When *men multiplied on the earth*, transgression multiplied, till GOD's *jealousy* was awakened and provoked to destroy the *whole world*, except *eight persons*, (1 Pet. iii. 20.) by a flood of waters.

Afterwards we see *Sodom* and *Gomorrah*, with the *five cities of the plain*, together with their *inhabitants*, destroyed by *fire and brimstone rained down upon them from the* LORD *out of heaven.* Gen. xix. 24.

Not to dwell on general topics, let us for a while descend to particulars, and we shall find GOD's *jealousy over His laws* displayed throughout the scripture. Even the *ceremonial* institutions furnish us with examples of this. For instance, in the case of *Nadab* and *Abihu*, Lev. x. 1.—of *Korah, Dathan*, and *Abiram*, and all that appertained unto them, Numb. xvi. 32, 33. who were swallowed up by the earth—the 250 who were *consumed by fire, for burning incense*—and beside these, 14,700 who *died of the plague*, ver. 35, 49. In 1 Chron. xiii. 10. we see *Uzza* struck dead for only *touching the ark*, which belonged alone to *Aaron and his sons* to do. Numb. iv. 5, 15. To these instances may be added that of 50,070 * men struck dead for looking into the ark at *Bethshemesh*, 1 Sam. vi. 19. Comp. *Numb.* iv. 19, 20. See 1 Chron. xv. 13. So that, even in respect of breaches of the *ceremonial* law, the men of *Bethshemesh* might well say—*who is able to stand before this holy* Lord God!

Likewise on the breach of *positive precepts,* though but *occasional* and *temporary,* the *jealousy* of God *over his laws* is terribly manifested; as in the case of *Achan,* Josh. vii. 25. —in the case of *Saul,* king of *Israel,* 1 Sam. xv. 23.—of the *disobedient prophet,* 1 Kings xiii. 21.—of *Ahab, king of Israel,* 1 Kings xx. 42.

From hence let us look to the *moral law,* which was ordained to be a *rule of life* to all nations, people, and tongues upon the face of the earth, whithersoever the word of God *should come.* This can never vary nor decay, because it is founded in the very nature of *that relation* which men bear to God and each other. The *commandment* which stands *first,* and is evidently the ground of all the rest, saith—*Thou shalt have no other* Gods *but me.* How all contempts of this law were punished may be seen in the fearful destruction

---

* Thus it stands in our translation: but there is not any absolute necessity to understand it of so many, or of more than 70 *men out of* 50,000 *men*—Septuaginta viros quinquaginta millia virorum. Mont.—which may certainly be looked upon as a fair rendering of the *Hebrew.*

See some ingenious remarks on this passage in *Letters of certain* Jews to M. de *Voltaire,* vol. i. 320—1.

of

of the *seven* nations in the *land of Canaan—* also in GOD's delivering the *Gentiles* into the hands of those worst of tyrants and destroyers, their own *vile affections*, so strikingly described by the *apostle*, Rom. i. 21, &c.—As to what the *Jews* suffered for *turning from* GOD *to idols*, it is so often mentioned, as to form a chief part in the history of all the calamities which were brought upon them by the righteous judgment of GOD. Not only the actual breach of this commandment, but even the enticing another to it, whether the enticer prevailed or not, was punished with death, and that without *mercy*, even though the enticer was a man's *dearest friend*, his *nearest relation*, the *wife of his bosom*. See Deut. xiii. 6, &c.

As the first commandment was to secure GOD's honour, as the *only object of worship*, so the *second* was like unto it, for it was to secure that *worship*'s being paid Him in the way which He Himself had appointed. Hence the worship of Him under the form of images, *molten* or *graven by art and man's device*, was expressly forbidden. What *His jealousy* over this *law* was, may be learned from Exod. xxxii. when the people *changed their glory into the similitude of an ox that eateth grass*. (Ps. cvi. 19, 20.) And there *fell in that day about* 3000 *men* (ver. 28.) besides what fell by the *plague* afterwards, ver. 35. Nay GOD would have *destroyed them (all) had not* MOSES *His chosen stood before him in the breach, to turn away His wrath, left He should destroy them.* Pf. cvi. 23.

All *image*-worship was absolutely forbidden by this law, whether the *idol* was meant as representative of the *true* GOD, as in the case of the *golden calf* (see *Exod.* xxxii. 4, 5,) or of the deities of the *Heathen*, as was the case of the *Israelites* in the matter of *Baal Peor*. The *apostle* (1 Cor. x. 8.) alludes to this, when he says—*Neither let us commit fornication, as some of them committed, and fell in one day* 23,000. The words πορνεύωμεν and ἐπόρνευσαν here, answer to the word לזנות Numb. xxv. 1. which we translate *committed whoredom*—but the word *whoredom* in this place, said to be *committed with the daughters of Moab*, and the *fornication* spoken of by the *apostle*, are not to be understood in the *common* acceptation of those terms, as merely signifying intercourse with *harlots*, but also an *idolatrous prostitution* of the women in honour of the *idol*, which among many nations was looked upon as a *religious rite*. This was the case with the *Moabites*, as appears from the whole chapter; and the sin of the *Israelites* was, first, their yielding to the temptation of the *Moabitish* women, ver. 1, and then their mixing in the idolatrous *impurities* which were practised in honour of the *Moabitish* idol. Comp. Numb. xxxi. 16. Hence the holy *zeal* of *Phineas*, who slew *Zimri* and *Cozbi*, is marked with such applause, ver. 11, 12, 13. Pf. cvi. 30. as he thereby
vindicated

vindicated the honour of *Jehovah*, in being an instrument in his hands of punishing those monstrous defilers of his law. And indeed their sin was a complicated insult on the *first* and *second* commandments. How GOD's *jealousy over His laws* operated on the occasion, may be learned from the judgment He inflicted. Numb. xxv. 3, 4, 5, 9. To this we may add the history of *Jeroboam*, king of the *ten tribes* of *Israel*, whose devilish policy led him to set up *two calves*, one in *Bethel*, the other in *Dan*, that the people might worship *there*, and not go to *Jerusalem*, thinking hereby to prevent their being drawn into a revolt from him to the king of *Judah*; but his sin is marked, as it were, with a *pen of iron*, as *cutting off and destroying the house of Jeroboam from the face of the earth*. 1 Kings xiii. 34.

The *third* commandment was to secure the honour due unto the *holy and reverend name* (Pf. cxi. 9.) of *Jehovah Aleim*—the LORD GOD—that it should not be mentioned in a *vain, irreverent*, or *profane* manner. In *Lev.* xxiv. 10. we find a man, by GOD's express order (solemnly delivered by *Urim* and *Thummim*) stoned to death for a breach of this commandment, though seemingly not done in a *deliberate*, but *hasty* manner, while *striving with another* man.

The *fourth* commandment, which, as to the moral intendment of it, was to secure a stated portion of our time to be set apart as *hallowed*, and sacred to the more immediate worship

worship of GOD, was not less an object of GOD's jealousy; for we find the same judgment as before, delivered and inflicted in the same solemn and awful manner, and terribly executed, for a breach of this law, and that too in the instance of a man, who only *gathered* a few *sticks on the sabbath-day*.

GOD having, in the *first table* of the law, provided for His own glory, worship, and service, proceeds in the *second* to publish His will concerning those relative duties, which men owe each other as children of one common *Father*. Accordingly—the *fifth* commandment enjoins duty * to *parents*—Honour
thy

---

* The words of this law shew it to belong, in a very particular and especial manner, to the *Jews*—" *That thy days may be long in the land which the* LORD *thy* GOD *giveth thee.*" The *land* here meant is doubtless the land of *Canaan*, to take possession of which they were now journeying from *Ægypt*.

But doth this *clause* so restrain this commandment to the *Jews*, as to exempt *Christians* from an obedience to it? Certainly not—because the *reason* of this law must ever survive, it having a moral intendment, in its enjoining reverence and duty of children to parents, which can never cease, 'till those relations shall cease from the earth. And this, as I have elsewhere observed, is the best rule to judge of every part of the *divine law*:—where the duties which that law enjoins, or those apparent mischiefs which it was intended to remedy, equally concern or affect mankind at all times and places alike, there can be no reason for the cessation of the law itself, but its *duration* must be commensurate with that of the objects of it.

On this principle, those *laws* of Exod. xxii. 16. and Deut. xxii. 28, 29. which were apparently made for the security and protection of the *female* sex, must be as obligatory upon *Christians* as upon *Jews*. The mischiefs
which

thy father and thy mother, &c. God's *jealousy* over this law is such, that when the *curses* from mount *Ebal* were solemnly pronounced, *Deut.* xxvii. one of them runs thus—Ver. 16. *Cursed is he that setteth light by his father or his mother; and all the people shall say*—Amen. In what a dreadful manner disobedient children were to be punished, appears from Deut. xxi. 18—21. Lev. xx. 9. See Prov. xxx. 17. The fearful example of *Absalom* is recorded 2 Sam. xviii. 9, 14.

The *sixth* commandment forbids *murder*. The breach of this law stands marked with the heaviest doom on the offender, Gen. ix. 6. *Whoso sheddeth man's blood, by man shall his blood be shed.*—Numb. xxxv. 31. *Ye shall take no satisfaction for the life of a murderer which is guilty of death, but he shall be* surely *put to death.* Here is another instance of the reduplicatory emphasis in the *Hebrew* language —מות יומת—*Moriendo moriatur*—dying he shall die—noting the *certainty* of what is said. See the terrible examples of *Agag*, 1 Sam. xv. 33. *Ahab* and *Jezebel*, 1 Kings xxi. 19. xxii. 34, 35, 38. xxi. 23, 24. 2 Kings ix. 30, &c.

The *seventh* commandment saith—*Thou shalt not commit adultery.*—We have already observed, that the uniform and unvaried use of the word נאף—which we have as uniform-

which have accrued from laying them aside, are dreadful to think on, but never can be remedied or put a stop to, but by the restoration of *those laws* to the respect and honour which are due to them.

ly and unvariedly tranflated *adultery*, relates to the defilement of a *betrothed* or *married* woman—that this word is ufed to denote the turning from GOD, who is the *husband* of His church, to *idols*, called *ftrangers*, Jer. iii. 13. So that it carries its own fingle *idea* with it wherever it occurs throughout the whole *Hebrew* fcripture. That the *feventh* commandment therefore prohibits a woman's taking or going to any man but her *own*, *one*, *proper husband*, is too plain to admit of the leaft doubt. GOD's jealoufy over this law appears from the *penalty* inflicted on the breakers of it, which is certainly *death*, both of the *woman* who was defiled, and of the *man* who defiled her. Lev. xx. 10.

So jealous is GOD of the honour of this law, that even a *bare fufpicion* which a man entertained of the chaftity of his wife, fubjected her to a moft fevere and awful *trial*, where, if fhe was guilty, GOD pledged Himfelf to difcover it even by miracle—by turning a little harmlefs *duft* and innocent *water* into a deadly and deftructive *poifon*. Numb. v. 17, 22. None of this ever happened to a man who had taken, or was fufpected to have taken, a *fecond* wife to his *firft*—But why not, if the law equally reached his cafe? Can GOD be fuppofed to be lefs *jealous* of His law, if a man was *guilty*, or *fufpected* to be guilty, of a breach of it, than in the cafe of *guilt*, or *fufpicion* of guilt, on the woman's fide? Why is *fhe* to fuffer *fhame*, the moft excruciating *torments*, and even *death* itfelf, and

and the man on *his side* be free from even the least reprehenſion? Shall not the *Judge of all the earth do right?* Gen. xviii. 25.—But one good reaſon can be aſſigned for this difference, which is, that the woman *was condemned by the law*, the huſband *was not*. This apparent diſtinction meets us every where throughout the *Bible*. If a wife took a *ſecond* huſband, living her *firſt*, they were called *adulterer* and *adultereſs*, and both the wife, and the man who took her, were to be *ſtoned to death*, and if any *iſſue* was born of ſuch *commerce*, it was to be excommunicated *from the congregation of the* Lord, even to the *tenth generation*. Deut. xxiii. 2. Where is there any thing of this to be found on the man's ſide?—So far from it, the iſſue of a *ſecond* wife, living a *firſt*, was expreſſly, by God's poſitive law, to be looked upon as legitimate as the iſſue of the *firſt*, Deut. xxi. 15. No excommunication of the iſſue followed.— The direct contrary appears from the inſtances of the twelve ſons of *Jacob*, who were equally *heirs* to, and *inheritors* of the land of Canaan—of *Samuel*, who miniſtered to the Lord in the tabernacle in his very childhood—of *Solomon*, who built and dedicated the temple of God—and, in ſhort, in every other inſtance, without exception, which we meet with in *holy writ*.

When *David* took the wife of *Uriah*, he was ſeverely reprimanded by the prophet *Nathan*; but after *Uriah*'s death, he takes the ſame woman, though he had other *wives* before, and no fault is found with him; nor

is

is he charged with the least flaw or insincerity in his repentance on that account. The *child* which was the fruit of his intercourse with *Bathsheba*, during her husband *Uriah*'s life, GOD *struck to death* with His own hand, 2 Sam. xii. 15. *Solomon*, born of the same woman, begotten by the same man in a state of *polygamy*, is called *Jedidiah*, or *beloved of the* LORD—acknowledged by GOD Himself as *David*'s lawful issue, 1 Kings v. 5. and *as such set upon his throne*. All this, and much more which might be, and indeed has been mentioned, shews that *polygamy* is not, nor ever was, an object of the *seventh* commandment.—To assert that it is, is not only without evidence, but against all the evidence which the word of GOD affords us on the subject. Had this been an equal offence on the man's side as on the woman's, the *jealousy* of GOD *over His laws* would not have suffered Him to have been silent on a subject so important to the glory of His HOLY LAW. Had it indeed been *any* breach of that law whatsoever, we must have found some traces of His anger against it, not *every where* have met with His entire acquiescence and approbation. Otherwise I know not how we can say with *David*, or how he, of all men, could say—*Thy word is a lamp unto my feet, and a light unto my path.* Pf. cxix. 105. There is not a single breach of the *divine law* that is not marked out, somewhere or other, either *directly* or by *consequence*, with tokens of GOD's disapprobation and displeasure: but *this* is no where so marked; therefore

fore we muſt either conclude, that we are left *in the dark* concerning the meaning and import of the *ſeventh* commandment, or that *polygamy* is no ſin againſt it: to conclude the *firſt*, is an impeachment of the *holineſs, wiſdom*, and *juſtice* of GOD; to infer the *ſecond*, is to eſtabliſh the conſiſtency and harmony of the ſcriptures, in the character which they have given us of the *bleſſed* GOD, who is to judge His reaſonable creatures by that law, which He hath commanded, and made known unto them. To imagine that the holy LORD GOD—whoſe *jealouſy over His laws is ſuch*, as to command a man to be *ſtoned to death* for a ſingle breach of the *fourth* commandment, and that only *in gathering* a few *ſticks* on the *ſabbath-day*—ſhould allow, bleſs, own, and promote a breach of the *ſeventh* commandment, without a ſingle inſtance to the contrary for *fifteen hundred* years together—and of the original *inſtitution of marriage* (which is as *poſitive* a law as the other) for about *four thouſand* years together—is wholly irreconcileable with the ſcripture-account of Him, whoſe glory it is to be of *purer eyes than to behold evil, and who cannot look on iniquity*. Hab. i. 13. Comp. Pſ. v. 4.

Superſtition itſelf ſeems abaſhed at the idea, and, in order to maintain its empire over the minds of men, to retire behind thoſe intrenchments of error, which, even in the days of the *apoſtles*, began to be thrown up by the heretic *Cerinthus*, in that horrid poſition, that " the bleſſed *Æon*, who took on him
" the

" the person of the man JESUS, constantly
" opposed the God of the *Jews.*" However
shocking this may sound in words, yet in
truth and fact it is maintained in substance,
by those who represent the LORD JESUS
CHRIST as a *new lawgiver*, and as enacting
laws contrary *to*, or inconsistent *with*, the
laws of the Old Testament; or who say with
Socinus, that " CHRIST's mission upon earth
" was to exhibit to mortals a *new law*, dis-
" tinguished from *all* others by its unble-
" mished *sanctity* and *perfection.*"—Let us
weigh the position, that " GOD allowed *po-*
" *lygamy* under the Old Testament—but
" CHRIST forbad it as *adultery* under the
" New Testament," in this balance, we shall
find, in all sense and reason, their *avoirdupois*
is so equal, that the weight of an hair, or the
breath of a fly, would turn the scale.

Such is GOD's *jealousy over His laws*, that
He positively commanded—none should *add
to* them, or *diminish from* them. Deut. iv. 2.
Whosoever did *either*, would be guilty of a
breach of *this express* command; as such
would be a *sinner*; *for sin is the transgression
of the law.* To fix this on CHRIST, is an
horrible blasphemy; and could it be proved,
that in any one instance CHRIST *added to* or
diminished from the law of GOD, by ordaining
any thing contrary to or inconsistent with
it, it would, as before observed, be making
Him a greater impostor than *Mahomet*, who
openly declared that he was sent to " de-
" stroy the law of the scripture, and to set
up

" up another of his own:"—whereas CHRIST declared, He *came not to destroy the law, but to fulfil it, and that not one jot or tittle should pass from the law*. But how could this be so, if CHRIST made that *sinful* which GOD made *lawful?*—if He repealed the *old* moral law, and set up a *new* one of *His own?* Those who can imagine such things, little consider the scripture-character of that *jealous* GOD, who declares so peremptorily by the pen of Divine inspiration—*I am JEHOVAH, that is* My *name, and* MY GLORY *I will not give to another*. If. xlii. 8. The power of the *divine legislation* is an essential part of HIS GLORY, which is incommunicably *His own*, and which never *was*, or *will*, or *can* be communicated to * any other. When one of the *persons* in JEHOVAH covenanted to take on Him the name and office of a *Son* (see *Heb.* i. 5. latter part, with Matt. iii. 17.) and was to assume the human nature as the *second Adam*, He was to be *made of a woman*, made *under the law* (Gal. iv. 5.) not *above* it. He was so under the bond of the law, that He was a *debtor to do the whole*. Comp. Matt. iii. 15. with Gal. iii. 3. This ill suits with the idea of His abrogating, changing, altering, or repealing any part of it. It is said, Phil. ii. 7. that He—ἐκενωσε—*emptied Him-*

---

* Therefore the MAN CHRIST JESUS (1 Tim. ii. 5.) had it not, any more than He had certain other prerogatives which the FATHER kept in *His own power*. Comp. Matt. xxiv. 36. Mark xiii. 32. Acts i. 7. ἐν τῆ ἰδίᾳ ἐξουσία —in his own—proper—peculiar *authority*, or *jurisdiction*.

self

self—that is, of the *glory which He had with the Father before the world was* (John xvii. 5.) and was made man—*took on Him the form of a servant* (Δȣλȣ—of a flave) not of a *sovereign* and *lawgiver*. So far from exercising such a power, He even refused to interfere in determining a question of *private property*, Luke xii. 13, 14. saying—*Man, who made me a judge, or a divider among you?* And so far from aiming at *kingly power* (a main branch of which is *legiflation*) when He *perceived that they would come and take him by force, and make Him* KING, *He departed into a mountain Himfelf alone.* John v. 15.—He had indeed a *kingdom*, but *not of this world.* John xviii. 36. not an *earthly*, but an *heavenly kingdom*, where *they neither marry nor are given in marriage*, but *are as the angels of* GOD. Matt. xxii. 30.

The small attention which the primitive *Chriftians* and *fathers* paid to the *jealoufy* of GOD *over His laws*, was greatly owing to their ignorance of the *Hebrew* scriptures, consequently of the true meaning of the Old Teftament. They too much feparated the New Teftament from it, making the *latter* a sort of * *new fyftem* by itfelf, and governing themfelves

---

* MARCION and the MARCIONITES, early in the second century, corrupted the book of the New Teftament, by cutting out every paffage which they thought to favour the *Jewifh religion*. They contracted the whole New Teftament into two books, the firft of which they called *the Gofpel*, the greateft part whereof was compofed from *St. Luke*, and then completed by paffages from

themselves by what they called *the precepts of* CHRIST, not considering that *these precepts* had their foundation and authority from what was written in the Old Testament. Hence, for want of comparing the New Testament with the Old, they got into their extravagant and wild opinions about *marriage*. For instance—CHRIST said—*There be eunuchs which have made themselves eunuchs for the kingdom of heaven's sake; he that is able to receive it, let him receive it.*—This was presently turned into a discouragement of *marriage*, as less pure and *holy* in itself than a *single life*, insomuch that the famous * *Origen*, who allegorized all the rest of the New Testament, took this passage literally, and actually *castrated* himself. His example was

from the other *Evangelists*. The other book they called *Apostolic:* it contained several of the *epistles*, to which they added an epistle to the *Laodiceans*. See *Wetstein*, Proleg. p. 79.

* *Origen* flourished in the *third century*, and was almost the only one among those early *fathers* who understood *Hebrew*; but the advantage which this might have been to him, was all lost by an irregular and wild fancy, which led him to interpret the scripture upon the principles of the *Platonic* philosophy, and which this great man set up as a test of all *religion*. He so allegorized the scripture, that the *letter* of it lost all its meaning and importance.—Thus did he open a secure retreat for all kind of *errors*, that a wild and irregular imagination could bring forth. See 1 *Mosheim*, p. 140, 141, 142.——The practice of *castration* lasted a great while, as appears by the *canons*, which were made and revived, during many *centuries*, to prevent such as made themselves *eunuchs* from being admitted into holy orders.

followed by many others, till the practice was condemned, under the name of *autophony*, or *self-murder*. Those who committed this violence on themselves, " were called " by the *Apostles Canons*, Ἀυτοφονεύται, *self-* " *murderers*—Ἐχθροὶ τῆς τȣ Θεȣ δημιȣργίας, " *enemies of* God's *workmanship.*" See *Hammond* on *Matt.* xix. 12. Others, who did not go so far as this, yet held marriage to be a *carnal* thing, and unfit for the *chastity* and *purity* of *Christians* †. Thus, to avoid what the *Devil*, transformed *into an angel of light*, taught them to esteem a *filthiness of the flesh*, they fell into the *spiritual filthiness* of making themselves *wiser* and *holier* than God. Had they gone to the only fountain-head of all true interpretation, the Old Testament—had they enquired by *whom*, and for what purposes, *marriage* was instituted—they would have seen that the *law was holy*, and the *commandment holy, just, and good* which ordained it. They would have likewise seen that the *first blessing* which ever came from *Heaven* to earth, after the creation of man upon it, was annexed to that command —*Be fruitful and multiply, and replenish the earth.* Gen. i. 28.—that, so far from a *single* life being more *holy* than a *married* life, *the* Lord God said—*It is not good for man to be alone, I*

---

† The persuasion was almost general in the *third century*, that they who took *wives*, were of all others most subject to the influence of malignant *dæmons.* 1 Mosh. 137.

will make him an help meet *for him*. Gen. ii. 18.
—that *marriage* itself was ordained by GOD *Himself*, as consistent with the *perfect* innocence of man's state in *Paradise*, while he stood in the *likeness* and *image* of GOD, therefore no impurity or defilement could belong to it. For all these reasons, it is impossible that CHRIST should mean by what He said, that *marriage* is less *holy* and *pure* than a state of *celibacy*, or less becoming the *Christian* profession. This He did *not* mean. What He *did* mean, Matt. xix. 12. was (as we may humbly suppose) that in the times of the *infancy* of the *church*, when surrounded by persecution, and every opposition that earth and hell could give it, even death itself threatening on all sides the profession of the gospel, it was expedient that those who were to *preach* and *profess* it, in the midst of a *crooked and perverse* generation (Phil. ii. 15.) should keep themselves *disentangled* from worldly engagements as much as possible (see 2 Tim. ii. 4.) and especially from those ties which might tempt them to withdraw from the work they were called to, by attention to *family concerns* (see 1 Cor. vii. 32, 33, 35.) or perhaps to deny the *faith*, if they were called to *suffer* for it. Now, whoever preferred these considerations before even the

---

* *As before him.* Eng. Marg.—*I will make for him an help, one like himself.* BATE.—*A counterpart, or one corresponding to himself, such as the reflection of a man's self with a glass or water sets* (נגד) *before him.* Id. note on Gen. ii. 18.

lawful indulgence of a *married* life, for the sake of the *gospel*, so as to remain *single* on this account, might truly be said to * *make himself an eunuch* for the *kingdom of heaven's sake*. This exactly harmonizes with 1 Cor. vii. in which the *apostle* says so much in favour of a *single life*, but explains the whole drift of his discourse, ver. 26. to relate to the then *distressed* state of things:—but as for *marriage itself*, he says, Heb. xiii. 4. *It is honourable in all* †. Had it not been so, we should hardly have seen our *Saviour beginning His miracles* at a *marriage-feast*—thus sanctifying by His presence this *primary ordinance* of GOD. *John* ii. 1—11.

From this want of comparing *spiritual things with spiritual*, they ran into all those extravagancies about *second* marriages, looking on them as abominable, forbidding *ecclesiastical* persons to be present at them, and

---

* The *Rhemists* comment thus, on Matt. xix. 12. "They *geld themselves for the kingdom of heaven*, which "*vow chastity*. Aug. de Virginitate 24 :—which proveth "these kind of vows to be both *lawful*, and also *more* "*meritorious*, and more *sure* to obtain *life everlasting*, "than the state of *wedlock*—contrary to our *adversaries* "in all respects."

† The apostle adds ϰ ἡ ϰοίτη ἀμίαντος, *and the bed* (that is the *marriage-bed*) *is undefiled*. For I take it the verb εϛι—*is*—must be supplied here as well as in the preceding sentence—τίμιος ὁ γάμος, which our translators have rendered—*marriage* is *honourable*.—Why not also render ϰ ἡ ϰοίτη ἀμίαντος, *and the bed* is *undefiled?* that is, not *less pure* than the bed of a *single person*. This connects the latter clause with the former, and makes the sense entire and complete, and would have saved a deal of *commentatorial* ingenuity on the word *undefiled*.

counting

counting little better than *whoredom* and *adultery* a man's marrying a *second* wife after the death of a *first*; thus making out notions of *purity* and *holiness*, which consisted in nothing better than *calling that which* God *hath cleansed, common and unclean. Acts* x. 15. All this, in part at least, is what we may suppose the *Apostle* to mean by τα πνευματικα της πονηριας εν τοις επυρανιοις—literally—*spirituals of wickedness in heavenlies*—such as spiritual pride, hypocrisy, error, and deceit relating to *heavenly things*, (Eph. vi. 12.) which are all the *works of darkness*, more eminently so when dignified with the name of *sanctity* or holiness. These things led the way to monkery, nunnery, and schemes of unnatural *celibacy*, which have been attended with practices too *unnatural*, *beastly*, and *abominable* to mention particularly.

Nearly allied to their disparagement of marriage, and condemnation of *second* marriages, and indeed the natural consequence of their wild opinions on these subjects, was their rage against *polygamy*, ranking it under the sins against the *seventh* commandment, and vouching Christ's authority for their proceedings; wresting that text Matt. xix. 9. to their own purposes, and making it contradict the whole united testimony of the Old Testament. In this particular we have trodden in their steps, the generality of our *commentators* make it *adultery*, and our *municipal* law, which does not punish *adultery*, yet adjudges a *polygamist* as worthy of *death*,

Q 4   actually

actually makes him a *felon*, and ranks him, in this respect, with *thieves* and *murderers*. This *wise* law was made in the *wise* reign of the *wise James* I. and stands in the statute-book next before the act which forbids persons to " *consult with*, covenant with, enter- " *tain, employ, feed*, or *reward* any *evil and* " *wicked spirits*."—This was repealed 9 Geo. II. though it had *some* countenance from scripture—but *polygamy* has still the brand of *felony* remaining upon it, though there is not a tittle in the word of GOD against it. Exod. xxii. 18. saith—*Thou shall not suffer a witch to live:* but no where does the law of GOD forbid *polygamy:* so that all that has been written, spoken, or enacted against it, from the days of the primitive *Christians* and *fathers* to this hour, or may continue so to be, is as void of all warrant from GOD's law, nay, is as opposite to it, as hanging a *priest* for *marrying at all*, under the statute of 31 Hen. VIII. c. 14. while it remained in force—or the *ousting a man of his clergy* under the stat. Ed. I. for having been *twice married*—or for *roasting* a fellow-creature alive under the writ *de hæretico comburendo*. All these things were most highly honoured, and most *piously* respected in their day, however inhuman, barbarous, antiscriptural, and unjustifiable, they may now appear to us.

Had the *jealousy* of mankind over the *law* of GOD, been at all times what it ought to have been, that *divine rule of right* had never been deformed and disgraced by *human invention,*

vention, and we never should have found men taking upon themselves to sport with the *consciences* and *lives* * of their fellow-creatures,

* In the Commentary on the *Marquis* of *Beccaria's* Essay on *Crimes* and *Punishments*, c. xiii. the *commentator*, who is supposed to be M. de *Voltaire*, exclaims—" Is it
" credible that there formerly existed a supreme tribunal
" more horrible than the inquisition, and that this tri-
" bunal was established by *Charlemagne?* It was the judg-
" ment of *Westphalia*, otherwise called the *Vhemic* court.
" The severity, or rather the cruelty, of this court,
" went so far, as to punish, with death, every *Saxon*
" who broke his fast during Lent. The same law was
" also established in *Franche-comté*, in the beginning of
" the 17th century.
" In the archives of a little place, called *St. Claude*,
" in *Burgundy*, are preserved the particulars of the sen-
" tence, and verbal process of execution, of a poor
" gentleman named *Claude Guillon*, who was beheaded
" 28th July, 1629. Being reduced to the utmost po-
" verty, and urged by the most intolerable hunger, he
" ate, on a *fish*-day, a morsel of horse-flesh. This was his
" crime. He was found guilty of sacrilege. Had he been
" a rich man, and had spent two hundred crowns in a
" supper of sea-fish, suffering the poor to die of hunger,
" he would have been considered as a person fulfilling
" every duty."

However horrible the above instances may appear, however shocking to humanity, as well as to all true religion, it may be, for one set of mortals thus barbarously to sport with the lives of another—yet there is not any thing above mentioned, which is not as much founded on the authority of GOD, as making a man a *felon, and to suffer death as such*, for having *two wives* at a time.

The very sensible reasoning of the *commentator* upon the fate of *Claude Guillon*—" Had he been a rich man," &c. will also, with very little variation, apply to the other case—for, had the man who was doomed to death for having *two wives* of his own, only debauched a dozen *wives* of other people, he would have been free from that

creatures, as the humour, fashion, or superstition of the times dictated. What the answer of the *Barons* was to the request of the *Prelates,* as related in the famous statute of *Merton,* 20 Hen. III. would, with a small, but important variation, have been the language of every succeeding parliament, and, instead of *Nolumus leges Angliæ mutare*—it would have been said *Nolumus leges Dei mutare.*

Still *the* LORD *is King*—His dominion is over all—the laws of His kingdom, both in *heaven* above, and in the *earth* beneath, are as unchangeable as Himself—they are the transcripts of His mind and will, and the *unalterable rule* of His moral government over His reasonable creatures. No time, place, or age can change their obligation. As His law is the same, so is *His jealousy over it.*—Were the first causes of *public* and *private* distress and calamity more attended to than they are, men might see this truth, written in legible characters on all their afflictions and miseries—GOD *is a jealous* GOD.

I have before spoken on the notion of *antiquating* the laws of GOD, and leaving them out of our *system,* as " having nothing to do
" with the more modern days of *Christia-*

---

that sanguinary law. One would almost think, that such laws as these were made " that there might remain no species of atrocious folly, which hath not entered into the heart of man."

" *nity;*

" *nity;* that *Christians* are governed by an-
" other *rule,* and people are not to do *now* as
" they did under the *Jewish* law." This
may appear plausible to those who want to
break His *bonds asunder, and cast away* His
cords from them—Pf. ii. 3.—without the
trouble and vexation of a guilty conscience;
or who are ignorant enough of the *nature,
use,* and properties of the *divine law,* to imagine that it is superseded by what they call
the *law of the gospel.* This idea is so general,
that it would ill become a writer on the subject of this *chapter,* to spare the pains of once
again considering these *dangerous* but *fashionable tenets.*

It is a true and solid maxim, with respect
to the *laws of* God, as well as in *human ju-
risprudence,* " ubi eadem ratio ibi idem jus—
" where there is the same reason for it, there
" the law must be the same." This is a good
criterion by which we may judge between
those laws which *are waxed old and vanished
away,* and those whose obligation must ever
remain. According to this rule, we may
safely determine on the *obsoleteness* of the
whole *ceremonial law*—as likewise on that of
those *particular laws,* which could only relate
to the peculiar situation of a peculiar people.
But there is the same reason *now* as ever, why
we should *have no other* Gods *but* Jehovah
—why we should not *make images and worship
them*—why we should not *take the name of
the* Lord *our* God *in vain*—why we should

set

set apart a portion of our time for the immediate service and worship of HIM *that made us*—why we should *honour our parents—do no murder—not commit adultery*, by *defiling our neighbour's wife*—why we *should not steal—bear false witness*, or *covet that which is another's :*—we have therefore very properly adopted these commandments into our *public service*, read them in the ears of the people every *sabbath-day*, and pray for *mercy* on account of our sins against them, and that GOD would *write* all these His laws *within our hearts, inclining our hearts to keep them*. We have made *other* commands of GOD the ground of some of our *penal laws*—such as those against *unnatural lusts*—and doubtless there is the highest reason why this should be so. Why then do we *make void* other laws? why *make* other commandments of GOD of none effect *through our traditions?* Why is a *virgin*, who gives *her person* into the possession of the *man of her choice*, less *one flesh* with him *now*, than when GOD said—*She shall be his wife*, &c? Why do we *now* put asunder those whom GOD *then* joined together? Is there not the same reason of their indissoluble union *now* as when it was said—*They shall be one flesh; because he has humbled her, he may not put her away all his days?* Is the divorcing or putting away the woman less against GOD's ordinance, or attended with less mischief and inconvenience, than it was *three thousand* years ago? Let the poor, deluded, helpless,

and

and forsaken * wretch, who is wasting with disease, perishing with cold and nakedness, fainting with hunger, give the answer!—let thousands, that, like her, have been deceived and ruined, declare what answer can be given. Could the unhappy, desperate creature, who is sharpening her knife for her *new-born infant's* throat—the wretch whose horror makes her *forget her own child, so that she has no compassion on the fruit of her womb*, If. lix. 15.—could she be asked the reason of her cruelty, she would tell us that it originated from *shame* and *fear* (fixed on her by the *inventions of men*) which prompt her to avoid the *censure of the world* so as to overwhelm every other consideration. Nor could it be made to appear, that such misery finds more alleviation from the want of *power* in a *married* man, than from the want of *will* in a single man, to prevent it.

All this is owing to the frame of our

---

* An affecting description of such an one, is to be found in Dr. *Goldsmith*'s Poem—*The Deserted Village*—

————— *Ah turn thine eyes,*
Where the poor houseless shiv'ring female lies:
She once, perhaps, in village plenty blest,
Has wept at tales of innocence distrest;
Her modest looks the cottage might adorn,
Sweet as the primrose peeps beneath the thorn.
Now lost to all her friends, her virtue fled,
Near her betrayer's door she lays her head;
And, pinch'd with cold, and shrinking from the shower,
With heavy heart deplores that luckless hour,
When idly first, ambitious of the town,
She left her wheel, and robes of country brown.

laws—to the unscriptural and *antiscriptural* power assumed by man in *things relating to* GOD—to our making *marriage* and its *obligation* consist, not in what GOD hath made them to consist, that is to say—simply in the *union* of the parties—but in the words of a *priest*, in the sanction of an human outward ceremony, in a *lye* *, invented at *Rome*, adopted by the ambition and avarice of *Pope Innocent* the IIId. and his clergy, and from them handed down and received, by the credulity of mankind, ever since. Hinc illæ lachrymæ! Hence flow the tears of the seduced, the deserted, the ruined *female*—hence heave those *sighs* which affect none but the heart they come from, and which serve to little other purpose than to grace the tri-

---

* *Viz.* That *marriage* is a *sacrament*, and as such must be administered by the hands of *priests*. Afterwards the Council of *Trent* decreed—" If any shall say that *matri-*
" *mony* is not one of the *seven sacraments* instituted by
" CHRIST, and doth not confer grace—*Let him be ac-*
" *cursed.*"
Again—" If any shall condemn the *benedictions* and
" other *ceremonies*—*Let him be accursed.*" See Brent Counc. Trent. p. 784.

† It is granted, that *Protestants* do not receive that part of the *lye* which turns *marriage* into a *sacrament*; but the other, and perhaps the most *mischievous* part of it, as far as *female ruin* is concerned, namely, " that there can
" be no *marriage-obligation*, but by the act of a *priest* in
" a church," is not only a general belief, among *Protestants* as well as among the *Papists*, but is honoured with the sanction of a public statute (26 Geo. II. c. 33.) *exceptis excipiendis* for special licence among the *Protestants*, and the Bishop's *licence*, or the POPE's *dispensation* among the *Papists*.

umphs

umphs of luſt, perfidy, and treachery, over *juſtice*, *mercy*, and *truth*. Cuſtom has fixed the odious name of *whore*, on her whom GOD accounts a *wife*—*whoredom and fornication* on that which he eſteems *marriage*, by poſitively eſtabliſhing it as ſuch in *His word*—*baſtardy* is ſtamped on thoſe whom GOD *legitimates*—and thoſe are *put aſunder* whom GOD for ever *joins together*.

The *Hebrew* זונה—which we tranſlate an *harlot or whore*—like the Greek πορνη, denotes a woman, who from a principle of luſt, idleneſs, or avarice, beſtows or ſells her favours promiſcuouſly to all men alike: whereas the *virgin* who beſtows *her perſon* on the man of her choice, with an intent to be *his* and *his alone*, ſo long as both ſhall live—or being *enticed*, or even on a more ſudden occaſion *ſeduced*—is in the language of ſcripture the אשה—or γυνη—the *woman* or *wife* of that man from that moment. He is bound to maintain, protect, and provide for her as ſuch; and no ceremony of man's invention can *add to* this obligation, or the want of it make any *diminution* from it, in the ſight of GOD. Our ideas of *baſtardy* are derived from the former error, and are very conſiſtent with it: we firſt, without all warrant from ſcripture, make the woman an *whore*, and then as unwarrantably ſtamp the name of *baſtard* on the iſſue: whereas the word ממזר denotes the iſſue of a זונה or *harlot* (εκ πορνης—ſay the LXX, *Deut.* xxiii. 2.) who by having promiſcuous intercourſe with different men, muſt render the iſſue *ſpurious*, and uncertain to *whom it belongs*. For this reaſon the iſſue of an *adultereſs* is alſo properly a *baſtard*; becauſe if a *wife* gives her perſon to others beſides her *husband*, the iſſue muſt be as uncertain to whom it belongs as the iſſue of an *harlot*.

Nor was a man who, having *one wife*, took another, ever called or reckoned an *whoremonger* or *adulterer*—nor was the woman which he ſo took called an *whore*, or ſaid to commit *adultery* with the man—nor was the *iſſue* of ſuch woman by that man deemed a *baſtard*;—but the whole was by the *divine law* ratified, confirmed, and deemed *lawful* and *right*, as hath already been ſhewn at large.

In ſhort, the whole ſyſtem of our laws, in theſe reſpects, is like the ſyſtems of the *Scribes* and *Phariſees*, who took as much of GOD's *law* as ſuited with their own *traditions*, and rejected all the reſt. The paſſage Mark vii. 9, &c. is very ſtriking—*He ſaid unto them, Full well ye reject the commandment of* GOD, *that ye may keep your own traditions. For Moſes ſaid, Honour thy father and mother, and whoſo curſeth father or mother, let him die the death*;—*But ye ſay, If a man ſhall ſay unto his father or mother, it is* Corban, *that is to ſay a gift (beſtowed and devoted by me to the temple-treaſury, for the repairs or ſervice of the temple,* according to King *Jehoaſh*'s inſtitution, 2 Kings xii. 9.) *by whatſoever thou mighteſt* (otherwiſe) *be profited by me, he ſhall be be free; and ye suffer* (or permit) *him no more to do aught for his father or mother, making the word of* God *of none effect through your traditions which ye have delivered: and many such-like things do ye.* Let us *modernize* this—*Moses* said, that if *any man* (כי איש) *entices a virgin not betrothed, and lies with her, he shall surely endow her to be his wife. She shall be his wife; becauſe he hath humbled her, he may not put her away all his days.* But ye say, that *if a man entice a virgin,* &c. and say unto her—" I have not been *married by a prieſt* at " *church,* according *to act of parliament—* " therefore I have no more to do with thee"—he ſhall be *free,* and ye *suffer him* no more *to do aught for her,* nor *permit her* to *claim him* as her huſband.

Again, *Moses* said—*If a man have two wives, the* one *beloved, and the* one *hated, and they have borne him children,* &c. *then it ſhall be, when he maketh his ſons to inherit that which he hath, he may not make the ſon of the beloved firſt-born, before the ſon of the hated, which is indeed the firſt-born. But he ſhall acknowledge the ſon of the hated for the firſt-born, by giving him a double portion of all that he hath; for he is the beginning of his ſtrength, and the right of the firſt-born is his.* But ye say, that if a man, having a *wife, marrieth another,* ſuch marriage is *null* and *void;* that the iſſue is not inheritable, but ſhall be *baſtardized.*

Again, *Moses* said—*The man who committeth adultery with another man's wife, even he that committeth adultery with his neighbour's wife, the adulterer and adulteress shall surely be put to death.* But ye say, that if a man hath *two wives* of his own, he shall be deemed a *felon, and suffer death as such*—whereas if he *committeth adultery with another man's wife, he shall be free:*—thus *condemning* those whom God *acquits,* and *acquitting* those whom God *condemns, making the word of* God *of none effect, through your traditions which ye have delivered: and many such-like things do ye.*

Still God is a *jealous* God; that is His character with respect to His laws, indelibly written on the sacred page, and awfully manifested throughout the volume of *divine revelation.* So those wretched *Jews* found it in the dreadful destruction which He sent upon them. They could not justify themselves by appealing to their *traditions,* nor repair the dishonour which they had done to the divine law, by vacating its obligations in order to establish their own inventions. However *pious* or *pure* they might seem in their *own eyes,* or in the eyes of those who were deluded into as high an esteem for *human tradition* as they themselves were, yet they found to their cost—and so will every one, sooner or later, who sets up human wisdom against the *wisdom of* God, and *human inventions* against the *ordinances of Heaven*—that *the wisdom of this world is foolishness with* God, (1 Cor. i. 20.) and—*that which is highly esteemed among men is abomination in the sight of* God. Luke xvi. 15.

Happy those whose passions have so *little*
power

power over them, and those who have so *much* power over their passions, as to steer clear of all difficulties. But this is not the lot of all. The *apostle*, speaking on this subject, 1 Cor. vii. 7. says—*Every man hath his proper gift of* God, *one after this manner, and another after that.* So His *Divine Master*, speaking also on the gift of continency, saith —Matt. xix. 11.—*All cannot receive* (ȣ χωρȣσι, *do* not receive) *this saying (viz.* it is not good to marry, ver. 10.) *save they to whom it is given.* The scriptures shew us, that no one, while in a *body* of *sin and death,* is out of the reach of temptation: therefore *let him that is thinking to stand* (ὁ δοκῶν ἑϛάναι) *take heed lest he fall.* 1 Cor. x. 12. Comp. Gal. vi. 1. Yet when persons are involved in difficulties, by means of any of the things heretofore discoursed upon; let them not consult with *flesh and blood,* and, by following *vulgar error,* under the influences of *superstition* and *prejudice of education,* endeavour to right themselves by *wrong* methods, and be led, under a notion of *repentance,* to act contrary to God's word, and to every principle of humanity, gratitude, truth, benevolence, and even common honesty, by abandoning and forsaking those who have a right to their assistance, comfort, and protection: —Let them, under the guidance of *real* prudence and *found* discretion, regulate their outward conduct so as to avoid all needless offence; but let the *inward* conduct of the *conscience* be subject *only* to the *law* of God.

As to the *world,* it *loves its own* (John

xv. 19.) its own maxims, customs, and inventions, and, above all, its *own* ease, too well to give itself the trouble of enquiring into the foundation on which either what it *believes* or *professes* is *built*. The *Papist* jogs on with his *Mass-book*—the *Turk* with his *Koran*—the *Persian* with his *Zendavesta*—the *Gentoo* with his *Shaster*—the *Chinese* with his *Confucius*—the *Englishman* with his *Marriage-Act*; and nothing is so ill received—because nothing so attacks the *pride* and exposes the *ignorance* of one part of mankind, and the *knavery* of another—as the discovery of the superstition, folly, and opposition to God, which cleaves to *worldly systems*, especially those of the *religious* kind. Still individuals may be profited, and thankful, to be shewn, by some diligent enquirer after truth, that, in many things, perhaps the most important, whereon the preservation of *millions* may depend, they have been taught to *believe a lye*, and that while they have been following the *opinion* of the world, even of what passes (like the *Pharisees)* for the *devout* and *pious* part of it, they have been only *following a multitude to do evil*. Exod. xxiii. 2.

CHAP.

CHAP. X.

Of POPULATION.—*Comparison of the* JEWISH LAW *with* OURS.

WHEN we search the scripture, and take an impartial view of the *divine law*, we must acknowledge its harmony and consistency, both with respect to itself, and all things which are the objects of it. It perfectly agrees with its original designs, the glory of GOD and the happiness of his creatures. In no instance doth this observation appear more true, than in that part of the sacred code which is to regulate the *commerce of the sexes*. The brute part of this lower creation is restrained by a sort of *physical necessity*, which is usually called *instinct*, within due bounds; so that the several species may be kept distinct, and not create a monstrous confusion from unnatural or improper mixtures; and though, partly from the inventions and contrivances of men, contrary to the positive law of GOD—Lev. xix. 19.—animals, both among beasts and birds, have been generated, yet it can go no farther; it is stopped in the first instance, and no *mule* *

is

---

* I believe no instance can be produced of the male and female *mule* propagating with each other. As to what *Buffon*, or others, may have said of the *she-mule's*

bringing

is known to carry the confusion any farther than itself.

With regard to reasonable beings, it pleased the CREATOR to enact and publish *written laws*, the moral obligation of which, was to circumscribe and regulate their actions. Whether these wise statutes are departed from by those whose infidelity and malicious contempt reject them utterly—or by those who, under a mistaken notion of greater *purity* and *perfection* than they are supposed to prescribe, make themselves *wiser* and *holier* than the divine *Law-giver*—the effect will be much the same, as to the grand objects which these laws are to promote. These are, 1. The *propagation* of mankind. 2. The prevention of *confusion, and every evil work*.

The first general commandment was—*Be fruitful and multiply, and replenish the earth, and subdue it.* Gen. i. 28; which last words, taken in connection with the beginning of the verse, and with what follows, clearly prove, that this command was addressed in an especial manner to the human * species, *then wholly in the loins* of their *first parent*. To suppose that every law given to mankind subsequent to this first ordinance, was calculated

bringing forth, I cannot help entertaining great doubt of it, as well as of the *he-mule* engendering with a *mare*; as I never heard of such a thing being attested, on the knowledge of any person whom I have yet met with.

* It is remarkable that this command was repeated a second time, to *Noah* and his sons, with a *blessing* also, on the renovation of the earth after the flood. Gen. ix. 1, 7.

to promote it, is certainly confonant with the higheft reafon, and accordingly we find this to have been the cafe. *Celibacy* was hardly known among the antient *Jews*, they looked on it with abhorrence, and confidered it as a reproach; and we find, that their whole œconomy, with refpect to marriage, all tended to the fulfilment of that promife to *Abraham*, Gen. xv. 5. that his *feed fhould be as the ftars of heaven for multitude.* *Mofes*—Deut. i. 10. —even at their arrival on the borders of *Canaan*, declares this to be the cafe. Marriage was looked upon as a facred duty, whofe chief end was population, and population as the riches, ftrength, and blefling of the ftate. No impediments or difficulties were, therefore, laid in its way—all promifcuous intercourfe of women with men, which *Montefquieu* juftly ftyles the bane of population, pofitively forbidden—the honour of their wives, the chaftity of their daughters, were fecured by the wifeft inftitutions; and thus they became populous, profperous, and happy.

From this fcene of things, let us advert to that which is daily before us, fince *Chriftian* churchmen have invented other *fchemes* of *marriage*, and *Chriftian* politicians have found out other *maxims* of *population*. What fwarms of unmarried people fill our capital and counties! fome through caprice and voluptuoufnefs, others through mifery and indigence.—Could we form a juft calculation of the *marriageable* of both fexes, who have no thought of altering their condition, and of those multitudes who live and die in *celibacy*, we should see the true reason why our *fleets* want sailors, our *armies* men—why we so sensibly feel the emigrations of people to our colonies abroad—why we complain of scarcity of people, and see so many thousands of acres lie uncultivated and uninhabited—and why we are forced to have recourse to *foreign auxiliaries* in our days of common danger. The reason of all this is, we have not *people enough*; the cause of which is, that the whole system of our laws is inimical to *population*; whereas the *divine law*—which we have banished, as not *pure* and *holy* enough for *Christians*, but which was sufficiently so under God's *own immediate government* of His *own people*—has every ingredient in it, which, were it sufficiently understood and attended to, would remedy all the evils we complain of. There * luxury is forbidden, debauchery, and all enticements to it, are proscribed, under the severest pe-

---

* Mr. *Coxe*—*Sketches of Switzerland*, p. 311.—observes, that *Lausanne*, and the whole *Pais de Vaud*, is much less *peopled* than in the *last* century: This depopulation, says he, "is owing to the encrease of luxury, which prevents "the gentry from entering into matrimonial engage-"ments so generally as they were heretofore accus-"tomed."

We may certainly, in a great measure, apply this observation to our own country, and look upon *luxury*, for the same reason, as one cause of our *depopulation:* but more especially when we cannot confine its mischiefs to *one part* of the people, but must consider it as pervading the *whole mass*, from the *highest* to the *lowest* orders of men.

nalties,

nalties. No publications of banns, inconvenient terms of refidence, expenfive licences, nor human ceremonies, were then invented, as conftituting the marriage in GOD's fight; all ftood on the fimplicity of the divine inftitution: the confent of the parties formed the contract; the *union* of their *perfons* completed it, and GOD's bleffing crowned the whole. The demands for women in marriage were too great, and the punifhment of forbidden lewdnefs too fevere, to leave a portion for the purpofes of profligacy and proftitution: whereas, with us, I queftion whether the numbers of *married women* are greatly beyond thofe of *harlots* and *proftitutes*, at leaft in many parts of the kingdom; however this may be, the *married* bear no fort of proportion * to the *unmarried*.

I muft confefs myfelf to have but little genius for the fcience of calculation; but perhaps *Demoivre* himfelf would not find fault with my fuppofing, that to every marriage we may allot, on an average, *four chil-*

---

* For the proportions which marriages bear to births, and births to burials, in feveral parts of *Europe*, Mr. *Derham* has given us a curious table; from which it appears, that *marriages*, one with another, do each produce about *four births*, both in *England* and other parts of *Europe*. And by Mr. *King's* computation, about *one* in an *hundred and four* perfons *marry*; the number of people in *England* being eftimated at *five millions and an half*, whereof *forty-one thoufand* annually *marry*. See *Chambers*, tit. Marriage.

dren.

dren. Let us say, that 20,000 * females are, in the space of seven years, rendered *barren* by *prostitution*, who would otherwise, under the sobriety of matrimony, have produced *four children* each. Here is a defalcation of 80,000 people from the community. To these let us add 100,000 more, who, from various causes † unknown to the *Jewish* polity, die *unmarried*, and who might otherwise have produced four children each. Here is a subtraction of 400,000 more. These make together 480,000. Let us suppose all this to happen in *every seven* years, then the average of our loss, in every space of *twenty-one* years, will be 1,440,000. Deduct for casualties of various kinds happening to the children, *two thirds*, and there will remain a loss of 480,000 people to the community in that space of time. Let us carry on this calculation for but *one century*, and the loss will, in that time, amount to 2,400,000 and upwards. This small imperfect sketch will serve to shew why the *Jews* were, in the space of about ‡ 215 years, that

is

* In this calculation I include the whole of *Great Britain*: were it to be extended to *Ireland*, and to the rest of the *British* dominions, it must be very short of the truth.

† Among others, the unlimited power of the men to seduce and abandon women at their pleasure—which must promote *celibacy* in the men, and of course leave an amazing number of females unsolicited in marriage.

‡ The *sojourning* of the children of *Israel*, who dwelt in *Ægypt*, is said (Exod. xii. 40.) to be 430 *years*, but this does not mean that they were so long in *Ægypt*—

for

is to say, from *Jacob*'s coming into *Ægypt* with *seventy* souls, to the *Israelites* arrival on the borders of *Canaan*, increased as the *stars in heaven for multitude*—Deut. x. 22.—and why we are complaining for *want of people*. It is true, that the increase of the *Jews*, which, even under the disadvantages of the *Ægyptian* bondage, was so prodigious as to alarm the government (Exod. i. 9, 12.) was by a special blessing from Heaven, in fulfilment of that promise to *Abram*, Gen. xv. 5; but then the means by which this was effected, was their having a law, which respected the *great first command* of the Creator—was favourable to marriage, and of course to *population*. Though this law was not reduced to writing till after the *Exodus*, yet enough of it was known by tradition, to check *adultery, whoredom*, and all destructive intercourse of the sexes, and thus to promote the interests of *population*. They did not hang people for † *polygamy*, but honoured marriage in all, where God had not forbid-

---

for they were *strangers in a land that was not theirs* (see Gen. xv. 13.) partly in *Canaan*, partly in *Ægypt* (see Exod. vi. 4.)—It is to be noted, that from the birth of *Isaac*, when the 400 years mentioned in Gen. xv. 13. began, to their deliverance out of *Ægypt*, was just 405 years; if we add to this the 25 years from *Abraham*'s coming into *Canaan* to the birth of *Isaac*, the total is 430 years. This, divided into equal parts, makes 215 years in *Canaan*, and 215 years after they went into *Ægypt*.— This is the computation of the *antients*, as well as of the later writers. See *Patrick* on Gen. xv. 13.

† In antient times *celibacy* was rare, *polygamy* almost universal. *Jews* letters to *Voltaire*.

den it. The permanency and unchangeableness of their law, accounts for the permanency and unchangeableness of its effect; the populousness of the *Jewish* nation, is at this hour incredible; if all that are dispersed throughout the globe were gathered together, I doubt whether they would not appear to be as * numerous as at any period of their most prosperous estate.

As for the *Christians*, they sat out on a plan opposite † to all this; they began very early

---

* The Italian rabbi, *Simon Luzatier,* reckoned up 90,000 *Jews* at *Salonica* and *Constantinople*, and more than a *million* of them in the *Turkish* dominions. When we consider that there is no part of the world where *Jews* are not found, we may well suppose their numbers to be immense. Vide *Jews* letters to *Voltaire*, vol. ii. 173—176.

† " *Constantine,* the first *Emperor* under whom the
" state forsook the gods of their forefathers, and became
" *Christian,* together with this alteration, abrogated
" those antient *Roman* laws, *Julia* and *Papia*, wherein
" the *desire of women and married life* were so much pri-
" vileged and encouraged, and *single and unmarried life*
" disadvantaged. Hear it in the words of *Sozomen,*
" lib. i. chap. 9. *Hist. Eccl.*—*There was,* saith he, *an*
" *antient law among the* Romans, *forbidding those, who*
" *after* 25 *years old were unmarried, to enjoy the like pri-*
" *vileges with married ones ; and besides many other things,*
" *that they should have no benefit by testaments and legacies,*
" *unless they were next of kindred: and those who had no*
" *children, to have half their goods confiscated. Where-*
" *fore the* EMPEROR, *seeing those who for* GOD's *sake*
" *were addicted to* chastity and virginity, *to be, for this*
" *cause, in a worse condition; he accounted it a folly for men*
" *to go about to increase their kind with such carefulness and*
" *diligence, when as nature, according to Divine moderation,*
" *continually receives as well* diminution *as* increase.

" *Therefore he published* a law—*that, both those who*
" *lived*

early to represent *celibacy* as most pleasing to God, condemned marriage, of course exe-

"lived a single life, *and those who had* no children, *should enjoy like privileges with others:* yea, he enacted *that those who lived in* chastity and virginity, *should be privileged above them;* enabling both sexes, though under years, to make testaments, contrary to the accustomed polity of the Romans. This alteration of the Roman law by Constantine, Eusebius *also witnesseth*, lib. iv. chap. 26. *de vita Constantini;* and again chap. 28. where he saith, *that above all, he honoured most those that had consecrated their lives to* divine philosophy—he means a *monastical life*—and therefore *he almost adored the most holy company of* PERPETUAL VIRGINS.

"That which the fathers had thus enacted, the sons also seconded, and some of the following *Emperors*, by new edicts, 'till there was no relique left of those antient privileges, wherewith married men had been respected; which *Procopius* saith (how rightly I examine not) was the cause of the ruin of that *empire*, which was so much enfeebled and weakened, that it was not able to match the numerous armies of the barbarous nations.

"This was the first step" (he must mean by *public authority of government*) "of the disregard of *marriage*, and the *desire of wiving*; which was not an absolute prohibition, but a discouragement. No sooner had the *Roman* bishop and his clergy got the power into their hands, but it grew to an absolute prohibition, not for *monks* only, but for the whole *clergy*: which was the highest disrespect that could be, to that which God had made *honourable among all men*." MEDE's *Works*, p. 672.

Nobis & monachis (saith *Chrysostome*, who was made Bishop *of Constantinople* anno 398.) *omnia mandata legis sunt communia*, πλην τε γαμε· "All the commandments of God's law are common to us with monks, besides marriage." Wherefore in the council of *Chalcedon* is an express *canon*—c. 16.—*Ut nec Deo dicata virgo nec monachus nubant.*—"That no *nun* or *monk* should marry." See *Mede*, p. 688.

Such were the *saints of Antichrist!*

crated

crated all *second* marriages, found out schemes of *holiness* by which millions of men and women have been lost to the world, and held forth the gospel as inimical to the first great commandment;—*purity* was to be found in *celibacy*, which they miscalled *chastity*, and *defilement* * in marriage, which they reckoned " too carnal for the *Christian* dispensation." The conceits of enthusiasts, the dreams of monks, the sophistry of schoolmen, were enlisted against the ordinance of Heaven, 'till the church of *Rome* made it the object of its *tyranny* † and *ambition*—Protestants, a *creature* ‡ *of the state*—and the great Author of our religion is called in, as an abettor of their monstrous opposition to the divine law. —They have changed His truth into a lye, and have set Him at the head of their ‖ rebellion

---

* *Epiphanius*, a writer of the fourth century, mentions a set of early heretics called *Severians*, who were so *pious* as to affirm, that, " woman was the work of " *Satan*, and that marriage was *diabolical*."

† Witness *Pope Innocent the Third*'s throwing it into the hands of Ecclesiastics, and establishing ceremonies, without which the contract has long been deemed *null* and *void*. Witness also the prohibiting marriage to the *clergy*.

‡ Witness the stat. 26 Geo. II. for *preventing clandestine marriages*.

‖ Witness making *polygamy* a capital felony—citing CHRIST's authority for calling it *adultery*—deeming all *polygamous* contracts null and void—and *bastardizing* the issue, contrary to Deut. xxi. 15—17.

We find the antient legislators and politicians of *Greece* and *Italy* well apprized of what *Moses* has taught us— that the numbers of the people are the *riches of the state*. Therefore every difficulty laid in the way of marriage is, even

bellion againſt the *holy commandment* once delivered to His people.

Our laws may truly ſay of *themſelves*, as we may ſay of *ourſelves—Mutamur in horas.*—As to thoſe which relate to marriage, they have gradually changed from bad to worſe, 'till, at laſt, the *marriage-act* has left little room for any farther mutability of this ſort. The letters of *Certain Jews to Mr. de Voltaire,* contain many ſtriking obſervations on theſe ſubjects, and account for the profligacy of *Chriſtian* governments, with regard to women, on principles too found and true to admit of any fair contradiction. Some of the above obſervations are extracted from them; and whoever reads thoſe excellent pieces of the learned * *Jews,* will get much entertainment and inſtruction for his pains; and will find, that *wiſdom* and *decency* breathed from the ſpirit of the laws of *Iſrael,* as much as *folly* and *libertiniſm* are derived from that ſyſtem which we have eſtabliſhed in its ſtead.

---

even in a political view, abſurd; but how much more abſurd in a maritime and commercial *iſland,* whoſe opulence and greatneſs is the conſtant object of envy to its powerful and ambitious enemies, who have long meditated its deſtruction! How, humanly ſpeaking, can this be avoided, unleſs, by encouraging marriage, we promote population, and thus are enabled to recruit our armies, and man our fleets, without ſtripping the country of its *huſbandmen, manufacturers,* &c.? Our dependence on foreign mercenaries is precarious, and may be dangerous.

* I ſpeak of them according to the title, but they are ſaid not to be written by *Jews,* but by *M. Guenné,* a learned *Frenchman.*

In p. 47. vol. ii. where a comparison is made between the *civil laws of the Jews,* and those of *other nations,* what cutting reflections doth the truth compel the learned writers to cast on the latter! Among others is the following — vol. ii. p. 63.—" † Our *code* says, " *There shall be no whore of the daughters* of " *Israel*—all your cities are full of them! " and if we are to believe your wife men, " there ought to be public endowments for " them, and their calling ought to be held " honourable." It is true, this is immediately addressed to a *Frenchman;* but if a total stranger was to visit both these *Christian* countries, I believe he would, from the *manners* of the inhabitants, be pretty much at a

---

† I refer to the English translation of *Dr. Lefanu,* octavo, Dublin, 1777. The editor of these masterly performances is so candid as to own, that the word here rendered *whore,* is קדשה—which properly signifies a *prostitute,* or a woman set apart for *prostitution,* in honour of the *idols* of the heathen. To the shame of human nature be it spoken, there were *prostitutes* of both sexes; which may serve to explain Deut. xxiii. 17. throughout. However, these women followed also the trade of *harlots,* wore a particular dress, and seated themselves in the highways and other places of public resort, to invite the passers by. See Gen. xxxviii. 14, the history of *Tamar,* who disguised herself so as (ver. 15.) to be taken for זונה—an *harlot,* whose trade it was to expose herself for hire (ver. 16, 17, 18.)—at ver. 21. she is called קדשה— *a consecrated prostitute* — which proves what is above asserted, that these women followed the trade of prostitution in both senses. These were *heathen* women, and therefore called in the book of PROVERBS, *strangers.* See chap. ii. 16. v. 20. vii. 5. No daughter of *Israel* could be either קדשה or זונה on pain of death.

loss to know whether *France* or *England* most espoused such a sentiment, and, of course, to which of *the two* it might, with the greatest justice, be attributed.

As to the second point, the prevention of *confusion,* and every *evil work.* This was secured on the woman's part by the severe laws against *adultery* and *whoredom,* and on the men's part also by the *moral* impossibility they were under, to forsake and abandon the *virgins* with whom they had *once* been *connected,* and thus to expose them to the danger and temptation of those dreadful violations of the divine law; therefore the prohibition was wisely extended to all men alike without exception. I will not repeat here what has been so largely before treated; but only observe, that the banishment of this law, has proved the banishment of decency and good order, to an alarming degree, from among us, and has plunged millions into irrecoverable ruin, who, had they lived under the *morality* of the *divine law,* had been *mothers* of children, instead of *prostitutes* in the streets.

To say that our *blessed Saviour* came to restore the institution of marriage to its primitive obligation, is as true as that He bore His testimony, on the footing of that institution, against all unlawful *divorce:* as true as, that by citing the very *words of union,* which were pronounced at the *beginning,* He shewed what was the mind of GOD as to the indissolubility of the contract. But where does

does He authorize the man who has *taken* a *virgin*, to put her away? Where does He *deny*, what the very scriptures which He cites *affirm*, that the being *joined* * to her, makes her the man's wife? Where does He *deny* the truth of the Hebrew scripture, by *affirming*, that if a man takes *two women together*, they are not equally *his wives?*— See Deut. xxi. 15. 1 Sam. i. 2. xxv. 43. Where doth He *bastardize the issue*—or consign either of the women to dereliction and ruin, by declaring the latter marriage *null and void?* and yet we plead His sacred authority for all this, as confidently as the *church of Rome* pleads it in defence of their persecutions of *Protestants*, because our LORD once said—*compel them to come in*—with relation to the call of the *Gentiles* into the *Christian* church. Such notions may pass with people who look no deeper than *popular opinion* for the foundation of what they believe; but how it is possible they should pass with *thinking* men, who *search the scriptures*, is only to be accounted for on the score of *prejudice*. Where this can be got rid of, they surely must appear lyes—" gross and palpa-" ble as the father that begat them." John viii. 44.

That the populousness of the *Jewish* nation proceeded *merely* or *wholly* from the prac-

---

* Compare דבק—Gen. ii. 24; προσκολληθήσεται, Matt. xix. 5; κολλώμενος, 1 Cor. vi. 16; and see before p. 134, note.

tice of *polygamy*, as contradistinguished from *monogamy*, I do not suppose; because the same number of women married each to a different man, is as likely to produce as *many* children as if married all to *one* man, perhaps *more*: but the scandal of *celibacy*, the esteeming *marriage* as a *sacred duty*, and a number of children *a blessing from the* Lord (see Ps. cxxvii. 5. and Ps. cxxviii. throughout) occasioned their eagerness after the marriage-state: add to this, the promise † of the *Messiah*, of whom each woman was led to hope she might be the happy mother. This accounts for the behaviour of certain women, whose desires after children seem very extraordinary. See Gen. xxx. 1, 15, 16. Judges xi. 37, 38. 1 Sam. i. 11. *Barrenness* was a *reproach*, probably from the same cause, and therefore the removal of it was looked upon as a special blessing. Gen. xxx. 23. 1 Sam. i. 27. and ii. 1, 5. The authors of the Antient Univ. Hist. vol. iii. p. 139, observe, that—" though the *Mosaic* law doth no
" where oblige men to marry, yet the *Jews*
" have always looked upon it as an indispensi-
" ble duty, implied in the words—*Be fruitful*
" *and multiply*, Gen. i. 28. ix. 1. So that a
" man who did not marry before he was

---

† This incentive to marriage, it is allowed, cannot now subsist among us. But still it must be true, that all incentives to marriage, be they what they may, must tend to encrease the number of *married women*, and of course *population*. For this reason *polygamy* must contribute to *population*, as increasing the number of *married* women. See before vol. i. p. 98, n.

" *twenty*

"*twenty* years of age, was counted acceſſary to any irregularity which the young women might be tempted to for want of being timely married. They had a proverb in the *Talmud—Who is he that proſtitutes his daughter, but he who keeps her too long unmarried, or gives her to an old man?* For this reaſon they uſed to marry them as ſoon as they came of age, which, with them, was at * *twelve.*" The populouſneſs of the *Jewiſh* nation, therefore, moſt evidently aroſe from the *univerſality of marriage*, whether *monogamous* or *polygamous:* ſo that there was not to be found, as among us, thouſands of young marriageable women devoted to *barrenneſs* for want of *husbands,* or conſigned to infertility by the miſchiefs of *proſtitution.*

As long as we hold it good *philoſophy* to ſay, that " the ſame cauſe will produce the ſame effects"—ſo long will it be true, that the reaſon of the populouſneſs of the *Jewiſh* nation was owing to the wiſdom of their laws which concerned the *commerce of the ſexes,*

---

* However matters ſtood before with us, it is very clear, that, ſince the *marriage-act*, the parties are neither of them *ſui juris*, as to the diſpoſal of themſelves in marriage, till the age of 21 years; which, with regard to young men particularly, is often attended with bad conſequences, ſuch as laying them under temptations to *acts,* and ſo to *habits* of profligacy, which in ſome end in ruin, in others in a ſettled and fixed diſlike to the ſober duties of a married life; and thus many young men of *rank* and *fortune* never marry at all. It is, I am afraid, too true, that this is daily increaſing among us.

and that our *want of people* is owing to our discarding the system of government which the *Jews* lived under in these respects, and establishing another in its place, big with every inconvenience, which that was so exactly calculated to prevent.

We are so overwhelmed with *luxury*, so sunk in *dissipation*, that the expence of a family is looked upon, as it certainly is, under such circumstances, an intolerable burden. The bringing up and maintenance of children is dreaded even by the opulent, because the enormous expence they are at upon their pleasures, reduces them to a level with the poorer sort. This is no uncommon reason for celibacy. Among the *Jews*, the frugality and industry of individuals left no room for such an excuse. Their very *women* contributed to provide for the * children which they

---

* Which children, as soon as able, contributed to the riches of the family by their labour, and in this sense they were a *blessing* instead of a *burden*. See Ant. Univ. Hist. vol. iii. p. 186. note B. The *Jews* permitted no *drones* in their *hive*. Their maxim was—" *he that will not work, let him not eat*"— Comp. Prov. xix. 15. and 2 Thess. iii. 10.—whereas with us, an increase of children is too often an increase of idleness and extravagance. Witness the crowds of, what we call, the *higher sort of people*, who fill our numerous places of public diversion, *gaming-houses*, &c. the *bankruptcies* among our *tradesmen*, and the shoals of *thieves*, *vagrants*, beggars, &c. among the lower orders of men.

It is a remarkable thing, that among other ingredients of ruin to the apostate *Jews—idleness—abundance of idleness*, was *one*. Ezek. xvi. 49. We do not find that God changed His law, because they had departed from

they brought, and ate not the *bread of idleness*. See a beautiful account of this, *Prov.* xxxi. 10, &c. Whereas, among us, it is no very uncommon thing to hear a person say—" I won't *marry*, because I can't afford it." Every man may *afford to marry*, who is sober and industrious, but certainly none can who are idle and profligate.

The *Jewish* law also, by its severity against *adultery*, inflicting certain death on the *adulterer* and *adulteress*, so checked the evil, that married men had little to fear on that account; whereas, among us, our laws having inflicted no punishment on *adulterers* as *public offenders*, leave the punishment of it to what *Judge Blackstone* well calls, " the fee-" ble coercion of the ecclesiastical courts," which is about as well calculated to restrain it, as the strength of a *pigmy* would be to repel the force of a *giant*; and even this, such as it is, is within the reach * of money to buy off. See 1 *Burn, Eccl. Law*, quarto, p. 663. Hence it is, that this *giant-vice*, with such large strides, marches through our

their observance of it; but maintained its holiness and unchangeableness, in the fearful punishments He sent upon them for their dissoluteness and disobedience.

* About the year 1735, the *Bishop of Chester* actually cited his *commissary* into the *Archbishop*'s court at *York*, to exhibit an account of the money received for commutations. *Oughton* says, that " commutation-money is to " be given to the poor, or applied to other pious uses, " at the discretion *of the Judge*." See Burn. Eccl. Law, tit. *Penance*. Also post, Append. to this Chapter.

land,

land, and may probably be the means of terrifying not a few from marrying.

Having elsewhere observed the wisdom of the divine laws for the prevention and punishment of *whoredom*, I will here say once more, that our banishment of them from our system of government, is another reason of the alarming frequency of *celibacy* among us.

As for *polygamy*, it certainly was *allowed*, as much as marriage † itself was; to say the contrary, is to deny the whole testimony of the *Hebrew* scripture:—but this was not that wild, licentious, wicked practice of it, which is now maintained at the expence, not

---

† For which plain and evident reason, it may be concluded, that the several attacks on *marriage*, which the *Christians* have made from time to time, under notions of greater *purity* and *holiness*, are wholly *unjustifiable*, because *unwarranted* by the scriptures. GOD forbad marriage under certain circumstances, but in no one precept or example did he prohibit *polygamy*, where marriage itself was allowed. Wherefore, I own, I cannot in the least doubt, that the stat. of 1 Jac. chap. 11. which forbids *polygamy* under pain *of death*, is just as opposite to the divine law, as the stat. of Hen. VIII. which hangs a *priest* for marrying *one wife*, as well as the man who should assert it lawful in the sight of GOD, for a *priest* to *marry at all*. There *was* a time when it would have given great offence to have found fault with this law of Hen. VIII. just as much as to arraign the propriety of that of 1 *Jac.* may give *now*;—but this proves no more than that both are equally absurd—that superstition is always the same—and that men are apt to take their ideas of religious truths, more from custom, and vulgar opinion, than from the word of GOD.

S 4 only

only of decency, but even of humanity itself, among the *Mahometans*; but a holy and sober use of marriage, circumscribed by holy laws and institutions, in *all* cases permitted, in some *commanded*. And what was the consequence to the state? A numerous issue, which contributed to its riches and strength —the demand for women in marriage increased, and few were left either to be a burden or a disgrace to it. But is this so with us? Our making *polygamy felony* has destroyed * it. — But in what respect are we gainers * by this?—Why, we have gained —what

* * That is, we have abolished the public and open marriage of *more* women than *one at a time*—and thus have we shut *one door*, against the private inexpediency and inconvenience to individuals, which, as things are constituted among us, might accrue in many instances.

But, on the other hand, what has the public gained? for *marriage* is not to be considered as only concerning *this* or *that* individual, or *this* or *that* private convenience or inconvenience, but as respecting the *public*—the *whole* in general. And this, no doubt, the ALL-WISE CREATOR had in view, when—*He blessed them, and said, Be fruitful and multiply, and replenish the earth*—Gen. i. 28, with Gen. ix. 1, 7.—as well as when he framed HIS LAWS for regulating the *commerce of the sexes*.

Baron *Montesquieu* observes, and very truly, that " *public incontinence* may be regarded as the greatest of " misfortunes."—Now, considering mankind, not as what *they ought to be*, but as what they really *are*—what a *door* to *public incontinence* is opened, by making it impossible for *married men*, who *seduce virgins*, to be under that *responsibility* towards them which the *divine law* enjoins—Exod. xxii. 16. and Deut. xxii. 28, 29?—by this means *thousands* are turned out friendless and helpless, to public *infamy*, *prostitution*, and *ruin*.

Another

—what *Israel* never saw, till they regarded the divine law as little as we do—thousands of women for the purposes of *prostitution* and destruction, by making it impossible for their seducers to do them that justice, which *reason*, *nature*, and the *divine law*, intitle them to demand. This may be reckoned also among the causes of our want of people; for I believe it would not be very hard to prove,

Another *door* is opened to that most horrid *practice* (it is so common as to be a practice) of *child-murder*, either by procuring *abortion*, or by *destroying infants* in or after the birth—for concealment, in such cases, has more, much more to plead, than where single men are concerned.

These, and other dreadful appendages of making ourselves more *wise*, *pure*, and *holy*, than the GOD who *knoweth whereof we are made*, are the consequences of an indiscriminate and total prohibition of *polygamy*—so that, whatever we may have gained in point of casual, private, or domestic *convenience* in *one* respect, we are losers in point of public, as well as private mischiefs, in *ten thousand!*

If we advert to the scripture, we shall not find a single instance of these things among the antient *Jews*—their law was so framed as to prevent them.—If we attend to the daily evidence of our own eyes and ears, they are frequently happening among us, because *our laws* are so framed as to be the *occasions* of them—and perhaps no one part of our *system* is chargeable with more of them, than our *sanguinary* prohibition of *polygamy*. 1 Jac. c. 11.

To lay a foundation for all this mischief, by charging HIM, who came *not to destroy men's lives, but to save them*, with repealing the *divine law* which was made to prevent it, is an *impious* and *infamous* slander, and its wearing the guise of *purity* and *piety* makes it so much the *worse*.

that almost every woman, who is driven into *common* prostitution, is a loss of one *breeding-woman* to the public. *Physical* reasons may be given for this, which I do not chuse to discuss, but which the learned uniformly agree in, and which experience demonstrates to be generally true.

I would therefore conclude upon the whole —that all restraints and impediments with regard to marriage, are equally inimical to *nature, reason,* and *scripture*—to sound policy and good government, as well as to that which is the strength, riches, and safety of all governments—an INCREASE of the PEOPLE. —These are *like arrows in the hand of a mighty man.*—Happy we, had we *our quiver full of them! we should not be ashamed to speak with our enemies in the gate.* Ps. cxxvii. 4, 5.

As a proper conclusion of this *chapter*, let the following *contrast*, between the *divine system* and our *system* of *human invention*, stand before us—let it bear its own testimony, as to the *advantages* and *disadvantages* of the *change* which has taken place, and as it may serve to introduce a *parallel* between us and the *Jews*, when they left the plain and simple road of *duty* which their *law prescribed*, and followed their *own imaginations* and *inventions*.

CONTRAST.

CONTRAST.

Divine System.	Our Human System.
Male and female created he them. Gen. i. 27.	
And God *bleſſed them—and* God *ſaid unto them—Be fruitful and multiply, and repleniſh the earth.* ver. 28. ch. ix. 1, 7.	To ſay nothing of the *Popiſh* ſchemes of *celibacy*, which have been ſet up againſt the command of God—let us look nearer home, and conſider the numbers of *un-married* people among us—one reaſon of which is, the *facility* of *ſeduction*, and *dereliction*, as well as the *difficulties* laid in the way of *marriage*—for all *marriages* had and ſolemnized contrary to 26 Geo. II. c. 33. ſhall be "utterly void, "to all intents and "purpoſes whatſoe-"ver."
And the rib which the Lord God *had taken from man, made He a woman, and brought her unto the man.*	
And Adam ſaid—This is now bone of my bone, and fleſh of my fleſh, ſhe ſhall be called woman becauſe ſhe was taken out of man.	
Therefore ſhall a man leave his father and mother, and ſhall cleave דבק—*be joined unto his wife—and they ſhall*	And no ſuit ſhall be had in any *eccleſiaſtical court*, to compel the celebration of any marriage, by reaſon

shall be one flesh. Gen. ii. 22—24.

If a man entice a maid that is not betrothed, and lie with her—*he shall surely endow her to be his wife.* Exod. xxii. 10.

If a man find a damsel that is a virgin, which is not betrothed, and lay hold on her and lie with her, and they be found—SHE SHALL BE HIS WIFE, BECAUSE HE HATH HUMBLED HER, HE MAY NOT PUT HER AWAY ALL HIS DAYS. Deut. xxii. 28, 29.

He that is joined to a woman (κολλωμενος) *is one body* — for *two,* saith GOD (i. e. who are thus joined) *shall be one flesh*—Gen. ii. 24. 1 Cor. vi. 16.

son of *any contract whatsoever,* any law or usage to the contrary notwithstanding.

Therefore—

If a man entice a maid, &c. he *shall not* SURELY *endow her to be his wife.*

Or if *he find a damsel that is a virgin, which is not betrothed,* &c. she shall *not* be his wife, unless he chuses it—though he has humbled her, he *may* put her away *as* and *when* he pleases.

Nothing shall make her his wife but marriage - ceremony administered by a *priest,* by *banns* first published, or by *licence* first had and obtained in some *parish church* or *chapel,* &c. or if elsewhere,

If

[269]

If a man have two wives, he shall not make the son of the beloved first-born, before the son of the hated, which is indeed the first-born.

But he shall acknowledge the son of the hated for the first-born, by giving him a double portion, &c. Deut. xxi. 15—17.

If a man be found lying with a woman married to an husband, then they shall both of them die. Deut. xxii. 22.

So if with a *betrothed virgin*, &c. ver. 23, 24.

In *Israel*, while these laws were observed, we read of no *adulteries* for many centuries together.

elsewhere, by *special licence* from the *Archbishop of Canterbury*.

If a man, having a wife, marry another, living the first, he shall be deemed a *felon*, and *suffer death* as such. The *second* marriage be utterly void, and the issue *bastards* and uninheritable.

If a man lie with other people's *wives*, he is no object of *criminal* judicature.

If a man lie with a *betrothed virgin*, he is not even liable to an action for damages, she to no penalty whatsoever on account of her situation.

Among us, the abolition of the *divine system* has been attended with daily *adulteries*, which have increased

No

No street-walkers, whores, and common prostitutes—no medicines taken to procure *abortion* — no *child-murder*—no *venereal* disease*, infecting increased the more, as mankind have felt the privilege of *impunity*.

Our streets are filled with *prostitutes*, our *brothels* also with *harlots*; *abortion* is sought after, *child-murder* is frequent; the *venereal disease* rages like a plague,

---

* This horrible disease is supposed to have made its first appearance in *Europe* in the year 1493; but some have thought it of much older date, even in this country, from a constitution of the stews, antiently kept at the *Bank-side, Southwark*, under the jurisdiction of the *Bishop of Winchester*, dated 1162, where it is supposed to be called *burning* or *brenning*. It is also supposed to be mentioned in a manuscript of *John Arden*, surgeon to *Rich*. II. and *Hen*. IV. Many have contended for its being known among the *antients*, only under different names. Some have gone so high as the days of *Job*, and suppose it to be the ulcerous distemper with which that great man was afflicted; insomuch, that in a *Missal* printed at *Venice*, anno 1542, there is a *mass* in honour of St. Job, to be said by those recovered of this disease (See *Chambers*, tit. *Venereal Disease*) as owing their deliverance to his intercession. Others contend that *David* was afflicted with it, as a punishment for his sinful commerce with the wife of *Uriah*, and this he complains of Pf. xxxviii. 3—8. But, omitting *fable* and *conjecture*, it is certain, whether we interpret that passage *literally* with some, or *allegorically* with others, it contains something like a description of *this disease*, as to many of its *symptoms*.

However this may be, one thing may, I believe, be asserted as a fact, established by long experience, that this *disease* has never been known to exist, but from a *promiscuous* intercourse of the sexes.—This will produce something very like it even in *brutes*—therefore I can

ing and destroying	plague, to the de‑
the people.	struction of thou‑
	sands.
Their *population* was	Our *depopulation* is
almost incredible.	alarming.

PARAL-

see no reason against dating its origin as early as common *whoredom* itself, as the same cause may very fairly be presumed to produce the same effects, though not perhaps in equal degree, nor at all times and places alike.

If we understand the word מבישה—*she that maketh ashamed*, or is an *instrument of shame* (Prov. xii. 4.) to denote an *harlot* or *common prostitute*—for of such it may be a very apt and descriptive *periphrasis*, and especially as the root בש signifies *to be ashamed through a sense of guilt* (see *Parkh.* sub voc.) and in this sense an *harlot* is מבישה—an *instrument of shame* to those who are *joined to her* (see 1 Cor. vi. 15, 16, 18.)—therefore I say, if we understand this passage of *an harlot* or common *prostitute*, how many men can at this moment bear testimony to the truth of what is here said!—whose bitter experience must lead them to subscribe to the words of Pf. xxxviii. 3. *who have no rest in their bones by reason of their sin*—who have to mourn that those *bones* are *rottenness* itself—and, as *Virgil* expresses himself on another subject—

Truncas inhonesto vulnere nares.

But whether the scriptures above-mentioned, or any other parts of *holy writ*, do, or do not, allude to the symptoms of the *disease* in question, or whether it was or was not known in *Europe* till the year 1493 (a very able and learned discussion of both which points may be found in *Astruc*, de Morb. Ven. lib. i. chap. 1—10.) surely a restoration of that *law* is to be wished for, which is contrived by infinite *wisdom*—*Concubitu prohibere vago*—thus to prevent *prostitution*, and, of course, every dreadful consequence of it to mankind.

" The shameful, loathsome, and often fatal disease" (says the late excellent *Dr. Hartley*, Obs. on Man, p. 229.)

PARALLEL.

When the *Jews* forsook the law which GOD set before them, *obeyed not His voice, nor walked therein, but walked after the imagination of their own heart.* Jer. ix. 13, 14.

Then they fell into all manner of *spiritual* and *fleshly* abominations.

They then *committed adultery, and assembled themselves by troops in the harlots houses.*

They were as fed horses in the morning, every one neighed after his

We see, in this *Christian* country, the *same* cause producing the *same* effects.

As the DIVINE LAW is laid aside for a *system* of *human imagination* —all manner of *lewdness* overspreads the land, under the various forms of *adultery* and *whoredom*—and no doubt helps to fill the measure of our *national* iniquity.

Surely this is a time for our deepest and most serious recollection, when GOD seems to be visiting our *iniquities* upon us, not

p. 229.) " which peculiarly attends the vice of lewd-
" ness, may be considered as a most unquestionable
" evidence of the *divine* will. This disease, with all
" its consequences, would cease among mankind, could
" they be brought under the restraints of *marriage*,
" but must ever continue while licentiousness conti-
" nues."

To this I will venture to add, that, *licentiousness* ever must *continue*, and even increase, while the *divine laws*, which are made to prevent and restrain it, are laid aside.

his neighbour's wife. Jer. v. 7, 8. Jer. xxiii. 10, 14. & al. freq. See Ezek. xxii. 9, 10, 11. Hosea iv. 14.

Shall I not visit for these things, saith the LORD, *shall not my soul be avenged of such a nation as this?* Jer. v. 9.

not the *least* of which, is forsaking the LAW which He hath set before us, with respect to the *commerce of the sexes,* and following a *system* which, in the nature of things, must lead us into the very state in which the *Jews* were, when the *prophets* were sent to call them to *repentance,* or to foretell their *destruction.*

APPENDIX to CHAP. X.

See p. 262, Note.

IT may not be amiss to lay before the reader the doctrine of *penance* and *commutation* as to their original, and then it will be seen how disgraceful such notions are to an enlightened Protestant church. *Theodore* of *Tarsus,* a Grecian monk, restored among the *Latins* the discipline of *penance,* as it is commonly termed, which had been for a long time

time almoſt totally neglected, and enforced it by a body of ſevere laws borrowed from the *Grecian* canons. This zealous prelate, who was raiſed to the *ſee of Canterbury*, A. D. 668, reduced to a regular ſcience that branch of eccleſiaſtical law, which is known by the name of *penitential diſcipline*. He publiſhed a *Penitential*, which was entirely new to the Latin world, by which the *clergy* were taught to diſtinguiſh *ſins* into *various claſſes*, according as they were more or leſs heinous, private or public. This new *Penitential* alſo contained the methods of proceeding with reſpect to offenders, and pointed out the various *penalties* that were ſuitable to the different claſſes of tranſgreſſions. This new diſcipline, though of *Grecian* origin, was eagerly adopted by the *Latin* churches. Its duration however was but tranſitory, for in the *eighth* century it began to decline, and was at length entirely ſupplanted by, what was called, the new *canon of indulgences*, in which the *biſhops* and *clergy* began to *trade* in the *twelfth century*, when the univerſal reign of ignorance and ſuperſtition was dexterouſly, but baſely, improved to fill their coffers, and to drain the purſes of the deluded multitude. All the various ranks and orders of the *clergy* had each their peculiar method of fleecing the people.

The *biſhops*, when they wanted money for their private pleaſures, or for the exigencies of the church, granted to their flock the power of purchaſing the *remiſſion* of the *penalties*

nalties imposed upon transgressors, by a *sum of money*; which was to be applied to certain religious purposes; or, in other words, they published *indulgences:* which became an inexhaustible source of wealth to the *Episcopal* orders, and enabled them, as is well known, to form and execute the most difficult schemes for the enlargement of their authority, and of the external pomp and splendor of the church.

When the *Roman Pontiffs* cast an eye on the immense treasures, which the sale of these *indulgences* brought in to the *inferior rulers* of the church, they limited the power of *bishops* in *remitting the penalties imposed on transgressors*, and assumed, almost entirely, this profitable traffic to themselves. In consequence of which, *Rome* became the general magazine of *indulgences*; and the *Pontiffs* in order to supply their coffers, published, not only an universal, but also a complete, or, what they called a *plenary* remission of all the *temporal* pains and penalties which the church had annexed to certain transgressions.

Afterwards they proceeded farther, and not only remitted penalties which the civil and ecclesiastical laws had enacted against transgressors, but audaciously usurped the *divine prerogative*, and impiously pretended to abolish even the punishments of the next world; a step this, which the *bishops*, with all their pride and presumption, had never once ventured to take.

Such proceedings stood in need of a plau-

sible defence, but this was impossible. To justify, therefore, these scandalous measures of the *Pontiffs*, a most monstrous and absurd doctrine was invented—" that there actually
"exifted an immense treasure of *merit*, com-
"posed of the pious deeds and virtuous ac-
"tions which the *Saints* had performed *be-*
"*yond what was necessary for their own sal-*
"*vation*, and which were therefore appli-
"cable to the benefit of *others*—that the
"guardian and disposer of this *precious trea-*
"*sure* was the *Pope*, and therefore he was
"empowered to *assign* to such as he thought
"proper, a portion of this inexhaustible
"source of *merit*, suitable to their respective
"*guilt*, and sufficient to deliver them from
"the punishment * due to their crimes."
This horrible superstition is retained and defended in the church of *Rome* to this day! it was happily banished from *England* at the *reformation*; pity but the former sort of indulgences had followed it out of our *church!* but they are still retained, under the more *plausible*, but more *explicit* term of *commutation*, which signifies *changing one thing for another*, as the punishment of *sin* for *money*. Though therefore *indulgences* and *commuta-*

---

* *Bellarmine* says of these indulgences, that they extend as well to the high *forum*, or tribunal of our *Saviour* CHRIST, as to the internal *forum*, or court of holy *church*; that they even profit the *dead*, and avail them by way of satisfaction or application. See Abs. of Hist. of Popery, vol. i. p. 173. quarto, 1735. and *Bellarm.* de Indulg. Lib. i. c. v. p. 28, 31.

tions

tions differ in *name*, they entirely agree in their *nature*. Their being given, or pretended to be given, to *pious uses*, no more salves the offence of taking * such money, than a *certain lady's* giving, or pretending to give, her *winnings* to the *poor*, atoned for her playing at *cards* on a *Sunday*.

Whatsoever these things may be called, they are certainly *judicial absolutions*, and such as never were heard of in the *Christian* church till *Popery* introduced them. See *Mosheim*, vol. i. 327, 595. edit. *Maclaine*.

That there were censures on offenders against religion and good manners in the *apostolical times*—such as *private admonition*, 2 Thess. iii. 15.—*public rebuke*, and even of a *sharp kind*, Tit. i. 13.—*rejection* for obstinate heresy, Tit. iii. 10.—and even *excommunication* itself for grievous and scandalous offences, (1 Cor. v. 1—5.) is most evident; but I should imagine, that if a sum of money had been offered to buy off the censures

---

* To make laws for the punishment of offences, and then to waive or suspend their execution, for a sum of money paid by the offender, and especially where such laws are made on no better principle than with a view to such extortion—which I take to have been chiefly the case with respect to the laws of *penance*—may bring to one's mind *Virgil's* account of one of the tormented in *Tartarus*; concerning whom he saith—Æn. vi. l. 622.

―――― *Hic fixit leges pretio atque refixit.*

He made, and unmade, laws for gold.

Which sufficiently shews even an heathen's sentiments of such a practice.

of the church, the *offerer* would have been anfwered as *Simon Magus* was—*Thy money perifh with thee*, &c. Acts viii. 20.

See 13 Edw. I. ftat. 4. commonly called the ftatute of *Circumfpecte agatis*; and 9 Edw. II. ftat. 1. c. 2. and c. 3.

See alfo before, vol. i. p. 64, n. and *Burn*. tit. *Penance*.

CHAP. XI.

CONCLUSION.

HAVING thus far finifhed what I had to fay on the foregoing fubjects—which are not of an indifferent or trivial nature, but of the utmoft importance for every body's confideration—it may be proper, by way of *conclufion*, to recapitulate, and to *commend* what has been faid *to every man's confcience in the fight of* GOD. 2 *Cor*. iv. 2.

While our laws are what they are, and fuffer men to take *virgins* into their poffeffion, and then put them away, not all the devices of *human wifdom*, nor the moft ftrenuous efforts of the moft difinterefted and beft-contrived plans of *reformation*, can have
any

any greater effect on the mischiefs which they would remedy, than a few buckets of water taken out of a *river* would have upon the *stream*. The *water* would soon *unite* again, and flow on with the same apparent *fulness*. So, though a few *prostitutes* may be taken from among the countless *herd*, and some of them so reformed as not to mix with it again, yet no apparent diminution meets the eye, no lessening of their numbers strikes the observation. The *brothels were* full—they *are* full—the streets *were* infested with *prostitutes*,—they *are* still infested with them as much as ever—there is no more difference as to *numbers*, than there is in an *army*, from whence an *hundred* soldiers are discharged, and an hundred fresh recruits are listed in their room. The man who thinks it can ever be otherwise, as *our laws* with respect to *marriage* now stand, may go with *Horace*'s rustic to the brink of a *river*, and expect that it will run itself dry.

———*At ille*
Labitur & labetur in omne volubilis ævum.
It still flows on, and will for ever flow.
FRANCIS.

If an expedient could be found to dry up its *source*, and thus stop it at the *fountainhead*, the *streams* must cease, and the *bed* of the river become *dry ground*. So if a law be devised which can prevent *seduction* and *dereliction*, and thus stop *prostitution* at its remotest

test apparent causes, the thing itself must cease.

This has not been left for the invention of man, he never could have been equal to the task.—The ALL-WISE GOD Himself, who could alone be possessed of *wisdom* and *authority* sufficient for this, hath done it. His law delivered to *Adam at the beginning*, and afterwards in more explicit terms to *Moses* at *Mount Sinai*, stands as a record of the *divine mind and will*, and, if duly observed by mortals, is adequate to the prevention or remedy of all the *moral evils under the sun*, among the rest, the dreadful and destructive evil of *prostitution*.

This law has been disregarded, a *system* very different from it has been set up in its place. This *system*, being of human contrivance, must of course oppose itself to the law of GOD—for *His ways are not our ways, nor His thoughts our thoughts.* Is. lv. 8. In short, that which GOD hath *bound*, man hath *loosed*. The *obligation* which is created by GOD's own *fiat*, must now give place to the inventions of men, which declare GOD's *ordinance* of *marriage null and void*, unless ratified by * man's authority. What are the *righteous* consequences of all this? Misery, ruin, desolation.—Let men but keep clear

* " As if the links of that eternal chain, whose be-
" ginning is in the breast of the FIRST CAUSE of all
" things, could ever be disunited by the institutions of
" men !" Essay on Crimes and Punishments, ch. xvi.

of the *human ceremony*, and they may bid defiance to the *divine inſtitution*. The lewd, the deſigning, the mercileſs and cruel, are turned looſe upon the *female* world, to make what ravages they can. *Seduction* precedes, *violation* follows, *dereliction* comes next, and *proſtitution* cloſes the monſtrous iniquity! Shame and diſgrace attend the *divine inſtitution*, honour and reverence await the *human ordinance!* Thus MAN IS EXALTED—GOD DESPISED! This is attended with the moſt fatal conſequences to thouſands, whoſe *protection* is provided for and ſecured by the laws of GOD, and whoſe *ruin* is invited and inſured by the neglect of them.

What an alteration would it make in the regions of *profligacy*, was the whole entire law of GOD to be obſerved? If no man, let his *ſituation* be what it might, *could entice a virgin*, &c. and not *ſurely endow her to be his wife*? This in every caſe whatever? What a ſecurity would this be to the *lower* order of *females*, on which the licentiouſneſs of the *higher* order of *men* uſually falls the heavieſt? It is hardly to be imagined that men of *family* and *fortune* would pay their *addreſſes*, or rather lay their *ſnares*, where the accompliſhment of their deſires muſt be attended with an *union*, unſuitable in all reſpects to their rank in life. This would force them early to match themſelves with their equals; they would not gratify their luſt at the expence of their pride, and we ſhould not ſee ſo many victims of luſt, treachery, and cruelty,

elty, filling the *brothels*, and walking our *streets*, till difeafe conveys them to an *hofpital*, and from thence to the grave: cut off and loft to the public in the bloom of youth; when, had the *protection* which the *law of* GOD hath ordained for them, been afforded them by their *feducers*, they might have been happy in themfelves, and bleffings to fociety.

Nor does the rejection of GOD's *law*, by the fubftitution of man's *inventions*, confine its mifchief even within the dreadful bounds above-mentioned, it extends itfelf even to *murder*, and that of the moft foul and unnatural kind, that of *infants* by the hands of the *mothers who bare them*. As fomething elfe than GOD's ordinance is required to make parties *one flefh*, perfons who are actually married in GOD's account, are under no *legal* obligation to each other. The *unhappy mother* of what is called a *baftard-child*—though as really *married* to the *father* of it as *Rebekah* was to *Ifaac*, or *Leah* and *Rachel* to *Jacob*—is placed in fuch a light by the *fuperftition* of the world, as to make her prefer an act of barbarity, which her own *bowels muft yearn at*, to the treatment which it is the cuftom * of the world to beftow upon her.

* " The murder of baftard children is the effect of a
" cruel dilemma, in which a woman finds herfelf, who
" has been feduced through weaknefs, or overcome by
" force. The alternative is, either her own infamy,
" or the death of a being who is incapable of feeling
" the lofs of life. How can fhe avoid preferring the
" laft

her. *Fear* unsheaths the fatal instrument of *death*, and *shame* plunges it into the vitals of the *helpless innocent*. The wretched *mother* (for concealment seldom covers the offence of *murder*) is apprehended, and by the hand of justice consigned to the pain and ignominy of a public death.

The father of the child looks upon himself as *free*; no outward ceremony had passed, and the tragical end of his *gallantry* deters him not from endangering a like scene of horror, with respect to the next woman he can *seduce*.

God's law arrests the man on his first intercourse with the woman, and pronounces them *one flesh*, so that he cannot forsake, or *put her away all his days*. Were this observed, and that deemed a *marriage*, which God hath made so, the woman could be under no *temptation* to *such* an act, or to any * other, than that,

---

"last to the inevitable misery of herself and her unhappy infant? The best way of preventing this crime would be effectually to protect the weak woman from that tyranny, which exaggerates all vices that cannot be concealed under the cloak of virtue.

"I do not pretend to lessen that just abhorrence, which these crimes deserve, but to discover the sources from whence they spring; and I think I may draw the following conclusion—That *the punishment of a crime cannot be just, that is,* necessary, *if the laws have not endeavoured to prevent that crime by the best means which times and circumstances would allow.*" Beccaria, Crimes and Punishments, chap. 31.

* Here I mean to include the frequent, though horrible, and, to many, fatal practice of taking medicines to cause *abortion*. That this, in a *moral* sense, is a
species

that, which the law would put in *her power*, that is to say, making the man do her the *justice* which it is now so amply in *his power* to *refuse*. From what has been said, let the *reader* revolve in his mind every species of injury and *female* ruin, which he ever heard of, red of, has seen, or can conceive, and he will find that it has all originated from the abolition of the *divine laws*, which so

species of *murder*, there can be no doubt, which was severely punished by the divine law. See Exod. xxi. 22, 23. There indeed the case is put of injury arising from only accidental violence to the woman; yet, even there, if it occasioned the *death* either of the mother or *the child*, if *quick*, it was a capital offence. *Life* was to go for *life*. The word אסון—which we translate *mischief*, comes from the root סן—which signifies to *pour out as water*; and as a noun, אסון—*effusion, diffusion, dissipation, dissolution.* —*Ar. Mont.* renders it by *Mors—death*. Comp. 2 Sam. xiv. 14. In the translation of the LXX, or rather their paraphrase on this place of *Exodus*, they distinguish between the παιδίον μὴ ἐξεικονισμένον, *the child not formed*, and ἐξεικονισμένον—*formed*, or, as we may say, between the *embryo*, which is *inanimate*, and the *fœtus*, which, being full formed and *animated*, may be said to be capable of *losing life*.

The frequent *abortions* which are procured by medicines, no doubt fall within the reason of this law.

But when we take into the account, the numbers of *women*, who, by the use of medicines to cause abortion, have destroyed *themselves*, as well as the *children* within them, and thus have died, under the *double guilt* of SUICIDE and CHILD-MURDER, it ought to fill us with horror, to think that a *system*, which, in the very nature of it, must afford numberless *temptations* to this, and be productive of frequent *instances* of it, should be the *system* of a people who profess a belief of DIVINE REVELATION, wherein the causes of such mischiefs are provided against by the *wisdom* and *goodness* of the CREATOR HIMSELF.

amply

amply provide for the security of women, and from the introduction of those human inventions, which have turned *marriage* into a mere *civil contract*, for in no * other view does our *municipal law regard it*, thus *vacating* obligations which GOD hath made, and *laying* obligations which GOD hath not made.

As for appointing certain outward acts, rites, or ceremonies, for the public recognition of the *marriage* as to *civil purposes*, these are in the breast of the state to ordain or alter, as may seem most expedient; but as to *marriage* itself, it neither being ordained *of* men nor *by* men, but *of* and *by* the GOD *of Heaven*, no power on earth can change or alter it. It is no more within the jurisdiction of man, or the power of mortals, to do this in a *moral* sense, than it is, in a *natural* sense, to change the rising of the sun, or stop the flowing of the tide. For the same reason that a child is completely and perfectly baptized, without the *sign of the cross*, or without *godfathers* and *godmothers*, a man and woman, whose *persons* are *united*, are completely and perfectly *married in the sight of* GOD, without any human ceremony whatsoever; that is to say, because this is no part of GOD's *ordinance* of marriage, therefore cannot be *essential* to the perfection of it as *in his sight*.

It is therefore truth, even the *truth* of GOD, that no man can receive the person of a

* See before vol. i. p. 65.

virgin

virgin into an *union* with his own (suppofing her not betrothed to another man) without her becoming *his* אשה—*woman* or *wife*—*fa femme*—from that moment. This law is as *general* as it is *abfolute*; though exceptions of *betrothing* or efpoufals are made on the *part of the woman*, no fuch thing appears on the *part of the man*: therefore, whatever his *fituation* may be, it makes no difference—having *taken* the woman and HUMBLED HER, *he may not put her away all his days.*

That this law * involves *polygamy*, fo as even to *command* it, and therefore to make it a *duty*, where the man is *married* who takes the *virgin*, is evident from the very *terms* in which the *law* is conceived: *If a man*—muft mean † *any* man—*every* man who does fo. The liberty which *commentators* have taken with this text, in order to accommodate it to their own prejudices, is an inftance of that fort of conftruction which the *Papifts* make ufe of in the underftanding of τίμιος ὁ γάμος ἐν πᾶσι—Heb. xiii. 4.—*Marriage is honourable in all:* that is, fay they, in *all things*, not *in all men*; for the *Rhemifts* fay, on 1 Cor. vii. 9. that " the marriage of *priefts* is the worft " fort of *incontinency*, and fornication, or " burning." Thus we fpeak of *polygamy*,

---

* Deut. xxii. 28, 29.

† As in ver. 22. IF A MAN *be found lying with a woman married to an hufband*—here כי איש—*if a man*—muft be underftood without limitation or reftraint, as to the fituation of the *adulterer*—fo doubtlefs of the feducer at ver. 28.

with

with juſt as much ground from God's word. We can condemn the *liberty* which the *Papiſts* take with one part of the ſcripture, little adverting to *that* which * *we* have learned from *them* to take with *others*.

Had *polygamy* been permitted on the ſide of the *woman*, the moſt material part of the ſacred hiſtory muſt have loſt its evidence: as no *genealogy* could have been preſerved with the leaſt certainty, it could not have been proved beyond a doubt that Christ is the *Meſſiah*, of the ſeed of *Abraham*, and of the *houſe and family* of *David*, to whom the promiſes were made; conſequently, that He is the *prophet which was to come, and we are to look for no other*. Matt. xxii. 42. and we muſt have been aſking, in another ſenſe than our Lord himſelf did—*What think ye of* Christ, *whoſe Son is He?* This fatal ſtroke to all our hopes muſt have been the conſequence of a precarious iſſue. In a more private view of the matter, all modeſty, decency, order, inheritance, relationſhip, and every bond of ſociety, muſt have been broken aſunder; whereas, on the *man's ſide*, polygamy

---

* N. B. I could wiſh that ſome of my learned and ingenious readers would favour me with a poetical tranſlation of the following elegant *apologue* of Phædrus.

Peræ Duæ.

Peras impoſuit *Jupiter* nobis duas:
Propriis repletam vitiis poſt tergum dedit;
Alienis ante pectus fuſpendit gravem.
   Hac re videre *noſtra* mala non poſſumus:
Alii ſimul delinquunt, *cenſores* ſumus.

is not attended with any of these things: what the wickedness and vileness of men have introduced, must be looked upon as *abuse* and *perversion*, but are no more * arguments

---

* To argue against any thing from the abuse of it, is the most unfair of all methods of refutation. There are no absurdities, and indeed no lengths of *impiety* and *blasphemy*, into which, by such means, we may not be carried.

We may even dispute the *wisdom* and *holiness* of the CREATOR in making the human species of different sexes—in ordaining the means of *increasing and multiplying* the human race, by the union of the *male* and *female*—in implanting, for this purpose, a desire towards each other—for if all this had never been, *adultery, fornication,* and *whoredom,* could not have existed:—Nay, we may carry the argument so far, as to conclude against the *divine wisdom* and *holiness* in the *creation* itself—for if this had never been, no evil, either *moral* or *natural,* could have ever been known. See vol. i. pref. p.

Let us go a little farther, and we shall get into *scepticism*—and from thence into *atheism*—like those

——— who tread the high *priori* road,
And argue downward 'till they doubt of GOD.
POPE.

In 1536, Archbishop *Cranmer,* who was projecting the most effectual means for a reformation of doctrine, moved in *convocation,* that they should petition the *king* for leave to make a translation of the *Bible.* But *Gardiner,* and all his party, opposed it, both in *convocation,* and in secret with the *king.* It was said, that all the *heresies* and *extravagant opinions,* which were then in *Germany,* and from thence coming over to *England,* sprang from the *free use* of the scripture: and whereas in the *May* last year, nineteen *Hollanders* were accused of some *heretical* opinions, for which opinions *fourteen* of them were *burnt* in *pairs* in several places; it was complained, that all those drew their *damnable errors* from the indiscreet use of the scripture. And to offer the *Bible* in the *Eng-*
lish

ments against the thing *itself*, when used according to GOD's regulation and disposition of the matter, than the *murders* and *massacres* by the Heathens of *old Rome*, or by the *Papists* of modern *Rome*, are to be reasonably urged (as they have been falsly by infidels) against the truth of the *gospel*. Had not *polygamy* been allowed to men, the provision made for the protection and defence of the *weaker sex* had been deficient; whereas GOD's law hath made it *complete*, and no man upon earth can, on the footing of *that law*, plead his *situation*, either as a *privilege* or a *disability*, against providing for, maintaining, and protecting as a *wife*, any or every woman whom he may chuse to *seduce*.

---

lish tongue to the whole nation, would prove the greatest *snare* that could be. See *Burnet* Hist. Ref. vol. i. p. 195, second edit.

Whoever reads with attention this excellent and entertaining *history*, will see what reliance the *Popish* party had on this mode of argumentation against the *Reformers*, their *writings*, and indeed against the *Reformation itself*. The great Sir *Thomas More*, in his writings, exercised all his dexterity in exposing the *ill consequences* that could follow on the doctrine of the *Reformers* Ibid 356.

Assuming certain prejudices as true, and thence drawing *conclusions*, which rest singly on such prejudices, is not only *unfair*, but is one of the meanest and most despicable *sophisms* that error can have recourse to. It is that sort of *deceit* and *imposition*, which " imports the
" misrepresentation of the qualities of things and actions
" to the common apprehensions of men, *abusing* their
" minds with false notions; and so, by this artifice,
" making *evil* pass for *good*, and *good* for *evil* in all the
" great concerns of life." SOUTH's *Sermons*.

That GOD should establish this *security*, by the positive laws which have been so often mentioned—and *that* in *all cases* where the woman was *free*—that it should be so uniformly and openly maintained, for so many ages together, in the practice of the *best people*; and then, all of a *sudden*, it should be found out to be against the *primary law* of marriage, a sin against the *seventh* commandment, and that which was a *moral duty* by Exod. xxii. 16. and Deut. xxii. 28, 29. should be a damnable *sin* under the *gospel*—is either to suppose the world so much *better* than it was before, and therefore no *such law* any longer *needful*—or that a *law-giver* came under the New Testament to oppose the *law-giver* under the Old Testament, and to set mankind free from their allegiance and obedience to Him. The former of which suppositions is not *true* in point of *fact* any more than the latter—our own senses may convince us of the *first*, and CHRIST's own declaration, that He *came not to destroy the law* (καταλῦσαι, to *demolish* or *loosen* its obligation) may assure us of the *second*. Urging that CHRIST has altered the law of the Old Testament, by forbidding *polygamy*—which was, in all cases where *marriage itself* was *lawful*, *allowed*, and in some instances positively *commanded*—is only saying, in other words, that he lessened that *security* which the weaker sex have against the stronger, and facilitated the *ruin* and *prostitution* of women, by cutting off a considerable part of that *protection* which
the

the law of GOD afforded them, and which He so strongly maintained in His whole dispute with the *Pharisees* on the subject of *divorce*, in no one part of it more strongly than Matt. xix. 9. the very *verse* which *superstition* has so long taught men to quote for an opposite purpose; for there He shews that *all divorces* (except what He had before excepted, ch. v. 32.) are absolutely forbidden.

So far as we believe GOD's law, so far *must* we believe that if a man *(having a wife) entices a virgin, and lies with her,* this *last* shall SURELY be *His wife*, as much as the *first*; and it would be equally criminal to *abandon her* as to *put away the first*. For saying this, I appeal to the whole *Bible*, from beginning to end. There are many instances recorded of men's taking a *second* to a *first*, but not one where such a thing was either forbidden, or where the *second* marriage was declared less *valid* than the *first*, or the *first* looked upon as a ground of *divorce* from the *second*, any more than the *second* was a ground of *divorce* from the *first*.

We have run into much confusion on the subject of *marriage*, by the terms *husband and wife*. The ideas which custom hath taught us to annex to them, have superseded the *scripture-definition* of that relation, and have substituted another, which is not to be found in the *Bible*. Our notion is, that when a man and woman have been at a church, and had the *matrimonial* service red over them, and the ceremonies therein contained observed, ferved, they are *man* and *wife*; not otherwife: whereas the fcripture has no *fpecific* name for the relation, as *husband** and *wife* —but a *man* and *his woman* איש ואשתו. When a man *took* a *virgin*, fhe became *his woman*, i. e. his *property*, not by any outward ceremony, but by the furrendering *her perfon* into his *poffeffion*; this, either *anticipatively* by promife or *betrothing*, or *actually* by *carnal knowledge*, where no betrothing or efpoufal went before; this, and this *only*, made them *one flefh*—this did, and it *ever* muft have the fame effect in the *fight* of God; for *He changeth not*. As fhe was called אשתו— *his woman*, by his having the *poffeffion* of her *perfon*, in a fenfe exclufive of *all other men*, fo in the fame fenfe *he* was called אישה—*her man*—ἴδιος ἀνηρ, (See vol. i. p. 217—222.)— the man fo *appropriated* to her that fhe could give herfelf to no other. This was fo in all cafes; the woman who gave *her perfon* into

---

* The author hath, notwithftanding, ufed the terms *hufband* and *wife* throughout this whole treatife, in compliance with our tranflators of the fcripture, and as the moft concife way of expreffing the *marriage-relation* which our language is acquainted with. However, fo far from implying that none can be *man* and *wife*, but thofe who are joined by fome outward ceremony adminiftered by a *prieft*, the words איש ואשתו are ufed to denote the pairing or coupling together of *brute animals*. See *Gen.* vii. 2. where we have tranflated them—the *male* and *his female*. Mont. *Virum & uxorem ejus*.— ἄρσεν και θηλυ. LXX.—See before vol. i. p. 43.

So Virgil—*Vir gregis*. Eclog. vii. l. 7.

And Horace—*Olentis uxores mariti*. Lib. i. Ode xvii. 7.

the *poffeffion* of a man, whatever the man's fituation might be, could not go to *another*, nor could the man *put her away all his days*. Were this fo with us, it would be as difficult to find a *brothel*, or even a *proftitute*, as it was in *Ifrael*, while thefe things were obferved and kept.

That the laws of Exod. xxii. 16. and Deut. xxii. 28, 29. would fometimes be attended, in their execution, with no fmall inconveniences in the cafe of *married* men, muft be allowed—but what are the *worft* of thefe which can be fuppofed, when put in competition with the tremendous and horrible mifchiefs of feduction and proftitution, either to individuals or to the public? The *man* has it in his own option whether he will incur the danger of the former, GOD has gracioufly provided in his *law*, that the *weaker fex* shall not * be expofed to the latter.

As to the murder of *baftard children*, as they are called, an attempt was made fome years ago to prevent this, by the charitable and well-meant inftitution of the *Foundling Hofpital*; if I recollect aright, this very purpofe is mentioned, either in the *king's charter*, or in the *petition* which preceded it.—I wifh not to *remember*, much lefs to *repeat*, leaft of all to *enlarge* upon, the mifchief which enfued to the lives of children, from the evil practices of thofe who were to convey them

---

* See before, p. 159—161.

to the *hospital*; this from all distances, at a time when the tenderness of their age made them unable to support the fatigue of *jolting waggons*, &c. by which means many died on the way:—suffice it to observe, that not one *murder*, of the sort above mentioned, could probably be prevented by the plan of this *charity*; because, in order to have the child conveyed to the *hospital*, somebody must be trusted with the *secret*, as the unfortunate mother can hardly be supposed in a condition to carry it herself, and these *murders* are always committed that the *secret* may not be divulged. Did the *law of* GOD prevail, that which no human contrivance can effect, would be done; such intercourse as we call *whoredom*, in *contempt* of GOD's *law*, and in *honour* of a *human* * *ceremony*, would be deemed, what the scriptures deem it, a *marriage*, and the *magistrate*, as in *Israel*, at the woman's request, might compel the man to a *public* recognition of it, in any manner which should be required by the *state*.

Something like this once prevailed in the kingdom of *France*, as appears by a passage in

---

* I should imagine that the following *syllogism* cannot be denied.

Nothing can be of the essence of marriage in GOD's sight, but that which he hath himself ordained and revealed as such in his word.

But—No outward marriage-ceremony, as essential to marriage in his sight, hath GOD ordained and revealed in his word.

Therefore—No such ceremony can be of the essence of marriage in GOD's sight.

the *Causes Célèbres*, published 1777 at *Paris*, wherein one of the *advocates*, in *Cause* LXXVII. says,—" On condamnoit autrefois les jeunes " *gens* qui abusoient de la foiblesse des filles, " sous promesse du marriage, a etre *pendus* ou " a les epouser."—" Formerly young men, " who abused the weakness of girls under " promise of *marriage*, were condemned, ei- " ther to be *hanged* or to marry them." This was something like reverence to the *law* of GOD; for though that does not say what the punishment was to be, in case the man refused to comply with the law which said *He shall surely endow her to be his wife*—yet if such a case had happened, and *Moses*, as in the case of the man who *gathered sticks on the sabbath* (Numb. xv. 32.) had consulted GOD by *Urim* and *Thummim*, he probably would have received the same answer; disobedience to a commandment so *emphatically* delivered would scarcely have met with a milder punishment in this case than in the other. However, we may with certainty pronounce that *death* would have been the consequence on the wilful and obstinate offender, as it appears to have been a capital offence to despise the *sentence of the judges*, (Deut. xvii. 11, 12.) and they must have passed *sentence according to law*.

But the *French* as well as ourselves are *improved* in their *manners*, therefore the said advocate adds—" Depuis on s'est relaché de " la severité de cet usage, & l'on s'est con- " tenté de les condamner a doter ces filles,
" ou

" ou a leur donner de dommages interêts."
" —Since then we have relaxed from the
" severity of that custom, and content our-
" selves with condemning them to give
" portions to these girls, or to pay them
" damages." So amongst us, a woman may
bring an *action* on a breach of *promise* of *marriage*; but then *actual promise* must be proved, or she will be nonsuited. This therefore does not reach the original cause of the evil complained of. GOD does not make an *actual promise* of *marriage* necessary, Deut. xxii. 28, 29.—but the man *lying with the woman* was to be considered as a *marriage*, and as such ought to be enforced under the severest penalties.

The *French advocate* farther saith—that this giving a portion, or pecuniary damages —" est le seul parti qui reste, lorsque le
" seducteur est mariè—" is the only * thing
" that remains, where the *seducer* is already
" a married man." So speaks *human wisdom*
—but not so the *law of* GOD; that made not the least difference as to the *situation* of the man, though it so expressly does as to that of the *woman*. *Portioning* such a woman out to marry another man, would have been *causing her to commit adultery*, as she was the wife

---

* The cause in question was instituted against a married man who had gotten a young woman with child; and ended with the DEFENDANT's being condemned to pay the *plantiff* 400 liv. damages—to take the whole charge of the *child*, as to its maintenance and education, upon himself—and to pay the whole costs of suit.

of the *first* man, by *that act* which made her *one flesh* with him. The man who married such an *unjustly-divorced* woman, would also be *guilty of adultery*. It might seem strange to go into an house, and to see a man with *two wives*; but this would be much better than to go along the street, and see a *number* of young women perishing with disease and filthiness, some of them because the men *would* not, others because they *could* not, marry them.

I have been lately informed, that by the laws of *Switzerland*, though *polygamy* is not tolerated there, yet if a single man gets a girl with child, he is obliged to marry her, be his rank in life what it may. Here is at least a *partial* remedy against *child-murder* and *prostitution*; but then it must be observed, that it is only just *so far* extensive as it agrees with the *divine law*.

The *Jews* are more *righteous* and *merciful* in the respects above mentioned than *we Christians* are; for the law of GOD is, as far as their difficult situation will admit, observed in all cases of this kind; and if any man refuses to submit to it, he is put under sentence of *excommunication*; which, as they have no public government, is the utmost which can be done. On conversing with a gentleman who is a *Jew*, on this subject, he told me, that some time ago a rich young *Jew* at *Amsterdam* seduced a poor *Jewess*, who was a servant-girl: she insisted on his *publicly* marrying her, which he refused.

She

She complained to the *synagogue*; who summoned him to appear before them, that they might enquire properly into the fact. Finding it true, they sentenced him to *marry* her publicly. He would not—urging the difference of his rank from her's; but this plea was not allowed, they urged the *law of* GOD against him; but he continuing obstinate in his refusal, they excommunicated him. He applied to some of the *States* of *Holland*, that they would interfere; but they refused it, saying—" the *synagogue* had a " right to enforce their own laws." I asked the *gentleman*, with whom I was conversing, " what would have been the case if this " young man had been before *married* to *an-* " *other* woman *then living* ?"—he answered —" *Just the same*—for by the law of *Moses*, " *no man* can take a *virgin*, and afterwards " abandon her at his pleasure." So that the very *Jews* may shame us *Christians* for the little respect we pay to the *preservation* of the *female sex*, or to those *laws of* Heaven which were made to insure it! Our saying that the SAVIOUR of the world (whom we call *Lord and Master*—and *in this we say well, for so he*

* As the *Jews* conform to the *laws* of the countries where their lot is cast, they do not use *polygamy*, where it is not the custom of the part of the world where they live. Therefore, in this latter case, a *public marriage* could not be meant; but, as I have been since informed, " the man would be obliged to *maintain her as his pro-* " *perty, as long as he lived*." And that " if he were " not able to do this, he would be stigmatized with the " *forty stripes*." See Deut. xxv. 3.

is—John xiii. 13.) came to set *those laws aside*, is only going a step farther out of the *way of truth*, and into the *way of abomination*.

I would observe, that if the young *Jew* above mentioned had lived in the days of *Moses*, he would not have come off so cheaply as with a bare excommunication, but *death* had also been the consequence of his contumacy. (Deut. xvii. 11, 12.) On which I cannot omit remarking—that what GOD positively commanded to be done in *all cases*, *we Christians* do not enforce in *any*—nay, by the *marriage-act* we have absolutely prohibited—that " any suit shall be instituted to " compel a marriage *in facie ecclesiæ*, by rea-" son of ANY CONTRACT of matrimony " WHATSOEVER." So that *single men* are absolutely *released* from all enforcement of the *divine law*—and as for *married* men, they are prohibited, on pain of *death*, to do what, under GOD's *own government*, they would on pain of *death* have been compelled * to.

Here we find an adequate cause of female ruin, prostitution, and misery! corrupt human nature is left to itself, uncontrouled,

---

* *Calixtus*, a writer of the 17th century, in his treatise *de Legibus*, saith very truly——

Nulla lex humana potest prohibere, quæ lege divinâ, sive naturali sive positivâ, fuerunt mandata; neque mandare quæ fuerunt prohibita.

" No human law can prohibit those things which by " the divine law, either natural or positive, were com-" manded, nor command what was prohibited."

unchecked

unchecked by the power of God's positive precepts, unpunished for an avowed rebellion against them. To say that we have laws to take up a poor *street-walker*, and send her to *Bridewell*, is only saying that we have laws to make the *miserable* still more *miserable*, and the *profligate* more *profligate*; for in those places of confinement, they help to corrupt each other, and they usually come forth more *abandoned* than when they went in. It is a sad remedy which increases the disease. All these things considered, can it be otherwise than that *adultery* should *increase*, in defiance of God's *law*, when we have not a single *statute* to enforce *that law?* that *whoredom* and *fornication* should *abound*, when the *only* method of preventing them is utterly laid aside, though prescribed and enjoined by the God *of Heaven?*—To punish a poor deserted creature for being a *prostitute*, when it is put out of her power to force her *seducer* to provide for her as the *divine law* enjoins, is equally cruel and foolish: not very unlike the man who threw his child into a ditch, and then beat him for being dirty.

I pretend not to the gift of *prophecy*; but without that, only by comparing *effects* with their *causes*, and weighing in the balance of reason and common sense *circumstance* with *circumstance*—unless recourse be had to the remedy which God hath provided in his *law*—I may venture to pronounce (as all evil is of a progressive nature, the more so the less check is given to it) that all our well-meant schemes

schemes of *reforming prostitutes*, and all our absurd and severe methods of *punishment*, will end just where they began; only with this melancholy difference, that for *one reformed* we shall find *twenty seduced*, and for *one* reclaimed by punishment, an *hundred* will be made the worse. I fear we shall have to say with *Seneca*—de Benef. l. i. c. 10. *Hoc majores nostri questi sunt, hoc nos querimur, hoc posteri nostri querentur, eversos esse mores, regnare nequitiam, in deterius res humanas & in omne nefas labi.* " This our ancestors *have*
" complained of, this we *do* complain of,
" this our posterity *will* complain of—that
" morals are overturned, that wickedness
" reigns, that human affairs go from bad to
" worse, and fall into all manner of im-
" piety." Or with *Horace*,

<blockquote>

Ætas parentum, pejor avis, tulit
Nos nequiores, mox daturos
Progeniem vitiosiorem.

" More vicious than their fathers' age,
" Our sires begat the present race,
" Of actions impious, bold, and base:
" And yet, with crimes to us unknown,
" Our sons shall mark the coming age their own."
FRANCIS.
</blockquote>

I cannot close the foregoing observations better, than by inserting a very affecting illustration of their truth, which appeared in the *General Advertiser* of *Oct.* 16, 1778.

" Mr.

"Mr. Editor,

"Seeing a *very young girl* wandering about the streets late in the evening of yesterday, I was induced to ask her—whither she was going? She told me that an officer encamped at *Coxheath* had, about a fortnight since, stolen her away from her friends at *Rochester*, and carried her by force to his *marquée*, where he debauched her; and after having kept her about a week after he had satisfied his licentious inclinations, he had sent her to *London* with a *guinea* in her pocket, to get her living as she might. This wanton act of barbarity so affected me, that I could not refrain from cursing aloud the author of it, in the most vehement manner, as I walked home.

"How much more does this cruel destroyer of innocence deserve the discipline of flagellation, than a poor deserter! I hope the officer who has thus taken from a young girl that recommendation, without which she will find it difficult to earn an honest livelihood, is not quite so nearly related to the Devil, as to suffer this unhappy victim to seek her bread by *prostitution*."

How far the case, as above stated, may be true, I will not pretend to say; but could we know *every thing* of this sort which daily passes in the world, we should find much

reason

reason to credit the facts in this letter. Many men there are, whose rank, and education, and fortunes, as well as their personal endowments, might intitle them to the affections of the most respectable and exalted of their own degree in the female world, with whom they might be the *happy husbands* of *happy wives*, who, devoting themselves to the indulgence of their appetites, lay out all their time and substance to inveigle and betray the lowest of the *other sex*, and then serve them as the *officer* above mentioned is represented to have served the *poor girl*. Sooner than fail, they will employ their mean dependents to be their *factors*; and numbers there are, of *both* sexes, who actually live upon the spoils of *female innocence*.

The *judges* of *Israel* would have saved the poor girl from destruction, by forcing the *officer* to a public recognition of his *marriage* with her, on the facts appearing to them as they are stated.—But he lives in a *Christian* country—he is *free*—the poor helpless girl irremediably undone! so are thousands and *tens* of thousands on the same principle.

By abolishing the connected, wise, and salutary laws of GOD, relative to the *commerce of the sexes*, and setting up a law of man's device in their place, the strongest barrier which words can form, for the preservation of the *weaker sex*, is thrown down; the strong holds of *female security* are razed to their

their very foundations; and the following *mischiefs* are *apparent*.

1. *Adultery* has not any punishment to stand in dread of from our *penal* laws, therefore we can be at no loss for its bare-faced appearance, and increase beyond the example of former times—for *evil* of all kinds is of a progressive nature.

2. There being no obligation on men to marry the *virgins* they *seduce*, thousands of helpless girls are enticed, seduced, and abandoned at the pleasure of their SEDUCERS; by which means the *brothels* and *streets* are filled with *harlots* and *prostitutes*.

3. These poor creatures, grown hardened and desperate in the ways of sin, are, in their turns, the *seducers* and debauchers of the young and heedless of the *other sex* who may fall in their way.

4. A *disease* little better than a *plague*, which *Providence* has seemed to set as a brand of *infamy*, as well as punishment, on the forbidden and promiscuous *commerce of the sexes*, spreads its *poison* far and wide, to the destruction of *thousands*.

5. *Depopulation* must, in its degree, ensue—not only from the ravages of the *venereal disease*, among young persons especially, of *both sexes*; but numbers of such females as would otherwise be *breeding women*, enervated by *prostitution*, rotted by *disease*, and consigned to the *grave* in the very bloom of youth, drop, like withered blossoms from the tree,

tree, leaving no fruit behind. Should they for a few, or even for many years, be able to withstand the assaults of intemperance, so as to survive them (which here and there may be the case of *one* * in an *hundred*) yet, *barrenness* and *prostitution* are so usually connected, as to make it amount at least to improbability that such women should ever breed.

6. Another source of *depopulation* must arise from the temptation which men are under to a *single life*, from finding an easy way of gratifying their appetites—without the burden and care of a *wife* and *family*—either with women whom they can *seduce*, and *leave* at their pleasure, or by a small sum purchasing the favours of those who have been *seduced* and abandoned by other men. This is one grand incentive to *celibacy* on the side of the men, and a reason why so many young women, however beautiful and deserving they may be, pass on to old age neglected by the other sex, and die unmarried.

7. By putting an *human ceremony* in the place of the *divine ordinance*, and men being under no obligation to *marry* the women they *seduce*, *whoredom* and *fornication* must increase, in proportion to the numbers of *profligate men*, who chuse to gratify their

* Usually most of these turn *bawds*, and make it the great end of their *professional industry* to live by keeping *brothels*, not only for the reception of young women *already ruined*, but for the inveigling and drawing into *ruin*, numbers of unwary and deceived females.

passions at a cheaper rate than the charge of a *wife* and *family*, and to indulge their love of *variety* at no greater *trouble* and *expence*, than may be incurred by the *seduction* of *youth* and *innocence* among the lower order of females.

8. By representing *polygamy* as a sin, the word of GOD is discarded as the *only rule of faith*—the *wisdom* and *holiness* of his *positive laws*, for its *regulation*, called in question—a very considerable part of the *security* which they afford the *weaker sex, destroyed*, and of course the seducing, abandoning, and prostituting women, by *married * men*, greatly facilitated. Vouching the authority of CHRIST, as forbidding *polygamy* under the notion of *adultery*, is a misrepresentation of his *prophetical character*, like that of *Cerinthus*, who taught that—" JESUS opposed the GOD of " the *Jews*."

9. By stamping *infamy* on the only *institution* and *ordinance* of *marriage* which GOD

---

* More especially by those who are under divorces *a mensa & toro*, or, from some unhappy differences, are for ever separated by mutual agreement, which are far the greater number of the two, and who are exposed to all the temptations of a *single life*, without having it in their power to use the appointed remedy against them.

Forbidding such men *to marry*, is as unscriptural, unauthorized, and dangerous a tyranny over the rights and consciences of makind, as the *Pope's* forbidding the marriage of the *clergy*.

It may however be observed, that those who are divorced " by sentence in the ecclesiastical court," are not liable to the pains and penalties of Jac. I. c. 11; from which it should seem, as if the *statute law tacitly* admits of such marriages.

ever appointed or revealed, and denying its *obligation* without the super-addition of an *human ceremony*, which was first made essential to *marriage* by a *Pope* of *Rome*, the *murders* * of new-born *infants* have been and are frequently occasioned, and, by this means, the *deaths* of many women by the hands of the public executioner.

10. Numbers of children are destroyed, as well as women, by the wicked practice of taking medicines to cause abortion.—To this may be added,

11. The many instances of *female suicide*, which have happened in the unspeakable moments of distress and desperation, when pregnant women have been basely † deserted by those

---

* Mr. *Guthrie*, Geograph. Gram. p. 185, edit. 1776, in the account of the *religion* of *Scotland*, says—" It is " said, that even that relic of *Popery*, the obliging *for-* " *nicators* of both sexes to sit upon what they call a " repenting-stool in the church, and in full view of the " congregation, begins to wear out; it having been " found, that the *Scotch women*, on *account of that pe-* " *nance*, were the greatest *infanticides* (or murderers of " infants) in the world." See also Memoirs of Cranstoun, p. 31, 32.

† A recent instance of this was in one of the public prints, about the latter end of July 1779. " A young " woman at ———, in Essex, was lately found drowned " in a pond. The occasion of this rash action was her " being deserted by a gentleman in the neighbourhood, " by whom she was pregnant." Many such instances may doubtless be found in the annals of human misery!

The *Morning Chronicle*, of *November* 12, 1779, furnishes us with a record, which, though almost enough to freeze the very blood of the humane reader, I cannot omit on this occasion.

those who ought to have become their protection and defence, and thus exposed to infamy and ruin—defenceless—helpless—hopeless!

Such

"On the 31st ult. one *Hannah Hoggarth*, of the township of *Hawsker* cum *Stainsiker*, in the parish of *Whitby*, in Yorkshire, was delivered of a male bastard-child alone. On the 2d inst. her neighbours, suspecting she had been so delivered, prevailed on the officers to get a surgeon and man-midwife to examine her; who, on the 3d, went to her house, examined, and talked to her about such her delivery, which she, at first, denied; but on a closer examination, she said she had a miscarriage, which being dead, and very small, she burnt; and would then confess no further. On the 5th instant the same persons went and examined her again, when she confessed she had been delivered alone of a boy, who crying very much, she, *to avoid a discovery*, took an axe, with the broad end of which she several times struck the infant on the head, and thereby greatly crushed and fractured his skull, and with the sharp end she endeavoured to cut off its head; that having thus killed the child, she laid it under the bolster of a bed in the room where she lay, until the evening, when she got up, took up one of the flags of the floor, and underneath it buried the child; where it was, by her directions, found, and the *coroner* made acquainted therewith, and summoned a jury, who met last Saturday afternoon, and, on examination of the witnesses, found that the said *Hoggarth* had murdered her child in the manner above related. Soon after the *jury* had left the place, she took an opportunity, in the absence of the person set to watch her, to HANG HERSELF, and was quite dead before it was discovered."

Whence arose this double tragedy?—From the same source which must account for all things of the same kind—that is to say, from the fooleries of *priestcraft*, first set on foot by Pope *Alexander* the IIId, and gradually brought into an *article of faith* by the superstition and credulity of mankind. We read of no such thing

happening

Such are the effects of *worldly systems*—such the fruits of the inventions of those who would make themselves *wiser* and *holier* than the GOD *who made them!* Nor can any thing put a check on the prevalence of such calamities, but a restoration of the WHOLE—UNIFORM—CONSISTENT—and * BENEFICENT LAW OF GOD. This, and *this* alone, is a remedy against *adultery*, and *whoredom* in all its forms. Long and sad experience has shewn us that all *other schemes*, whether of *prevention* or *remedy*, are vain and chimerical, and can no more stop these evils, than *Jeroboam*'s discarding the law of *Moses*, and setting up the *calves* in *Dan* and *Bethel*, could secure the *kingdom of Israel* to himself and family.

Nothing can be more pernicious to the pursuit and investigation of truth, than supposing the *antiquity* of an opinion is a certain proof of its *solidity*, or that the *universal* reception *of*, or veneration *for*, a *doctrine*, is a conclusive argument of its *truth*. We have but to travel into *China* or *Japan*, *Mexico* or *Peru*, or into any other idolatrous countries,

---

happening in *Israel*; the motives of *fear* and *shame*, which drove this poor creature to such desperation, could not exist, but under those circumstances of *infamy*, which the tyranny of custom has annexed to certain *actions*, without any warrant or foundation from that *law*, by which we must *all be judged at the last day.*

* *Grotius* saith well—*Lex divinæ* HEBRÆIS *data, ut omnis virtutis, ita & humanitatis magistra.* "The divine "law given to the *Hebrews*, is as well the sovereign of "all *humanity* as of all *virtue.*" De B. & P. lib. ii. c. 19. § 4.

and we shall find the most horrible and monstrous forgeries that *Satan* himself can invent, all depending on the *antiquity* of their establishment, the *universality* of their reception, as well as of the *veneration* which is paid them. Let us not think that we are by *nature* wiser than the inhabitants of those countries—*we are all the children of one man*, the *naturally-engendered* offspring of fallen *Adam*.—He *that giveth to all life and breath, and all things*, hath *made of one blood all nations of men, for to dwell on all the face of the earth. Acts* xvii. 25, 26. The *human mind*, like the *human nature*, is in all men and in all places *alike*. Prov. xxvii. 19. Were the people who are born in *Mexico* born among us, they would not be worshippers of the idol *Vitziputzli*; were we born among them, we certainly should. The mind of fallen man, having no *innate ideas* of *divine things*, is impressible by the *first that offer*, and as he grows up, these grow up with him. Hence the *Bramin* is as much wedded to the adoration and * worship of *Vistnou*,

as

* The force of custom and education is seen in all countries, in *civil* as well as *religious* matters—" Let a
" *Hottentot* be well daubed from head to foot with *soot*
" and *grease*—let him be equipped too with a sheep or
" wild-beast skin upon his shoulders, and adorned *a la*
" *mode de son païs*, with *trinkets*, and he will strut with
" as much affectation and parade as the vainest *European*
" in the most sumptuous habit—the noblest robes, the
" richest and most glittering brocades, all the beauty
" and magnificence of the *European* attire, fall infinitely
" short, in the eye of a *Hottentot*, of the grandeur and
" attractions he fancies there are in the full dress of his
" own

as a *Papist* is to the adoration and worship of the *Virgin Mary*. The only difference between them is, that the blind *Heathen* has been taught his *religion* by those who have *no revelation*, and the *ignorant Christian* has been instructed in *his*, by those who have perverted and abused the *revelation* which GOD hath given them. Such is the human mind—so fallen, so lost to the possession and love of truth—that it will suffer itself to be led blindfold into the acknowledgment of propositions as *true*, which even the outward senses demonstrate to be *false!* Witness the absurd, unprofitable, self-contradictory notion of *transubstantiation*, whose *antiquity*, and *universal reception* and *veneration* in the church of *Rome*, have prevailed on men to relinquish the demonstration of their outward senses, and to embrace *a lye*, though it bears its own detection upon the face of it.

" own country." *Kolben*, vol. i. p. 264. The custom and education of the *Hottentot*, and those of an *European beau*, are the only causes of any difference between them, and why the one is scenting his locks with essenced pomatum and powder, the other with *sheep's fat* and *buchu*—why the one is sighing after a mistress in silk and brocade—why the mouth of the other waters for the *tripe* and *guts* on the *legs of his dear* TOTTA.—See Prior's Alma, Canto II. Now all this does not happen from human nature's being different in different parts of the world, but from its being the *same every where*; therefore *every where* duped alike by *custom* and *education*. The same principle of *vanity*, which would lead an *European* to be pleased, with being told, that he was the best-dressed man in the *drawing-room*, would make a *Hottentot* plume himself on being the best *greased* and *footed* man in the whole *kraal*.

The *credulity* of the *human mind* was hardly ever more plainly evinced, than by an experiment which was tried upon the *public* about thirty years ago:—A certain noble *Duke* was conversing on this subject with some company at his own house, and said—" He was certain that no absurdity could be " proposed, which mankind would not be-" lieve. I dare say," continues he, " that " if it was advertised in the papers, that at " one of the *theatres* a man would get into a " *quart-bottle*, the house would be crowded." This was thought to be carrying the matter too far. " No," said *his Grace*, " if you " will promise to keep my counsel, I will " try the experiment." Accordingly it was announced in one or more of the papers, that " at such a *theatre*, on such an evening, " a man, with all his *cloaths* on, would " come on the stage, get into a *quart-bottle*, " and there play several *tunes on the German* " *flute*." The *evening* arrived, the experiment succeeded, the house was full from top to bottom; numbers tried to get places, but were forced to go away for want of room. The company waited patiently a considerable time, at last they grew noisy, and called, but in vain, for the *artist*; then they began to be angry and riotous, insisting on a return of their *money*, which they had *paid at going in*; this was equally vain, the *offices* were all locked up, the *receivers* decamped with a large sum, which, it was said, was afterwards distributed among some public charities.

If

If the human mind is capable of such impositions as these, in things wherein the *outward senses* must be supposed to be competent judges, what must it not be capable of believing, where spiritual and invisible things are the objects proposed to it? more especially when those objects are presented before it under the venerable guise of piety and religion, and are recommended to its observance by the authority of *usage, custom,* and *law?*

That there should be a set of people who could persuade themselves that "marriage is a carnal thing, which, though allowed to the *Jews* under the Old Testament, is unlawful * for *Christians* under the New Testament"—that there should be *others,* who, though they "allowed marriage for once to be *lawful,* yet condemned *all second* marriages as only a more specious and decorous kind of *whoredom and adultery*"—that others should, in the very face of the scripture, hold *polygamy* to be a *damnable* † *sin,* and even punish the having *two wives*

---

* See *Broughton,* Hist. Lib. tit. Marriage.

† In *N. Brent*'s translation of *Polano*'s Hist. of the Council of Trent, p. 784, are to be found the following anathemas:

1. Against him that shall say, that matrimony is not one of the *seven sacraments* instituted by CHRIST, and doth not confer grace.
2. Or that it is lawful for *Christians* to have *many wives* at once, and that this is not forbidden by any law of GOD.
3. Or that only the degrees of *affinity* and *consanguinity*

wives at once, which the scriptures do *not condemn*, more severely than the *defiling* the *wives of other men*, which the scriptures *do condemn*

    nity expressed in *Leviticus*, may nullify the marriage, and that the *church* may not add others, and dispense with some of *them*.
4. Or that the *church* cannot constitute impediments, or hath erred in constituting them.
5. Or that ecclesiastics in *holy orders* may marry, as also all those who find they have not the gift of chastity, or that shall prefer the state of marriage to virginity and chastity.
6. Or that the prohibitions of marriage in certain times of the year is superstition, or shall condemn the benedictions and other ceremonies.

I have selected these *synodal* determinations of that famous *Popish* council, that the reader may be apprized of the origin of systematical opposition and contrariety to the divine law. *Ab inferis ad Romam, a Româ ad nos.* As to the matter of *polygamy*, I cannot, from the history of those times, have the least doubt of its being branded with a CURSE on such as should assert its " not " being contrary to the law of GOD," in order to make *Luther, Zuinglius, Bucer, Melancthon*, and the other reformers, the more odious in the sight of the world, they having given this as their opinion, in the business of *Philip Landgrave* of *Hesse*.

  I the more readily believe this, because many of the most celebrated *Popish* writers, as *Durandus* à *St. Portian*, in the 14th century—*Alphonsus Tostatus*, Bishop of *Avila*, in the 15th century—and particularly Cardinal *Cajetan*, who disputed with *Luther* at *Augsburg*, in the 16th century—do confess—that " a plurality of *wives* is lawful, " according to the divine law, and that it hath no in- " decency in it by the law of nature; but it would be " lawful even to priests, unless prohibited by the dis- " cipline of the church"—*Jure divino uxorum pluralitatem esse licitam, idque naturali jure nullam habere indecentiam quin & sacerdotibus hoc licitum fore, nisi ecclesiastica prohiberentur disciplina.* Cardinal Bellarmine acknowledges the same—Lib. 1. De Matr. c. 10. See before, p. 82, n,

Rainold

condemn to *capital punishment*—that the whole legiflative body of this kingdom fhould determine it to be *againſt the law of* God that a *clerk in orders* fhould marry; that this fhould be made *felony*, in *both parties*, as alfo in thofe who fhould only maintain it *to be lawful*:—that all thefe things fhould gain fuch an afcendency over the minds of men, as, in their turns, to be believed as fo many folemn truths of *religion*, affords, furely, reafon enough for every thinking man to be upon his guard, and to examine well into the foundation of things before he makes them articles of his *creed*.

When the holy fcriptures are applied to in a partial and defultory manner, *words* taken out of *ſentences*—*ſentences* from the entire *text*—*texts* wrefted from the *context*—the *context* from the *reſt of the* fcriptures, and then the *ſound* of the words detached from their *ſenſe*—matters are ſtill made worſe, the deception is ſtrengthened by the fuppoſed authority of fcripture, and *Error*, having counterfeited the feal of *Truth*, thus commends itfelf to the minds and confciences of men.

A little before *our bleſſed Saviour* left this

Rainold de lib. Apoc. tom. i. *prælect* 4, exprefsly faith —" *Cajetanus* afferit pluralitatem uxorum nufquam a " Deo prohiberi, adeoque *Paulum*, cum *epiſcopum* vetet " habere plures uxores, reliquis concedere." " *Cajetan* " afferts, that a plurality of wives is no where pro- " hibited by God. And therefore *Paul*, when he for- " bids a *Biſhop* to have a plurality of wives, grants it " to *others*." See before, vol. i. p.

world,

world, He *thus* prayed for His *difciples—(not for them only,* but *for them alfo which fhould believe on Him through their word*—John xvii. 17, 20.) *Sanctify them through Thy truth, Thy* WORD IS TRUTH. Whatever contradicts that WORD muft be a *lye,* for *no lye is of the truth.* 1 John ii. 21. However *facred* thefe *lyes* may have become, by people's efpoufing them as *truths,* under notions of *purity* and *holinefs,* yet are they of *their father the Devil, who, when he fpeaketh a lye, fpeaketh of his own, for he is a lyar, and the father of it.* John viii. 44. Whatever will bear the *teft* of the *Hebrew* fcripture, muft be *true*—but if it will not bear this, we may be certain it is *falfe,* however it may be dignified with the opinions of the *learned* and *pious,* or come recommended to us under the fanction of the higheft human authority. I much queftion whether *fuperftition* and *error* owe their afcendency over the minds of profeffing *Chriftians* to any thing more, than to detaching the Old and New Teftaments from each other, and thus looking upon the *latter* as an entire *new* fyftem, unconnected *with,* and independent *on,* the *former.* Whereas, in truth and in fact, the New Teftament owes its whole importance and glory to the *Hebrew* fcriptures; it is entirely built upon them; we therefore find a conftant reference to them throughout the whole New Teftament. *Search the fcriptures, they teftify of Me.* John v. 39.—For *if ye had believed* MOSES, *ye would have believed Me, for he wrote of Me;*

but

but if ye believe not his writings, how shall ye believe My words? John v. 46, 47. Here, by the way, I would aſk, how it is poſſible to conceive, that OUR LORD ſhould appeal to the *writings of* MOSES for the truth of what he ſpake, if *his words* eſſentially differed from them? *They have* MOSES *and the prophets, let them hear them*—Luke xvi. 29. And in that exquiſitely fine apology of *Paul* before *Agrippa*, Acts xxvi. he declares, that he ſaid nothing in his public miniſtry, but what MOSES *and the prophets did ſay ſhould come to paſs*. As we find ſome of the books of the Old Teſtament refer to others preceding, ſo do we find the New Teſtament referring itſelf for its authority to the Old Teſtament; which ſhews, that *both together* form one connected ſcheme, one uniform plan of *divine wiſdom and truth*. The *goſpel* in the Old Teſtament, and the *goſpel* in the New Teſtament, differ only as the *ſhadow* of a man *upon a wall* differs from the *image* of the ſame perſon ſeen *in a glaſs*; we ſee the repreſentation of the *ſame* identical perſon in *both* caſes, only more diſtinctly and plainly in the *latter*. *The law had a ſhadow of good things to come, not the very image of the things.* Heb. x. 1. But under the New Teſtament, *we all with open face* (the veil of the typical diſpenſation being removed) *behold, as in a glaſs, the glory of the* LORD. 2 Cor. iii. 18.

It is ever to be remembered, and therefore cannot be too much or too often inculcated, that though the *Bible* conſiſts of different

ferent *books*, written at different and distant *times*, by different *penmen*, yet one and the same truth pervades the whole; one uniform *design* appears; nor is there, throughout, the least appearance of a departure from it;—the reason of which is, that the AUTHOR is *one*—his WILL is one—and therefore his WORD is *one*:—the least real contradiction, inconsistency, or variation, must destroy the authority of the *whole*, and leave the *infidel* in full enjoyment of his triumph over the credibility of the scripture.

If this was more attended to and considered, people who profess themselves to be *friends* of *revelation*, would be very cautious of granting its enemies their favourite arguments of *inconsistency* and *contradiction*; for this they certainly do, in allowing a difference between the Old Testament and the *New* in point of *moral obligation*: little thinking that if this could once be proved, and that the *latter* is more *pure* and *holy* than the *former*—it would shake the credit of *both*, as the work of *one* and the *same* SPIRIT; and perhaps we must be led to give up *one* in order to support the *other*, or, to be entirely consistent, deny the authority of *both*.

Thus it was with *Manes*, that famous *heretic* of the third *century*.—In order to remove the obstacles which lay in the way of his monstrous system, which was a motley mixture of some tenets of *Christianity*, mixed with the ancient philosophy of the *Persians*, in which he had been instructed in his

youth

youth—and to establish a scheme of *purity, holiness*, and *mortification*, which, among other things, consisted in total abstinence from *marriage*, and all comforts which arise from the bonds of conjugal tenderness—he affirmed that the Old Testament was not the work of God, but of the *prince of darkness*, who was substituted by the *Jews* in the place of the true God: and afterwards, finding that the New Testament would not fully answer the designs of this enormous *fanatic*, he threw a total discredit on the *four Gospels*, the *Acts of the Apostles*, and on *Paul's Epistles*, and supplied their place by a *gospel* which he pretended to be dictated to him by God himself. See *Mosheim*, Maclaine's edit. vol. i. 155.

Another *fanatic* arose in this *century*, whose name was *Hierax*—who maintained, that "the principal object of Christ's ministry "was, the promulgation of a NEW LAW, "more *severe* and *perfect* than that of *Moses*; "and from hence he concluded, that the "use of *flesh, wine, wedlock,* and of things "agreeable to the outward senses, which "had been permitted under the *Mosaic* dis- "pensation, was absolutely prohibited and "abrogated by Christ." *Mosheim*, ib. 156. Mosheim also mentions a wild *sect*, that troubled the *church* during the 12th century, which he calls *Catharists*. "Their religion" says he, "resembled the doctrine of the *Ma-* "*nichæans* and *Gnostics* in many respects; "particularly on the subject of *marriage*, "from

" from which they enjoined a rigorous ab-
" ftinence, as well as from wine and animal
" food; they moreover treated with the ut-
" moft contempt all the books of the *Old*
" *Teftament*, but expreffed an high degree of
" veneration for the *New*, particularly for
" the four *gofpels*." See *Mofheim*, cent. 12.
part ii. c. 5. fect. 4.

Many more inftances of this kind might eafily be mentioned, but thefe may fuffice to fhew, whither men may be led, if once imagination fets to work, and notions of *religion* are entertained, which fet the Old Teftament and *New* at variance:—to maintain, therefore, their uniformity, harmony, and confiftency, fhould be the endeavour of every writer on religious fubjects; the moment we lofe fight of thefe, we muft be loft in endlefs mazes of contradiction and inconfiftency—how can it be otherwife, if the *book*, from whence we muft derive the matter of our difcourfe, be *inconfiftent* with itfelf?

In vain are we *all* called upon—1 Cor. i. 10. —*to fpeak the fame thing—that there be no divifions among us—that we be perfectly joined together in the fame mind and in the fame judgment*—if the facred writers of the Old and New Teftament are at variance—or if MOSES faid one thing and CHRIST another—or if GOD can be fuppofed to differ from *himfelf*; for thefe confequences cannot be avoided, if there be one *law of lefs purity* in the *Old Teftament*, and another of *greater purity* in the *New Teftament*.

This latter notion has filled the world with more enthusiasts, fanatics, and mad religionists, than convents and cells could contain; it has peopled desarts, caves, dens, and forests, with anchorets, hermits, demoniacs, and other wild and gloomy mortals, who have represented human nature under such a form, as almost to countenance the *Manichæan* notion of the creation of the world by the *prince of darkness*.

It were endless to attempt a recapitulation of all the *mischiefs* which have arisen, from setting the Old Testament and the *New* at variance—and from contending that the *holy law*, or *rule of life*, which GOD revealed for the government of the *Jews*, is not *holy and pure* enough for CHRISTIANS.

The condemnation of *marriage*, and other instances of rebellion against the *wisdom* of GOD, are but a part of that *spiritual wickedness*, which, through the prevalence of this notion, has taken possession of so great a part of mankind—those *mischiefs* which are the subjects of this *treatise*, all flow, as has been before observed, from the same principle, though they operate in a different manner.— I know not that the *fanatic* *, who took it into his head to live for thirty-seven years together on the top of an *high pillar*, by way of devotion, hurt any body but himself, unless it were those who were *mad* enough to

---

* See an account of this *pillar-saint*, and his sect, 1 Mosh. p. 254.

follow

follow his example :—but when the law of *juſtice, mercy,* and *truth* (for ſuch is the moral law of GOD) is laid aſide, for a ſyſtem of the moſt atrocious baſeneſs and cruelty, which diſſolves all *marriage-contract* whatſoever, and renders all *ſecurity* ariſing therefrom utterly *null and void,* unleſs ratified by *human authority*—then laying aſide the *law which was given by Moſes,* annihilating its obligations, and ſetting up a *new law* not of GOD's ordaining, but of *man's device,* is ſeverely felt by thoſe, whoſe aggravated ſufferings are the natural and infallible conſequences of it.

As for the *moral law,* it is founded in the *relation* which men bear to GOD and *one another*; and therefore, as that *relation* is incapable of alteration, change, addition, or diminution—but muſt ever remain *one* and the *ſame*—ſo muſt that *rule of life* and *conduct,* which was eſtabliſhed *by that law.* Therefore, when *our bleſſed* SAVIOUR, who came *not to deſtroy,* but to *magnify the law, and make it honourable,* Iſ. xlii. 21. and this by His own perfect, ſinleſs, and moſt holy *obedience,* even *unto death,* is ſumming up the whole under *two* general heads, which *He* calls the *two great commandments of the law,* He ſays, *On theſe two commandments hang* (or depend) *all the law and the prophets.*—There is not ἀκ ἐςι (not there *was not* in the days of *Moſes,* but) there IS *not* NOW, *any other commandment greater than theſe.* Matt. xxii. 40. Mark xii. 31.

Hence, when the primitive *Chriſtians* and
Fathers

Fathers took it into their heads to confider the New Teſtament as a diſtinct new ſyſtem of faith and manners, which abrogated the *old law*, and ſet up for *itſelf*, they laid the foundation of the hereſies and errors which have infeſted the church of Christ, as in other things ſo with reſpect to *marriage*. Had they interpreted what Christ ſaid on the ſubject of *celibacy*, not by detaching the words, and taking them by their *ſound*, but by comparing them with the Old Teſtament, thus taking them by their *ſenſe*, they would not have ſtigmatized God's holy ordinance of *marriage* as an *impure and carnal thing*, and accordingly have thought the *married leſs* holy and pure than the *unmarried*—they would not have treated it as merely *allowable* (much leſs, like the blaſphemy of *Jerome*, have reckoned it, as ſome did, among the things *quæ ſunt per ſe mala ac vitioſa*) but as a thing commendable, yea, *honourable in all*. Heb. xiii. 1. They would not have *raved*, as they did, againſt *ſecond* marriages, calling them little better than *whoredom and adultery*, and holding men as *heathens and publicans* who entered into them; but they would have ſeen in the Old Teſtament, that when men, though already *married*, took *ſecond wives*, ſuch marriages were approved, bleſſed, owned, and even promoted by God Himſelf.—Thus would they have *learned not to have condemned the guiltleſs*. In ſhort, they would have ſeen that *marriage*, in all the forms in which it appeared in the Old Teſtament,

tament, was an obedience to that firſt command uttered with the *firſt bleſſing* from Heaven—*Be fruitful, and multiply, and repleniſh the earth*—that their ſchemes of *celibacy*, and their other reſtraints of *marriage*, under notions of greater *purity and perfection*, were oppoſite to that command, and tended to the * deſtruction of the *human ſpecies*—and that there was no more difference between their plans of feigned † *chaſtity*, and *murder*, than

---

* Whatever hypocrites auſterely talk
Of purity, of place, and innocence;
Defaming as impure what GOD declares
Pure ———— ———— ————
Our Maker bids increaſe; who bids abſtain
But our *Deſtroyer*, foe to GOD and man?
        Parad. Loſt. B. 4.

† For, after all, the *chaſtity* they pretended to was but ill obſerved. Witneſs the proceedings of the *clergy* in the *third century*, who, to humour the people, abſtained from *marriage*; but they did this ſo as to offer no great violence to their own inclinations — for they formed connexions with thoſe women who had vowed *perpetual chaſtity*; and it was an ordinary thing for an *eccleſiaſtic* to take one of theſe fair ſaints to his bed, ſtill under the moſt ſolemn declarations, that nothing paſſed that was contrary to the rules of *chaſtity* and *virtue*. Theſe *holy concubines* were called συνείσακ]οι by the *Greeks*—and by the *Latins—Mulieres ſubintroductæ*. And it was a long time before the more pious and zealous of the *Biſhops* could entirely aboliſh this practice. See 1 *Moſheim*, 137, 138.

The order of the Counteſs of *Guaſtalla*, inſtituted in 1537, was made up of *monks* and *nuns*, who, to *overcome fleſhly luſts*, did lay together, a *monk* and a *nun* in the ſame bed, putting a big wooden *croſs* between both; which (as they gave out) had the virtue to quench *rebellious concupiſcence*. But this *croſs* being but a very low wall of partition, and ſcandalous diſorders, and *works of darkneſs*,

than between the prevention of a child's birth, and destroying it after it is born.

Our BLESSED SAVIOUR (John viii. 44.) describes the *arch-enemy* of mankind, the *Devil*, as a *lyar and a murderer from the beginning*. His grand plan is the destruction of the *human species*. He brought *sin and death* into the world, by being the father of that *lye* which he induced our *first parents* to believe, and which stands recorded Gen. iii. 4. His end and aim has ever since that hour been uniformly the same, therefore he is fitly styled in the *Hebrew* tongue, ABADDON *(destruction, perdition)* and in the *Greek*, APOLLYON—the *destroyer*. Rev. ix. 11. In how successful a manner his plans have been carried on, by preventing the propagation of children, the history of the church, from the days of the primitive *Christians* and *fathers*, abundantly declares, especially that part of it which respects the *church of Rome*. The *celibacy* of the clergy hath for * many ages been universal—millions of men and women have been taught to turn the *particular* and *occasional* recommendations of a *single*

---

darkness, arising from this foolish institution, this infamous order came to an end, being destroyed all over *Italy*. I know not that this instance of *conventual chastity* is recorded in any printed book, but accidentally meeting with it in an old *manuscript*, I thought it too curious not to set it down.

* Bishop *Newton*, in his ingenious and learned *Diss.* on *Proph.* vol. ii. p. 444, seems to date the prohibition of *priests* marriage, by public authority, so early as the council of *Eliberis* in *Spain*—Anno 105.

life,

life, into general injunctions against *marriage* itself; thus *changing the truth of* God *into a lye, forbidding to marry*, and shutting themselves up in *convents, cloisters*, and other uncommanded retirements. *Satan*'s grand plan is still carrying on among mankind, even where *Protestantism* prevails, witness the numbers of *females*, who are daily rendered unfit for the *ends of marriage* by *prostitution*. This would not be, if the *father of lyes* had not taught us to abrogate those salutary and beneficent laws of God, which were enacted in heaven, and delivered to *Moses* on *Mount Sinai*, to prevent this foul disgrace, and sad destruction of the *female sex*; and to substitute others, which render it more *safe* for a man to *ruin* an hundred *virgins*, than to *steal* a *sixpence*. As far as this is attended with *depopulation*—which it must be in proportion to the numbers of women *seduced*, and abandoned to *prostitution*—so far doth *Satan* succeed in the destruction of the *human species*.

In this, and in many other ways, which have been mentioned in these *volumes*, doth the *enemy* of God and *man* find his account, from the substitution of *human invention* in the place of DIVINE LEGISLATION; which last, in every part of it, the more closely it is considered, the more it appears calculated to obviate those mischiefs, and to prevent those calamities, which, as *human nature* is now constituted, form so large and fatal a part of *female* misery.

How so considerable a portion of the *Christian*

tian world could ever be brought, through a long succession of ages, to imagine it possible that *a jot or tittle of the* DIVINE LAW *could ever pass away*—or that the change which has been supposed, could be derived from *divine authority*—or that GOD could be less *provident* for the *protection* and *security* of the *weaker sex*, under the *New-Testament dispensation*, than under *that* of the *Old Testament*—is one of those *problematical* questions, which I freely own to exceed all the apprehension which I am master of.—I therefore leave it to be resolved by those, whose genius for *the inexplicable*, may perhaps prompt them to attempt a solution of it.

All that I can say is, that if once we separate the New Testament from the Old, and set it up as a *distinct system*, explaining the words by the *sound* of them, we may prove CHRIST a *repealer* and *opposer* of GOD's *law* in *more* instances *than one*. As for example—Luke xiv. 26.—*If any man come to me, and hate not his father and mother, and wife and children, and brethren and sisters, yea, and his own life also, he cannot be my disciple.* However these words may *sound*, yet, when rightly understood, they are not to lessen *filial duty*—*parental* or *filial affection*—*brotherly love*—to weaken the great duty of *self-preservation*, or to dissolve the conjugal *union* and *affection* between a *man and his wife*;—but to shew that even *these* things, *obligatory* as they are in *themselves*, are but of *secondary* consideration, or indeed of *no* consideration at all,

when

when they stand in competition with *doing* or *suffering* for the glory of GOD, in the maintenance of His *truth*. So ver. 33. *Whosoever he be of you that forsaketh not all that he hath, he cannot be my disciple.*—This cannot mean, consistently with other scriptures, that a man cannot be a *Christian* without he leaves his *wife and family—friends and relations,* and throws his *substance* into the sea, and *himself* after it;—but that he is to prefer the *cause of* GOD, with the *loss of all things* (see Phil. iii. 7, 8.) to the *whole world* (see Matt. xvi. 26.) when in times of difficulty and danger, for the *truth*'s sake, he must either forsake one or the other. This, however, is not merely a New-Testament doctrine, or something imposed by a *new law* of CHRIST —it is all to be looked upon as an exemplification of the *first great commandment of the law*—*Thou shalt love the* LORD *thy* GOD, *with all thine heart, with all thy mind, with all thy soul, and with all thy strength.* Matt. xxii. 37. Mark xii. 23. Accordingly we find examples of as eminent *martyrs* under the Old Testament as under the New, as may be seen Dan. iii. 14—23. Dan. vi. 10, 16. See also 2 Maccabees vi. and vii. Heb. xi. 33, &c. —who forsook all for the cause of GOD, and *loved not their lives even to the death.* Again, Matt. x. 34. *Think not that I am come to send peace on earth: I came not to send peace but a sword. For I am come to set a man at variance against his father, and the daughter against her mother, and the daughter-in-law against her*

her mother-in-law, and a man's foes shall be they of his own houshold, ver. 35, 36. Comp. Luke xii. 51—53. What a character doth CHRIST here exhibit of Himself, supposing what He says is to be understood according to the mere *letter*, and construed according to the *sound*, instead of the *sense* and meaning of the passage! He may be said to disclaim the character of the *Messiah*, who was to bring *peace*—to be the *Prince of peace*, (see If. ix. 6, 7.) and of *the increase of whose peaceful government, there was to be no end*. Here then we must compare the Old and New Testament, and we shall find the true meaning of our LORD's declaration, which runs almost in the very words of the prophet *Micah*, vii. 6. and shews, that the spirit of opposition, and persecution of GOD's truth, are at all times alike, and that no obligation, even of the nearest kindred, relationship, or friendship, can shield us from the bitter effects of heart-enmity against GOD and His truth. We shall find the prophet's words abundantly verified in the character of persecutors—*The best of them is as a briar, the most upright is sharper than a thorn hedge*, ver. 4. But when people began to separate the New Testament from the Old, and to set up CHRIST as a broacher of a *new system*, established on *new laws*, then *folly*, being set at work by *ignorance*, *pride*, and *self-righteousness*, began to devise plans of *piety* and *holiness*, which were to be more pure and perfect than the *laws of* GOD. Hence arose

vows

vows of *perpetual chastity, voluntary poverty,* and numberless uncommanded mortifications, and refusals of the *good creatures* of GOD, *which He hath commanded to be received with thankfgiving of those who believe and know the truth.* 1 Tim. iv. 3. Hence also, as has been observed, came the disparagement of *marriage*—the condemnation of *second* marriages—the reprobation of *polygamy*.—These things might do very well for such *dwarfs* in grace as *Enoch*—*Abraham*—*Isaac*—*Jacob*—*David*, &c.; but as the *Christians* began to think, that what they called the *Christian law* was more *holy* and *perfect* than the *law of Moses*, so they invented schemes by which they were to think themselves *more holy* than the believers of *old time*, whom they esteemed to live under a less *pure* and *holy rule of life*, than what they ignorantly called the *law of* CHRIST. This *blasphemy* against GOD's *most holy law* (for it was no better) passed for very exalted *piety*, and was a part of that *mystery of iniquity*, which at length branched itself into so many orders of *monks*—*nuns*—*friars*—*hermits*—*anchorets*, among the *Papists*—and so many fanatical wild *sects* among the *Protestants*, well described by the ingenious author of *Hudibras*, where he says—

> *Religion spawn'd a various rout*
> *Of petulant capricious sects,*
> *The maggots of corrupted texts.*

Nearly allied to all this was the invention of a number of human *rites* and *ceremonies*, which were to attend upon the *ordinances* of
GOD,

GOD, and which in procefs of time began to be miftaken for the *ordinances themfelves*, or at leaft fo *effential* a *part* of them, as that the *ordinances* were looked upon as *nothing* without them. *Baptifm*, which fimply confifted in *dipping* a perfon in water, or *pouring* water upon them, in the name of the *ever-bleffed* TRINITY, was to be accompanied with *rites* of human *invention*, and *ceremonies* of *man's device*, or elfe it was good for nothing—fuch as *anointing*—*prayers*—*impofition of hands*—*the fign of the crofs*—*exorcifm*—*falt*—*fpittle*—and certain *fureties* called *godfathers* and *godmothers*.—So the facrament of the *Lord's Supper*, as fimple an inftitution as the other, and confifting in *eating bread* and *drinking wine* in remembrance of CHRIST's *death* and *facrifice*, was * loaded with *rites* and *ceremonies*, by which, in procefs of time, a piece of *wafer* was fuppofed to become the *flefh*—*bones*—*body*—and *blood* of *a man*, firft to be *worfhipped* and then *eaten*. No marvel then that *marriage*, when the Popifh vifionary, *Peter Lombard*, had found

* To this we may add—loaded with fo many ftrange opinions and devices, by the imaginations and inventions of writers of "*treatifes* on the *facrament*"—"*preparations* for "the altar"—"Devout communicants"—and books of the like kind, that a moft fimple and fignificant rite, is become too complex and unintelligible for the generality of mankind.—A late writer, Dr. BELL, has done worthily, in his *attempt* to extricate this *fimple* inftitution of CHRIST, from the difficulties which have been caft upon it by the conceit of human reafoning, by examining into the *only fource* of information, from which any true knowledge of it can be authentically deduced, the SCRIPTURE ITSELF.

it

it out to be a *sacrament*, and *Pope Innocent* III. threw the administration of it entirely into the hands of the *priests*, should also have ceremonies invented and annexed to it, which, by degrees, wrought upon the *credulity* and *superstition* of the people, so as to obscure the *real* nature of the *institution*, as *ordained of* GOD, be put in its place, and, in length of time, be mistaken for the *thing itself*. *Superstition* is always ready to give an helping hand to such sort of things, by obtaining the sanction of *custom* for their support. Still the ordinances of GOD are just the same *in* themselves and *by* themselves, as well as in their *validity, operation*, and *effect* ; they are not *added* to in these respects by the *inventions of men*, nor *diminished* by the *want* of them. What *was baptism* when CHRIST ordained it, *is baptism* still—what *was* the sacrament of the *Lord's supper*, *is* still the same—and that which made a *woman* a man's *wife*, when it was said—they shall be *one flesh*, makes her so at this moment, and *will* do to * the end of

the

* If any would be for confining this mode of marriage, *simply* by the *personal union* of the *male* and *female*, to our *first parents* ; and *that* from the necessity of their situation, they being *alone* on the earth ; and therefore no *rite* or *ceremony* to be administered by another on the *occasion*, could exist, but that afterwards this *simple union* of the parties, was not sufficient to constitute a valid marriage in GOD'S sight—let such consider the whole passage together, and they will find it, in some respects, more applicable to *Adam's* posterity, than to himself. If we believe in the notion of *Præadamites*, then indeed the words—" *a man shall leave his father and mother*"—

may

the world.—This is clearly laid down in the New Teſtament, as well as in the Old Teſtament, by CHRIST, Matt. xix. 6. and St. Paul, 1 Cor. vi. 16. See before, vol. i. p.

The various alterations which the *ſuperſtition* of *ſome* have introduced into theſe matters, and which the credulity of *others* have received, ſtill leave the *things themſelves* juſt as they were. Though the Pope denies the *cup* to the laity—though he ſtrikes out the *ſecond* commandment of the *decalogue,* and divides the *tenth* into *two,* in order to make up the number *ten*—though he, or any other earthly power, ſhould invent a ceremony, without the obſervance of which *all marriage* is *null* and *void*—though they ſhould *vacate* marriage on account of *impediments* of their *own* deviſing—ſtill all this only proves the height of human pride and preſumption—the ordinances and commandments of GOD *are* juſt what they *were,* and are equally binding *on every man's conſcience in the ſight of* GOD. As a man who makes to himſelf a *graven image,* and bows down before it and worſhips, falls

---

may apply to *Adam*; but otherwiſe, theſe words muſt apply, not to *Adam,* who had no "*father and mother,*" but to thoſe who *have,* that is to ſay, to all the *naturally-*engendered offspring of *Adam* throughout all *generations.*

This is clearly laid down by OUR SAVIOUR, Matt. xix. 5, 6. and by *Paul,* 1 Cor. vi. 16. Eph. v. 31, 32. We are therefore authorized to look on Gen. ii. 24. as the true, *original,* and *unalterable* inſtitution, by which the *male and female* become *one fleſh,* from the moment it was revealed, to the end of all things.

as much under the condemnation of the *second* commandment, though it be left out of the *decalogue* by the *authority of man*, as if it had been retained; so a man, who, on *human authority*, can imagine himself to be at liberty to *forsake* the *virgin* which he has *taken*, because he *has* not—*will* not—or *can* not go to a church with her, and hear a *form* of words of *man's device* red over him by a *priest*, is as great a sinner in the sight of GOD, as if he had done such a thing the very moment after hearing *Moses* pronounce those laws, Exod. xxii. 16, and Deut. xxii. 28, 29, which positively forbid it, and which neither *man* nor *angel* can invalidate the force and obligation of.

That the observance of these laws must be attended, in some instances, with *polygamy*, is certain. The *all-wise legislator* must foresee this, as nothing can be hidden from Him—yet no exception, no qualifying clause, no restriction, is found in these laws as to the circumstances or situation of the *man*; and that no such thing was intended, appears, not only from the construction of the *Hebrew* words—כי איש—*if any man*—but also from the *evident* care which is taken of the honour of the *seventh* commandment, by adding the words לא ארשה—non desponsata—*not betrothed*—to the description of the *damsel*.—Some such exception must certainly have been found with regard to the man, if the honour of *that law* had been endangered by *polygamy* on *his* side, as on the *side of the woman*.

woman. Another reason why no exception is made, is, the apparent objects of these laws themselves—which were, to secure the validity and obligation of the *marriage ordinance*, so that no man should put away and abandon the *virgin* he had *taken*; thus also to secure and protect the *weaker sex* from seduction and dereliction, consequently from *prostitution*; thus to prevent *whoredom* and *fornication*, and all other evils arising from wanton and causeless *divorces*. But even *polygamy* itself was regulated and circumscribed: it did not follow that a man might take any number of *wives* he pleased, because he might take more than one. The *maintenance* and *provision*, as well as the due *communication* of *his person*, (called by *Moses* עֹנָה—*duty of marriage*, Exod. xxi. 10. and by St. Paul, 1 Cor. vii. 3. ʼΟφειλομενην ʼΕυνοιαν—*due benevolence*) were not to be withdrawn from any *first* or *preceding wife*; so that much depended on the circumstances of the man.— All beyond * this was called *multiplying wives*,

---

* Doubtless in this, as in all things else, which, however lawful or innocent in themselves, may become sinful by abuse and excess, we may say with *Horace*—

Est modus in rebus—sunt certi denique fines,
Quos ultra citraque nequit consistere rectum.

Some certain mean in all things may be found,
To mark our virtues, and our vices bound.
FRANCIS.

That *polygamy* is *lawful in itself*, and in many cases *expedient* (see before, p. 178—80, and n.) in some *duty* (see vol.

wives, and, like other unreasonable excesses, forbidden even to persons of *royal* dignity. Deut. xvii. 16, 17. What *Solomon* suffered for his neglect of this law, may be seen, 1 Kings xi. 1—14.

I have said so much on this subject of *polygamy*, because it is so little understood, owing to its being taken for granted to be *sinful*, because every body is taught to believe so, though the reason of this belief is not to be found in GOD's word, but in the imaginations of people, who derive their notions upon the subject from *prejudice* and *vulgar error*, just as the *Papists* do their notions of *purgatory* or *praying to saints*. However, it is highly necessary that every part of the *divine plan* for regulating the *commerce of the sexes* should be considered upon the footing of the *divine law*, that all stumbling-blocks may be removed out of the way of that *retributive justice* so strongly commanded in that law to *every man*, and therefore which *every man* owes to the *virgin* which he has once received *into his possession*. Declaring *polygamy* to be a *sin*, that it is a *transgression of the law*,

---

vol. i. 255, and n.) none can deny, who will yield to the testimony of the scripture, and plain matter of fact. But where it is entered upon with no other view than to pamper the appetite, and to indulge a love of variety, it degenerates into *evil*; and seems to be to *marriage*, what gluttony and drunkenness, and excess of apparel, are to *food* and *raiment*—a sinful, because a forbidden, *abuse* of lawful and necessary things. See before vol. i. preface——and this vol. p. 288, and n.

when

when there is *no* * *law* against it, is, to say the least of it, an horrid and unwarranted piece of presumption, and is attended with these mischiefs among many others—It furnishes the man who has *no conscience*, with a ready excuse for leaving to distress, prostitution, and ruin, the helpless object of his brutal lust—And it deters the man who has *some conscience*, from thinking it his duty to maintain, protect, and provide for *as a wife*, the woman whom he has made so in the sight of GOD, and whom, if ever it be in his power, he ought to make so in the *sight of the world*. Whereas the *law of* GOD, the only criterion of good and evil, leaves the *former* without all excuse for *not doing*, and the *latter* without all fear *of doing*, what, if done in *every* case, would save thousands from ruin both in *this* world and in the *next*.

To maintain this, is to maintain the word of GOD—to contend *for the faith once delivered to the saints*—to defend the bulwarks of *female* security—to throw down the *strong holds* of *seduction, debauchery,* and *prostitution*—and, by sapping the foundation, to demolish the whole fabric of *adultery, whoredom,* and *fornication;* which are all *supported*, as well as *built*, by systems of human invention—policy of man's device—and maxims of *worldly wisdom*. But again let me say, be it

* *Where no law is, there is no transgression.* Rom. iv. 15. *Sin is not imputed when there is no law.* Rom. v. 13.

remembered—*the wisdom of this world is foolishness with* God. 1 Cor. iii. 19.

Into whose-soever hands these papers may come, I must at the *end*, as at the *beginning*, enjoin the *reader* to take his *Bible*, and examine thoroughly into the truth of what has been said—to weigh it in the *balance of the sanctuary*—to let no prejudice or pre-conceived opinion (if possible) bias his judgment—no traditions of men usurp the place of God's *commands* within his *conscience*—no popular opinion plead, from its *antiquity*, a right to deceive his understanding—remembring that it is written—*Let* God *be true, but every man a lyar*, Rom. iii. 4. Therefore, notwithstanding all the *plausible* and seemingly *pious* objections, which human pride can devise and raise against God's *dispensations*, and all the best-connected plans, which human wit and wisdom can oppose to that *uniform* and *holy* system of *moral government* over men's actions, which is revealed in the *Bible* —as well as all the inventions of uncommanded *rites* and *ceremonies*, which have *obscured*, and even *made of none effect*, the simple *ordinances* of God—*still* God *will be justified in His sayings, and clear when He is judged.* Rom. iii. 4. *He will destroy the wisdom of the wise, and bring to nothing the understanding of the prudent.* 1 Cor. i. 19; and it will appear at *that day*, that *what is highly esteemed among men, is abomination in the sight of* God. *Luke* xvi. 15.

By this time, it is to be hoped, that the *reader*

reader will give the *author* credit, for having considered the foregoing subjects, not in a light, hasty, desultory, or careless manner, but with all the diligence and ability of which he is capable. The *author* for himself can truly say, that he hath not wilfully overlooked the *divine testimony* on either side of the question, but hath faithfully transcribed what he apprehends to be the mind and will of GOD, as revealed in scripture, on every subject which has been considered. Notwithstanding which, if he could suppose that *second causes* were at the disposal of ignorance, superstition, vulgar error, and inveterate prejudice, he could expect little more than to adopt the complaint in Is. xlix. 4. *I have laboured in vain, I have spent my strength for nought and in vain.*—But when he looks *higher*, and recollects by whose power and providence it was, that those *very truths* of scripture, for maintaining of which *Wickliffe*'s bones, and † *Bucer*'s *books*, were publicly and ignominiously burnt, and hundreds of the wisest and best of men were committed to the flames, are now the *standards* of our *national faith*—when he recollects, that being

---

† *Bucer* died at *Cambridge* anno 1551, and was buried with the highest solemnities that could be devised. In 1557 his body was dug up, and burnt, together with that of *Fagius*, for *heresy*—and the very *churches*, where they had been buried, laid under an *interdict*.

Another proof this, of the *wisdom* and *stability* of HUMAN OPINION!

See *Burnet*, Hist. Ref. vol. ii. 163, 345.

a *bigamist*,

a *bigamift*, or *twice* fucceffively to be married, was once *infamous*, but now *honourable*—that for a *clergyman* to *marry at all* was, a little more than two hundred years ago, *felony* * both in the *man and wife*—but that now the truth of fcripture prevails, and *marriage is honourable in* ALL—when he reflects that if
" any taught their children the LORD's *Prayer*
" —the *Ten Commandments*—and *Apoftles*

* The words of this moft horrible law, 31 H. VIII. c. 14. are—" or any man which is or hath been a *prieft*,
" do carnally ufe any woman, to whom he is or hath
" been *married*, or with whom he hath contracted matri-
" mony, or openly be converfant or familiar with any
" fuch woman, both the man and the woman fhall be
" adjudged *felons*."

Let us fuppofe a *prieft* indicted on this ftatute—he is arraigned, and pleads *not guilty*. In the courfe of the trial it comes out, that the *woman* in queftion is a common *harlot*; his *intimacy* with her is proved, but *no marriage.*—He muft be *acquitted*.—So if the *woman* was proved to be *only* the *wife of another man*.—Here *whoredom* or *adultery*, fairly proved, would have faved the man's life—*marriage* would have deftroyed it.

On the fame principles, let us argue as to an indictment for *bigamy* on 1 Jac. c. 11. where the faid *peccadillos* of *whoredom* or *adultery* would equally befriend the prifoner.

Then let us afk ourfelves—how much *wifer*, or *more* conformable to GOD's *law*, this is than the other?

This *age* has learned to look upon the *firft* of the above laws with indignation and juft abhorrence—as no doubt *future ages*, if the world grows *wifer* as it grows *older*, will look upon the *fecond*.

Be it remembered, that, in both cafes, the man is indicted as a *capital* offender—his *life* put in *jeopardy* for fuppofed crimes, which the *divine law* no where condemns—and that his life is faved, by *only* having committed one or other of what are *capital offences* by the *law of Heaven*—or by claiming the *benefit of clergy* if convicted.

" *Creed,*

"*Creed,* in the vulgar tongue, it was crime
"enough to bring them to the *ſtake,* as it
"did *ſix men* and a *woman* at *Coventry,* in
"the *paſſion-week,* 1519."—(See *Burnet* Hiſt.
Ref. vol. i. p. 31.)—but that now, on the
baptiſm of our children, a ſolemn charge is
given to the ſponſors, that—"they *chiefly*
"provide that the children may learn the
"*Creed*—the LORD's *Prayer*—and the *Ten*
"*Commandments,* in the *vulgar tongue*"—I
ſay, when the author reflects on theſe and
many other inſtances of the like kind, he
owns himſelf inclined to adopt the advice of
the wiſeſt of the ſons of men—Eccl. xi. 1.—
*Caſt thy bread upon the waters, for thou ſhalt
find it after many days ;*—and not to be without hope that a day may come—when *adultery*—which, though it be the moſt malignant ſpecies of *robbery,* does not amount
with us to the guilt of a *petty larceny*—will
become terrible even to think of, much more
ſo to *perpetrate,* when men cannot indulge
their *gallantry,* but at the peril of their lives.
A time may alſo come, when ſeduction, proſtitution, and the ruin of the *weaker ſex,* ſhall
be put a ſtop to, by our adopting the ſalutary
proviſions of the *divine* law—when *child-murder, female ſuicide,* and all the other diſmal effects of men's villainy, falſhood, and
treachery, ſhall be prevented—when *fear*
and *ſhame* ſhall no longer be the concomitants
of GOD's *own ordinance,* but the magiſtrate, as
in *Iſrael,* be armed with a ſufficient power to
enforce a public recognition of it:—then will

marriage be promoted—*population* increased—GOD honoured—millions saved from destruction!

To recommend all this is the purpose of these pages.—As for the Author—*Modò hæc tibi, lector Christiane, usui sint, quemvis authorem fingito*—All that remains for him, is, to endeavour not to be *misunderstood*. He therefore desires to conclude, with explaining himself, as to those ERRORS, which appear to him to result from the present *system* of things, and which, therefore, he would wish to be rectified in the apprehensions of mankind.

1.

That the GOD and CREATOR of all things is not the *sole* legislative power, with respect to the *moral* actions of His reasonable creatures, as they relate to HIMSELF.—Therefore,

2.

That the laws, customs, and inventions of men, are to supersede, and set aside, the obligations of the *divine law*, and to correct the ways of Him who is *perfect in knowledge*.—Therefore,

3.

That *marriage* is *not* that which GOD's law makes it, but that which has been established by the authority of the church of *Rome*—adopted by *Protestants*—and confirmed by *act of Parliament*.—Therefore,

4.

The *seduction*, &c. of *virgins* creates no legal obligation in the man to marry, or to provide

provide for them in any wife, unless an *human ceremony* be performed :—on the contrary, they are to be reputed INFAMOUS—and, under the temptations of *fear* and *shame*, be reduced to the horrid and unnatural barbarity of either *murdering* their infants, in order to concealment, thus exposing their own lives to the hands of the public *executioner*—or, with the loss of *friends* and *reputation*, be driven as vagabonds on the face of the earth, to seek a wretched maintenance in common *prostitution*, and thus incur all the consequences of disease, misery, ruin, and destruction :—while the *men*, who are the guilty and inhuman authors of their calamities, are under no responsibility or obligation whatsoever.

5.

The releasing and absolving men from their *promises, vows*, and even *oaths*, so that no *private* contract of marriage, though " becom-
" ing *matrimony* by *consummation*" (see vol. i. p. 31. and vol. ii. p. 52.) shall be binding—to the great dishonour of Almighty GOD—in defiance of his laws—and to exposing numbers of the *female sex* to ruin and destruction. And this by,

6.

Adding impediments, and laying difficulties in the way of *marriage*, which are not warranted by the LAW of GOD.

7.

That *adultery*, though a capital offence by the law of GOD, subjects neither party to
any

any indictment or prosecution whatsoever, in any of our courts of criminal judicature; and is of less *penal* consequence to the guilty parties than the stealing a *sixpence*.

8.

It being held no cause of divorce from *the bond of matrimony*, without an *act of parliament*, none but the * *rich* can do themselves justice, or be at liberty to resort to that remedy, to which they are intitled by *nature, reason,* and *scripture*.—Therefore,

9.

It may be, and doubtless is, the fate of numbers of injured husbands, either to cohabit with adulterous wives—or to be reduced to all the *inconveniences* and *temptations* of a *single state*, without being able to help themselves; and at the same time to all the *burdens* and *inconveniences* of a *married state*, yet unavoidably deprived of all the comforts of it—to the grievous and irremediable distress of the injured.

10.

That *polygamy* is against the law of God—

---

* A certain eminent professor of music, of my acquaintance, had the misfortune to marry a woman, who, after bringing him a large family of children, was detected in *adultery*.—Notwithstanding the clearness of the evidence, and the notoriety of the fact, it cost him near a *thousand pounds* to get a *divorce* by *act* of *parliament*. In this account, he told me that he included his loss of time, as a master in his profession; the expence of the suit in *Doctor's Commons*; and the *fees* and *expences* which attended the *act of parliament*.

or " though allowed to the *Jews* under the " *law*—yet is in *no case* lawful to *Christians* " under the *gospel*." By *our law* it is totally and indiscriminately prohibited, on *pain of death*.—Hence it follows, that men who are *once married*, though deprived utterly of the ends and benefits of *marriage*, by *barrenness*, distemper of *mind*, or disease of *body*, in their wives—or unavoidably compelled to *separation*, by the most reasonable and justifiable causes—must be content to submit to all the inconveniences of *celibacy*—whether it be to the *extinction* of their families, which is one means of *depopulation*, or, the being exposed to all the temptations to *vice* which attend an *unmarried* state, and to all their dreadful consequences, rather than break through the laws which *men* have *imposed* on them, by using the remedy to which they are intitled by the *law* of GOD. See before, p. 178. and n.

These, and many other consequences of our present system which regards the *commerce of the sexes*, equally dangerous to the peace, happiness, comfort, and welfare of society, as well as destructive, more especially to the *weaker sex*, and dishonourable to the government of the world, as established by the *divine Legislator* at *Mount Sinai*, are what, from visible and daily proofs, the *author* apprehends, call loudly for *reformation*. This on the *basis* of that wise, holy, uniform,

uniform, and confiſtent ſyſtem of *moral government*, which *was not made for the righteous*, (i. e. for man in a ſtate of innocence and perfection) but for the *lawleſs and diſobedient*, &c. (1 Tim. i. 9.) i. e. for mankind in a fallen and corrupted ſtate—and therefore neceſſarily containing many *poſitive precepts*, which are wiſely contrived to obviate the ſad conſequences of thoſe *evils*, which, in a ſtate of *innocence* and *perfection*, could not have exiſted.

To point out theſe defects—to ſet forth their remedy on the evidence of DIVINE REVELATION—to recommend the whole to the moſt ſerious conſideration of *all men*, but more eſpecially to the *legiſlative powers*—is the author's *real deſign*.

How this has been executed, is left to the reader to determine.

As for *favour*, the *author aſks* none.—If what he hath written be contrary to the *law of* GOD—he *deſerves* it not—If, on the contrary, what hath been ſubmitted to the *reader*, be agreeable to the *divine* LAW and TESTIMONY—the *author* puts himſelf entirely out of the queſtion; and as for *critics, cavillers, objectors,* and *diſputers of this world*—whether they be of the ſect of the SADDUCEES, who ſay *there is no reſurrection, neither angel nor ſpirit*—or of the ſect of the PHARISEES, *who confeſs* both—but prefer *tradition* to ſcripture—

Quid curet LUNA *latratus canum ?*

Which,

Which, if the reader pleases, he may thus paraphrase—

> As when, with radiant majesty, the Moon,
> In her full orb, afcends her higheft noon,
> The bark of dogs, and howl of wolves, in vain
> Infult the glories of her peerlefs reign:
> Thus, beaming forth from Scripture's holy page,
> Tho' fcoffers cavil and oppofers rage,
> Fix'd in its facred orb, THE TRUTH will fhine,
> Ever be GLORIOUS—ever be DIVINE.

I conclude the whole, with recommending to the *reader*'s ferious recollection and meditation, that moft folemn, moft noble, and moft fublime *teftimony*, which MOSES, THE MAN OF GOD, under the immediate *infpiration* of the HOLY SPIRIT, bare to the holinefs, perfection, purity, and tranfcendent excellency of the LAW OF JEHOVAH.

DEUT. iv. 5, &c.

Behold, I have taught you ftatutes and judgments, even as the LORD *my* GOD *commanded me, that ye fhould do fo in the land whither ye go to poffefs it. Keep, therefore, and do them; for this is your wifdom and your underftanding in the fight of the nations: which fhall hear* ALL THESE STATUTES, *and fay, Surely this great nation is a wife and underftanding people. For what nation is there fo great, who hath a* GOD *fo nigh unto them, as* THE LORD OUR GOD *is, in all things that we call upon Him for? And what nation is there fo great, that hath* STATUTES AND JUDGMENTS SO RIGHTEOUS, *as*

ALL

ALL THIS LAW *which I set before you this day?*

PROV. xxx. 5, 6.

Every word of GOD is pure—ADD *thou not unto* HIS WORDS, *lest He reprove thee, and thou be found a* LYAR.

APPENDIX,

[349]

APPENDIX, Nº I.

Referred to vol. i. p. 108.

In which the cafe of *Hannah*—1 Sam. i.—is more *particularly* confidered.

AS I fhould be forry to be mifled myfelf, fo I fhould be equally anxious not to miflead others, with refpect to any fcripture quoted, referred to, or explained in the foregoing pages, and fo many of which have been employed to prove that *polygamy* is neither againft any law given before the *Sinai-covenant*, nor againft any law *then* delivered; confequently, is not *finful—for fin is not imputed where there is no law—and where there is no law there is no tranfgreffion.* Rom. v. 13. iv. 15.

As a proof of GOD's *own* fentiments on the matter, I have produced the ftriking inftance of *Elkanah the Levite*, and his *two wives, Peninnah* and *Hannah*; and by confidering *Hannah* as taken after, and in the lifetime of *Peninnah*, have drawn arguments, which appear to me concluſive, with regard to the main point, viz. that if *polygamy* was a tranfgreffion of the *original inftitution of marriage*—of the *feventh commandment*—or of any other *pofitive law* of GOD, it is highly unreaſonable and abfurd to fuppofe, that GOD fhould fo fignally *blefs,* and *own* it as lawful,

in

in so many instances, and *particularly* in that of *Hannah*.—But I find it is an usual opinion, and that several *commentators* rather seem to embrace it, that *Peninnah* was the *second wife, and Hannah the first*; I have the more earnestly and more diligently examined the *whole* passage, as willing to retract what I have said if it be *false*, as to abide by it if it be *true*.

The ground on which the opinion that *Hannah* was the *first* wife is built, is a very uncertain one, *viz.* that "*she is* * *named first*,"

---

* The *Hebrew* words—אחת ושנית—though they may be rendered *first* and *second*, yet are so frequently used for *one* and *the other* (as in our translation) that nothing conclusive can be gathered from them in this place. See Exod. i. 15. Numb. xi. 26. Ruth i. 4. 2 Sam. iv. 2. The best way of considering the matter, is to advert to the whole of the following context; in which it appears from many circumstances, that *Hannah* was the *second* or *after-taken wife*.

And indeed there is a very natural and obvious reason why *Hannah*, though the *second*-taken wife, should yet be named *first* in the beginning of the *history*—because the subsequent parts of it *principally* relate to *her* and her son *Samuel*.

For a like reason we may suppose *Shem* to be mentioned first of the *sons* of *Noah*—Gen. x. 1.—though not the eldest, *Shem* and his descendents being the chief subject of the *sacred* history.

So *Moses* is commonly placed before *Aaron* (though *three years* younger, See Exod. vii. 7.) wheresoever they are named together, *Moses* being the *principal* person treated of.

When the sons of *Levi* are mentioned, Numb. iii. 17. they stand thus—*Gershon, Kohath,* and *Merari*. In Numb. iv. where their several *charges* are set forth, they stand in a different order—*first*, the sons of *Kohath*—then the sons of *Gershon*—and then the sons of *Merari*.

1 Sam.

1 Sam. i. 2. But the very next sentence furnishes us with just as good a reason for supposing *Hannah* was the second, for there *Peninnah* stands *first*—*And Peninnah had children, but Hannah had no children:*—and the reason still grows stronger for supposing *Peninnah* to be *first*, ver. 4. for there she is not only mentioned *first*, but has the precedency of a *first* * wife given her by her husband *Elkanah*, who served her *first* of the *peace-offerings*:—*And when the time was come that Elkanah offered, he gave to Peninnah his wife, and to all her sons and daughters, portions;* † *and to Hannah he gave a more worthy portion, for he loved Hannah*; i. e. she was his favourite, as *Rachel* was *Jacob*'s, Gen. xxix. 30. The custom of placing the *eldest first* was very ancient, as we find, Gen. xliii. 33. *And they set before him, the eldest according to his birth-right, and the youngest according to*

---

* The *first wife* among the *Jews*, as among the *Turks* at this day, was the *principal*, and had distinguishing honours paid her.

Lady M. W. Montague says, that among the *Turks* the first made choice of, *was*, always after, *the first in rank*.

See that very ingenious, learned, and instructive writer, Mr. HARMER—*Outlines of a new commentary on Sol. Song*, p. 52, 53.

† The particle ו Vau is sometimes rendered by *postea, et postea*—*afterwards*—*and afterwards*. See Nold. part. sub ו, Nº 41.

This sense of it occurs 1 Sam. ii. 16. and in numbers of other places cited by *Noldius*; he mentions this also to be the sense of καὶ in some passages of the New Testament.

his youth — *and he took and sent messes to them from before him; but Benjamin's was five times as much as any of theirs.* Benjamin was distinguished as the favourite of his brother *Joseph*, though younger than all the rest; so was *Hannah*, the youngest or *after-taken wife*, distinguished as the favourite of *Elkanah*, and though, as *youngest*, helped after *Peninnah*, and *her sons and daughters*, yet had a larger *share*, or, as it is mentioned in the margin, a *double portion*. This is our translation; but the words מנה אחת אפים literally signify—" *a piece, part,* or *portion* of the *roasted meat*"—some more *choice part*, we may suppose, which he had reserved for her. *Elkanah*'s love, and preference of *Hannah* in his affections, would hardly have suffered him to place her after *Peninnah*, if *Hannah* had not been the youngest and after-taken wife; any more than *Joseph*'s affection to *Benjamin* would have suffered him to have placed him below the rest of his brethren, had it not been against all rule to have done otherwise.

But if we look more deeply into this scripture, we may gather from *Hannah's song*, chap. ii. 1—10, a certain proof that *Hannah* was the *second wife*. The *song* itself is evidently *prophetical*, it treats upon the same subject as that of the *Virgin Mary*, which is recorded Luke i. 46—54; and these *two wives of Elkanah*, are spoken of as typical of what should *come to pass in the latter days*, when the *Jews*, the *elder* professing people of GOD, and who *brought forth professing* children, should become *barren*, and the poor *barren Gentiles* become fruitful. *Hannah* says, chap. ii. 5. *The barren hath borne seven, and she that hath many children is waxed feeble.* A clear *prophecy* of the rejection of the *Jews*, and the *calling of the Gentiles*, the former typified by *Peninnah*, and the *latter* by *Hannah*. So Is. liv. 1.—alluding to the same interesting and wonderful events—says, *Sing, O barren, thou that didst not bear; break forth into singing, and cry aloud, thou that didst not travail with child; for more are the children of the desolate, than the children of the married wife, saith the* LORD. In this view of the matter, *Hannah* must certainly be the *second wife*, as the *Gentiles* were called subsequently to the *Jews*, or else the whole similitude of this *prophetical* transaction, as to the fulfilment of it, in the rejection of the *Jews*, and calling of the *Gentiles*, is destroyed at once.

For all these reasons, it is surely manifest, that *Peninnah*, who was a figure of the *Jews*, was the *first-taken wife*, and that *Hannah*, who was a figure of the *Gentile church*, was the *second in point of time*. Nor is it likely that *Elkanah*, having a wife whom he liked better, should take *another* he *liked worse.*—The contrary is very probable.

That *Hannah* should delay her anxious requests for a child, till after a *second* wife had been taken by her husband, and till by this second he had *sons and daughters** grown up, is inconceivable; but that *Peninnah, the first wife*, who had left off *breeding* (see chap. ii. 5, latter part)—full of rage, and jealousy, and indignation, from observing *Elkanah*'s partiality to an *after-taken wife*—should become her bitter *adversary*—say every thing to vex her, with bitter taunts upon the subject of her *barrenness* (which was reckoned a matter of disgrace among the *Jewish women*) and thus afflict and grieve her, 'till, in the sorrow, grief, and anguish of her spirit, she prayed earnestly to have *her reproach taken away* (see Gen xxx. 23.) is surely the plain, obvious, natural sense of the history. Something like this may be supposed to have happened between *Leah* and *Rachel, Gen.* xxx. 15, 22, 23.

But let us suppose, for *argument's sake*, what, for the reasons above mentioned, can never be allowed, that *Hannah* was the *elder wife*, still the history affords a very conclusive proof that *polygamy* is no *transgression of any law of* God, therefore *no sin*. *Elkanah*

---

* By ver. 4, where it is said, that, *when the time was that Elkanah offered, he gave to Peninnah his wife*, and to ALL *her sons and daughters, portions*—it should appear that *Peninnah* had brought him *many* children. Comp. chap. ii. 5.—Their being *grown up*, may be gathered from their attendance on the tabernacle, and partaking of the sacrifices, and this for *several years* together, as may be gathered from ver. 7.—*And as he did so*—שנה בשנה—*Anno in anno.* Mont. *Annuatim.* Pagn. *Year by year.* Eng. Transf.

was

was a *Levite*, who came *up to worship and sacrifice to the* LORD, probably *peace-offerings*, which were wont to accompany others at the great *festivals*, all of which—except the *fat*, which *was burnt upon the altar*, and the *breast and right shoulder*, which belonged to *the priests*—belonged *to him that offered them*; with the rest the *sacrificer* made a feast * for *himself*, his *family*, and *friends*, giving to every one a *portion* of the sacrifice.—But no one could *offer*, or *feast* upon the sacrifices, unless he was *clean*, on pain of being *cut off from his people*. Lev. vii. 20, 21. Hence we hear *Saul* accounting for *David*'s absence from the *feast, on the offerings at the new moon*. 1 Sam. xx. 26. *The touch of any thing* that was *unclean*, or having some bodily disorder upon him, such as the *leprosy*, and the like, rendered a man *unclean*, so that he could neither offer, or *feast upon the offerings*. But what must have become of that man, whose *moral* uncleanness must have been what *Elkanah*'s was, if he could be deemed to live in adultery? for that he certainly did, if *polygamy* was a sin against the *seventh commandment*. Could he have come up, year after year, to worship and to sacrifice to JEHOVAH, under such a state of *moral* defilement and uncleanness? Could he have found blessing and acceptance, while in the sink of *moral* filth and pollution? *Hophni* and *Phineas*, *Eli*'s two sons, were both cut off in one day,

* See Deut. xii. 12. xvi. 11. 2 Sam. vi. 18, 19.

for the abuse of the offerings of GOD, and for their uncleanness, 1 Sam. ii. 17, 22, 34; but *Elkanah* remains in his, accepted of GOD, and happy in being blessed with a *son* (and such a *son* as *Samuel*) by miracle. Again, what was *Peninnah?* a partaker, a partner, in *Elkanah's* iniquity, if their marriage was unlawful.—What were the sons and daughters who were born of *Peninnah*, under a forbidden marriage? *Bastards.* Therefore *Peninnah's* eating of the sacrifices, as well as her *children's*, were absolutely forbidden things. Even the *hire of an whore* was forbidden to be *brought into the house of the* LORD. Deut. xxiii. 18. how much more the *person* of an *adulteress?* and as for a *bastard*, or one born of her who was with child by *whoredom*, he was not even to *enter into the congregation of the* LORD, *even to his tenth generation.* Deut. xxiii. 2. How then could *Elkanah* himself —how could *Peninnah* (supposing her the *second wife)*—how could the *children born of these parents*, go to the *house of the* LORD in *Shilo—feast upon the sacrifices*, and *return in peace*, with GOD's *blessing* and *acceptance*, unless the *second marriage* was as *lawful* in GOD's sight as the *first*, and no more than *that*, an offence against GOD's law? In whatever view we take this *chapter*, it proves, that neither the *words* of the *primary institution*, nor those of any *subsequent commandment*, prohibited *polygamy*; for if they had, these things respecting *Elkanah, Peninnah*, and their *children*, could not have been as they were, consistently confiftently with the fcripture-character of that HOLY GOD, *who is of purer eyes than to behold evil, or to look on iniquity.* Hab. i. 13.

Here I might once more mention the cafe of *Solomon,* the fon of *David* by *Bathfheba,* whom *David,* having other *wives* before, *took to wife* after the deceafe of *Uriah.* The *law,* which pofitively excluded *baftards,* or thofe born out of lawful wedlock, *from the congregation of the* LORD, *even unto the tenth generation,* (Deut. xxiii. 2.) is wholly inconfiftent with *Solomon's* being employed *to build* GOD's *temple*—being the *mouth of the people* to GOD in *prayer*—and *offering facrifices* in the *temple* at its *dedication*—unlefs *David*'s marriage with *Bathfheba* was a *lawful marriage*—*Solomon* the *lawful iffue of* that marriage—confequently *polygamy* no fin, either againft the *primary inftitution of marriage,* or againft the *feventh commandment.*—But fo far from *Solomon's* being under any legal difqualification from the *law* above-mentioned — he is appointed *by* GOD *himfelf to build the temple,* 1 Kings viii. 19. *His prayer is heard*—*and the houfe is hallowed,* chap. ix. 3. and *filled with fuch glory, that the priefts could not ftand to minifter,* chap. viii. 11. *Solomon,* therefore, as well as *Samuel,* ftand as a demonftrable proof, that a child born under the circumftance of *polygamy* is no *baftard*—GOD *Himfelf being the judge, whofe judgment is according to truth.*

A more ftriking inftance of GOD's *thoughts,*

on the total difference * between *polygamy* and *adultery*, does not meet us any where, in any part of the *sacred history*, than in the account which is given us of *David* and *Bathsheba*, and their *issue*.

When *David* took *Bathsheba*, she was another's *wife*—the *child* which he begat upon her in that situation was begotten in *adultery*—*and the thing which David had done displeased the* LORD, 2 Sam. xi. 27. And what was the consequence? We are told, 2 Sam. xii. 1. *The* LORD *sent Nathan (the prophet) unto David*. *Nathan* opened his commission with a most beautiful parable, descriptive of *David's* crime; this parable the *prophet* applies to the conviction of the delinquent, sets it home upon *his conscience*, brings him to *repentance*, and the poor penitent finds *mercy*—his life is spared, ver. 13. Yet GOD will vindicate the honour of His *moral government*, and that in the most awful manner—the murder of *Uriah* is to be visited upon *David* and *his house*—*The sword shall never depart from thine house*, ver. 10. The *adultery* with *Bathsheba* was to be retaliated in the most aggravated manner—*Because thou hast despised Me, and hast taken the wife of Uriah the Hittite to be thy wife*—*Thus saith the Lord, I will raise up evil against thee out of thine own house*—*and I will take thy wives and give* † *them unto thy neighbour*

---

* See also vol. i. p. 265—8.

† GOD's taking and giving *David's* wives to *Absalom*, is to be understood in a very different sense from His giving the deceased *Saul's* wives into *David's bosom*, ver. 8.

This

neighbour before thine eyes—*and he shall lie with thy wives in sight of this sun*—*for thou didst it secretly, but I will do this thing before all Israel, and before the sun.* All this was shortly fulfilled in the *rebellion* and *incest* † of *Absalom*, chap. xvi. 21, 22. And this was done in a way of *judgment* on *David*, for taking and defiling the wife of *Uriah*, and was included in the *curses* threatened, Deut. xxviii. 30. to the despisers of God's laws.

This last is peculiarly mentioned as a *favour* done to *David*, and therefore spoken of as an ingredient to heighten his ingratitude in taking the wife of *Uriah*—the other was *threatened* as a *judgment* (see Deut. xxviii. 30. Jer. viii. 10. former part) and permitted, as many other *evils* are, in a course of *providence*, as a sore punishment on *David* for what he had done. But *Absalom* was nevertheless guilty of *adultery* and *incest*, in taking his father's *wives* and *lying with them*, and is no more excusable, than he was in drawing his sword in *rebellion* against his father, because this, as the other, was a fulfilment of God's threatening—ver. 11. *I will raise up evil against thee out of thine own house.*

So when it is said—*Ezek.* xx. 25.—*I gave them statutes that were not good, and judgments whereby they should not live; and I polluted them in their own gifts*, &c. it appears from ver. 24, where the reasons of this are set down, that all was in a way of *judgment* for their departure from the *statutes* of JEHOVAH. *Wherefore*—God left them to follow the deceit of their own hearts, the consequence of which may be described, Ps. cvi. 39. *Thus were they defiled in their own gifts, and went a whoring with their own inventions.* As if God had said—*I gave them*—that is—*I permitted them to follow*—such *statutes* and *precepts*, as a *judgment* on their departure from ME. See JEWS *Letters* to M. de VOLTAIRE, vol. i. p. 339—341, a very sensible solution of this passage of *Ezekiel.*

† For the tragical story of *Amnon*, see 2 Sam. xiii. throughout.

[360]

As to the issue of *David's* adulterous commerce with *Bathsheba*, it is written—2 Sam. xii. 15.—*The* LORD *struck the child which Uriah bare unto David, and it was very sick.* What a dreadful scourge this was to *David*, who could not but read his *crime* in his *punishment*, the following verses declare; wherein we find *David* almost frantic with grief: however *the child's sickness was unto death*, for, ver. 18, *on the seventh day the child died.*

Now let us take a view of *David's* act of *polygamy*, when, after *Uriah's* death, he added *Bathsheba* to his *other wives*, ver. 24, 25. *And David comforted Bathsheba his wife, and went in unto her, and lay with her, and she bare a son, and he called his name* (שלמה) *Selomoh* (that maketh *peace and reconciliation or recompence)* and *the* LORD *loved him.* Again, we find *Nathan*, who had been sent on the former occasion, sent also on this, but with a very *different* message.—*And He* (the LORD) *sent by the hand of Nathan the prophet, and He called his name* JEDIDIAH (DILECTUS DOMINI—*beloved of the* LORD) *because of the* LORD—i. e. because of the favour GOD had towards him, ver. 24. Comp. 1 Chron. xxviii. 5, 6.

Let any read onward through the whole history of *Solomon*—let them consider the instances of GOD's peculiar favour towards him already mentioned, and the many others, that are to be found in the account we have of him—let them compare GOD's dealings
with

with the *unhappy offspring of David's adultery*, and this *happy issue* of his *polygamy*—and if the *allowance* and *approbation* of the *latter*, doth not as clearly appear, as the *condemnation* and *punishment* of the former, surely all distinction and difference must be at an end, and the scripture itself lose the force of it's own evidence.

APPENDIX,

APPENDIX, Nº II.

See before, Vol. i. p. 374.

HAVING mentioned *Barbeyrac's* note ee, on *Grotius* de Jure, lib. ii. c. v. sect. 9. —in which the latter is represented as having changed his opinion, with regard to a *new law* of CHRIST on the subject of *polygamy*—I was much inclined to examine farther into this matter, and therefore procured *Barbeyrac's* French translation of *Grotius de Jure*, with the *French annotations*, to which *Barbeyrac* refers in the above note—imagining that I might there meet with a more ample account of the matter.

On searching the *notes* of this learned *Frenchman* on his translation of *Grotius de Jure*, I find abundant proof of a very great change of sentiment in that great man.

I will lay this before the reader in the very words of *Barbeyrac*; whose proofs are incontestible, because taken from the writings of *Grotius* himself.

The first passage which I would mention, is, *Barbeyrac*'s note on Grot. de Jure, liv. ii. c. v. sect. 9. No. 7. which, as far as it relates to this matter, stands thus:

" Pour éclaircir la matiére, & pour savoir
" en même tems ce que pensoit nôtre auteur
" depuis la premiere édition de cet ouvrage,
" ou

" ou il ne fit neanmoins aucun changement
" dans cet endroit; il eſt bon d'ajouter ici
" quelques unes des reflexions que l'on
" trouve dans ſon commentaire ſur le *Nou-*
" *veau Teſtament*, Matt. v. 32. Il remarque
" donc d'abord, que notre Seigneur JESUS
" CHRIST ne pretend point, dans ce paſſage,
" non plus que dans tout le reſte de ſon diſ-
" cours fait ſur la montagne, abolir aucune
" partie de la loi de *Moïſe :* il veut ſeule-
" ment montrer de quelle maniere, & en
" quel cas un homme-de-bien peut profiter
" de la permiſſion du *divorce* accordée par
" un des reglemens politiques de cette loi,
" qui ſubſiſtoit encore dans le tems qu'il
" parloit. Il ne s'agit point par conſequent
" d'une cauſe de divorce portée devant les
" juges : car, outre qu'un mari, qui vouloit
" repudier ſa femme, n'étoit point obligé,
" ſelon la loi, de le faire par voie de juſtice ;
" lors qu'il accuſoit ſa femme d'adultére de-
" vant les juges, cela alloit à la faire punir de
" mort, ſelon la loi, & non pas obtenir une
" diſſolution de marriage.

" Ainſi quand nôtre ſeigneur par le de l'a-
" dultére, comme d'une juſte cauſe de divorce,
" il ſuppoſe ou un mari doux & clement,
" qui ne vouloit point faire punir ſa femme,
" quelque coupable qu'elle fut d'infidelité,
" comme *Joſeph* en uſa à l'egard de *Marie*,
" dans le tems qu'il ne pouvoit encore ſavoir
" la cauſe miraculeuſe de ſa groſſeſſe ; ou
" bien un mari, qui n'avoit pas dequoi
" prouver en juſtice l'infidelité de ſa femme,

" quoiqu'il

" quoiqu'il en fut perſuadé, ou que même
" il en eut des preuves indubitables pour
" lui."

" To elucidate the matter, and to know
" at the ſame time what our author *(Grotius)*
" thought ſince the firſt edition of this work
" *(De Jure)*—in which neverthelefs he
" made no alteration of this paſſage—it is
" proper to add here ſome of the reflections
" which we find in his *notes on the New
" Teſtament*, Matt. v. 32. He remarks then,
" firſt, that our LORD JESUS CHRIST doth
" not intend at all in this paſſage, any more
" than in the whole of his ſermon upon
" the mount, to * aboliſh any part of the
" law of *Moſes*—he means only to ſhew after
" what manner, and in what caſe, a *good
" man* might avail himſelf of the permiſſion
" of divorce, which was granted by one of
" the political regulations of that law which
" ſtill ſubſiſted at the time he ſpake. The
" queſtion, conſequently, was not concern-
" ing a cauſe of divorce brought before the
" judges; for, beſides that an huſband who
" would repudiate his wife was not obliged,
" according to the law, to do it in a judicial
" way, it muſt be obſerved, that when he
" accuſed his wife of adultery before the
" judges, that would have tended to her be-
" ing puniſhed with *death*, according to the
" law, and not to the obtaining of a diſſolu-
" tion of the marriage.

* See before, vol. i. p. 300—3.

" Alſo,

"Also, where our LORD speaks of *adultery*
as a just cause of divorce, he supposes, either
a mild and kind husband, who would not
have his wife punished, however guilty
she might be of infidelity—as *Joseph* acted
with respect to *Mary* at the time when he
could not know the miraculous cause of
her pregnancy—or else an husband who
had not full legal proof of his wife's infidelity, though he was persuaded of it, or
even had indubitable proofs with respect
to himself."

Then follows a long passage on the subject
of divorce; after which, *Barbeyrac* gives us
Grotius's thoughts on the latter part of the
verse.

" Dans les paroles suivantes—*& celui qui*
epouse la femme repudiée, commet adultére—
la loi de Moïse subsistant encore, comme
nous l'avons dit, il faut entendre les paroles de JESUS CHRIST de celui qui epousoit une femme repudiée, avant qu'on eût
tenté toutes les voies possibles de la recon-
cilier avec son mari, comme l'Apôtre St.
Paul le prescrit, 1 Cor. vii. 11, ou ce qui
est encore pis, de ceux qui etant devenus
amoureux des femmes d'autrui cherchoient
à s'en emparer par un divorce.

" C'est aussi à cela que se rapporte ce qui dit
notre *Seigneur*, Matt. xix. 9. ou il explique plus au long sa pensée. *Celui qui*
répudiera sa femme, ET EN EPOUSERA UNE
AUTRE, &c. car & celui qui epousoit la
femme repudiée, empechoit par là qu'elle
" ne

" ne retournât avec son mari, qui n'auroit
" pû après cela la reprendre, quand il l'auroit
" voulu; & le mari de la femme repudiée,
" des-là qu'il en epousoit une autre, donnoit
" lieu de croire qu'il n'étoit point disposé à
" reprendre la premiere, & ainsi il lui four-
" nissoit occasion, entant qu'en lui étoit, ou
" de s'abandonner à l'impudicité, ou de s'en-
" gager avec un autre mari: car c'est ainsi
" qu'il faut entendre le terme $\mu o\iota\chi\alpha\tau\alpha\iota$ que
" l'on traduit *commet adultére*, mais qui doit
" signifier la meme chose que $\pi o\iota\epsilon\iota\ \mu o\iota\chi\tilde{\alpha}\sigma\theta\alpha\iota$
" *fait commettre adultére*, dans l'autre passage
" parallel du même evangeliste; selon le stile
" des *Hebreux* qui attribuent à quelqu'un di-
" rectement, ce à quoi il donne occasion par
" quelque action propre. Voiez. Rom.
" viii. 26. Gal. iv. 6.

" Voila en substance ce que dit notre au-
" teur dans ses notes sur le *Nouveau Testa-*
" *ment*. D'ou il paroit, que ses idees n'étoi-
" ent pas tout-à-fait les mêmes, quand il
" composa l'ouvrage que nous expliquons,
" quoiqu' il n'aît depuis rien changé dans
" cet endroit.

" De tout ce que l'on vient de voir, il s'en-
" suit, que dans les passages de l'evangile
" qu'il cite ici en marge pour montrer que
" nôtre Seigneur JESUS CHRIST a defendu
" par une de ses loix la *polygamie*, il ne
" s'agit que du *divorce*; & cela par opposi-
" tion aux fausses idées des *Juifs*, qui le croi-
" oient permis en conscience pour quelque
" cause que ce fût. Matt. xix. 2.

" Aussi

" Auſſi voyons nous que notre auteur dans
" ſon traité *de la verité de la religion Chrétienne*,
" publié pour la premiere fois en 1639, c'eſt
" à dire, environ deux ans avant ſes *notes ſur*
" *le Nouveau Teſtament*; lorſqu'il parle du
" marriage d'un avec une, après avoir dit,
" qu'il y en a peu des nations dans le pa-
" ganiſme parmi leſquelles on ſe ſoit conten-
" té d'une femme, comme faiſoient les *Ger-*
" *mains* & les *Romains*; ajoute ſeulement,
" que les Chrêtiens ſuivent cette maniere de
" marriage, lib. ii. § 13. & dans les notes il
" ne cite aucun paſſage de l'evangile, mais
" ſeulement ces paroles de 1 Cor. vii. 4. *Une*
" *femme n'eſt pas maitreſſe de ſon corps, mais*
" *ſon mari; de meme un mari n'eſt pas maitre*
" *de ſon corps, mais ſa femme.* Or, dans ſes
" notes poſthumes ſur les epîtres, il explique
" ces paroles conformément à la ſuite du diſ-
" cours, comme n'emportant autre choſe que
" le droit qu'a une femme d'exiger que ſon
" mari ne lui refuſe point le devoir conjugal;
" parce que en vertu du marriage, elle en-
" tre avec lui dans une ſocieté qui demand
" l'uſage reciproque de leurs corps: Ουκ'
" εξουσιαζει *hic eſt, non habet jus plenum atque*
" *integrum; nam non vitæ tantum, ſed & cor-*
" *porum eſt initia* κοινωνια. *In re autem ſociali,*
" *nemo ſociorum jus plenum habet.*
" Mais il n'enſuit point de là, qu'un mari
" ne puiſſe avoir plus d'une femme : car les
" ſocietéz ne ſe ſont pas toujours ſur un pié
" egal. Ainſi ce n'eſt que par accommoda-
" tion que notre auteur applique ici les pa-
" roles

" roles de St. *Paul*, & pour donner à enten-
" dre que les Chrétiens ont renoncé à la *po-*
" *lygamie*, plûtot pour fuivre l'efprit & le
" genie de l'evangile, qui porte à eviter ce
" dont on peut abufer facilement, que pour
" obeïr à une loi expreffe de nôtre *Seigneur*, ou
" de fes apôtres. Voiez Mr. *Le Clerc*, Hift.
" Eccl. Prolegom. fect. 3. c. iv. fect. 5. num. 9.
" p. 162. Il n'y a nulle apparence que Jesus
" Christ aît voulu obliger ceux qui avoient
" plufieurs femmes, avant que de devenir fes
" difciples, à les renvoier toutes, hormis
" une."

" In the words which follow—*And he
" that marrieth her that is put away, commit-
" teth adultery*—the law of *Mofes* yet fubfift-
" ing, as we have before obferved, we muft
" underftand the words of Jesus Christ to
" concern him who married a *divorced wo-
" man*, before all poffible ways had been
" tried to reconcile her to her hufband, as
" St. *Paul* prefcribes 1 Cor. vii. 11.— or,
" what is worfe ftill, of thofe who having
" become fond of the wives of others, en-
" deavoured to get * poffeffion of them by
" means of a *divorce* in order to poffefs
" them.

" It is to this alfo, that what our Lord
" faith, Matt. xix. 9. relates, where he ex-
" plains his meaning more fully—*Whofoever
" putteth away his wife, and* marrieth an-
" other, &c.; for both he who married

* See before vol. i. 357, 358.

" the

"the *divorced* woman, hindered her by that
"means from returning to her hufband, who
"could not, after this, have taken her if he
"would; and the hufband of the divorced
"wife, from the inftant he married another
"woman, gave occafion to think, that he
"was not at all difpofed to retake the firft
"woman; and thus he gave occafion to her,
"as far as in him lay, either to abandon her-
"felf to lewdnefs, or to engage with another
"hufband*. For it is thus we muft under-
"ftand the term μοιχᾶται, which they tranflate
"—*committeth adultery*, but which ought to
"fignify the fame as—ποιει μοιχᾶσθαι—*caufeth
"to commit adultery*; as in the parallel place
"of the fame *evangelift*—(ch. v. 32.)—ac-
"cording to the ftyle of the *Hebrews*, who
"attribute that to a perfon *directly*, which by
"any action of his own he is the *occafion*
"of." See Rom. viii. 26. Gal. iv. 6.

"This is the fubftance of what our author
"fays in his notes on the *New Teftament*:
"from whence it appears, that his ideas
"were *not altogether the fame* when he com-
"pofed the work which we are now explain-
"ing, though he has not fince made any al-
"teration in this paffage.

"From all that we have been obferving,
"it follows, that in the paffages of the gof-
"pel, which *Grotius* here cites in the mar-
"gin, to fhew that OUR SAVIOUR prohibited,
"by one of his laws, *polygamy*, the fubject
"was only concerning *divorce*; and that in

* See before, vol. i. 370—373.

"oppofition

"oppofition to the falfe notions of the *Jews,*
"who believed that in confcience it was per-
"mitted for any *caufe whatfoever.* Matt. xix. 2.

"Let us obferve alfo, that our author, in
"his treatife of the *truth of the Chriftian*
"*Religion,* firft publifhed in 1639, that is to
"fay, about two years after his *notes on the*
"*New Teftament,* fpeaking of the marriage
"of *one man with one woman,* after having
"faid that there were few heathen nations,
"among which people contented themfelves
"with *one wife,* as the *Germans* and *Romans*
"did, only adds, that the *Chriftians* followed
"this manner of marriage, lib. ii. fect. 13;
"and in the notes he does not cite a fingle
"paffage from the gofpel, but only thefe
"words of 1 Cor. vii. 4. *The wife hath not*
"*power of her own body, but the hufband: and*
"*likewife alfo the husband hath not power of*
"*his own body, but the wife.* But in his
"pofthumous notes on the *Epiftles,* he ex-
"plains thefe words conformably to the fe-
"quel of the difcourfe, as importing nothing
"elfe but the right which a wife hath to
"require that her hufband fhall not refufe
"her the conjugal duty; becaufe, in virtue
"of the marriage, fhe enters with him into
"a fociety which demands the reciprocal
"ufe of their bodies. 'Ουκ εξουσιαζει, here
"fignifies—*he has not a full and entire right*—
"*for a communion, not of life only,* but of their
"*bodies* alfo, is entered into. However, in
"a matter of *partnerfhip, neither of the par-*
"*ties have a full right.*

"But

" But it doth not follow from thence,
" that a man can have but *one wife*; for
" partnerships are not always made upon an
" equal footing. So that it is only by way
" of accommodation that our *author* applies
" these words of *St. Paul,* and to give us to
" understand, that *Christians* renounced *po-*
" *lygamy,* rather to follow the spirit * and
" genius

* The " spirit and genius of the *gospel,*" as far as it relates to the *spirit* and *temper* of its *professors,* speaks thus by the Prophet *Isaiah,* chap. ii. 11. *The lofty looks of man shall be humbled, and the haughtiness of men shall be bowed down, and the* LORD *alone shall be exalted in that day.* Comp. ver. 17. and 1 Cor. i. 31.

This, in the very early days of *Christianity,* seems to have been forgotten, and, instead of exalting *Jehovah,* by making HIS PURE AND PERFECT LAW (Pf. xix. 7—11.) the holy directory of their obedience, the *Christians* (as has been before observed) sat about inventing schemes of *devotion* and *piety,* not only inconsistent with, but opposite to, the DIVINE LAW—they detached the *New Testament* from the *Old,* and ran into as much folly and extravagance, as, before the end of the *first century,* branched themselves out into those *heresies,* which, in one shape or other, have been the disgrace of the *church* ever since. If we look onward to the end of the *second century,* we may say of the *heretics* and their *heresies,* as is said of the men which arose from the *bones.* Ezek. xxxvii. 10.—*they stood up upon their feet an exceeding great army.* See Chron. Tab. Mosheim, Maclaine edit. vol. ii. 581—2.

To alter GOD's LAW relative to marriage, for fear of *abuse,* is about as wise and holy, and as respectful to the wisdom of the DIVINE LAWGIVER, as taking the *Bible* away from the Popish laity, in order to prevent *heresy and schism,* and to preserve the *unity of the church.* See before, 288, n.

When persons speak of the *spirit and genius of the gospel,* as distinguishable from the *spirit and genius of the law,* with respect to *purity* and *holiness,* they usually say

a great

"genius of the gospel, which carries us to avoid what may be easily abused, than to obey any express law of OUR LORD or of His *Apostles*. See *Le Clerc Hist. Eccles. Prolegom. sect.* 3. c. iv. *sect.* 5. *numb.* ix. p. 162. There is no appearance that JESUS CHRIST had any intention to oblige those who had several wives, before they became his disciples, to send away all but one."

a great deal more than they are authorized from the *scriptures* to speak, or, perhaps, than they themselves understand.

If the New Testament says—*As He which hath called you is holy, so be ye holy in all manner of conversation*—it is added—*because it is written, Be ye holy, for I am holy.* Comp. 1 Pet. i. 15, 16. with Lev. xix. 2. and xx. 26. Deut. xiv. 2. with Tit. ii. 14. and 1 Pet. ii. 9.

I went down to the potter's house (saith *Jer.* xviii. 3.) *and behold he wrought a work on the wheels. And the vessel that he made of clay was marred* (נשחת—*spoiled*) *in the hand of the potter ; so he made it again another vessel, as seemed good to the potter to make it.*

Certainly the poor *potter* could do no otherwise ; if he *spoiled* the *vessel in the making*, he must repair his loss by *making it over again* ;—but shall we imagine that the *all-wise* GOD, either for want of *wisdom* or *foresight*, miscarried, or *failed*, in point of *holiness* and *purity*, with respect to the LAW which he framed for the *moral government* of his creatures under the Old Testament, and therefore corrected his *mistake*, and made *another* and a *better* LAW for that purpose under the New Testament?

Contending for a *purity* and *holiness* in the New Testament, which is not in the Old Testament, is but saying all this in other words, and coinciding with the *principles* of *Cerinthus, Mahomet,* and *Socinus.* See before, vol. i. chap. v.

Manes and *Cerinthus* were consistent, for as they rejected the *law* of the Old Testament, they at the same time rejected the GOD of the Old Testament.

Barbeyrac,

Barbeyrac, in another part of the *French* notes on his tranſlation of *Grot. de Jure*—viz. *Liv.* i. c. 1. ſect. 15. n. 3.—expreſſes himſelf thus—

"Quand *Moïſe* dit que *l'homme quittera ſon pere & ſa mere, pour s'attacher à ſa femme, & qu'ils deviendront une ſeule chair*; cela ne fait rien ni pour, ni contre, la *polygamie*, ou le *divorce*; l'expreſſion, *devenir une ſeule chair*, ſignifie ſeulement par elle-même, qu'il y auroit, entre un mari & ſa femme, une union très étroite : mais elle n'emporte point qu'un mari ne puiſſe avoir en même tems une ſemblable liaiſon avec *deux* ou *pluſieurs femmes*; & a l'egard de la diſſolution du marriage, tout ce qu'on en peut inferer, c'eſt qu'il ne doit pas être rompu legerement, & ſans quelque bonne raiſon. Selon le ſtile des *Hebreux*, le mot de *chair* marque toute liaiſon, tant d'affi-nité que de conſanguinité, comme l'a re-marqué Mr. *Le Clerc*. C'eſt ainſi que *La-ban* dit à *Jacob*, Gen. xxix. 14. *Tu es mon os & ma chair*—c'eſt-à-dire, je vous recon-nois pour un des mes parens. Comme donc tout autant de parens qu'a une per-ſonne font ſa *chair*, de même rien n'em-pêche qu'un homme ne puiſſe être dit, ſelon ce ſtile, *une même chair* avec pluſieurs femmes."

"When *Moſes* ſays, that *a man ſhall leave his father and mother, and cleave to his wife, and they ſhall become one fleſh*—this makes nothing for or againſt *polygamy* or *divorce*;
"the

"the expression—*become one flesh*—signifies
"only by itself, that there should be be-
"tween a man and his wife a most strict
"union: but it does not import that an
"husband may not have at the same time, a
"like bond with *two* or *more wives*. As to
"the dissolution of the marriage, all that one
"can infer from it is, that it ought not to
"be broken lightly, and without some good
"reason. According to the style of the
"*Hebrews*, the word *flesh* denotes all rela-
"tion, as well of affinity as of consanguinity,
"as Mr. *Le Clerc* has observed. Thus *Laban*
"says to *Jacob*, Gen. xxix. 14. *Surely thou
"art my bone and my flesh*—that is to say, *I
"acknowledge thee for one of my relations.*—As
"therefore all the relations which any person
"hath * are his flesh, so nothing hinders,
"but that a man, according to this style of
"speaking, may be called *one same flesh* with
"many wives."

On that part of *Liv.* ii. c. v. sect. 9. where
Grotius says—that "GOD's giving but one
"woman to one man, sufficiently shews what
"is most agreeable to GOD, and consequent-
"ly this has always been comely and com-
"mendable; but it does not follow, adds
"*Grotius*, that one cannot do otherwise with-
"out a crime: for where there is no law,
"there is no violation of law: now at that
"time there was no law about the matter."

---

* See Judges ix. 2. 2 Sam. v. 1. 1 Chron. xi. 1. 2 Sam. xix. 12, 13.

Grotius

Grotius has a long note on part of this paffage, which *Barbeyrac* tranflates; and then adds——

"A juger de cette queftion, indépendam-
"ment des loix civiles, il eft certain que
"fouvent on ne pourroit ufer de la liberté
"de la *polygamie*, fans pecher contre quelque
"vertu, & s'engager dans des inconvéniens
"facheux; à caufe defquels la prudence des
"legiflateurs a demandé qu'on defendît en-
"tierement d'avoir plus d'une femme à la
"fois. Mais on ne fauroit inferer de là que
"la chofe foit mauvaife en elle-même, felon
"le droit naturel : tout ce qu'on peut dire,
"c'eft que c'eft une des ces chofes indiffe-
"rentes de leur nature, dont il eft facile
"d'abufer, comme le jeu, par exemple, &
"plufieurs autres divertiffemens, dont le plus
"fûr eft de fe priver, pour peu qu'on fe fente
"de la difpofition à en faire mauvais ufage."

"To judge of this queftion, independent-
"ly of civil laws, it is certain, that often one
"cannot ufe the liberty of *polygamy* without
"offending againft fome virtue, and engag-
"ing in grievous inconveniences; on ac-
"count of which, the prudence of legiflators
"has required, that the having more than
"*one* wife at a time, fhould be prohibited *
"entirely.

---

* The Marquis of *Beccaria*, in his ingenious effay on Crimes and Punifhments—c. xl. *On falfe Ideas of Utility*—obferves, that—" A principal fource of errors and in-
"juftice, are falfe ideas of utility. For example—that
"legiflator has falfe ideas of utility, who confiders *par-*
"*ticular* more than *general* inconveniences; who had
"rather

" entirely. But we cannot infer from thence,
" that the thing is evil in itfelf, according
" to natural right: all that can be faid is,
" that it is one of thofe things indifferent in

" rather *command* the fentiments of mankind, than *excite*
" them, and dares to fay to reafon—" be thou my flave;"
" —who would facrifice a thoufand real advantages, to
" the fear of an imaginary or trifling inconvenience; who
" would deprive men of the ufe of fire, for fear of their
" being burnt, and of water, for fear of their being
" drowned; and who knows of no means of preventing
" evil but by deftroying it."

The indifcriminate and total prohibition of *polygamy*, in order to prevent its *abufe*, falls directly within the above obfervation, and is one of thofe proofs of human abfurdity, with which the hiftory of mankind abounds, even taken in a temporal view, as might be inftanced in many *fituations* to which married men may be unavoidably reduced. See before, vol. i. p. 175—178. Their being condemned to fuffer all the inconveniences, and to be expofed to all the mifchiefs of *thofe fituations*, becaufe others, who are not in the fame, may *abufe* that mode of relief which the law of GOD affords, is an attack upon the *divine legiflation*, an arraignment of the *divine wifdom*, and an unauthorized encroachment on the *natural rights* of mankind.

The fame may be faid of the prevention of *clandeftine marriages*, by vacating the *bond of marriage*, and releafing the parties from all matrimonial obligation whatfoever.

Thus alfo, depriving a contracted woman of the exaction of that right which GOD's law pofitively gives her, and the law of this land once afforded her, to the deftruction of her character, comfort, and peace of mind for ever—this, becaufe, now and then, a *clandeftine marriage* might hurt the pride, or difappoint the avarice or ambition, of a few individuals.

In fhort, the whole is replete with *folly*, and, as far as the *divine law* is concerned, with *wickednefs*; and reminds one of the *blackfmith*, who, feeing a *fly* on the forehead of his fleeping infant, ftruck at the *infect* with his *fledge-hammer*, killed the *fly*, and at the fame time dafhed out the brains of his child.

" their

" their nature, which it is easy to abuse;
" such as *gaming*, for instance, and many
" other amusements, of which it is the
" surest way to deprive ourselves, if we per-
" ceive in the least a disposition in ourselves
" to make a bad use of them."

Barbeyrac, on Grot. de Jur. liv. i. c. 1.
§ 17. note 3. lays it down as a rule, that—
" God cannot absolutely permit the least
" thing which is evil in itself, though he be
" considered as acting in the quality of a
" temporal monarch"—(as under the theocracy)—" for this character does not strip
" him of his holiness, nor does it hinder us
" from supposing that he approves, as inno-
" cent at least, all that he permits, either
" in formal terms, or by necessary conse-
" quence from any express law or ordinance.
" Here then, in my opinion," adds he, " are
" the consequences which we may draw from
" the divine permission, where reasons drawn
" from the nature of the things themselves,
" to which attention is always to be paid,
" may appear doubtful."

He then proceeds to lay down two general rules, which are well worth our attention.

" I. *Quand* Dieu *permet une chose en certain*
" *cas, ou à certaines personnes, ou par rapport*
" *à certaines gens; on doit inferer de là, que*
" *cette chose permise n'est point mauvaise de sa*
" *nature.*"

" I. When God permits a thing in a cer-
" tain case, or to certain persons, or with
" respect to certain people, we ought to infer
" from

" from thence, that the thing which is per-
" mitted *is not evil in itself.*"

After giving other examples to illustrate this rule, he proceeds—

" Il est défendu aux Rois, par la loi de
" *Moïse* (Deut. xvii. 17.) *D'avoir un trop
" grand nombre des femmes*, de peur qu'elles ne
" les portent à violer la loi : par là le legisla-
" teur permet tacitement à eux, & à tous les
" autres, d'avoir plus d'une femme sans quoi
" la défense seroit fort superfluë. Donc la
" *polygamie* n'est pas mauvaise, & illicite de
" sa nature."

" By the law of *Moses* (Deut. xvii. 17.) the
" kings (of *Israel)* are forbidden to have *too
" great a number of wives*, lest they should
" carry them into a violation of the law: by
" this the *legislator* tacitly permits them, and
" all others, to have more than one wife,
" otherwise the command were * superfluous.
" From

---

* The intention of the commandment relative to the *kings* of *Israel* (Deut. xvii. 17.) appears plainly from the very words of it—which are not—that they *shall not have more than one wife at a time*—but that the *king*—לא ירבה —*non multiplicabit*, Mont.—*shall not multiply (or increase to a multitude)* נשים לו *women to himself*—so as to imitate the *kings* of the *heathen*, who had numbers of *women* of all nations, partly for *state*, partly for the provocation and indulgence of *sensuality*, and this to such a degree, as wholly to neglect all public affairs, and to sink into the most shameful sloth and effeminacy. Therefore it is added—ולא יסור לבבו—*that his heart turn not away*—not only from the affairs of the *kingdom*—but into *apostacy* from God to *idols*, being solicited thereto by the fondness he might entertain for a variety of *women* taken to supply his pleasures, some of them perhaps *heathens*, to
which

[379]

" From hence it follows, that *polygamy* is not
" evil and illicit in itself."

" II. *Lorsque* Dieu *regle la maniere d'une
" chose, ou qu'il fait par rapport à cette chose,
" quelque autre reglement, qui suppose necessaire-
" ment qu'elle est permise ; il faut voir s'il s'agit
" d'un seul acte passager, ou d'une chose qui par
" elle-meme, ou par ses suites, se reduise à une
" habitude, & une pratique continuelle.*"

" II. When God regulates the manner of
" a thing, or makes, with respect to the
" thing, some other regulation, which ne-

which he might be attached, if once he gave a loose to an unbounded appetite. The wisdom of this command, appears from the melancholy history of *Solomon*, as recorded 1 Kings xi. 1—8.

Mr. *Prior*, in one of the most beautiful poems that our language ever produced, has finely, and indeed *scripturally*, represented *Solomon* as saying—

" Charm'd by their eyes, their manners I acquire,
" And shape my foolishness to their desire:
" To each new *harlot* I new altars dress,
" And serve her God, whose person I caress."

Sol. B. ii.

To guard against this, as well as other effects of a provoked, indulged, and unbounded sensuality, appears to be the intention of this law. But as to *polygamy*, as considered in itself, its lawfulness must be supposed, otherwise (as *Barbeyrac* rightly concludes) there could be no place for such a *law* as this, which is to moderate and regulate it with regard to those who, from their *station*, must have so full a *power*, and consequently so much *temptation*, to abuse it.

If the *reader* considers the whole context of this passage (ver. 16, 17.) he will perceive, that it only concerns the *abuse* or *excess* of things *lawful* in themselves, as the instances of *horses*, and *gold and silver*, clearly demonstrate.

" cessarily

"cessarily supposes the thing itself permit-
"ted; we should consider whether this con-
"cerns a single transitory act, or something
"which in itself, or by its consequences,
"may reduce itself into habit and continual
"practice."

"Dans le dernier cas la permission emporte
"toujours une veritable approbation de la
"chose dont il s'agit, comme licite par elle-
"même. Il est impossible que DIEU per-
"mette, par exemple, le metier de *brigand,*
"de *pirate,* d'*assassin,* de *duelliste,* &c. sous
"quelques conditions que ce soit. Lors donc
"qu'on voit qu'il règle certains cas qui sup-
"posent la *polygamie* permise, comme dans
"Deut. xxi. 15. on a tout lieu d'inferer de
"cela seul que la *polygamie* n'est pas necessaire-
"ment contraire au droit naturel.

"In the latter case, the permission always
"implies a real approbation of the thing in
"question, as lawful in itself. It is impossi-
"ble that GOD should allow the trade, for in-
"stance, of a *robber*—of a *pirate*—of an *assas-
"sin*—of a *duellist*, &c. under any conditions
"whatsoever. As then we see that He re-
"gulates certain cases, which suppose a per-
"mission of *polygamy*—as in Deut. xxi. 15.
"—we are at full liberty to infer from thence,
"that *polygamy* is not necessarily contrary
"to *natural right.*"

More transcripts might be made from this very learned and ingenious man, to the same purpose; but these are sufficient to shew the force of TRUTH, over a liberal and candid mind,

mind, where *scripture* is made the one standard of decision as to *good* and *evil*. Influenced by this, the great *Grotius* shall vary from his first opinions, and *Barbeyrac*, though no friend to *polygamy*, yet does not offer, in a single instance, to condemn it on the footing of *divine revelation*; he fairly and *honestly* owns, that its abolition has been owing to *human legislation* ONLY—and of course, that it is not *evil in itself*—not forbidden either in the *Old* or *New Testament*;—so far from it, most certainly approved and allowed—and, as such, *regulated* by the *divine law*.

I would not be understood to have quoted *Grotius*, *Barbeyrac*, or any other great and learned *author*, in the course of this work, with the least view of determining any matter of *faith*, or of *deciding*, either one way or the other, as to what is agreeable, or otherwise, to the *mind* and *will* of GOD, touching any of the points which have been discoursed upon. The writings of *men* are evidence of their *opinions*; but whether those *opinions* are *right* or *wrong*, can only appear from their conformity or disagreement with the scriptures. To these *alone*, therefore, we must appeal, for all decision in religious matters—if we think with *these*, we need not concern ourselves who differs from us; if our notions of *religious truths* are only derived from the *opinions* or *reasonings* of fallible men like ourselves, we are on no better footing than our *Popish* neighbours, or our *heathen* ancestors, as to any reason *which we can give for the hope that is in us*.—

us.—Therefore let me *finish* the whole of this WORK, as I *concluded* the *Introduction* to it— TO THE LAW AND TO THE TESTIMONY.— If. viii. 20.

As for any thing else, whether it be the wisdom of *Plato, Aristotle, Cicero,* &c. among the *antients*—of *Sir Isaac Newton, Mr. Locke, Bishop Warburton,* or the *old woman* that sells *apples* at the corner of a street, among the *moderns*—the *author* esteems it all equally venerable, equally to be depended upon, where GOD's *mind and will* is concerned, *independently of revelation;* and he does earnestly hope, that every *reader*—if the *author* might presume to name himself after such *great authorities*—will, throughout the perusal of *these volumes,* treat him in the *same way,* and not believe one word, but as it appears consonant to the *scriptures*—For *what man knoweth the things of a man, save the spirit of a man which is in him? Even so, the things of* GOD *knoweth no one* (ὐδεις) *but the spirit of* GOD. 1 Cor. ii. 11.

END OF THE SECOND VOLUME.

INDEX

TO VOL. I.

A

ATHEISTS and *Hobbists*, their principles relative to *civil contracts*, 37, n.
ADULTERY, 57. Defined, ib. A capital offence by the divine law, 62, 63. So by the law of England in 1650, p. 64, n. Not so now, ib.
AKIBA, 83.
AUSTIN, St.—his testimony concerning concubinage, 32, n. On the antient polygamy, 98, n. A foolish saying of his on the subject, 243, n.
ADULTERY, mischiefs of, 66.
ABRAHAM and *Hagar*, 117, and n.
ALEXANDER III. Pope, his constitution concerning post-legitimation, 35.
ADAM and *Eve*, their creation—no precedent to be drawn from it against polygamy, 139 and n.
ABIGAIL and *Ahinoam*, wives to David, 148.
ABISHAG the *Shunamite*, 164—5.
ANSELM, Archbishop of Canterbury, makes a canon against *sodomy*, which is never published, 171, n.
ANTHONY, St.—preaches to FISHES, 193.
ACT OF GENERATION, not sinful in itself, 46 & seq.
אִישׁ—explained in all its senses, 255—6.
ABIMELECH, case of, 265.
ARTICLE, SEVENTH, of the church of England, quoted and explained, 282.
ABIGAIL, her pleading for *Nabal*, 320.
ABROGATION, doctrine of, borrowed from the *Mahometan* doctors, 390, n.

B BOLINGBROKE,

INDEX TO VOL. I.

B

BOLINGBROKE, Lord, a sentiment of his, 7, n.
BUSBEQUIUS, his distinction between a *wife* and *concubine*, 55, n.
BURNET, Bishop, quoted on the subject of the dissoluteness of the unmarried clergy before the Reformation, 65, n. A quotation from him on polygamy, 249. His opinion at large thereon, 291.
BACON's Abr. quoted on pre-contracts, 31.
BUXTORF, on Deut. xxi. 1—4. p. 86, n.
BIGAMY, statute of 1 Jac. c. 11, preamble of, 175, n. *Bigamists*—clergy censured, 189, n. Ousted of clergy, 199.
BELLARMINE, his testimony for the *Pope's* power to make and unmake sins, 183, n.
BANTAM, more *females* than *males* born there, 105.
BEZA—talks nonsense, 151.
BEREANS, their example to be followed, 237.
BOTTLES, *leathern*, mistaken for *glass*, 350.
BUCER, on *concubinage*, 396.
BARBEYRAC observes that *Grotius* changed his opinion concerning the interpretation of Matt. xix. 9. p. 374. See also vol. ii. Append. No. 2.
BAPTISM, no *new law* of CHRIST, 333.
BERNARD, on celibacy, 170, and n.

C

CRUCIFIX, an heathen invention, Pref. p. vii. n.
CONSTANTINE, his laws about marriage, 32, n. Establishes Christianity by law, 203, n.
CONCUBINE, what, 53, 54, and n.
COROLLARIES on the nature and obligation of marriage, 40.
COMMANDMENT, the *seventh*, does not forbid *polygamy*, 120.
CHURCH, in 4th century, made no distinction between *wife* and *concubine*, 32, n.
COKE, Lord, on *Jointenancy*, 151, n.
CELIBACY condemned, 168 & seq. Of the clergy, 200, 201.
CONTINENCY, where to be prayed for, 179.
CARTHUSIANS would not eat *flesh* to save their lives, 183.
CERBERUS, *Popish*, his three heads, 202, n.
CORINTH had a temple of *Venus*, 211, n.
CORINTHIANS lewd and debauched to a proverb, ib.
——————— Paul's answer to their letter, 211. Explained, ib. & seq.
CÆSAR, his account of community of *wives* among the *Britons*, 220, n.
CONCUBINES approved in the church, 32, n.
CECROPS establishes *monogamy* at *Athens*, 232.

CAVE,

INDEX TO VOL. I.

CAVE, Dr. allows that the primitive *Christians* carried matters too far with respect to second marriages, 245.
CEREMONIAL law, its morality must ever remain, 260.
CASTRATION practised by some of the antient *Christians*, 286, n.
CERINTHUS, his creed, 327.
CLARKE, Dr. makes the New Testament the only criterion of truth to *Christians*, 328, n.
CHRIST not a giver of a *new law*, 300. His *offices*, 337. His commission, 388.
COMMERCE of the *sexes*, an object of the *moral law*, 342.
CARVILIUS RUGA, the first *Roman* who *divorced* his wife, 346, n.
CANON LAW, Popish, affirms the church to be above the scripture, Pref. viii. n.
CLERGY, their marriage made felony, 200, 201.

D

DOWER among the *Jews*, 27.
DEUT. xxiv. 1. considered and explained, 85, 86, 87, and n.
DEUT. xxii. 28, 29. explained, p. 28, 29.—red in the church as the first lesson, March 4th, at evening service, 161.
DIVORCE, *Jewish*, did not operate as a dissolution of the marriage, 88. Bill of, 347. Attended with difficulties, 346, n.
DEUT. xxi. 15. a conclusive argument for polygamy, 109.
DAVID has many wives given to him, 115.
DIOGENES held community of women, 214, n.
DELANEY, *Dean*, his reflections on *polygamy*, 116, 117, 249, 250—1. Examined, ib. and 252—3.
DAVID and *Jonathan*, their friendship, 321.
DRUSILLA forsakes her husband and marries *Felix*, 364, n.

E

ERASMUS, a saying of his adversaries, 5, n.
EXOD. xxii. 16. explained, 25. Red in the church as the first lesson, Feb. 8, p. 161.
ECCLESIASTICAL courts, their views of marriage, 31.
——— ——— ——— their oppression and tyranny, 67, n. Ought to be abolished, 68.
ESPOUSALS, 26, and n.
EXAMPLES of the saints in old time are for our instruction, 84, n.
EUNUCHS, mentioned Matt. xix. 11, 12, what, 173, n.
ELIJAH, a bold reprover of sin, 130.
EZRA x. 1, &c. and x. 2. quoted, 133.
EDWARD I. stat. of, adopting the Pope's constitution at *Lyons*, concerning *bigamists*, 199.

EDWARD VI. ſtat. of, repeals the former, 199.
ECCLESIASTICUS xxiii. 22, 23, deſcribes *adultery*, 276.
ENEMIES, love of, equally a doctrine of the *Old* and *New Teſtaments*, 314, 315.

F

FATHERS, antient, their writings not to be depended on, 16, and n. ib. Their notions of Gen. i. 28. p. 119, n.
FALLIBILITY of councils, churches, &c. confeſſed by the church of England, 6.
FORNICATION defined, 51, n.
FATHER and SON, names of office, not of nature, 18, n.
FORSTER, Dr. his voyage quoted, on the proportion of *males* and *females* born in *Africa*, &c. 103.
FLESH, one, the meaning of the phraſe, 151, n.
FRANCIS, St. preaches to the beaſts, 193.

G

GEN. ii. 23, 24, explained, and compared with 1 Cor. vi. 15, 16. p. 18, 19.
GENERATION, act of, not ſinful in itſelf, 46, 47.
GRANT, *Major*, his notion about males and females examined, 101, n.
GABRIEL brings the celibacy of prieſts from heaven, 200, n.
GOSPEL always one and the ſame, 229.
GREEKS polygamiſts, 232, n.
GROTIUS, his thoughts on what makes a marriage, 22, n. Owns the *Jewiſh* law allowed *polygamy*, 240, n. His notions on the law of *Chriſt* relative to polygamy, 302.
——— changes his opinion, 374.

H

HENRY II. of France, a ſaying of his on *papal* diſpenſations, 13, n.
HILLELL, 82.
HUSBAND, defined, 44, n.
HORACE quoted on navigation 101, n. On the mutability of words, 59, n.
HAGAR's marriage with *Abram* not ſinful, 117, n.
HEN. VIII. ſtatute of, againſt prieſts' marriage, 200, 201.
HALL, *Biſhop*, a ſaying of his, 331.
HERODIAS leaves her huſband, and marries his brother, 364, n.
HIPHIL-*conjugation*, how expreſſed by the *Helleniſts*, 373, n.

INDEX TO VOL. I.

I

JUDGES xix. 1, &c. confidered, 55.
JENKINSON, *Ann*, her hard cafe, 67, n.
IGNORANCE not the caufe of the *Jewifh* polygamy, 92, & feq.
IGNATIUS introduces the faying of a Jew on the credibility of the New Teftament, 93, n.
JOASH a polygamift, by the act of the high-prieft *Jehoiada*, 94.
JACOB and the *angel*, 115, n.
JOB xxxi. 1, explained, 124, n.
JESUIT'S continency, ib.
JOSEPH and *Potiphar*'s wife, 139, n.
INFANTS heads found in Pope *Gregory*'s fifh-pond, 201, n.
JOHN the *Baptift*, his reproof of *Herod*, 243. His commiffion and preaching, 245—6. Appeals to the Old Teftament for his miffion, 305, n.
JOSEPHUS on *Ruth* iv. 6. p. 253. A faying of his on *David*'s marrying *Saul*'s wives, ib.
JEWS, the modern, forbid *polygamy*, why, 264, n.
JOHN xiii. 34. explained, 316.
JUVENAL, on the manners of the *Roman* women, 368—9.

K

KEMPFER, his account of the *males* and *females* in *Meaco*, 104, n.
KENNEDY, Mr. on the fabbath, 159.

L

LUTHER, his quarrel with LEO X. one means of the reformation, 3.
LAW of *God* immutable, 10, 78.
LANGUAGE mutable, 58, n. Not fo the *Hebrew*, ib.
LAMECH and his *two wives*, 143, 149.
LEV. xviii. 18, on the marriage of two fifters, explained, 152—157.
LYONS, conftitution of, excluding *bigamifts* from all *Clerks* privilege, 199. Law of *Ed.* VI. againft it, ib.
LUTHER, a faying of his upon fin-making, 203, n.
LANDGRAVE of *Heffe* marries two wives at once, on the opinions of the *reformers* at *Wittemburg*, 204, n.
LYCURGUS, his law about men's lending their wives, 212, & feq.
LEVIRATUS, Deut. xxv. 5—10. p. 250. Reafon of that law, 251.
LYING, a maxim of the fathers of the fourth *century*, 285, n.
LAW of *nature*, what, 301, n.
LACTANTIUS, his notion of CHRIST'S miffion, 304, n.
LAW of CHRIST, mentioned Gal. vi. 2, explained, 322. And illuftrated, 323, and n.

INDEX TO VOL. I.

LAW, *moral*, founded in the relation which *reasonable* creatures bear to the *Creator*, 341. Like a *golden chain*, 344. Its nature, use, and properties, 323, n.
LUKE xvi. 18. paraphrased, 383—385.
LEFT-HANDED wife, what, 404.

M

MONTESQUIEU, his sentiments on prostitution, 8, n.
MATT. v. 18. explained, 14.
MARRIAGE, original institution of, 18. Ordinance defined, ib. n.
——————— ceremony, an human invention, 22, and n. Useful, 41.
——————— condemned as unlawful for *Christians*, 184.
MERTON, statute of, concerning marriage, 32.
MATT. xix. 3, &c. explained, 80, & seq.
MISTRESS, kept, 53.
MOLIERE quoted, 79.
MATT. v. 28, explained, 122, and n.
MAL. ii. 14, 15, explained, 132, & seq.
MARRIAGES, second, condemned, 140, and n. 184.
——————— of the *clergy*, 189, and n.
MIRACLES, Popish, said to be wrought by CHRIST, and the *Virgin Mary*, on prayers for continency, 180.
MONTANISTS and *Novatians* condemn second marriages, 185.
MILTON quoted on the creation of woman, 141, n.
MANES, or *Manichæus*, his errors about marriage, 211, n.
MAHLON's next kinsman will not redeem his land, why, 251—2.
MALES and *Females*, proportion of, 100, &c. and n.
MAHOMET, his account of the *prophets* who brought *new laws*, 304. This necessary for his plan, ib. His art with respect to the authority of the Scripture, 305, and n.
MADNESS, argues *right* from *wrong* principles, instanced in the *Socinian* plan, 308—9.
MOSES, his love for the people, 319. Said nothing of marriage-ceremony, 24, n.
MELCHIZEDECK, 332.
MATT. v. 31, 32, farther considered, 345.
—— xix. 9, ditto, 349.
MORAL law, unalterable, binding on *angels* as well as *men*, 341.

N

NOLDIUS quoted on the subject of dispensation for *polygamy*, 90, n.
NAIRES, tribe of, *Polyandrists*, 195, n.

NICHOLAS, Pope, restrains priests from marrying, 200, n.
NISUS, his speech to the *Rutulians* on behalf of *Euryalus*, 320.
NEW-LAW scheme, pregnant with mischiefs of the most alarming kind, 334—5.

O

ORDINANCES of men to be submitted to, 42, n.
OCCASION of CHRIST's discourse with the *Pharisees*, MATT. xix. 4, &c. 353.

P.

PIUS, Pope, Articles of his Creed, Pref. viii. n.
PROSTITUTION, dreadful consequences of, 8, n.
PARISIAN divines make doctrines for the people, 9.
PENANCE and commutation, 68, and n. at bottom.
1 PET. ii. 13, quoted and explained, 42, n. See also Vol. II. 66, n.
PUBLIC WISDOM, a mere *Proteus*, 5, n.
POLYGAMY, 74. Defined, 75, and n. Whether it tends to population, 98, n.
POPE, Mr. on criticism, 81, n. On the pride of human reasoning, 99.
PLURALITY of persons in the Godhead revealed in the Old Testament, 57, n.
POLYGAMY not mentioned in the New Testament, 120, 121.
——— probably frequent among the first Christians, 185, 232.
PATRICK, Bishop, his comment on Lev. xviii. 18. p. 154.
PUFFENDORF leaves the matter of *polygamy* uncertain, whether against the *law of nature*, or not, 74, n.
PAPHNUTIUS, his speech at the council of NICE, about the *clergy* putting away their wives, 188, n.
PREJUDICE against *married priests*, instances of, 205, n.
PLATO held community of women, 211.
PAUL, St. no law-giver, 229.
PATRICK on *Ruth* iv. 6. p. 253.
PARADIGM setting forth GOD's dealings towards *Monogamists* and *Polygamists*, 269.
POLYGAMY how first condemned in the *Christian* church, 171, 275. Why allowed to men and not to women, 276—279. Necessary to be so, 280—1.
PERFECTION of the *divine law* attested by the *Old* and *New Testaments*, 307, 308.

INDEX TO VOL. I.

R

RELIGION of anceſtors to be followed, an Heathen maxim, 1, n.
ROME, ancient, three kinds of marriage, 33.
RUTH, iv. 5, 6. conſidered, 251, & ſeq.
RABBINICAL explanation of אֵן—281, n.

S

SCRIBLERUS quoted, 10.
SPOUSALS de futuro, &c. what, 26, n.
SCOTLAND, cuſtom of with reſpect to marriages—after cohabitation, and children born, 34.
SHENSTONE, Mr. of the Spiritual Court, p. 67, n.
SHAMMAH, 82.
SWEDEN, more *females* than *males* born in the laſt century, 104. An inſtance of ditto at a village in *England*, ditto, n.
SAMUEL no baſtard, 108.
SALMON in the water, experiment of, 102, n.
2 SAM. xii. 8, Dean *Delaney*'s interpretation refuted, 116, 117, 118.
SIXTUS V. grants a diſpenſation for *ſodomy*, 172, n.
SEPARATION of man and wife, where neceſſary, 176, n.
SOCRATES put to death, why, 2. Has two wives, 232, n.
SUPERSTITION of the *Jews*, in not reſiſting their enemies on the *Sabbath-day*, 183.
——————— of the *Chriſtians* with regard to the marriage of prieſts, 205, n.
STOICS held community of women, 214, n.
SINGULAR words, have often plural meanings, 222, n.
SELDEN, on *Ruth* iv. 6. p. 254.
SERMONS, two, on the marriage-act, 262.
SOCINIANISM, 303, 308—9.
SERMON on the *Mount*, explains and aſſerts the honour and obligation of the *divine law*, 309—15.
SACRAMENTS, of *baptiſm* and the *Lord's ſupper*, prefigured in the Old Teſtament, 331—33.
SALOME repudiates her huſband, 364, n.
SENECA, his account of the *Roman* women, with reſpect to leaving their huſbands for others, 368, n.
SYNESIUS, a *Chriſtian* Biſhop, his duplicity, Pref. xii.

T

TOLEDO, council of, decree about concubinage, 32.
TALPÆ, among the *Jews*, a Phariſaical ſect, 124, n.
TYMPIUS, his notes on *Noldius*, relative to *Lev.* xviii. 18, p. 153, n.
TERTULLIAN's reaſons for the celibacy of the antient *Chriſtians*, 170, n.

1 TIM. iii. 2. and TIT. i. 6. explained, 194, & seq.
TRENT, council of, obliged to those who defend their *anathema* against *polygamy*, 230, n.
TESTAMENT, *Old* and *New*, to be compared together, 237—9. See also vol. ii. 316, & seq.

U V

USHER, *Archbishop*, sensible of the evils of the *spiritual courts*, p. 67, n.
VOLTAIRE misled by translations, 15, n. 351, n.
VATABLUS on *Deut.* xxiv. 1—4, p. 87.
VASHTI, Queen, her disobedience—her punishment no bad precedent, 176, n.
VENUS, temple of, at *Corinth*, 211, n.
VALESIANS castrated themselves, 286, n.
VENEREAL *disease*, not in *Israel*, 289, and n.
UNION between CHRIST and the *Church*, no argument against *polygamy*, 240—3.

W

WICKLIFFE, first reformer in Europe, 3, n.
———'s bones burnt, ib.
WHORE defined, 19, n.
WHOREDOM and fornication, 46. Defined 51.
————, odious in GOD's sight, 50. Punished with death, ib.
————, supposed original of, 49.
WOMEN not suffered to approach the altar, or to receive the *Eucharist* without gloves on, 180, n.
WHISTON, *William*, on second marriages of the *clergy*, 190, n.
WHITTINGTON and his bells, an emblem of people who are deceived by the *sound* of words in favour of preconceived opinions, 236.
WHITBY, DR. his comment on 1 *Cor.* vii. 4. p. 230. His concession respecting *polygamy*, 231, n.
WETSTEIN, his explanation of *Matt.* xix. 9. and *Mark* x. 11. p. 363, & seq.

INDEX

TO VOL. II.

A

ADULTERY not a cause of *divorce a vinculo matrimonii*, a Popish tenet, 3, n.
ABRAHAM and *Hagar*, no exception to the rule against *divorce*, 24, n.
ALEXANDER, Dr. *History of Women*, observes the protection which *Deut.* xxviii. 29. affords to female chastity, 32, n.
ATHENÆUS, his account of a custom relative to old *batchelors*, 57.
ARRAGON, Catherine of, her marriage with Henry VIII. 70, n.
ANTIPODES, the doctrine of, once reputed heresy, 99, n.
ALBIGENSES, 140, and n.
AMBROSE, a violent stickler for celibacy, 117, n.
ALANUS de Rupe, his blasphemy on priesthood, 194, n.
APOSTOLICAL constitutions, forgeries, 194, n.
ABORTION, procurement of, a species of murder, 283, n.
ABUSE, an unfair ground of argument, 288, n. Much used by the *Papists* against the *Reformers*, ib. n.
ANTIQUITY of a doctrine, no proof of its truth, 309, 310.

B

BEDFORD, *Duke* of, makes a motion for the repeal of the marriage-act, 38, n. Part of his speech thereon, 58.
BELLARMINE allows of *polygamy*, 89, n. Contradicts himself, ib
BECCARIA, *Marquis* of, on conjugal fidelity, 54, n. On child-murder, 282, n.
BLACKSTONE, his opinion on restraints upon marriage, 54.

BRAZEN

INDEX TO VOL. II.

BRAZEN SERPENT, broken by *Hezekiah*, 104, n.
BASIL, clock at, 128, n.
BLACKSTONE, his account of the first invention of marriage by *priests*, 141.
BANNS of *marriage*, when invented, 147. The true reason thereof, ib. n.
BOURDEAUX, a young *lady* at, stoned to death, 164.
BONNER, Bishop, his speech on the dignity of priests, 189, n.
BURNET's *Hist. Ref.* referred to concerning the visitation of monasteries, 112, n.
BASTARD, the term improperly used, 239.
BELLARMINE of indulgences, 276, n.
BOTTLE-CONJUROR, 312.
BELL, Dr. on the *sacrament*, 331, n.
BARBEYRAC, his account of *Grotius*'s change of opinion with respect to CHRIST's altering the law of *Moses*, 362, & seq.
BECCARIA, *Marquis* of, on false ideas of utility, 375, n.
BLACKSMITH and his child, 376, n.

C

CRIM. CON. actions for, 75, n.
CONGO, the Christians of, *polygamists*, 89, n.
CLANDESTINE MARRIAGES, provided against by several *statutes*, 54.
CELIBACY discouraged by the *Heathens*, 56, 57. By the *Jews*, 259.
CANON against clandestine marriages, 59.
CUSANUS, *Cardinal*, his saying, at the council of Trent, on the subject of expounding Scripture, 71, n.
CEREMONY, marriage, necessary, and to be enforced in every case, 64, 67.
CHRISTIANITY, considered as in itself, and as abused, 94, n.
COPERNICAN system, once accounted an heresy, 99, n.
CAVE, Dr. William, an historian of primitive *Christianity*, 112, 115, 125. *White-washer* of the *antients*, 124, n.
COXE's *Sketches of Switzerland*, quotations from, 127, n. 248, n.
CHILD-MURDER, cause of, 162, 237, 309, n. An horrid instance of, 308, n.
CONTRACTS of *marriage*, of all sorts, vacated, 46—48, and n.
1 COR. iv. 3, 4. explained, 157, n.
CONSCIENCE, what, 168. The evidence on which it should determine as a *judge*, 169.
CARTHAGINIANS, their method of appeasing their idol *Saturn*, 169—70.
CAPUCHIN *Friar*, conversation with, 179, n.
CONFARREATION, a mode of marriage among the antient *Romans*, what, 185, n.
CHURCHMEN, their pride and insolence of early date, 194, and n.

CYPRIAN

INDEX TO VOL. II.

CYPRIAN, St. his high notion of episcopal dignity, 194, n.
CAMPEGIUS, *Cardinal*, a saying of his on priests' marriage, 209, n.
CERINTHUS, a position of his, 223.
CASTRATION, practised by *Christians*, 227—8.
CHRISTIANS, *primitive*, their condemnation of marriage, the occasion thereof, 226.
CORBAN, what, 240.
CELIBACY frequent among us, and why, 247—8.
CALCULATION on our loss of people, 249, 250.
CONSTANTINE encourages celibacy, 252, n.
CHESTER, Bishop of, cites his *commissary* into the *spiritual court*, 262, n.
CONTRAST between the *divine* and *human* systems, 267.
CONCLUSION, 278.
CEREMONY, not of the essence of marriage, 294, n.
CALIXTUS, a sentiment of his on the obligation of the divine law, 299, n.
COROLLARIES arising from the banishment of the *divine law*, 304—8.
CAJETAN, *Cardinal*, asserts St. *Paul*'s allowance of *polygamy*, 315, n.
CATHARISTS, in the 12th century, their doctrine, 319.
CHASTITY of the *clergy*, in the 3d century, but ill observed, 324, n.

D

DINAH, the case of, 9, n.
DAVID, his lamentation for *Absalom* different from that on account of his child by the wife of *Uriah*, 19.
DIVORCE causâ precontractûs on the man's side, unauthorized by Scripture, and illegal under the divine law, 21, and n.
——— *bill* of, its intention, 4, n. 77, n.
——— too expensive for the generality of people, 75, n.
DOCTORS-COMMONS, a sentence of *divorce* there, on a clause in the marriage-act, 48, n.
DRYDEN, a saying of his, 73.
DIDO, her vow against a second marriage, 114, n.
DEUT. xxi. 13, explained, 189, n.
DESERTED VILLAGE, quoted on the misery of a *prostitute*, 237, n.
DÆMONS, married people supposed to be most subject to their influence, 228, n.
DERHAM, Mr. his tables of births and burials, 249, n.
DISPENSATION of the *Pope* to the King of *Portugal*, to marry his own niece, 144, n.
DESIGN, the Author's, in this Treatise, 346.
DAVID and *Bathsheba*, their adultery, 358. Their marriage afterwards, 360.
DEUT. xvii. 17, explained, 378, and n.

E ECCLE-

INDEX TO VOL. II.

E

ECCLESIASTICAL Courts, not of divine original, 45, n.
Their proceedings on marriage-*contracts* before the *marriage-act*, 50.
ECCL. iv. 1. on *oppression*, quoted, 151.
EUNUCHS, mentioned Matt. xix. 12, what 229.
EPH. vi. 12. explained, 231.
ERRORS, which this Treatise unfolds, and proposes a remedy for, 342—345.

F

FREE-ENQUIRY, a privilege and duty, 101.
——————— secured by the Church of *England*, 134, 135.
FEMALE-ruin, floodgates of, 160.
FORNICATION, how committed with a man's own wife, 124, n.
FULLER's-*earth* of reputation, what, 33.
FOUNDLING-*hospital*, not an adequate remedy against *child-murder*, 293.
FRANCE, laws of, with respect to seduction, 294—296.

G

GOTHS, compelled marriage in case of seduction, 29.
GERMANS, antient, their custom in case of *adultery*, ib.
GORDIAN knot, *Alexander*'s saying about it, 68.
GNATHO, an emblem of *worldly wisdom*, 71, n.
GALILEO invents telescopes, and forced to renounce the *Copernican* system as heresy, 99, n.
GOING IN *unto a woman*, what, 188, and n.
GUILLON, *Claude*, his sad fate, 233, n.
GUASTALLA, order of, 324.
GOSPEL, in the Old Testament and New Testament one and the same, 317.

H

HEATHEN women, marriage with them lawful and valid, if they were proselytes, 8, n. Otherwise not, 9.
HOLT, Chief Justice, his opinion on the validity of marriage-contracts, 49.
HORACE quoted on the presumption of mankind, 50.
HENRY VIII. his marriage with *Catherine* of *Arragon*, 70.
HARAM, sacred among the *Mahometans*, 85.
HUDIBRAS, on the influence of money in Church and State, 145, n. On *sectaries*, 373.
HOTTENTOT and *European* compared, 310, n.
HORACE, quoted on the subject of *error*, 182, n. On a happy marriage, 177. On the increase of evil, 301. On moderation, 335, n.

HICKES,

INDEX TO VOL. II.

HICKES, Dr. his tracts, in *Lord Sommers's* collection, on the dignity of Bishops, 190, n. On prayers for the dead, ib. n.
HEB. xiii. 4, explained, 230, and n. Popish gloss, 323.
HELP *meet*, &c. what, 229, n.
HARLOTS, antient, what, 256, n.
HUSBAND and *wife*, no such terms in Scripture, 291, 292, and n. Used by the author, why, ib.
HOGGARTH, *Hannah*, her melancholy case, 308, n.
HEBREW Scripture, the test of truth, 316.
———— ———— ———— the foundation of the New Testament, 317.
HIERAX, an heretic in the 3d century, 319.
HANNAH, her case more particularly considered, 349—357.
———— supposed, for argument's sake, the first wife of *Elkanah*, 354.

I

JEROME writes against marriage, 116. Against *Jovinian*, 117. Against *Vigilantius*, 118.
JEHOIADA orders a *chest* for the temple offerings, 130.
JACOB, Mr. his Dictionary quoted on the subject of marriage, 141.
INNOCENT III. *Pope*, gets marriage into the hands of the *priests*, 141, 142.
IMPEDIMENTS to marriage added or dispensed with by the *Council of Trent*, 28, n 69, n.
JESUITS expelled out of *Tonquin*, 82, n.
IGNATIUS to *Polycarp*—Epistle, on marriage before a Bishop, 138, n.
JOHN viii. 3, &c. applied to the *censorious* reader, 160—1.
JEWISH priesthood, dignities of, claimed by the *Christian* clergy, 196.
JUSTICES *of the peace*, marriages performed by them, 197, n.
JEALOUSY, GOD'S, over his laws, 212.
JEROBOAM, why he set up the calves, 217.
JEALOUSY, trial of, under the *law*, 220.
INSTINCT, a law to *brutes*, 245.
JEWS, numerous, 252, and n. Why, 258.
—— Letters to Mr. De Voltaire, 255—6.
—— married young, 259, 260.
IDLENESS partly the ruin of the *Jews*, 261, n.
JEWS more merciful to seduced women than the *Christians* are, 297.

K

KING, CHRIST refuses to be made one, 226.
KING, Mr. his computation on marriages, 249, n.

L LAWS,

INDEX TO VOL. II.

L

LAWS, their permanency, rules to judge of, 26, 27.
LOLME, Mr. De, his opinion of the marriage-act, 55.
LOLLARDS, 140, and n.
LAMECH the first *polygamist* mentioned, 152, n.
LEO, *Emperor*, publishes an edict against those who married *thrice*, 121. Caught in his own trap, ib.
LOMBARD, *Peter*, discovers *seven* sacraments, 139.
LUTHER, anathematized by the *Papists*, canonized by the *Protestants*, 155, n.
LYING prophet of *Bethel*, 192.
LUTHER, abuse of him, for defending the marriage of *priests*, 209, n.
LEGISLATION, the divine, inherent in *Jehovah*, 225, and n.
LE CLERC on Gen. iv. 19. p. 152, n.
LAUSANNE, and the country about it, less populous than heretofore, 248, n.
LUZATIER, *Simon*, his account of the numbers of *Jews*, 252, n.
LUXURY, one cause of *celibacy*, 261.
LETTER, affecting one, in the General Advertiser of October 16, 1778, p. 302.
LUKE xiv. 26 and 33. explained, 327.

M

MESSIAH, his genealogy considered, 14—17.
MARRIAGE, as a *civil contract*, and, as such, the object of human laws, 35, 94, n. What is the *essence* of it as a divine institution, 136, n.
MARRIAGE-ACT considered, 38, & seq.
———— ————, its *heathenism* and *popery*, ib. n.
MARRIAGES, among the *Jews*, with *heathen* women, 8, n. and 9, n.
MONTESQUIEU gives *physical* reasons for *polygamy* in some countries, 79, n.
MONTAGUE, Lady M. W. on the *sale* of women, 80, n.
MEHMET EFFENDI, the *Turkish* ambassador in *France*, a saying of his, 85, n.
MINOTAUR, the *Cretan* monster, 98.
MONKERY, established early in the *fourth century*, 111, n.
MARRIAGES, second, condemned, 125, and n. 230.
MARRIAGE-*ordinance*, as divinely instituted, 136, n. Whether solemnized by a *minister* of the church among the *primitive Christians*, 138.
———— ————, no scripture warrant for it, 184.
———— ————, a money-scheme, 145, n.
MOLOCH, children sacrificed to, 162.
MASKWELL, his saying, 171, n.

MASSACRES

INDEX TO VOL. II.

MASSACRES of Proteſtants, 170, and n.
MULES, ſome divines ſtiled ſo, 190, n.
MARRIAGE-*plan*, Popiſh, the model of ours, 202, n.
MARK vii. 9, &c. applied, 240—1.
MULES never breed, 245, and n.
MARCION corrupts the New Teſtament, 226, n.
MESSIAH, every *Jewiſh* woman excited to marriage, in hopes of bringing him forth, 259, and n.
MENSA & *toro*, perſons ſeparated from, not liable to the penalty of *Jac.* I. c. 11. p. 306, n.
MANES, his contempt firſt of the Old Teſtament and then of the New Teſtament, 318.
MARRIAGE, always the ſame in GOD's ſight, 332.

N

NORTHAMPTON, *Marquis* of, his caſe of *divorce*, 5, n.
NEOCÆSARIENSIAN *Council*, diſapproves of *ſecond* marriages, 125, n.

O

ORDERS of *miniſters* in the *Chriſtian* church, 191.
———— never had any thing to do with *matrimony*, ib.
OPPRESSION, remedileſs, as deſcribed Eccl. iv. 1, p. 151.
ORIGEN caſtrates himſelf, 227. Explains ſcripture on the principles of the *Platonic* philoſophy, ib. n.

P

PROSTITUTES, none in *Iſrael*, 30.
PAPIAN law, 38, n.
POLYGAMIA *triumphatrix*, quotation from, 81, n.
POLYGYNY, its difference from *polygamy*, 83, n.
1 PET. ii. 13. explained, 66, n.
PRIOR, on the human mind, when judging and determining for itſelf, and when led on by *vulgar opinion*, 97, n. On hereſy, as depending on human opinion, 157, n.
PHILOSOPHER's Stone, *marriage* has proved ſo to the *clergy*, 143, and n.
POST-LEGITIMATION of *marriage* and *iſſue*, a ſtrange method of, 148.
PORTUGUESE, their behaviour on the execution of *heretics*, 133.
POPERY, a curſe and plague, 171, n.
———— always the ſame, ib. n.
POLYGAMY, the queſtion of its lawfulneſs of the higheſt importance, 179, n. Not an object of the *ſeventh* commandment, 222—3.
PRIESTS, no ſuch order in the *Chriſtian* church, 192. A title belonging to all real *Chriſtians*, 194.

PHINEAS,

INDEX TO VOL. II.

PHINEAS, his zeal commended, and why, 216.
POLYGAMY, condemnation of, whence it arose in early times, 231. Restrained, 335.
POPULATION, and comparison of the *Jewish law* with ours, 245.
PROSTITUTE, as described by the *Hebrew* term קדשה, what, 256, n.
PHÆDRUS, the *two wallets*, 287, n.
POLYGAMY, consequences of, among the *Jews*, 264. Of its banishment from us, ib. and n.
PENANCE and *commutation*, the original of, 273.
PORTUGAL, King of, marries his own niece, 144, n.
PILLAR-*saint*, 321.
POLYGAMY, where *evil*, 335, n.
POTTER, parable of, *Jer.* xviii. 2—4, applied, 372, n.
PRIOR, his *Solomon* quoted, 379, n.

Q

QUAKERS, their marriages, 197—8.

R

REYNOLDS, *Archdeacon*, his account of the origin of marriage-ceremonies, 139.
RAY, *Miss*, her sad catastrophe, 307, n.
REDUPLICATION of *expression* denotes the certainty of the thing spoken of, 158.
RING, in marriage, derived from the heathen, 203, n.
REASON of law, a rule and measure of its continuance, 235.

S

SHYLOCK, his exclamation, 28.
SERAGLIO, laws of, abominable, 79, 80. Worse scenes in *England*, 86, 87.
SUPERSTITION, 91. Defined, 100. Its genealogy, 98. Caveat against it by the church of England, 134—5.
SOTER, fifteenth Bishop of *Rome*, throws *marriage* into the hands of *priests*, 143, n.
STYLE, alteration of, in the year 1751, the occasion of a curious piece of *superstition*, 128, n.
SERMONS, two, on the *marriage-act*, examined, 184.
SAMARIA, woman of, CHRIST'S discourse with her, about her having *no husband*, explained, 187, n.
SOCINUS, his doctrine, 224.
SOLOMON no *bastard*, though born under a *polygamous* marriage, 222, 387.
SEVERIANS, their opinion about marriage, 254. n.
SUICIDE, female, 283, n. Terrible instances of, 307—8, n.

SWITZERLAND,

INDEX TO VOL. II.

SWITZERLAND, law of, respecting seduction, 297.
SENECA, on the increase of wickedness, 301.
SCOTCH-*women*, *infanticides*, and why, 307, n.
SATAN, his plan to destroy the human species, 325.

T

TRENT, Council of, condemn clandestine marriages, 38, n.
——————————, its decree on the subject of *impediments*, 69, n. Other decrees, 313, n.
TURKS, their distrust, 84. Their opinion of an adulterer, ib.
TONQUIN, King of, banishes the *Jesuits* for preaching against *polygamy*, 82, n.
TERTULLIAN, on clandestine marriages, 147, n.
TAMAR and *Amnon*, 163.
TRINITY, the names of, used in the *Romish* ritual of *marriage*, to make the people believe a *lye*, 201, n.
TRANSUBSTANTIATION of evil into good, 163, n.
TALMUD, a saying of, respecting the marriage of daughters, 260.

U V

VOLTAIRE, on the ignorance of *Popish priests*, 101, n.
VIRGIL's account of the *Harpies* applicable to Popery, 171, n.
UZZIAH, King, his usurpation of the *priestly* office punished, 199.
VHEMIC *court*, its severity, 233, n.
VENEREAL *disease*, when supposed to have appeared in *Europe*, 270, n.

W

WOMEN less valued than beasts, 53.
————, their *passions* weaker than those of men, 181.
WHOREDOM, where a man may commit it with his own wife, according to the opinion of some of the *fathers*, 124, n.
WOMEN, means of their corruption, 181.
————, some owe their ruin to themselves, 30.
WHORE, the term improperly used, 239.
————, definition of, 164.
WORLD, the, loves it's own ways, &c. 244.
WOMEN not permitted polygamy, and why, 287.
WICKLIFFE's bones burnt, 339.

www.ingramcontent.com/pod-product-compliance
Lightning Source LLC
Chambersburg PA
CBHW031229290426
44109CB00012B/210